A MILLENNIUM OF BUDDHIST LOGIC

BUDDHIST TRADITION SERIES

VOLUME 36

Edited by
ALEX WAYMAN

A Millennium of Buddhist Logic

Volume One

Alex Wayman

MOTILAL BANARSIDASS PUBLISHERS
PRIVATE LIMITED • DELHI

First Edition: Delhi, 1999

ISBN: 81-208-1646-3

Also available at:

MOTILAL BANARSIDASS

41 U.A. Bungalow Road, Jawahar Nagar, Delhi 110 007
8 Mahalaxmi Chamber, Warden Road, Mumbai 400 026
120 Royapettah High Road, Mylapore, Chennai 600 004
Sanas Plaza, 1302, Baji Rao Road, Pune 411 002
16 St. Mark's Road, Bangalore 560 001
8 Camac Street, Calcutta 700 017
Ashok Rajpath, Patna 800 004
Chowk, Varanasi 221 001

PRINTED IN INDIA
BY JAINENDRA PRAKASH JAIN AT SHRI JAINENDRA PRESS,
A-45 NARAINA, PHASE I, NEW DELHI 110 028
AND PUBLISHED BY NARENDRA PRAKASH JAIN FOR
MOTILAL BANARSIDASS PUBLISHERS PRIVATE LIMITED,
BUNGALOW ROAD, DELHI 110 007

FOREWORD

It is a great pleasure for the author to include this Volume One of my long-time occupation with Buddhist logic in this series of Buddhist Traditions.

It may well be that this work on Buddhist logic is the first major effort in this translation field that deliberately avoids the use of Western philosophical terms, such as 'universal' and 'particular'. Since there is a sufficient scope of textual length for enabling the reader to judge whether this deliberate avoidance leads to more comprehensible sentences or not, I hope that interested and competent scholars will indeed observe whether I have or have not succeeded in this approach to these important texts.

And so I share with other scholars the relief that is felt when finally completing a task after many years; and I still have a Volume Two to offer when appropriate.

ALEX WAYMAN

PREFACE

Here I acknowledge with gratitude the grants that enabled me to carry out this research on Buddhist logic, although the completion of the promised task took much longer than was anticipated. The first research abroad was supported for three months in Japan (September through November, 1976) and three months in Switzerland (March through May, 1977) by the Social Science Research Council; and for the three months in India (December, 1976 through February, 1977) by the American Institute of Indian Studies. This varied research foundation has led, belatedly, to the present Volume One of the Millennium, devoted to texts. The next period of research abroad, completely in India, February 12 to August 11, 1987, was sponsored by a Faculty Fulbright fellowship through Columbia University; and this varied research foundation will lead, also belatedly, to the completion of Volume Two, devoted to topics and opponents, its MS. finishing expected in 1999 for announcing at the Dharmakīrti Conference, Hiroshima, Japan, in November, 1997.

The research abroad enabled the present author to acquaint himself with the standard of Buddhist logic research and study in Asia, Europe, as in the United States; and to amass a fine library of relevant works in Sanskrit, Tibetan, as well as in Western languages. I am also appreciative of the many scholarly offprints and copies of work in this area that were sent me, obviously with the expectation that I would use them in my Millennium. Some utilization has taken place in this Volume One, but the bulk of such usage will naturally occur in Volume Two.

Some scholars might have reasonably concluded that my promise to put out a large work called A Millennium of Buddhist Logic would never come to pass, since the years were passing without its appearance in modern published form. That I might well be one of those scholars—of which we know one or more—who keep promising to put out the 'great work' for years, finally retiring with the task incomplete; and who subsequently passes from this world without putting out the great 'work'.

The present writer did retire from Columbia University in 1991; but this is not the reason that the herein Volume One was completed now, to be followed by Volume Two. Indeed, all the texts presented in this Volume One, were edited (if necessary) and translated during the five years 1981-5, and one of these—Ratnākaraśānti's treatise on 'inner pervasion' I published in translation by date of 1985. Thus, this Volume One was present in a sort of draft form before I took my second (Fulbright) research abroad in India mentioned above. What delayed the improvement of these individual texts was my rejection of Western philosophical terms for rendition of important terms of the system—a rejection set forth in my Introduction the Second (herein), so I had to figure out appropriate renditions in ordinary English words. A decisive break-through for the present author was his collaborated lexical work on Śrīdharasena's *Viśvalocanam*, wherein I published the second volume, translation of the lexicon (Narita: Naritasan Shinshoji, 1994). For work on this lexicon I had to shift from my typewriter to a computer with appropriate software. After completing the lexical task, which improved my sensitivity to Sanskrit and Tibetan words, I put certain texts of this Millennium Volume One on the computer while inserting numerous corrections of my drafts.

In short, I am pleased to offer this Vol. One now in partial compliance in this area. Just as my initial grant-supported research in this area has been decisive for the production of this Volume One, so the second research period in India has been essential for finishing Volume Two.

Since I edit the series Buddhist Traditions for my publisher, Motilal Banarasidass, Delhi, I am sending this Volume One to this publisher, and plan to do likewise with Volume Two (of approximately the same size). I here express my appreciation to the Director of that Press, N. Prakash Jain, for undertaking to publish this work.

New York City
15 January, 1998

ALEX WAYMAN

PROLOGUE

Here I wish to inform the reader of the scope of the present work and the possible use thereof. The next introduction is concerned with translation.

This Volume One is devoted to Texts. Volume Two, being prepared, will be on Studies (Topics and Opponents).

By a 'millennium' I mean beginning with Asaṅga (latter 4th cent. A.D. to first part 5th cent.), his "Rules of Debate"; and ending with Tsong-kha-pa (1357-1419 A.D.), his *Mun sel* (a guided tour through the books of Dharmakīrti). Forty years ago I was completing my doctoral thesis on the text, *Śrāvakabhūmi*, a manuscript in which intruded the "Rules of Debate"—both parts of the encyclopedic *Yogācārabhūmi*; and published an article on these "Rules of Debate". Tsong-kha-pa's *Mun sel* is unusual as being his only work of which I am aware wherein he was not instructing, but rather showing how he had studied a topic. Both these texts on logic which begin and end this Volume One are not the main concerns of these two authors.

As I filled in this Volume One with other works, I tried to include as much as possible of Dignāga and Dharmakīrti—the leaders of Buddhist logic, or studies on their works.

This Volume One is divided into two parts. Part I is devoted to certain introductory texts. First, Asaṅga's "Rules of Debate" presents various terms and definitions that involve the state of logic prior to Dignāga's great contribution. We learn that there were two words used for the thesis, namely, *pratijñā* (one's own or the opponent's thesis) and *sādhya* (normally, one's own thesis). Later, the word *sādhya* apparently took over. Second is Dharmakīrti's *Nyāyabindu*, for which the Sanskrit was already available, followed by Kamalaśīla's rather short but important commentary thereon—preserved in Tibetan—stressing the opponents to the positions of the *Nyāyabindu*. Third is Ratnākaraśānti's *Antarvyāptisamarthana*, a sort of introduction to the rather technical theory of 'pervasion' (*vyāpti*), for which I present both the Sanskrit and English rendering.

Part II of this Volume One then deals with the Dignāga-Dharmakīrti system in different introductory ways. First I give five sets of 11 verses, namely, the first 11 verses of Dignāga's *Pramāṇasamuccaya*—as I count them; plus the first 11 verses in each of the four chapters of Dharmakīrti's *Pramāṇavārttika,* in both cases leaving out the initial 'bowing' *(maṅgala)* verses from the count. Then I present studies of two texts that represent two lineages that came into Tibet as to the Dharmakīrti texts, or parts thereof, that must go with the preceding Dignāga positions. In the case of Dharmakīrti's *Pramāṇaviniścaya,* I present an analysis of Bu-ston's Tibetan Commentary on this text, with the lineage that it was this text whereby Dharmakīrti showed the part of his system that directly went back to Dignāga's position. Then, by Tsong-kha-pa's *Guided Tour,* namely, through the seven books of Dharmakīrti I show the other lineage, stressing the *Pramāṇavārttika* as the Dharmakīrti text that goes with the Dignāga system.

As I do not include any texts pertaining to the ancient Chinese type of logic, may I call attention to two introductory works dealing with this topic: Hu Shih (Suh Hu), *The Development of the Logical Method in Ancient China* (Shanghai: The Oriental Book Company, 1928); and Chad Hansen, *Language and Logic in Ancient China* (Ann Arbor: The University of Michigan Press, 1983).

Now may I go into the possible use of the texts included in this Volume One. For example, there is Asaṅga's treatment of the thesis *(pratijñā)*, the reason *(hetu)*, and the example (*udāharaṇa*); and this study may be continued in Ratnākaraśānti's essay on 'inner pervasion'. Then one may notice Asaṅga's rather extensive treatment of 'direct perception' (*pratyakṣa*) and 'inference' *(anumāna)*, and then observe how these topics are continued in Dignāga and Dharmakīrti, how inference in this new system of logic divided into 'inference for oneself' and 'inference for others'. And in this Volume One there is much material on these two kinds of inference, in each of the three texts of Part II.

One may notice in Asaṅga's treatise the emphasis on 'lineage of the masters' (*āptāgama*), while this third kind of *pramāṇa* accepted by Asaṅga is denied in the Dignāga Dharmakīrti system.

Then, by Asaṅga's treatise one may see how all these topics were subservient to the debate; and how in the later system of logic the topics were taken out of the debate context and treated as individual topics. And in the form of the later system, the texts of Volume One furnish much material, for example, on 'direct perception' (*pratyakṣa*), so that the reader can read, say, just this topic, and derive much instruction. This is much more profitable than simply reading each text in the order presented.

Besides, it is my claim that the reader can indeed understand the system in this manner of approach, say, by paying attention to a particular topic in each text, because I have employed ordinary English words for rendering the texts here included. I need not continue this topic here, since it is treated in my Introduction.

INTRODUCTION

Upon offering to the public this first volume, on texts, of my Millennium of Buddhist Logic (about 5th cent. in India to 14th cent., A.D. in Tibet), may I admit that over the years of pursuing and laboring on this topic, to have gradually adopted renditions for technical terms differing from the terms almost ubiquitously used. Many such renditions by others are copies of Aristotelian-derived terms, then applied to Indian logic. Others are renditions in ordinary words of, say, English. These two kinds of former renditions will be treated, along with my alternatives, below in two parts: a. Regarding Western philosophical terms for translating Buddhist logic b. Regarding renditions with ordinary words.

A. REGARDING WESTERN PHILOSOPHICAL TERMS FOR TRANSLATING

At the end of this part a, I shall present a list of my renditions along with mention of the philosophical term renditions which I do not employ when translating texts of Buddhist logic.

It seems appropriate to explain why I adopted this course of translation, rather than, for example, using such renditions as 'universal' and 'particular' for the two kinds of *lakṣaṇa*. J. Brough has some appropriate remarks.[1]

> Logic, Mathematics, linguistics, science in general, all convey their messages in language, and this language, however technical, *cannot be understood* save in a manner which is fundamentally similar to the understanding of everyday language. As the ancient Indian might say, the utterances of the costermonger, the language of the great poet, and the formulae of the atomic physicist are all in some sense manifestations of the same divine Vāk.

---

1. John Brough, "Some Indian Theories of Meaning," *Transactions of the Philological Society*, 1953, p. 176c.

Brough's remarks remind us of the famous Hindu author Bhartṛhari, who emphasized the sentence to force meanings upon the individual words. When we demand of a sentence to reveal the meanings of the individual words, we ask too much that the sentence also reveal the meanings of Western philosophical terms. A reader should not ask a translator for the meanings of the Western terms, since the latter probably uses them because someone else used them. Ordinarily one must be a specialist in Western philosophy to know those selected terms in their classical senses.

An Indian pioneer in pushing the use of Western philosophical terms is Satis Chandra Vidyabhusana. He did this in his work, *A History of Indian Logic.* A section of his book even claims that the logical theories of Aristotle migrated from Alexandra into India during 175 B.C. and 600 A.D.[2] But Vidyabhusana failed to show use of any Greek words in the Indian syllogism, as we find adopted in Indian astronomy/astrology, such as *horā*, for which the Greek original is still in English as 'hour' for parts of the day. So Vidyabhusana's position reduces to that it must be true because he says so. Indeed, the basic part of a syllogism does not need borrowing, because in every language known of, people say something is the case (i.e. the thesis) because... (i.e. the reason, the *hetu*). Whether they go on to add an example does not matter because there was a dispute in India as to whether the example was necessary for what is called the pervasion (*vyāpti*).

The present author is not alone in rejecting these Western philosophical terms for rendering Buddhist logic. There are two scholars that I know of who have each rejected this imposed terminology, namely, H. Kitagawa and F. Staal.[3]

Besides, a well-known author, Ganganatha Jha, has a basic work called *The Pūrva-Mīmāṃsā-Sūtras of Jaimini* (Varanasi, Delhi, 1979); and going all through this fine work I could not find a single case of such imposition by Western terms. In Ganganatha Jha's *Pūrva-Mīmāṃsā in its Sources* (Varanasi, 1964) he does use the word 'universal' but as an ordinary English word, contrasting with 'individual' (see his pp. 65 ff.) His books remain fine reference works.

---

2. M.M. Satis Chandra Vidyabhusana, *A History of Indian Logic* (Delhi: Motilal Banarsidass, 1971 [author's Preface, Calcutta, 1920]), pp. 511-13.
3. Hidenori Kitagawa, "A Note on the Methodology in the Study in Indian Logic," *Journal of Indian and Buddhist Studies* (Tokyo), Vol. VIII, No. 1 (January 1960), pp. (19)-(29); J.F. Staal, "The Concept of *Pakṣa* in Indian Logic," *Journal of Indian Philosophy* 2 (1973), pp. 156-166.

My personal library of South Asia books includes some that are full of these Western philosophical terms applied to Indian logic, including the Buddhist type. I need not cite those books here to advertise or to chastise them, but their authors will readily recognize what I shall now mention. When such authors apply the one word 'universal' to *sāmānya-lakṣaṇa*–which has two terms, *sāmānya* and *lakṣaṇa*; and apply the one word 'particular' to *svalakṣaṇa*—a compound of *sva* and *lakṣaṇa*, there is an immediate shortcoming: If the 'universal' is just for the *sāmānya*, and the 'particular' is just for the *sva*, then to the users of such Western terms, the word *lakṣaṇa* in both cases is superfluous; but not superfluous to the author of Buddhist logic. Besides, those books indiscriminately apply the word 'universal' both to the individual term *sāmānya* and to the two-term compound *sāmānya-lakṣaṇa*. And what those books apparently do not take account of, is that the authors of Buddhist logic always distinguish between *sāmānya* and *sāmānya-lakṣaṇa*. To get the significance of this distinction, one should pay attention to the theory of Buddhist logic that there are four kinds of direct perception (*pratyakṣa*)—that of the five outer senses; that of the mind, called *mānasa-pratyakṣa*; the introspective kind (*svasaṃvedana-p.*), and that of the yogin (*yogi-p.*); and that each of these has as object the *svalakṣaṇa* (individual character). And also pay attention to the theory of this logic that the range of the *svalakṣaṇa* does not overlap that of the *sāmānya-lakṣaṇa*. Then notice in the essay included in this Vol. One, Bu-ston's Analysis of the Pramāṇaviniścaya, in the early part (*P-Vin-Bu*, 22b-4), that Dignāga explained the object of *mānasa-pratyakṣa* (i.e. its *svalakṣaṇa*) as a *sāmānyagocara*, which I render a 'global scope', because of the diverse contents of the object of this sort of *pratyakṣa*.

In fact, the texts in this volume show that usually *sāmānya* is indeed an abbreviation for *sāmānya-lakṣaṇa* in contexts of inference, but in contexts of *mānasa-pratyakṣa* it abbreviates Dignāga's *sāmānya-gocaram*, and that the authors keep this in mind. Notice that I could only discuss this in ordinary English words but that it could not be treated by users of the words 'universals' and 'particulars' because such words were applied always to those Sanskrit terms no matter what the context, while in fact there are two different contexts.

The following list of terms with my own renditions along with renditions of other authors (especially using Western philosophical terms) has the advantage of pointing out in this Introduction certain important terms of the system:

Term	*Translation here adopted*	*Some other translations*
svalakṣaṇa	individual character	a particular
sāmānyalakṣaṇa	generality-, generalizing-character	a universal
liṅga	evidence	a sign
trirūpa	(its) three modes	three marks or characters
sādhya	thesis	major term, predicate, probandum
hetu	the reason	middle term
pakṣa	[usually] locus	minor term
sapakṣa	similar locuses	homologue
asapakṣa	dissimilar locuses	heterologue
bādhaka	annulment	sublating

The foregoing should serve as an indication of why I decline to use the Western philosophical terms in my renditions, as demonstrated in the texts included in this Vol. One.

B. REGARDING RENDITIONS WITH ORDINARY WORDS

Probably the most important among the terms translated with ordinary words are *pramāṇa* and its object *prameya.* The brilliant Buddhist logician Dignāga is acknowledged to have made a great impact on Indian philosophy. His quarrel with the Naiyāyikas and the Mīmāṃsakas among Hindu schools of philosophy was especially over theories about this term *pramāṇa* and about its varieties. In short, he set forth two kinds of *pramāṇa,* namely, direct perception (*pratyakṣa*), and inference (*anumāna*), and had four kinds of *pratyakṣa.* He claimed that *pramāṇa* is a result (in Sanskrit, *phala or kārya*), and that its two kinds are respectively the results of a nonoverlapping individual character (*svalakṣaṇa*) and generality character (*sāmānyalakṣaṇa*).

Various Hindu and Jain authors disagreed with Dignāga's use of the word *pramāṇa* as a result, claiming the word has an instrumental meaning, giving rise to such renditions as 'source of cognition'. That the Hindu and Jain opponents employ the term differently does not in itself render Dignāga's use wrong, even though various modern books dealing with the topic talk that way, to wit, if one author correctly uses a term a certain way, that renders other ways incorrect. Such an attitude appears unaware that the medieval Indian lexicons with the term *anekārtha* or *nānārtha* in their full titles give different definitions for a headword. I have looked up several concerning this matter, but of course am mostly familiar with the lexicon I myself translated, the one by Śrīdharasena, whose definitions of the headword *Pramāṇaṃ* are mostly the same as are found in earlier lexicons.[1] Among these definitions are ones which support an instrumental interpretation and ones that support a fruitional interpretation. Thus, the definition 'a truth teller' (*satyavādin*) is instrumental, a source of truth; the definition 'boundary' (*maryādā*) fruitional, the result of measurement. It follows that if one wants to understand the Hindu, Jain, or Buddhist systems of logic, one must know how such systems are using their important terms. And so one cannot treat any of those systems properly if one insists on translating such a word as *pramāṇa* in a way that suits a rival system. Perhaps the different usages of such a term reflect a different education, or a different audience for such teachings. It is because Dignāga went about refuting certain rival systems in his *Pramāṇasamuccaya* that those other systems naturally responded with returning arguments; but such facts do not prove that either Dignāga's initial refutations, or the subsequent return attacks, are fair and judicious.

Therefore, I shall now explain why, in the context of Buddhist logic, I translate *pramāṇa* as 'authority' and its object *prameya* as 'sanction'. First, may I explain what is meant by the words 'authority' and 'sanction'. Take *Webster's New world Dictionary of the American Language* (College Edition, 1960). p. 1290, and select under 'sanction', "authorization, authoritative permission"—in short, "what authorizes". And from its p. 99, under 'authority', "power or influence resulting from knowledge, prestige, etc." Here, 'authority' is defined in a so resultative manner, much like we may say, "Some professors become authorities in their topics," so resultative. In contrast, when Monier-Williams Sanskrit-English Dictionary puts under *pramāṇa* (p. 685c), "The Vedas are authorities" *(vedāḥ pramāṇāḥ)*, the term 'authority' is employed in instrumental fashion, as we could rephrase, "The Vedas are source of divine knowledge."

As to my 'sanction' for *prameya*, this rendition might appear strange to some scholars, so it will justify the somewhat technical

4. *Abhidhānaviśvalocanam of Śrīdharasena*, tr. by Alex Wayman (Narita: Naritasan Shinshoji, 1994), p. 199.

approach that follows. We notice that according to Sanskrit grammar this term is a gerundive, based on the word *pramā*. Now it is a fact that the gerundive is generally understood as a future, so the Whitney *Sanskrit Grammar* heads its para. 961: "Future Passive Participles: Gerundives. Yet it is recognized that the gerundive may also be interpreted with present time. In illustration, see the same Monier-Williams dictionary (p. 728a) under the entry *bādhya*—a gerundive—"to be (or being) set aside..." But how to determine when the gerundive has present time? Fortunately the answer is deriveable from the treatment in Joshi's and Roodbergen's translation of Patañjali's commentary on Pāṇini (the 1973 issue, pp. 18-24).[5] We read on its p. 18, "*bādhya*: 'what is debarred'"—so attributed the present time—and the discussion continues with the pair, *bādhaka-bādhya*; and we learn how to impose the present-time option by this pair being considered in their relation independently of their suffixes. Thus, on p. 19, the general rule is prevented [or suspended] because the suffixes occupy different positions. On p. 21 we learn that a special rule could prevail over the general rule. The discussion here is quite subtle and complicated. The general rule applies when, e.g. *bādhya*, is employed adjectively to agree with another term, of course with their suffixes or endings. The present-time state of my rendition choice 'sanction' demands a special rule.

Then the non-suffixal relations of *bādhaka, bādhya*, apply as well to the pair *pramāṇa, prameya*. We notice that in both pairs, the second member is the object of the first member. Thus, 'what debars' (*bādhaka*) has as object 'what is debarred' (*bādhya*); while the 'authority' (*pramāṇa*) has as object 'the knowledge and prestige which authorizes' (*prameya*). And both first members are preceded by their respective objects. Thus, there should be 'what is debarred' so 'what debars' may operate; and there should be 'what authorizes' so there may be the 'authority'. Accordingly, the special relations between the two members of each pair enable a special rule to operate, permitting the present-time option for the gerundive.

My selection from possible English definitions of 'sanction' to arrive at "what authorizes" has been justified as a present-time companion to 'authority' (in a fruitional sense). This applicability also rejects the futuristic rendition 'inferable' of *prameya*.

5. S.D. Joshi and J.A.F. Roodbergen, *Patañjali's Vyākaraṇa Mahābhāṣya*, Tatpuruṣāhnika (Poona: University of Poona, 1973).

This rejection can also be made in a different way. Notice that *prameya* in Buddhist logic is of two kinds—'generality character' (*sāmānyalakṣaṇa*) and 'individual character' (*svalakṣaṇa*). The generality character' has been called *anumeya* (the inferable), which is the object of *anumāna* (inference). The other kind of *prameya,* 'individual character', is the object of *pratyakṣa* (direct perception), which cannot be inferred according to Buddhist logic. The rendition 'inferable' works for one kind of *prameya,* but is contradictive for the other kind. In contrast, the word 'sanction' works for both kinds, since the 'inferable' as 'generality character' is what authorizes (or sanctions) inference; and the 'individual character' is what authorizes (or sanctions) direct perception.

The present writer can further explain the adoption of the rendition 'sanction' for *prameya.* In the Tsong-kha-pa treatise which concludes the essays of this Vol. One, there is a section on variegating the 'sanction' (*prameya*) that first presents the two kinds, already mentioned ('generality character' and 'individual character'), then presents three kinds, which are *sākṣāt* (directly realized), *parokṣa* (beyond sight), and *atyantaparokṣa* (further beyond sight). Of these, the first is comprehended by direct perception, e.g. the color blue. The second is comprehended by inference authority, e.g. "The blue is impermanent." The third is comprehended by inference authority, taking recourse to a pure scripture by three examinations. Since Dignāga was criticized by some Buddhists for not including the Buddhist scriptures as a kind of authority (*pramāṇa*) [Asaṅga's *āptāgama*], for which he had only two—direct perception and inference, it is of interest that he or his successors included the scriptures in the second kind of the two inference-objects. As the Buddhist logicians thus included the scriptures within *prameya,* this supports my rendition 'sanction' which is lent an ethical touch for involving the Buddhist scriptures.

The foregoing is certainly enough for the terms *pramāṇa* and *prameya.* One other term will be briefly treated here. It is *svabhāva.* There is a tendency for Buddhist specialists, having arrived at their rendition of a term like *svabhāva,* to employ the same rendition wherever the term occurs in Buddhist texts. The position adopted here is that the term has one meaning when used in the Buddhist sect called Mādhyamika, perhaps 'self-existence'; another meaning in Yogācāra Buddhism, which speaks of three of them, also calling them the three *lakṣaṇa,* perhaps 'individual nature'; and still another in Buddhist logic, for which I have adopted the rendition, 'individual presence'. I learned about this rendition first from Dharmakīrti's *Nyāyabindu,* Chap. II on Svārthānumāna, where is set forth the three kinds of evidence, with the second one called the *svabhāvahetu.* I made sense of the definition by this rendition: "Individual presence is a reason when the thesis feature has a presence that amounts to the (concrete) existence of itself." This is followed by an example: "as, e.g. 'This is a tree, because it is an Aśoka.'" Here, the Aśoka is the individual presence (the object of direct perception) and is the reason for tree-ness, i.e. the class of trees. Here, the Aśoka is the concrete existence of itself—the tree. I found this rendition of 'individual presence' to help clarify numerous sentences of Buddhist logic where the word *svabhāva* occurred.

It is not feasible in this Introduction to give more reasons for translating individual terms, so I shall present this partial list of such terms with translations into ordinary language words.

Term	*Translation here adopted*	*Some other translations*
pramāṇa	authority	means of right knowledge [and other instrumental renditions]
prameya	sanction	inferable, cognized [and untranslated]
svabhāva	individual presence	identity, etc.
anvaya	similar presence (= presence in similar cases)	affirmation
vyatireka	dissimilar absence (=absence in dissimilar cases)	negation
sādharmya	feature concordance	homogeneous
vaidharmya	feature discordance	heterogeneous
svasaṃvedana	introspection	self cognition
vikalpika	with discursive thought	determinate
nirvikalpika	without discursive thought	indeterminate
kalpanā	constructive thought	reflection, etc.

As to other terms, not included in this b. list, or above in the a. list, over the years I have adopted the renditions of other scholars, or have renditions of my own. The adoption of various renditions of my own does not mean I do not appreciate the previous translations and studies of Buddhist logic which have their varying helpfulness.

If the present volume is more successful at expounding Buddhist logic, it would be so by the texts being more in focus, approaching close enough to be made out.

CONTENTS

Foreword v
Preface vii
Prologue ix
Introduction xiii
Abbreviations xxv

PART I: INTRODUCTORY TEXTS 1

Asaṅga's Rules of Debate (Sanskrit-English) 3-41
The Debate in Itself 5
Setting of the Debate 9
Foundation of the Debate 9
The Debate's Ornament 26
Points of Defeat in the Debate 31
Decision Whether to Undertake the Debate 37
Attributes of Much Utility in the Debate 40

Introduction to Dharmakīrti's *Nyāyabindu* and Kamalaśīla's *Nyāyabindupūrvapakṣasaṃkṣipti* 43
Dharmakīrti's *Nyāyabindu* (Sanskrit-English) 44-75
Pratyakṣa (Direct Perception) 44
Svārthānumāna (Inference for Oneself) 45
Parārthānumāna (Inference for Others) 51
Kamalaśīla's *Nyāyabindupūrvapakṣasaṃkṣipti* (NB-PPS) 75-100
Adversaries of Direct Perception 75
Adversaries of Inference for Oneself 81
Adversaries of Inference for Others 90

Antarvyāptisamarthana of Ratnākaraśānti 101-122
Paragraphs 1-10 105
Paragraphs 11-16 116

PART II: THE DIGNĀGA-DHARMAKĪRTI SYSTEM 123

Introduction to the Dignāga-Dharmakīrti
System by the 'Elevens' 125-145
PS-Prat, First Eleven Verses 126
PV-Sid, First Eleven Verses 132
PV-Prat, First Eleven Verses 135
PV-Sva, First Eleven Verses 138
PV-Par, First Eleven Verses 142

Analysis of P-Vin-Bu 147-254
Pratyakṣa (Direct Perception) 154
Svārthānumāna (Inference for Oneself) 183
Parārthānumāna (Inference for Others) 217

Tsong-kha-pa's Guided Tour Through the
Seven Books of Dharmakīrti 255-331
Object 259
Subject 266
Means of Understanding the Object 283

Bibliography 333

Index 339

ABBREVIATIONS

AK	*Abhidharmakośa* by Vasubandhu
AKBh	Vasubandhu's *bhāṣya* on *AK*
Bhāṣya.	See *PV-Bh.*
HB	*Hetubindu* by Dharmakīrti
JAOS	*Journal of the American Oriental Society*
JRAS	*Journal of the Royal Asiatic Society* (London)
Mun sel	Tsong-kha-pa's text (translated in this Vol. One)
NMu	The *Nyāyamukha* by Dignāga
Nyāyabindu-Par	Parārthānumāna chap. of *Nyāyabindu*
P-Vin	*Pramāṇaviniścaya* by Dharmakīrti
P-Vin-Bu	Bu-ston's commentary on *P-Vin*
P-Vin-Par	Parārthānumāna chap. of *P-Vin*
P-Vin-Prat	Pratyakṣa chap. of *P-Vin*
P-Vin-Sva	Svārthānumāna chap. of *P-Vin*
P-Vin-Par-Bu	Bu-ston's commentary on the *Par* chap. of *P-Vin*
P-Vin-Prat-Bu	Bu-ston's commentary on the *Prat* chap. of *P-Vin*
P-Vin-Sva-Bu	Bu-ston's commentary on the *Sva* chap. of *P-Vin*
PS	*Pramāṇasamuccaya* by Dignāga
PS-Par	Parārthānumāna chap. of *PS*
PS-Prat	Pratyakṣa chap. of *PS*
PS-Sva	Svārthānumāna chap. of *PS*
PTT	Peking Tibetan Tripitaka (Japanese reprint)
PV	*Pramāṇavārttika* by Dharmakīrti
PV-Bh.	*Bhāṣya* on *PV* by Prajñākaragupta
PV-Bh.-Par	*Par* chap. of *PV-Bh.*
PV-Bh.-Prat	*Prat* chap. of *PV-Bh.*
PV-M	The *vṛtti* by Manorathanandin on *PV*
PV-M-Par	The *Par* chap. of *PV-M*
PV-Par	The *Par* chap. of *PV*
PV-Prat	The *Prat* chap. of *PV*
PV-Sid	The *Siddhi* chap. of *PV*

PV-Sva	The *Sva* chap. of *PV*
PV-SV	Dharmakīrti's commentary on the *Sva* chap. of his *PV*
vṛtti	See *PV-M*
WZKS	*Wiener Zeitschrift für die kunde Sud-und Ostasiens*

PART I

INTRODUCTORY TEXTS

ASAṄGA'S RULES OF DEBATE

INTRODUCTION

The topic of Debate has a wide literature, and in recent years even separate volumes have been addressed to the topic. My Vol. Two of this 'Millennium' will have an essay on Debate, so here I shall restrict the material to a text by Asaṅga.

The text and translation herein presented and called "Asaṅga's Rules of Debate" is a portion of an encyclopedic work by Asaṅga, also called Ārya-Asaṅga, entitled *Yogācārabhūmi*, composed probably in the second half, fourth century A.D. in north India.

The first treatment of Asaṅga's debate section was by Guiseppe Tucci, who had available both the Tibetan and the Chinese versions, namely, in an article of 1929.[1] Then, when the present writer did his doctoral dissertation, *Analysis of the Śrāvakabhūmi Manuscript* (published 1961),[2] he noticed various intrusive folios in this Bihar photographic manuscript of the *Śrāvakabūmi* (photographed by Sankrityayana in Tibet) and among them folios belonging to another section of the *Yogācārabhūmi*, namely, belonging to the section on Rules of Debate. The present writer, even before finishing that dissertation, after gaining an initial control of the script, published in 1958 the essay "The Rules of Debate According to Asaṅga," which amounted to an outline, but informed interested scholars that the original Sanskrit for this section was available.[3] Years later, in the mid-70's, while teaching at Columbia University, I conceived a plan to write a book, A Millennium of Buddhist Logic, which would begin with this Asaṅga treatise and end with the Guided Tour

1. Guiseppe Tucci, "Buddhist Logic before Dignāga (Asaṅga, Vasubandhu, Tarkaśāstras)," *JRAS* for 1929, Part III, July, pp. 451-88; note, Part IV, October, pp. 870-1 (London).
2. Alex Wayman, *Analysis of the Śrāvakabhūmi Manuscript*, University of California Publications in Classical Philology, Vol. 17, Berkeley, California.
3. Wayman, "The rules of debate according to Asaṅga," *JAOS* 78:1, 29-40.

Through the Seven Books of Dharmakīrti by Tsoṅ-kha-pa (1357-1419). For this purpose I attempted to edit the entire text from the Bihar MS, difficult as it was, and produced my edition in early 1980's, along with a translation into English, but did not publish this until now. Earlier, Pradhan had edited Asaṅga's *Abhidharma-samuccaya*, which near its end has an abbreviated version of this debate section;[4] and when the commentary was edited with a citation from the debate section,[5] this helped for one part of my edition. However, while I did work on various Buddhist logic texts during the coming years, my major efforts remained in manuscript form, while I completed other projects in Tantric and non-tantric Buddhism.

Other scholars became interested in editing this text. I know of two other scholars who edited the same Sanskrit text here called the Rules of Debate and preceded me in publication. One, Jagadīśvara Pāṇḍeya, edited it from the same Bihar photo MS that I used, and translated his edition into Hindi (1986).[6] The other, a Japanese scholar named H. Yaita, edited it from a reproduction of the *Śrāvakabhūmi* MS, that had been taken from Tibet to Beijing, and translated his edition into Japanese (1992).[7] Yaita has references both to Pāṇḍeya's text and my old article. Naturally I consulted both of those editions to see if we agreed; and if not, to decide what be the correct reading. My edition is based on the Bihar Society MS, and the Tibetan translation.[8]

I decided to intersperse my translation with the Sanskrit edition by logical divisions such as paragraphs. When necessary in the notes I shall refer to alternate readings of Pāṇḍeya as Pa, and of Yaita as Ya. I shall use italics for Sanskrit words accepted for inclusion in the edition on the basis of the Tibetan, except for obvious corrections.

---

4. Pralhad Pradhan, *Abhidharma-samuccaya* (Santiniketan: Visva-Bharati, 1950).
5. Nathmal Tatia, *Abhidharmasamucaya-Bhāṣyam* (Patna: Jayaswal Research Institute, 1976).
6. Pāṇḍeya in *Homage to Bhikkhu Jagdish Kashyap*, ed. By P.N. Ojha (Nalanda, Bihar: Siri Nava Nalanda Mahavihara), Part II, pp. 315-49. I am appreciative of N.P. Jain of Motilal Banarsidass, Delhi, furnishing a copy of this honorary volume to me.
7. Yaita in *Naritasan Bukkyō Kenkyūsho*, Kiyō 15, special issue vol. "Bukkyō Bunka Ronshū II", May 1992 (Narita: Naritasan Shinshōji), pp. 505-76. I am appreciative of Yaita's furnishing an offprint of his essay to me.
8. The Bihar Society MS by intrusive folios; the Tibetan by the actual location of the *hetuvidyā* section (Tib. tr.) in the Tibetan canon, using the Peking version, *PTT* Vol. 109, starting p. 298-1-6.

ASAṄGA'S RULES OF DEBATE (SANSKRIT-ENGLISH)

// hetuvidyā katamā/ parīkṣārthena yad vijñanaṃ vastu/ tat punaḥ katamat / tadyathā vādaḥ vādādhikaraṇaṃ vādādhiṣṭhānaṃ vādālamkāraḥ vādanigrahaḥ vādaniḥsaraṇaṃ vāde bahukāra dharmāḥ /

What is the science of reasoning (*hetuvidyā*)? Whatever understanding (*vijñāna*) for the given thing (*vastu*) by virtue of examination (*parīkṣā*). And what is it besides? As follows: I. The debate in itself (*vāda*), II. Setting of the debate (*vādādhikaraṇa*), III. Foundation of the debate (*vādādhiṣṭhāna*), IV. The debates's ornament (*vādālaṃkāra*), V. Points of defeat in the debate (*vādanigraha*), VI. Decision whether to undertake the debate (*vādaniḥsaraṇa*), VII. Attributes of much utility in the debate (*vāde bahukarā dharmāḥ*).

/ vādaḥ katamaḥ sa ṣaḍvidho draṣṭavyaḥ vādaḥ pravādaḥ vivādo 'pavādo 'nuvādo 'vavādas ca /

I. THE DEBATE IN ITSELF

What is the debate in itself? It should be observed as six kinds: 1. Utterances of all kinds (*vāda*), 2. A popular message (*pravāda*). 3. Quarrels (*vivāda*), 4.Noxious talk (*apavāda*), 5. (Doctrinally) consistent discussion (*anuvāda*), 6. Precepts (of guidance) (*avavāda*).

/ vādaḥ katamaḥ savro vāgvyavahāro vāgghoṣo vāgniruktir vā ity ucyate vādaḥ/

1. What are utterances of all kinds? All (the following:) conventions of speech (*vāgvyavahāra*); enunciations of speech (*vāgghoṣa*); denotations of speech (*vāgnirukti*)—these are called "utterances of all kinds."

/ pravādaḥ katamaḥ / yo lokānuśraviko vādaḥ /

2. What is a popular message? Whatever message is being heard frequently by the people.

/ vivādaḥ katamaḥ / kāmān vārabhya pareṣām āchettukāma iṣṭasvaparigṛhīteṣu kāmeṣu, pareṣām ācchettukāma iṣṭapara-parigṛhīteṣu kāmeṣu; iṣṭasattvaparigṛhīteṣv ācchidyamāneṣv ācchettukāmasya vāparigṛhīteṣu kāmeṣu;[9] tadyathā naṭa-

9. From the part after *vārabhya* down to this point there are various differences in the editions of Pa and Ya from what is given here. Ya, p.512, n. 7, claims that the MS omits *parair ācchidyamāneṣu*, influenced by Pa's *parair ucchidyamāneṣu*. And then Ya, p. 512, n. 8, claims that the MS repeats *pareṣām ācchettukāma iṣṭasattvaparigṛhiteṣu kāmeṣu*, as though repeating in error both phrases. But, using the Tibetan as I did, I found almost everything in the MS applicable.

narttakahāsakalāsakādyupasaṃhiteṣu[10] *strīgaṇikopasaṃhiteṣu*vā punaḥ saṃdarśanāya yā upabhogāya vā iti / yad evaṃ prakāreṣu kāmeṣv avītarāgāṇāṃ sat(t)vānāṃ kāmarāgaraktānām adhyavasānahetor vibadhyahetoḥ parigredhahetoḥ saṃrāgahetor saṃrabdhānāṃ vigṛhītānāṃ vivādam āpannānāṃ nānāvādo vivādo vipratyanīkavādo/

3. What are [the entries to] quarrels? (1) Entey through desired things (*kāma*). There might be desires to gain for oneself what is wished while there is a desire to deprive others. Or there might be desires to gain for the others what is wished while there is a desire to deprive others. Or there might be deprived (i.e. failing) desires to gain for respected sentient beings; or nongained (i.e. also failing) desires on behalf of the desire to deprive. That is to say, (desires) involving actors, dancers, comedians, sensual performers, etc.; or involving women [in general] and harlots—whether to see them or to enjoy them. And when there are desires of such kind, belonging to sentient beings who are not free from cravings, who are attached to cravings for desired objects,—on account of clinging, on account of bondage, on account of greediness, on account of passion, they begin contending. Having fallen into quarrel, their quarrels or discordant declarations are of many sorts.

/ duścaritaṃ vā punar ārabhya svayaṃkṛte kāyaduścarite vāgduścarite parair anuyujyamānaḥ parakṛte kāyaduścarite vāgduścarite parānuyuñjana iṣṭasat(t)vakṛte kāyaduścarite parair anuyujyamāne paraṃ vā anuyuñjato '*kṛte* kāyaduścarite vāgduścarite kartum praṇihitasya iti / yad evaṃ prakāre duścaritasamācāre 'vigatalobhānām avigatadveṣāṇām avigatamohānāṃ lobhadveṣamohābhibhūtānām adhyavasānahetor vinibandhahetoḥ parigredhahetoḥ saṃrāgahetor anyonyaṃ saṃrabdhānāṃ saṃkliṣṭacittānāṃ vigṛhītānāṃ vivādām āpannānāṃ nānāvādo vivādo vipratyanīkavādaḥ /

(2) Or, entry through bad conduct (*duścarita*). When there is bad conduct of body or bad conduct of speech committed by oneself, one is reprehended by others. And when there is bad conduct of body or bad conduct of speech committed by others, one reprehends the others. And when there is bad conduct of body or bad conduct of speech committed by a respected sentient being, that one is reprehended by others, or reprehends another. Or when bad conduct of body or bad conduct of speech is not committed, they say

---

10. Ya, p. 512, n. 9, says he follows Tib. and Pa for correcting the MS *hāsakalāsakādy-* but I find the MS satisfactory here.

it is of one wishing to do it. And when there is such kind of customary behavior of bad conduct of those not free from covetousness, not free from hatred, not free from delusion—they are dominated by covetousness hatred, and delusion. On account of clinging, on account of bondage, on account of greediness, on account of passion, they have begun mutually with defiled mind, contending. Having fallen into quarrel, their quarrels or discordant declarations are of many sorts.

/dṛṣṭiṃ vā punar ārabhya tadyathā satkāyadṛṣṭim *ucchedadṛṣṭim ahetudṛṣṭiṃ*[11] *viṣama*[12]-hetudṛṣṭiṃ śāśvatadṛṣṭiṃ vārṣagaṇyadṛṣṭiṃ mithyādṛṣṭim iti/yā vā punar anyā pāpikā dṛṣṭir ity evambhāgīyadṛṣṭiṣu svaparigṛhītāsu parair vicchidyamānā paraparigṛhatāsu parān vicchindayataḥ / iṣṭasat(t) vaparigṛhītāsu parair vicchidyamānā parān vicchindayato vā aparigṛhītāsu vā punaḥ parigṛhītakāmatām upadāya avītarāgānām *sattvānāṃ* pūrvavad yāvan nānāvādo vivādo vipratyanīkavādaḥ / ayam ucyate vivādaḥ /

(3) Or entering through views (*dṛṣṭi*). (Through) the reifying view (*satkāya-d.*), the nihilistic view (*uccheda-d.*), the irrational view (*ahetu-d.*), the view with dishonest reason (*viṣamahetu-d.*), the eternalistic view (*śāśvata-d.*), the view of Vārṣagaṇya, the deviant view (*mithyā-d.*), or any other sinful view among views of like category adopted by oneself. These are reprehended by others after one reprehends others for what (views) were adopted by others. Or when they are among those adopted by respected beings, they are reprehended by others after one has reprehended the other (persons). Or when they are not among those adopted, by resort to the adopted state of desire of sentient beings not free from passion [they could be adopted], as previously, and so on up to, their quarrels or discordant declarations are of many sorts.

Those are called [the entries to] quarrels.

/apavādaḥ katamaḥ saṃrabdhānāṃ saṃkliṣṭacetasām anyonyam utsṛjya viprakṛtāṃ kathāyaḥ[13] pāruṣyopasaṃhito 'sabhyopasaṃhitaḥ sambhinnapralāpopasaṃhito vādaḥ yāvad durākhyāte dharmavinaye dharmadeśanā-saṃkathye viniścayo 'pavādānuśāsanam/ayam ucyate 'pavādaḥ /

11. Pa (p. 335) omits this; Ya (p. 513) mentions only the Tibetan, *rgyu med par lta ba.*

12. While I had favored the *pratikūla-* reconstruction from Tib. *mi mthun pa,* now I believe Pa, followed by Ya, is right with *viṣama.*

13. While admitting that this reading is in the MS, Ya, following Pa, changes it to *Kathāṃ yaḥ.* But the MS form, which I accept, is the genitive plural of *kathā,* with which the preceding word *viprakṛt* agrees in declination.

4. What is noxious talk (*apavāda*)? Among those (persons) beginning with defiled mentality, when there is mutual emitting of offensive discussions (*viprakṛt-kathā*). The talk exhibits coarseness, exhibits unworthiness to convoke a gathering (*asabhyopasaṃhita*), exhibits incoherence, and so on, up to, set in an account that [supposedly] teaches the Dharma, amounting to a badly expressed doctrine (*dharma*) and disciplinary code (*vinaya*), to wit, an instruction in noxious talk. This is called 'noxious talk'.

/ anuvādaḥ katamaḥ *yaḥ*[14] svākhyāte dharmavinaye dharmadeśanāsāṃkathye viniścayopaśāsanam utpannasya saṃśayasya chedāya[15] gambhīrasyārthapadasya prativedhāya jñānadarśanasya śuddhaye / mokṣasyānukūlo 'nulomiko vādaḥ tasmād anuvāda ity ucyate / ayam ucyate 'nuvādaḥ /

5. What is a (doctrinally) consistent discussion (*anuvāda*)? Whichever is an instruction set in an account that teaches the Dharma as a well-expressed doctrine (*dharma*) and disciplinary code (*vinaya*), for cutting off the arisen doubt, for penetrating the profoundly meaningful words, for purifying knowledge and vision. Being a consistent discussion that is compatible with liberation, it is therefore called 'a (doctrinally) consistent discussion'.

/avavādaḥ katamaḥ / adhicitte / 'dhiprajñe prayoktukāmasya pudgalasyāsamāhitasya vā cittasya samādhāya[16] samāhitasya vā cittasya vimokṣāya yo vādaḥ tat(t) vajñānāvabodhāya tat(t) vajñānāvagamāya vādaḥ tasmād anuvāda ity ucyate/ ayam ucyate 'vavādaḥ /

6. What are precepts (of guidance) (*avavāda*)? a. Whatever precept for concentrating the unequilibrated mind of a person desirous of exerting oneself to higher mind training (*adhicitta*), or for liberating that one's equilibrated mind. b. Or desirous of exerting oneself to higher insight (*adhiprajña*), a precept for awakening the knowledge of reality, and for comprehending the knowledge of reality. Therefore, they are called 'precepts (of guidance)'. This is called *avavāda*.

/ eṣāṃ ṣaṇṇāṃ vādānam kati vādā bhūtās tat(t) vā arthopasaṃhitāḥ sevitavyāḥ / kati vādā abhūtā atat(t) vā anarthopasaṃhitāḥ parivarjayitavyāḥ dvau paścimau vādau bhūtau *tattvav* arthopasaṃhitau sevitavyau / dvau madhyau vādav abhūtav atat(t) vav anarthopasaṃhitau (pari) varjayitavyau ādyayor dvayor vādayor bhedaḥ/

---

14. Pa, followed by Yā, has *yā*, agreeing with *dharmadeśanā*; but I accept the latter as part of a compound.
15. I accept Pa's correction, followed by Ya, of MS. *saṃśayacchedāyaḥ* to *saṃśayasya chedāya*.
16. Both Pa and Ya add to this MS expression, thus: *samādhānāya*.

Of those six (kinds of) 'debate' (in itself), which communications are genuine (*bhūta*), real (*tattva*), meaningful (*arthopasaṃhita*), and to be followed (*sevitavya*)? Which communications are false, unreal, meaningless, and to be avoided? The last two (i.e. nos. 5 and 6) are genuine, real, meaningful, and to be followed. The two middle ones (i.e. nos. 3 and 4) are the two that are false, unreal, meaningless, and to be avoided. The kind of the first two (i.e. nos. 1 and 2) is of both communications (to be followed and to be avoided).

/ vādādhikaraṇaṃ katamat tad api ṣaḍvidhaṃ draṣṭavyaṃ / tad yathā rājakulaṃ yuktakulaṃ parṣatsabhā dharmārthakuśalāḥ / śramaṇā brāhmaṇā dharmārthakāmāś ca sat(t) vāḥ /

II. SETTING OF THE DEBATE

What is the setting of the debate? It is also of six kinds, namely, 1. royal residence (*rājakula*), 2. residence of officials (*yuktakula*), 3. retinues (*parṣad*), 4. (formal) gatherings (*sabhā*), 5. ascetics and brahmins skilled in the doctrine (*dharma*) and meaning (*artha*), 6. persons desiring the doctrine and (its) meaning.

/vādādhiṣṭhānaṃ katamat/tad daśavidhaṃ draṣṭavyaṃ/sādhyo 'rtho dvividhaḥ/sādhyasyārthasya sādhanam aṣṭavidhaṃ/sādhyo 'rtho dvividhaḥ katamaḥ svabhāvo viśeṣaś ca/ tatra svabhāvaḥ/ sādhyaḥ sac ca sato 'sac cāsataḥ/viśeṣaḥ sādhyaḥ sottaraṃ ca sottarato 'nuttaraṃ cānuttarataḥ/nityo nityataḥ/anityonityataḥ/rūpī rūpitaḥ /arūpy arūpitaḥ/yathā rūpy arūpī tathā sanidarśano 'nidarśanaḥ sapratigho 'pratighaḥ sāśravo 'naśravaḥ saṃskṛto 'saṃskṛta ity evam ādinā prabhedanayena/viśeṣaya sādhyatā draṣṭavyā/

III. FOUNDATION OF THE DEBATE

What is the foundation of the debate (*vādādhiṣṭhāna*)? There are ten kinds. Two kinds are the two thesis topics (*sādhya-artha*). Eight kinds are the proving (*sādhana*) of the thesis topics.

What are the two theis topics? They are the individual presence (*svabhāva*) and the qualification (*viśeṣa*). Among them, a. The thesis individual presence is existence of an existent, and nonexistence of a nonexistent. b. The thesis qualification is the superior of what is superior; being without superior of what is without superior; permanence of the permanent; impermanence of the impermanent; the formed of what has form; the formless of what is formless. Likewise, by dividing into such (qualifications) as 'shown', 'unshown', 'with impediment', 'without impediment', 'with flux', 'without flux', 'constructed', 'unconstructed', there is the thesis state of a qualification.

/ sādhanam aṣṭavidhaṃ katamat/pratijñā hetur udāharaṇaṃ sārūpyaṃ vairūpyaṃ pratyakṣam anumānam āptāgamaś ca/

What are the eight kinds of proving? Thesis (*pratijñā*), reason (*hetu*), example (*udāharaṇa*) similarity (sārūpya), dissimilarity (*vairūpya*), direct perception (*pratyakṣa*), inference (*anumāna*), lineage of the masters (*āptāgama*).

/pratijñā katamā dvividhaṃ sādhyam artham ārabhya yaḥ anyonyaṃ svapakṣaparigraha [*taḥ*?][17] śāstraparigrahato vā svapratibhānato vā parānugrahato vā *paraśravaṇato vā tattvādhigamato vā* svapakṣāvasthānato vā parapakṣadūṣaṇato vā parābhibhavato vā paraparibhavato vā parānukampanato vā/

What is a thesis (*pratijñā*)? It is of two kinds [both required]. Starting with the thesis topic, whichever one another., due to being furnished with one's own side, and/or being furnished with a treatise, or due to one's eloquence, or due to assisting the other, or due to listening to the other, or due to understanding reality, or due ot dwelling in one's own side, or due to criticising the other's side, or due to overcoming the other, or due to defeating the other, or due to pity for the other.

/hetuḥ katamaḥ yas tasyaiva pratijñārthasya siddhaye udāharaṇāśritaḥ sārūpyavairūpyato vā pratyakṣato vānumānato vāptāgamato vā *jāto*[18] yuktivādaḥ/

What is the reason (*hetu*)? So as to prove the thesis-topic, it is whatever declaration of principle (*yuktivāda*), resorting to an example, that is engendered by similarity and dissimilarity, or by direct perception, or by inference, or by the lineage of the masters.

/udāharaṇaṃ katamat/ yas tasyaiva pratijñārthasya prasiddhaye hetvāśrayo lokocitaprasiddhavastv-ābharaṇo[19]pasaṃhito vādaḥ/

---

17. Pa, followed by Ya, adds here the *visarga*, which does not make the term agree with *pratijñā* or with *sādhyam*. The term has the rsame status as the following ones. Since the term *anyonya*, 'one another', means that the 'thesis topic' is 'one', and 'another' comes from the following list, the term *pratijñā* does not reaure an own side since it could be the opponent's thesis. This is clear from some later items of the list. It seems that the following list is not restricted to one choice.

18. Both Pa and Ya give *hito*, while I read in the MS *heto*. *Tib. bskyed pa'i* (at p. 299-1-5) suggests *jāto*. While it might be argued that about the same verbal intention could be interpreted for *hito*, Asaṅga would not, as I understand his way of writing, put the obscurity in this verbal expression, preferring to have the difficulty in the technical terms of the system.

19. Pa and Ya have *udāharaṇo*, which is suspicious as repeating the word to be defined in the definition, which I believe to be contrary to the rules followed by Asaṅga.

What is the example (*udāharaṇa*)? So as to prove the thesis-topic, is is a statement relevant to the reason (*hetu*) and furnished with embellishment (*ābharaṇa*) of the right thing (*vastu*) that is customary and well-known in society.

/sārūpyaṃ katamat yat kasya cid dharmasya sādṛśena[20] kasya cid eva sādṛśyaṃ tat pañcavidhaṃ draṣṭavyaṃ liṅgasādṛśyaṃ svabhāvasādṛśyaṃ karmasādṛśyaṃ *dharmasādṛśyaṃ* hetuphalasādṛśyaṃ ca/

What is similarity (*sārūpya*)? It is a certain resemblance by a likeness to a certain feature (*dharma*). It is of five kinds, to wit: a. similarity of evidence (*liṅga*), b. similarity of individual presence (*svabhāva*), c. similarity of activity (*karma*), d. similarity of natures (*dharma*), e. similarity of cause and effect (*hetu-phala*).

/ liṅgasādṛśyaṃ katamat/ yad varttamānena vā pūrvadṛṣṭena vā cihnanimittasambaddhena vānyonyasādṛśyaṃ /

· a. What is similarity of evidence (*liṅgasādṛśya*)? A mutual likeness by association with a sign (*cihna*) or sign-source (*nimitta*) that is present or formerly seen.

/ svabhāvasādṛśyaṃ katamat / yad anyonyaṃ lakṣaṇasādṛśaṃ /

b. What is similarity of individual presence (*svabhāvasādṛśya*)? A mutual likeness of character.

/karmasādṛśyaṃ katamat/yad anyonyam kāritrasādṛśyaṃ/

c. What is similarity of activity (*karmasādṛśya*)? A mutual likeness of operation.

/dharmasādṛśyaṃ katamat / yad anyonyaṃ dharmatayā sādṛśyam *tadyathā* anityaṃ duḥkhadharmatayā duḥkhaṃ nairātmyadharmatayā nirātmakānāṃ jātidharmatayā jātidharmakānāṃ jarādharmatayā jarādharmakānaṃ maraṇadharmatayā rūpyarūpisanidarśanānidarśana-sapratighāpratigha-sāśravānāśrava-saṃskṛtāsaṃskṛta-dharmatayā evaṃbhāgīyayā dharmatayā /

d. What is similarity of natures (*dharmasādṛsya*)? What is mutually similar by a continuum (*dharmatā*);[21] as follows: (similarity) to impermanence by the continuum of suffering. To suffering by the continuum of nonself. (Similarity) of those without self by the continuum of birth. Of those with the nature of birth by the

---

20. Pa, followed by Ya, admitting it is not in the MS, now interpose *kena cit*, calling attention to the presence of this form in the definition below of *vairūpyam*. Without disagreeing with their addition here, I shall attempt a translation on the basis of the MS, and its Tibetan version.

21. Cf. Wayman, *Untying the Knots in Buddhism* (Delhi: Motilal Banarsidass, 1997), for *dharmatā* as a group of *dharmas* in a category, pp. 268-70, 535; for the rendition 'continuum' for *dharmatā*, pp. 273-4, 536.

continuum of old age. Of those with the nature of old age by the continuum of death. (And similar to) the formed (*rūpin*), the formless (*arūpin*); to the shown (*sanidarśana*), the unshown (*anidarśana*); to the impeded (*spratigha*), the unimpeded (*apratigha*); to the fluxional (*sāśrava*), the nonfluxional (*anāśrava*); to the constructed (*saṃskṛta*), the unconstructed (*asaṃskṛta*) by continuums; (so) by continuum of like category.

/hetuphalasādṛśyaṃ katamat/yad anyonyaṃ hetutaḥ phalataś ca niṣpādananiṣpattisādṛśyam/

e. What is similarity of cause and effect (*hetuphalasādṛśya*)? The mutual likeness of the accomplishing process and the full accomplishment through cause and through fruit.

/idam ucyate sārūpyaṃ/

The foregoing is called similarity.

/ vairūpyaṃ katamat / yad kasya cit kena cid eva vaisādṛśyena kasya cid eva vaisādṛśyaṃ /tad apy etad viparyayāt pañcavidham eva draṣṭavyam/

What is dissimilarity (*vairūpya*)? There being a certain dissimilarity by dissimilarity to a certain thing; that being so, by way of the reversal [of similarity, a, b, c, d, e] there are five kinds.

/pratyakṣaṃ katamat yad aviparokṣam anabhyūhitam anabhyūhyam avibhrāntaṃ ca/

What is direct perception (*pratyakṣa*)? What is not out-of-sight, not already inderred and not to be inferred, and non-delusory.

/aviparokṣaṃ katamat yac caturbhir ākārair veditavyam aparibhinnendriye pratyupasthite manaskāre 'nurūpotpattitaḥ samatikramotpattito 'nāvaraṇato 'viprakarṣataś ca/

A. What is the not out-of-sight (*aviparokṣa*)? It is to be understood by four aspects. Given that the senses are unimpaired and that attention (*manaskāra*) is present, it is A-1, because of occurrence in conformity; A-2, because of occurrence with transcendence; A-3, because of lack of obscuration; A-4, because of accessibility.

/ anurūpotpattiḥ katamā kāmāvacarasyendriyasya kāmāvacaro viṣayaḥ ūrddhvabhūmikasyendriyasya ūrddhvabhūmiko viṣayo ya utpannaḥ samutpanno jātinirvṛttaḥ so 'nurūpotpattir ity ucyate /

A-1. What is occurrence in conformity (*anurūpotpatti*)? The realm ranging in desire for the senses ranging in desire, the realm of those in higher stages for the senses of those in higher stages, which has arisen, arisen together, been fulfilled in its *jāti* (common origin). This is said to be occurrence in conformity.

/samatikramotpattiḥ katamā ya ūrddhvabhūmikasyendriyasyādhobhūmiko viṣaya utpanna ity evam ādi samatikramotpattir ity ucyate/

A-2. What is occurrence with transcendence (*samatikramotpatti*)? When the realm of those in lower stages has arisen for the senses of those in higher stages.

/ anāvaraṇaṃ katamat tad api caturbhir ākārair veditavyam avacchādanīyenāvaraṇenāntardhāy[22]anīyenābhibhavanīyena saṃmohanīyenāvaraṇena yad anāvṛtaṃ tad anāvṛtam ity ucyate/

A-3. What is lack of obscuration (*anāvaraṇa*)? It also has four aspects, namely, what is unobscured by an obscuration that veils, or by that which makes disappear, or that overpowers, or by those which confuse, are said to be unobscured.

/avacchādanīyam āvaraṇaṃ katamat/tadyathā tamo 'ndhakāram avidyāndhakāraṃ rūpāntaraṃ cānaccham/

3a. What is the veiling obscuration (*avacchādanīya-āvaraṇa*)? As follows—pitch-black darkness, darkness of nescience, and the unclearness [or lack of definition] within shape (or color).

/antardhāyanīyam āvaraṇaṃ katamat/tadyathā auṣadhibalaṃ vā mantrabalaṃ vārddhyanubhāvabalaṃ vā/

3b. What is the obscuration that makes disappear (*antardhāyanīya-āvaraṇa*)? As follows—the power of herbs, or the power of incantations, or the power of magical might.

/abhibhavanīyam āvaraṇaṃ katamat/tadyathā parīttaṃ prabhūtenābhibhūtam nopalabhyate bhojanapānī[23] vā viṣaṃ keśāgraṃ vā yad vā punar anyad evambhāgīyaṃ/tadyathā parīttatejā ugratejasābhibhūto nopalambhate/ādityena vā candramasā vā/ tārakarūpāṇi/tadyathā vi[24]pakṣeṇa pratipakṣo 'bhibhūto nopalabhyate/aśubhā-manaskareṇa vā śubhatā; anityaduḥkhānātma-manaskāreṇa vā sukhatā; animitta-manaskāreṇa vā sarvanimittāni/

3c. What is the obscuration that overpowers (*abhibhavanīya-āvaraṇa*)? As follows—a tiny thing overpowered by a large thing, or not reaching food and drink, or the poison on a hair tip, or anything of the same category, to wit, a tiny radiance overcome by a fierce radiance and not apprehended, e.g. the forms of stars by the sun or moon; an adversary side (in the debate) overcome by the opponent

---

22. Pa, followed by Ya, read *-p-* where I read *-y-*.
23. MS: *bhojanapāne*.
24. Pa, followed by Ya, add the *vi* here; and I accept it on the basis of the Tibetan, which renders *vipakṣena* as *gñen pos*.

and no longer apprehended; an appealing state by a mental orientation to the repulsive; a happy state by a mental orientation to impermanence, pain, and nonself; or any sign-source by a mental orientation to nonsign-sources.

/saṃmohāvaraṇaṃ katamat/tadyathā māyākarma rūpanimittaviśeṣo vānusādṛśyaṃ vā ādhyātmaṃ vā pratyātmaṃ vā taimirikaṃ ca svapna-mūrcchā-māda-pramāda-unmādaś ceti/yadvā punar anyat tv evambhāgīyam āvaraṇam idam ucyate saṃmohāvaraṇam/

3d. What is obscuration that confuses (*saṃmohāvaraṇa*)? As follows—a work of illusion (*māyākarma*), the diverse sign-sources of form, a similitude (*anusādṛśya*), the inferior (*ādhyātma*), what is back inside (*pratyātma*), cauls (of the eyes), sleep, faint, intoxication, heedlessness, derangement; or some other obscuration of the same cateyory. This is called the obscuration that confuses.

/aviprakarṣaḥ katamaḥ trividhena viprakarṣeṇa yad aviprakṛṣṭaṃ deśaviprakarṣataḥ kālaviprakarṣato 'pacayaviprakarṣataś ca /

A-4. What is accessibility (*aviprakarṣa*)? In consideration of three kinds of inaccessibility, there is accessibility, namely inaccessibility of place (*deśaviprakarṣa*), inaccessibility of time (*kālaviprakarṣa*), and inaccessibility through metaphysical nature (*apacayaviprakarṣa*).

/tad etat sarvam abhisamayasyāviparokṣam aviparokṣataḥ pratyakṣaṃ pramāṇaṃ draṣṭavyam/

Taking together all those (kings of) 'not out-of-sight'for direct vision, one may observe the 'direct perception' authority by way of 'not out-of-sight'.

/anabhyūhitam anabhyūhyam pratyakṣaṃ katamat /yo grahaṇamātraprasiddhopalabdhyāśrayo viṣayaḥ/ yaś ca viṣayapratiṣṭhitopalabdhyāśrayo viṣayaḥ /

B. What is direct perception that is not already inferred and not to be inferred? The sence object which is a basis for acknowledged apprehension consisting of perceiving-only; and the sense object which is a basis established for apprehension of the sense object.

/grahaṇamātraprasiddhopalabdhyāśrayo viṣayaḥ katamaḥ/yo viṣayo grahaṇamātraprasiddhāyā upalabdher āśrayakṛtyaṃ karoti/ tadyathā bhiṣag āturāya bhaiṣajyaṃ dadyād varṇagandharasasparśasampannaṃ mahāvīryavipākaprabhāvaṃ ca /tasya varṇagandharasaparśā grahaṇamātraprasiddhāyā upalabdher āśrayabhūtā draṣṭavyā/mahāvīryavipākaprabhāvas tv akṛta ārogyo 'nabhyūhyo bhavati/kṛte 'nabhyūhita ity ayam evambhāgīyo grahaṇamātraprasiddhopalabdhyāśrayo viṣayo veditavyaḥ/

B-1. What is the sense object which is a basis for acknowledged apprehension consisting of perceiving-only (*grahaṇamātraprasiddhopalabdhyāśrayo viṣaya*)? The sence object which performs the function of apprehension acknowledged as perceiving-only, e.g. (Suppose) a physician would prescribe for an illness a medicine perfect in color, odor, taste, and touch, and having great effectiveness, result, and potency. Its color, odor, taste, and touch are observable as a basis by apprehension acknowledged as perception-only. Given that there are the great effectiveness, result, and potency—still, before being brought about, health is not to be inferred; and after being brought about, is not already inferred. And one should understand the sense object that is the basis of apprehension acknowledged as preceiving-only to be of like category.

/viṣayapratiṣṭhitopalabdhyāśrayo viṣayaḥ katamaḥ/viṣayapratiṣṭhitāyā upalabdher āśrayakṛtyaṃ kạroti tadyathā yogācārasya pṛthivyām āpastejovāyudhātūn abhyūhya pṛthivīm āpo 'dhimucyamānasya pṛthivīsaṃjñaivāvatiṣṭhate vyāvartate āpsaṃjñā pṛthivītejovāyum adhimucyamānasya pṛthivīsaṃjñaivāvatiṣṭhate vyāvartate / tejovāyusaṃjñā tasya yā pṛthivīsaṃjñā sā viṣayapratiṣṭhitā upalabdhiḥ /yā pṛthivī sā viṣayapratiṣṭhitāyā upalabdher āśrayaḥ yathā pṛthivī evam āpastejovāyur yathāyogaṃ draṣṭavyaḥ/ayam ucyate (viṣaya-[25]) pratiṣṭhāyā upalabdher āśrāyo viṣayaḥ[26]/ asau' 'nabhyūhito 'nabhyūhyaḥ /dhātavas tv aniṣpannāyām adhimuktāv abhyūhyā vidyanata iti / niṣpannāyāṃ tv abhyūhitā/idam ucyate 'nabhūhitam anabhyūhyam/pratyakṣaṃ pramāṇam/

B-2. What is the sense object which is a basis established for apprehension of a sense object (*viṣayapratiṣṭhito palabdhyāśrayo viṣaya*)? The one that performs the function of a basis for apprehension which is established upon the sense object. To wit—When there is the yoga-practitioner's inferring of water, fire, and wind element in earth; then may that one (mentally) change the earth to water, still just the idea of earth persists while the idea of water goes away. And may one (mentally) change the earth into fire or wind, still just the idea of earth persists while the idea of fire or wind goes away. Whatever is one's idea of earth, it is an apprehension founded on the (actual) sense object. Whatever is earth (as an object), it is a basis of the apprehension founded upon a sense object. Just as is earth, so

25. I accept Ya's suggestion, following Pa, that *viṣaya* should be inserted here.

26. Ya (p. 520.1-2, note 1), following Pa, accepts a phrase, not in the MS, which seems to me rather duplicative, so I shall not include it.

also water, fire, and wind are to be observed according to the circumstance. This is said to be a sense object which is the basis of an apprehension founded upon a sense object. And it (the sense object) is not already inferred and not to be inferred. But the elements are to be inferred when the (mental) change of them still has not succeeded, and were already inferred when the (mental) change of them has succeeded.

The foregoing is said to be the 'direct perception' authority as not already inferred, and not to be inferred.

/avibhrānto viṣayaḥ pratyakṣaṃ katamat/tat pañcavidhaṃ draṣṭavyaṃ saptavidhaṃ vā /

C. What is the direct perception when the sense object is nondelusory? [Not] the five kinds, or the seven kinds.

/pañcavidhaṃ katamat pañcavidhā bhrāntiḥ pañcavidhā bhrāntiḥ katamā saṁjñābhrāntiḥ saṃkhyābhrāntiḥ saṃsthānabhrāntiḥ/varṇabhrāntiḥ / karmabhrāntiś ca/saptavidhā bhrāntiḥ katamā asyām eva pañcavidhāyāṃ bhrāntau sarvatragaṃ dvividhaṃ bhrāntir miśrayitvā saptavidhā bhrāntir bhavati dvividhā bhrāntiḥ katamā cittabhrāntir dṛṣṭibhrāntiś ca /

What are the five kinds? There are five kinds of delusion (*bhrānti*), namely, delusion of idea, delusion of number, delusion of shape, deusion of color, delusion of activity. What arethe seven kinds of delusion? There are two delusions that pervade the five kinds. When one adds (to the list) the two kinds of delusion, there are seven kinds. The two kinds of delusion are delusion of thought and delusion of view.

/saṃjñābhrāntiḥ katamā / yā 'tallakṣaṇā[27] tatsaṃjñā tadyathā marīcikānimittāyāṃ mṛgatṛṣṇikāyām āpsaṃjñā /

C-1. What is delusion of idea (*saṃjñābhrānti*)? Any idea of something where there is no such characteristic; for example, the idea of water when there is the fancied appearance constituting a mirage-sign.

/saṃkhyābhrāntiḥ katamā/yo 'lpe bahv-abhimānaḥ/tadyathā taimirikasya/ekasmiṃś candre bahucandradarśanaṃ /

C-2. What is delusion of number (*saṃkhyābhrānti*)? The false confidence (*abhimāna*) of numerous when there is few, for example, for the person with an eye-caul, to see many moons when there is one moon.

---

27. Ya, following Pa, changes to *yātallakṣaṇā*.

/ saṃsthānabhrāntiḥ katamā yo 'nyasaṃsthāne tadanyasaṃsthānābhimānaḥ tadyathā: alāta[28]-cakrasaṃsthānadarśanaṃ /

C-3. What is delusion of shape (*saṃsthānabhrānti*)? The false confidence that there is a certain shape when there is a different shape: for example, to see the shape of the whirling fire-brand.

/ varṇabhrāntiḥ katamā / yo 'nyavarṇe tadanyavarṇābhimānaḥ tadyathā; kāmalena yādhinopahitendriyasyāpīte rūpe pītarūpadarśanaṃ/

C-4. What is delusion of color (*varṇabhrānti*)? The false confidence that there is a certain color when there is a different color; for example, the seeing of a yellow color when the color is not yellow, by a sense organ deceived (*upahita*) by the 'yellow eye' illness.

/karmabhrāntiḥ katamā / yo 'karmake sakarmakatvābhimānaḥ/ tadyathā gāḍhaṃ muṣṭim ūrddhvadhārato vṛkṣānuvrajadarśanaṃ/

C-5. What is delusion of activity (*karmabhrānti*)? The false confidence that there is activity when there is no activity; for example, to see a tree moving alongside while holding up a tight fist.[29]

/cittabhrāntiḥ katamā/anayaiva pañcavidhayā bhrāntyā vibhrānte 'rthe cittābhiratiḥ/

C-6. What is delusion of thought (*cittabhrānti*)? The delight of consciousness in the entity mistaken by reason of precisely those five kinds (C-1 through-5) of delusion.

/dṛṣṭibhrāntiḥ katamā yā pañcavidhayaiva bhrāntyā vibhrānte 'rthe rocanā-dīpanā-vyavasthāpanā-maṅgala-saṃjñābhiniveśaḥ/

C-7. What is delusion of view (*dṛṣṭibhrānti*)? The idea of, and the clinging to satisfaction, stimulation, encouragement, and auspiciousness, in regard to the entity mistaken by reason of precisely those (same) five kinds of delusion.

/tad etat pratyakṣaṃ kasya pratyakṣaṃ vaktavyaṃ/ samāsataś caturṇāṃ rūpīndriyaṃ pratyakṣaṃ mano'nubhavapratyakṣaṃ lokapratyakṣaṃ śuddhapratyakṣaṃ ca/

Now this direct perception is a direct-perception concern of

---

28. Ya, following Pa, and claiming consistency with Chinese and Tibetan, changes to *alate*.

29. What seems to be meant is an experience probably all of us have had, namely, when boarding a train, that when it starts to move there is the illusion (or here 'delusion') that it is not moving but that something outside the train is moving. Thus, it is claimed that a similar experience will be had by holding up a tight fist and while looking at it as well as the 'tree' outside, while slowly moving the upright arm in that pose, it does seem to get the outside upright element to somewhat move.

what? In short, of four, namely direct perception belonging to the formal sense organs, direct perception belonging to mental experience, direct perception belonging to the world, and pure direct perception.

/rūpīndriyapratyakṣaṃ katamat/rūpiṇāṃ pañcānām indriyāṇāṃ yo gocaraviṣayo yathānirdiṣṭena pratyakṣalakṣaṇena/

a. What is direct perception belonging to the formal sense organs? The sense object(s) for ranging (or, scope) of the five formal sense organs, according to the characteristic of direct perception, as was pointed out.

/ mano 'nubhavapratyakṣaṃ katamat/yo manogocaro viṣayo yathānirdiṣṭena saiva pratyakṣalakṣaṇena/

b. What is direct perception belonging to mental experience? The sense object which is the range of mind, according to the characteristic of direct perception as was pointed out.

/lokapratyakṣaṃ katamat/tad ubhayam ekadhyam abhisaṃkṣipyaṃ lokapratyakṣam ity ucyate/

c. What is direct perception belonging to the world? Taking the foregoing two together as one, there is 'direct perception belonging to the world'.

/śuddhapratyakṣaṃ katamat /yat tu tal lokapratyakṣaṃ śuddhapratyakṣaṃ api tat/syāt tu śuddhapratyakṣaṃ na lokapratyakṣaṃ yo lokottarasya jñānasya gocaraviṣayaḥ/sac ca sato 'sac cāsataḥ sottaraś ca sottarataḥ/asādhāraṇaṃ laukikaiḥ/idam ucyate pratyakṣaṃ pramāṇam/

d. What is pure direct perception? There is a pure direct perception that is the foregoing direct perception belonging to the world. But there can be a pure direct perception that is not a direct perception belonging to the world, namely the sense object which is the range of supramundane knowledge. And the knowledge of the existence of the existent, the nonexistence of the nonexistent, the superiority of what is superior, is the 'direct perception authority' not shared by worldlings.

/ anumānaṃ katamat/sahābhyūhayābhyūhito 'bhyūhyaś ca viṣayaḥ tat punaḥ pañcavidhaṃ draṣṭavyaṃ/liṅgataḥ svabhāvataḥ karmato dharmato hetuphalataś ca/

What is inference (*anumāna*)? What is attended with the inferable or what has already been inferred, and the sense object which is inferable. Besides, it is of five kinds:—from an evidence (*liṅgatas*), from an individual presence (*svabhāvatas*), from activity (*karmatas*), from natures (*dharmatas*), from cause and effect (*hetuphalatas*).

/liṅgato 'numānaṃ katamat/yat kena cid eva cihnanimittasambandhena varttamānena vā pūrvadṛṣṭena vā viṣayābhyūhanaṃ/ tadyathā dhvajena ratham anuminoti/dhūmenāgniṃ rājñā rāṣṭram patyā striyaṃ kakudaviṣāṇabhyāṃ gāvaṃ śiśukālaśīrṣa-pratyagrayauvanayā taruṇaṃ valīpalitādibhir vṛddhaṃ svena veṣagrahaṇena gṛhiṇāṃ vā pravrajitānāṃ vā āryāṇāṃ darśanakāmatayā saddharmaśravaṇena vītamātsaryatayā ca śraddham/ sucintita-cintitayā subhāṣita-bhāṣitayā ṣukṛtakarmakāritayā paṇḍitam anukampayā priyavāditayā dhairyena muktahastatayā gambhīrārthasaṃdhinirmocanatayā ca bodhisattvam auddhatya-drava-saṃcagghita-saṃkrīḍita-saṃkilikilāyitena/avītarāgaṃ sadāpraśānteryāpathena vītarāgaṃ tathāgatair lakṣaṇair anuvyañjanais tathāgatajñānenopaśamena pratipattyā prabhāvena tathāgatam arhat(t)vaṃ samyaksambuddhaṃ sarvajñaṃ kaumara-dṛṣṭena nimittena sa evāyam iti vṛddham anuminoti/ity evambhāgīyaṃ liṅgato 'numānaṃ veditavyam/

A. What is the inference from an evidence (*liṅga*)? The inferring of a sense object by association with some sign or sign-source, whether present or formerly seen; for example, one infers a battle chariot by means of an ensign (*dhvaja*); fire by means of smoke; a kingdom by a king; a wife by means of a husband; a bullock by the hump and horns; youth by the head at the time of childhood and the early juvenile; old age by the wrinkles, grey hair, etc.; whether one is among householders or among those in the religious life, by the individual wearing of clothes; a man of faith, by the āryas' desire for the (right) view, their listening to the illustrious doctrine, their freedom from jealousy; a wise man, by his reflecting on what was well thought over, by his speaking what was well spoken, by his doing the deeds that were well done; a bodhisattva, by his compassion, his kindly words, his steadfastness, his 'open handedness' [i.e. liberality], his unravelling the knots of the profound meaning [=the name of the basic scripture of the Yogācāra school, *Saṃdhinirmocana*]; one addicted to lust, by his frivolity, seductive attitude, laughing together, sporting together, making happy noises together with (others); one free from lust, by his dignified posture, which is continually tranquil; an omniscient Tathāgata-Arhat-Samyaksambuddha, by the Tathāgata characteristics and minor marks, by the Tathagata knowledge, tranquillity, accomplishment, and power; one infers that an old man is thingking, "I was that very one," by the sign-source seen (by him) that is related to his youth. And what agrees with this category may be understood as the inference by way of an evidence.

/svabhāvato 'numānaṃ katamat / yat pratyakṣeṇa svabhāvena viparokṣe svabhāve 'bhyūhanam ekadeśeṇa vā svabhāvasyaika-deśasyābhyūhanaṃ ' tadyathā varttamānenātītam anuminoti/ atītenānāgataṃ pratyutpannaṃ ca sannikṛṣṭena viprakṛṣṭaṃ pratyutpannenānāgatam anuminoti/annapānayānavastrā-laṃkārāṇāṃ caikadeśena stokena katipayena parīttena[30] parīkṣitena guṇadoṣaparīkṣayā kṛtyam annapānayānavastrālaṃkārānāṃ anuminoti/ekadeśāya kena vā pariśiṣṭāya kam ity evambhāgīyaṃ svabhāvato 'numānam veditavyaḥ[31]/

B. What is the inference from an individual presence (*svabhāva*)? The inferring, when an individual presence is out of sight by an individual presence directly perceived; or the inferring of an individual presence in another place, by one in a certain place. For example, one infers the past from the present. One infers the future and the present from the past; the remote from the nearby; the future from the present. One infers the purpose (*kṛtya*) of food, drink, vehicles, clothes, ornaments, by the particular place of the food, drink, vehicles, colthes, ornaments, and by an inspection that is meager, to some extent, brief, while inspecting the merit and demerit. (One infers) the 'whereby' (*kena*) for the particular place, and 'to what' (*kam*) for the rest [the 'merit' and 'demerit']. What is of the same category may be understood as inference from an individual presence.

/karmato 'numānaṃ katamat/yat kāritreṇa karmāśrayā-bhyūhanam/aspandana-pakṣiniḍīnādibhiḥ sthāṇum anuminoti/ praspandanāṅgavikṣepādibhiḥ puruṣaṃ padavikāreṇa hastinaṃ gātragativikāreṇālagardanaṃ /heṣitenāśvaṃ naditena siṃhaṃ narditenarṣabhaṃ/darśanena cakṣuḥ śravaṇena śrotraṃ/jighritena ghrāṇaṃ/svāditena jihvaṃ/sparśitena kāyaṃ vijñātena manaḥ/ āpsu darśanena pratighātena pṛthivīṃ/snigdhaharitapradeśa-darśanena āpaṃ/dahabhasmadarśanenāgniṃ/ vanaspati-praspandanena vāyuṃ/sadā nimīlitākṣitvena daṇḍabhṛd-paravyapadeśa-skhalitāpamārgagamanādibhiś cāndham uccaiḥ

30. The three adjectives beginning wth *stoka* are synonyms. I have previously experienced this device of three synonyms in Asaṅga's *Śrāvakabhūmi*.

31. My editing decision of this last sentence beginning with *eka-*, differs considerably from what is in Ya, following Pa, namely, *ekadeśapākena vā pariśiṣṭapākam ity...*

śravaṇena badhiraṃ/śraddhapaṇḍitāvītarāgavītarāga-bodhisattvatathāgateṣu karmato'numānaṃ pūrvavad draṣṭavyaṃ /

C. What is the inference from an activity (*karma*)? An inferring of the basis of the activity by the mode of action. For example, one infers a post from such features as the motionlessness and the downward swoop of birds. One infers a human from the pulsation, the movement of limbs, and so on; an elephant from the imprinting of his foot; a cobra (*alagardana*) from the swirling passage of its body; a horse from a neigh; a lion from a roar; a bull from its 'bu'; an eye from vision; an ear from hearing; a nose from smelling; a tongue from tasting; a body from touching; a mind from the understood (*vijñāta*); earth from the appearance in water and (its) resistance; water from the appearance of a place that is slippery and green; fire from the appearance of hot ashes; wind from the swaying of trees; a blind person (*qndha*) from the constantly closed eyes, the bearing of a staff, the being commanded by another,[32] the going the wrong way in stumbling manner, and so on; a person of hard hearing, by the loud sound. And among those of faith and those of learning, those not free from passion, and those free from passion, and (among) bodhisattvas and Tathāgatas;—one may observe, as previously, the inference from an activity.

/dharmato'numānaṃ katamat/yan nānuśliṣṭena dharmasambandhena tatsambandhāyā dharmatāyābhyūhanaṃ/tadyathā 'nityasambandhena duḥkhatām anuminoti/duḥkhasambandhena śūnyatānātmatāṃ jātisambandhena jarādharmatāṃ jarāsambandhena maraṇadharmatāṃ rūpisanidarśanasapratighasambandhena pradeśatāṃ mūrttatām anuminoti/sāśravasambandhena saduḥkhatām anāśravasambandhenāduḥkhatāṃ / saṃskṛtasambandhena utpādavyayasthityanyathātvadharmatām ity evambhāgīyaṃ dharmato 'numānaṃ veditavyam/

D. What is the inference from natures (*dharma*)? The inferring of the continuum (*dharmatā*) of its association by an associated nature (*dharma*) that is not (obviously) connected thereto. For example, one infers the state of suffering from one (i.e. *dharma*) associated with impermanence. One infers voidness and nonself from one associated with suffering; (infers) the continuum of old age from one associated with birth; the continuum of death from one (i.e. dharma) associated with birth; the continuum of death from one (i.e. dharma) associated with old age; the placement and corpore-

32. Cf. Franklin Edgeton, *Buddhist Hybrid Sanskrit Dictionary*, p. 515, under *vyapadeśate*, for our translation from the Sanskrit.

ality by association with the showing and the impeding of a material entity; accompaniment with misery by association with the fluxional (*sāśrava*); nonaccompaniment with misery by association with the nonfluxional; the continuum of arising, passing away, staying, and becoming otherwise, by association with the constructed (*saṃskṛta*); [and the continuum of not arising, not passing away, not staying, and not becoming otherwise, by association with the unconstructed (*asaṃskṛta*)].[33] Whatever agrees with this category should be understood as inference from natures.

/hetuphalato'numānaṃ katamat/yad dhetunā phalasya phalena vā hetor adhyūhanaṃ /tadyathā gatyā deśāntaraprāptim anuminoti deśāntarapraptyā gatim/rājarādhanena mahābhisāralābhaṃ/ mahābhisāralābhena rājarādhanaṃ sukṛtasampannakarmāntatayā mahādhanadhānyalābham mahādhanadhānyalābhena sukṛtasampannakarmāntatāṃ prāktanasucaritaduścaritena sampattivipattī sampattivipattibhyāṃ prāktanasucaritaduścaritaṃ/prabhūtabhojanena tṛptiṃ/tṛptyā prabhūtabhojanam/viṣamabhojanena vyādhiṃ/vyādhinā viṣamabhojanaṃ/dhyānena vairāgyaṃ vairāgyena dhyānaṃ mārgeṇa śrāmaṇyaphalaṃ śrāmanyaphalena mārgam/ity evambhāgīyaṃ hetuphalo'numānaṃ veditavyam/idam ucyate 'numānam/

E. What is the inference from cause and effect (*hetuphala*)? The inferring of an effect by means of a cause, or of a cause by means of an effect. For example:—One infers the reaching of another place by means of the travelling; and (infers) the travelling by the reaching of another place. Attainment of a great rendezvous by pleasing the king; pleasing the king by attaining a great rendezvous. The acquirement of much wealth and goods, by the condition of work that fulfills the well-done; the condition of work that is well-done, by acquirement of much wealth and goods. (One infers) good fortune or disaster, by former good deeds or bad deeds; former good deeds or bad deeds, by good fortune or disaster. Satiation, from the plentiful eating; plentiful eating, from the satiation. Illness, from wrong eating; wrong eating, from illness. (One infers) dispassion, by the meditation (*dhyāna*); meditation, by the dispassion (*vairāgya*). The fruit of monkhood, by the path; the path, by the fruit of monkhood. Whatever agrees with this category should be understood as inference from cause and effect.

The foregoing is called inference (*anumāna*).

---

33. This addition is according to the Tibetan at PTT edn, p. 300-5-7.

/ āptāgamaḥ katamaḥ / yat sarvajñabhāṣitaṃ/tato vā śrutvā tadanudharmaṃ vā sa punas trividho draṣṭavyaṃ/ pravacanāvirodhataḥ/saṃkleśapratipakṣataḥ lakṣaṇāvirodhataś ca/

What is the lineage of the masters (*āptāgama*)? What was expressed by the omniscient one, or was heard from him, or is a doctrine consistent therewith. Moreover, it should be observed as three kinds; resulting from compatibility with the sacred word, resuliting from the adversary to defilement, resulting from compatibility with the characteristic (of certainty).

/ pravacanāvirodhaḥ katamaḥ/yaḥ śrāvakabhāṣito vā buddhabhāṣito vā sūtrāntaḥ parasparāgataḥ/tatra yo dharmāvirodhaḥ/arthāvirodhaḥ/

A. What is compatibility with the sacred word (*pravacanāvirodha*)? Whatever *sūtra* passage that was expressed by the disciples (of the Buddḥa) or expressed by the Buddha, handed down in succession, therein the compatibility with the doctrine (*dharma*), the compatibility with its meaning (*artha*).

/saṃkleśapratipakṣaḥ katamaḥ/yo dharmo bhāvyamānaḥ rāgavinayāya saṃvartate/dveṣavinayāya mohavinayāya/ sarvakleśopakleśavinayāya saṃvartate/

B. What is the adversary to defilement (*saṃkleśapratipakṣa*)? Whatever *dharma* being contemplated (or cultivated) that conduces to the taming of lust, conduces to the taming of hatred, to the taming of delusion, to the taming of all defilements and secondary defilements.

/lakṣanāvirodhaḥ katamaḥ lakṣaṇavirodhaviparyayeṇa lakṣaṇāvirodho draṣṭavyaḥ/lakṣaṇavirodhaḥ katamaḥ/yathāpi tad asati lakṣaṇe salakṣaṇaṃ samāropayati/tadyathā ātmā vā sat(t)vo vā jīvo vā jantur vety evam ādi/śāśvato vā ucchidyate/rūpī vārūpī vety evam ādi ca/sati lakṣaṇa ekātiko 'naikāntikatāṃ vyavasthāpayati/ tadyathā anityāḥ sarvasaṃskārāḥ duḥkhāḥ sarvasāśravāḥ sarvadharmā anātmanaḥ ayaṃ caikatyaṃ nityaṃ vyavasthāpayati/ekatyam anityam / ekatyaṃ duḥkhaṃ vyavasthāpayati/ekatyam aduḥkham/ekatyam ātmā vyavasthāpayati/ekatyam anātmā/tathā yāny avyākṛtavastūni bhagavatā vyavasthāpitani/ekāntena teṣāṃ vyākaraṇaṃ/paryeṣate/ vyākaraṇataś ca vyavasthānaṃ pratyeti[34] /

34. I am pleased to reject my own reading here of *prāpyate* in favor of Pa's reading *pratyeti*, followed by Ya. The Tibetan *yid ches pa*, going with two *Mahāvyutpatti* entries nos. 6985 and 7147 (Sakaki edn.), confirms the *pratyeti* reading, with the meaning 'trusts'; and if Edgerton had come across this, we could have expected him to include it in his *Buddhist Hybrid Sanskrit Dictionary*.

C. What is the compatibility with the characteristic (of certainty) (*lakṣaṇāvirodha*)? One should observe compatibility with the characteristic as the opposite of incompatibility with the characteristic. What is incompatibility with the characteristic (*lakṣaṇavirodha*)? As follows: "When there is no characteristic, one attributes (or superimposes) possession of a characteristic, to wit, self, or sentient being, or living being, or progenitor, and so on; that it is eternal though cut off, or that it has form though formless, and so forth. When there is the characteristic, though it is certain one posits uncertainty; to wit, (it is certain), All constructions are impermanent," "All fluxional things have suffering," "All natures (*dharma*) are devoid of self." And while this is (so), one posits certain (constructions) as permanent, and certain ones as impermanent; posits certain (fluxional things) to have suffering, and certain ones to lack suffering, posits certain (natures) to have a self, and certain ones to lack a self. Likewise, among which things the Lord established indeterminate given things (*avyākṛtavastūni*), one searches for their determination by way of certainty; and trusts the establishment that is due to a determination.

/ anaikāntikam apy ekāntikena/vyavasthāpayati/tadyathā sarvasyāṃ sukhāyāṃ vedanāyāṃ rāgo 'nuṣeta iti/sarvasyāṃ duḥkhāyāṃ dveṣaḥ/sarvā sukhavedanā sāśravaikāntena sukheti/ sāṃcetanīyasya karmaṇaḥ/*ekāntena* duḥkham eva vipākaṃ pratisaṃvedayatīti evam ādi/

C. (continued). One also posits what is not certain as certain, to wit, "Lust is enhanced through all pleasant feeling;" "Hatred (is enhanced) through all painful feeling;" "All pleasant feeling that is fluxional is, to be sure, pleasure;" "From volitional *karma*, to be sure, one reaps just suffering maturation;" and so on.

/sati lakṣaṇe yad aviśiṣṭalakṣaṇaṃ tad viśeṣato vyavasthāpayati/ tad yā viśiṣṭalakṣaṇaṃ tad aviśeṣato vyavasthāpayati/tadyathā yat saṃskṛte viśiṣṭalakṣaṇaṃ tad asaṃskṛte 'pi vyavasthāpayati/yad asaṃskṛte 'viśiṣṭalakṣaṇaṃ tat saṃskṛte 'pi vyavasthāpayati/yathā saṃskṛtāsaṃskṛte evam rupiṣv arūpiṣu sanidarśaneṣv anidarśaneṣu sapratigheṣv apratigheṣu sāśraveṣv anāśraveṣv ity evam ādi yathāyogam veditavyaṃ/

C. (continued). When there is a characteristic (of certainty), what is an unqualified characteristic one posits by way of a qualification; and what is a qualified characteristic one posits by way of nonqualification. For example, given a qualified characteristic in the case of a constructed (nature), one posits it also for a non-constructed (nature). Or, given an unqualified characteristic in the case of an unconstructed (nature), one posits it also in the case of a constructed (nature). Just as in the cases of the constructed and the unconstructed (natures), so also in the cases of those with form and those without form, those shown and those not shown, those impeding and those unimpeding, those with flux and those wihtout flux, and so forth, one may understand according to circumstances (the same improper attribution).

/sati eva lakṣaṇe 'yogapatitaṃ hetuphalato lakṣaṇaṃ vyavasthāpayati/tadyathā sucaritasyāniṣṭaṃ phalaṃ duścaritasyeṣṭaṃ durākhyāte dharmavinaye mithyāpratipattito viśuddhiṃ svākhyāte dharmavinaye samyakpratipattitaḥ/saṃkleśaṃ vyavasthāpayati/

C. (continued). Only when there is the (correct) characteristic, may one establish by way of cause and effect the characteristic that belongs to false (even-perverse) positions, e.g. that good conduct has an undesirable fruit, while bad conduct has a desirable fruit; that in the badly expressed *dharma* and *vinaya* there is purity through deviant accomplishment, while in the well-expressed *dharma* and *vinaya* one establishes defilement through right accomplishment.

/apariniṣpanne lakṣaṇe prajñaptivādena pariniṣpannaṃ lakṣaṇaṃ/prajñaptivādena vyavasthāpayati/tadyathā nirabhilapyeṣu sarvadharmeṣu/abhilāpataḥ paramārthavyavasthānaṃ/ity evambhāgīyo lakṣaṇavirodho veditavyaḥ/etad viparyayeṇāvirodhaḥ/ ayam ucyate/lakṣaṇāvirodho 'yam ucyate āptāgamaḥ/

C. (concluded). When the characteristic is not perfect according to the position of worldly convention, one establishes it as a perfect characteristic according to the position of worldly convention, e.g. given that all *dharmas* are inexpressible, (claiming) there is the absolute (*paramārtha*) establishment (taking them) in terms of expression. Whatever agrees with this category (as illustrated by the foregoing wayward and/or perverse examples) should be understood as incompatible with the (correct) characteristic. The compatibility which is its opposite is said to be the compatibility with the characteristic (of certainty).

The foregoing is said to be the lineage of the masters.

/yadā svalakṣaṇataḥ siddhāḥ sarvadharmā vyavasthāpitāḥ svasyāṃ dharmatāyāṃ kena kāraṇena dvividho 'rthaḥ sādhya ity ucyate/ parasaṃpratyayotpattim ārabhya no tu lakṣaṇotpattiṃ/kena kāraṇena sādhyasyārthasya prasiddhaye āditaḥ pratijñā kriyate yāvad ev*ābhinkānkṣitasyā*rthasya paridīpanārthaṃ/kena kāraṇena hetur upasaṃhriyate/yāvad eva dṛṣṭavastvāśritayā yuktyā tasminn eva pratijñā*rthe* paragrahaṇārthaṃ/kena karaṇena dṛṣṭanta upasaṃhriyate/yāvad eva tasyām eva yukte dṛṣṭavastvāśrayaṃ darśanārthaṃ/kena kāraṇena sārūpyaṃ vairūpyam pratyakṣam anumānam āptāgamaś copasaṃhriyate/yāvad eva tayor hetūdāharaṇayor virodhāvirodha-paridipanārtham/sa punar virodho dvābhyām ākārābhyām veditavyam anaikāntikatvena ca sādhyasamatvena ca/avirodhaḥ/dvābhyām evākārābhyāṃ veditavyaḥ aikāntikatvena sādhyaviśeṣeṇa ca/yatra virodhaḥ/tat pratijñāsiddho na pramāṇīkriyata iti/kṛtvā na pramāṇaṃ/yatra tv avirodhas tat pratijñāsiddho pramāṇīkriyata iti kṛtvā pramāṇaṃ ity ucyate/idam ucyate vādādhiṣṭhānaṃ/

[Final comments on III. Foundation of the Debate (*vādādhiṣṭhāna*)]. Now, when all features are established each in its that two kinds of thesis topics are stated? It is to begin the generation of confidence in the other person (i.e. in the debate), and it is not for generating the characteristic (of certainty). Why is it for proving the thesis topic, at the outset the thesis (*pratijñā*) is announced? So as to point out the topic which one desires (to prove). Why is the reason (*hetu*) adduced? To draw the other person to precisely the thesis-topic by a principle based on a visible given thing. Why is the example adduced? Just so, when given that principle, as to show the locus of a visible given thing. Why are similarity, dissimilarity, direct perception, inference, and lineage of the masters adduced? So as to point out the incompatibility and the compatibility of the reason-and-example pair. Besides, one may understand the incompatibility by two aspects—uncertainty (*anaikāntikatva*) and equality with the thesis (*sādhyasamatva*). One may understand the compatibility by two aspects—certainty and divergence from the thesis (*sādhyaviśeṣaṇa*). When there is incompatibility, it is not authorized as thesis-proved; in effect, there is no authority (*pramāṇa*). When there is compatibility, it is authorized as thesis-proved; in effect, there is the authority (*pramāṇa*).

The foregoing is called 'Foundation of the Debate.'

/vādālaṃkāraḥ katamaḥ/sa pañcavidho draṣṭavyaḥ/tadyathā svaparasamayajñatā/vākkaraṇasampannatā/vaiśāradyaṃ sthairyaṃ dakṣiṇyaṃ ca/

IV. THE DEBATE'S ORNAMENT

There are five kinds of ornament of the debate: A. Knowledge of one's and the other's context, B. Accomplishment of speech art, C. Confidence, D. Control, E. Nobility.

/svaparasamayajñatā katamā /yathāpīhaikatyasya yo dharmavinayaḥ/abhirucito bhavaty asyābhipretaḥ/tatraśāstre samaye siddhānte pāṭhato *prītitaḥ*[35] śravaṇataḥ cintanataḥ paripākataḥ pratipattitaś ca/kṛtakuśalo bhavati/kṛtabhāsyaḥ kṛtavidyaḥ/yo vā punar dharmavinayaḥ nābhipreto bhavati/nābhirucitaḥ/tatra paraśāstre parasamaye parasiddhānte pāṭhato *prītitaḥ* śravaṇataś cintanataḥ paripākato no tu pratipattitaḥ kṛtakuśalo bhavati/ kṛtabhāṣyaḥ kṛtavidyaḥ/iyam ucyate /svaparasamayajñatā/

A. What is knowledge of one's own and the other's context (*svaparasamayajñatā*)? Now, there is someone here whom the doctrine-discipline (*dharma-vinaya*) has attracted and delighted; who has made oneself skilled, made for oneself the words, made for oneself the knowledge, in the treatise, the context, the special tenets —through rehearsal, satisfaction in, hearing, pondering, getting mature in, and accomplishing. And there is someone else here whom the doctrine-discipline has not attracted or delighted; who has not made oneself skilled, or made for oneself the words, or made for oneself the knowledge, in the treatise of the other, the context of the other, the special tenets of the other-through rehearsal, satisfaction in, hearing, pondering, getting mature in, and accomplishing. This is called the knowledge of one's own and the other's context.

/vākkaraṇasampannatā katamā/yathāpīhaikatyaḥ śabdena vaktā bhavati / nāpaśabdaiḥ / śabdaḥ katamaḥ pañcabhir guṇair yukto veditavyaḥ / agrāmyo bhavati / laghur bhavatī/ tejasvī bhavati / sambadho bhavati / svarthaś ca bhavati /

B. What is accomplishment of speech arts (*vākkaraṇasampannatā*)? Now, someone here has become a speaker with words, avoiding vulgar words. Speech here should be understood as endowed with five merits: It is not rustic, (rather) of easy style, inspired, coherent, and significant.

/kathaṃ agrāmyo bhavati / kudeśarāṣṭra-kujanapada-bhāṣāvarjanatayā/

B-1. How is it nonrustic (*agrāmya*)? By being free from the expressions of a bad district or bad countryside, or bad country.

35. Ya (p. 528), following Pa, gives *dhṛtitaḥ* here and where the term is repeated in the next sentence. My original reading of the MS gave *vṛttitaḥ*. However, since the Tibetan trs. shows *dga' ba*, this fits neither Ya and Pa, nor my former reading: rather, it suggests **prītitaḥ*.

/kathaṃ laghur bhavati/lokapratītayuktatara-bhāṣāprayuktayā/

B-2. How is it of easy style (*laghu*)? By endowment with expressions current in the world and very fit.

/ kathaṃ tejasvī[36] bhavati / yasyārthakathā viprakṛta[37] bhavati / tasyārthasya siddhaye suprayuktabalavattayā /

B-3. How is it inspired (*tejasvin*)? Of which the discourse of meaning has begun (and is not yet completed), so as to perfect its meaning—(namely,) by having the power of the well-expressed.

/ kathaṃ sambaddho bhavati / paurvaparyeṇa dharmārthaviśiṣṭatayā[38]/

B-4. How is it coherent (*sambaddha*)? By a distinguished (or, preeminent) meaning of *dharma* in the sense of prior and posterior.

/ kathaṃ svartho bhavati / abhyudayaṃ niḥśreyasaṃ cārabhyāviparyastatayā/

B-5. How is it significant (*svartha*)? Having started in an elevated and excellent manner, by not reversing (the standard).

/ tac caivaṃ śabdavādinaḥ navabhir ākāraiḥ sampannaṃ vā karaṇaṃ veditavyam / anākulam asaṃrabdhaṃ / gamakam mitam / arthayuktam kalena sthiram dīptaṃ prabaddham ca / tad etat sarvam abhisamasya vākkaraṇa-sampad ity ucyate / iyam ucyate vākkaraṇasampat /

B-6. And the composition (*karaṇa*) by the speaker of the words should be understood as perfect by nine aspects as follows: It is not confused (*anākula*), not violent (*asaṃrabdha*), understandable (*gamaka*), or proper length (*mita*), cogent (*arthayukta*), right-timed (*kālana*), held to the point (*sthira*), clear (*dīpta*), continuous (*prabaddha*).

---

36. Ya, admitting that the MS has *tejasvī*, still follows Pa's reading *ojasvī*, even though the Tibetan *brjid pa* as a verb meaning 'to shine' agrees with *tejasvī over ojasvī.*

37. The Tibetan equivalent, *skabs su bab pa*, is in Lokesh Chandra's *Tibetan-Sanskrit Dictionary*, shown to have a Sanskrit original *prastuta*, 'begun' (as a topic); while Edgerton's entry on *viprakṛta* in his *Buddhist Hybrid Sanskrit Dictionary*, has the meaning 'the uncomplete'. This leads me to conclude that the MS expression—with which both Pa and Ya agree—has here a special meaning of 'begun but not yet completed'.

38. Ya, though noting that the MS has *viśiṣṭatayā*, follows Pa in the reading *āśliṣṭatayā*. However, when the MS word makes perfect sense in the context, it does not seem proper to change it to something else.

Taking all the foregoing together, there is 'accomplishment of speech arts'. This is called *vākkaraṇasampat.*

/ vaiśāradyaṃ katamat / yathāpīhaikatyo bahunaikāyikāyām api parṣadi vicitra-naikāyikāyām apy *audārika*[39]-naikāyikāyām apy abhiniviṣṭa-naikāyikāyām api sabhā[40]-naikāyikāyām api kuśala-naikayikāyām api / alīnacittaḥ / adīnacittaḥ /abhītacittaḥ / asaṃsvinna-gātraḥ / apāṇḍumukhaḥ / agadgada-svaraḥ / ahīna[41]-vākyo vācam udāharati / idam ucyate vaiśāradyam /

C. What is confidence (*vaiśāradya*)? Now, there is here someone who, in an assembly, whether in a large group, or in a variegated group, or in a coarse group, or in a group of determined persons, or in a group of official gathering, or in a group of experts (on the topic), utters words with one's mind not timid, mind not depressed, mind not fearful, body not perspiring, face not turning pale, without stammering, without a loss for words. This is called 'confidence'.

/ sthairyam katamat / yathāpīhaikatyaḥ kāla*prāpto* 'tvaramāṇo vācaṃ bhāṣate / na tvaramāṇaḥ / idam ucyate sthairyam /

D. What is control (*sthairya*)? Now, there is here someone who, the time having arrived (for speaking), speaks words that are not hasty. Being not hasty, this is called 'control'.

/ dakṣiṇyaṃ katamat / yathāpīhaikatyaḥ sūrato bhavati / pareṣām viheṭhana-jātīyaḥ / sa yā sūratānāṃ sūratabhūmiḥ tāṃ nābhivṛtya[42] paracittānuvarttī vācaṃ bhāṣate / tac ca kālena bhūtenārthopasaṃhitena ślakṣṇena mitravarttayā / idam ucyate dakṣiṇyam /

E. What is nobility (*dakṣiṇya*)? Now, there is here someone who is kindly (*sūrata*), whose nature does not lend itself to scoff at others. Whatever be the level of kindness of kind people, one does not oppose it; and solicitous for the mind of the other, utters words in a manner timely, true, meaningful, gentle, and friendly. This is called 'nobility'.

/ asya khalu pañcavidhasya vāgālaṃkārasyaivaṃ viprakṛtasya saptaviṃśatir anuśaṃsā veditavyā / katame saptaviṃśatiḥ / saṃmatataro bhavati / ādeyavacanataro bhavati / parṣatsu;

39. Pa and Ya: *udāra.* Cf. Edgerton, BHS Dictionary, under *audārika,* as here with Tib. *rags pa.*

40. Pa and Ya: *satya,* for which one would expect Tib. *bden pa;* but instead the Tib. is *tshogs,* agreeing with what I saw in the MS, to wit, *sabhā.*

41. Pa and Ya: *adīna,* the same word used just above with *citta,* where Tib. had *dman pa med,* while here it has *bcom mi ruṅ bar,* agreeing with my MS reading of *ahīna.*

42. Pa and Ya: *anativṛtyaḥ.*

nirbhayataro bhavati /[43] parasamayadoṣajño bhavati / svasamayaviśeṣajño bhavati / anabhiniviṣṭo bhavati / apakṣarāgī śāstraparigraho bhavati / svakād dharmavinayāt pareṇokte āśutaraṃ pratipadyate / pareṇoktam āśutaram udgṛhnāti / pareṇokte āśutaraṃ uttaram pratipadyate / vāgguṇaḥ ca parṣadaṃ rañjayate/ tadvidyādhimuktaṃ *cārādhayati* / niruktam arthapadavyañjanaṃ karoti / avyathito bhavati /kāyena; avyathito bhavati / manasā vā / *na* sajjate / vadataḥ; *na* pratibhānaṃ paryādīyate / na kāyaḥ klāmyati / na smṛtir muṣyate / na cittam upahanyate / na kaṇṭhaṃ kṣiṇoti / vispaṣṭaṃ vijñeyaṃ bhavaty asya bhāṣitam / ātmānurakṣī svayaṃ na kupyati / paracittānuvartī paraṃ na kopayati / prativādinaś cittam abhiprasādayati / avaira-sapatna-vartmanī pratipadaṃ pratipanno bhavati / digvidikṣūdāro varṇakīrtiśabdaśloko 'bhyudgacchati / mahācāryo mahācāryo iti saṃkhyāṃ gacchati vighuṣṭaśabdo bhavati loke /

Now, it should be recognized that of those five kinds of speech ornaments thus inaugurated (*viprakṛta*[44]) there are twenty-seven benefits. What are the twenty-seven? (1) In the assembly (*parṣatsu*), one becomes more esteemed, receives nicer words. (2) One becomes completely fearless. (3) One knoes the faults of the other's context. (4) One knows the distinguishing character of one's own context. (5) One becomes not clinging. (6) One follows the śāstra without attachment to a 'side'. (7-9) Out of one's own doctrine-discipline, one quickly understands when another speaks, is able to grasp quickly what is said by another, and is able to reply quickly when someone has spoken. (10-11) The speech merit charms the assembly, and gratifies those convinced of one's clear vision. (12) One composes words and sentences with good words that are certain in meaning. (13-14) One is not disturbed in body, and not disturbed in mind. (15) One is not impeded in speech. (16) One's

43. Our numbering differs from Ya's. Ya (p. 530, his n. 7) observed, "In Tib. *parṣatsu* (*'khor gyi naṅ du*) is located before sammatataro," but Ya counts the first two statements as his nos. 1 and 2, and takes *parṣatsu* as going with his no. 3 (Pa unaccountably moves *parṣatsu* in front of what in Ya is no. 4). However, the Tib. interpretation is that *parṣatsu* goes with all 27 items, so put at the head; and Tib. must have understood the Sanskrit placement of *parṣatsu* to mean the same, but this could only be the case if *parṣatsu* goes with what precedes it, thus forcing the first two statements to be counted as no. 1, with no. 1 taken as the basis for the remaining 27 items. This is how I interpreted when I studied this text in the early 1980's. It means that Ya's and my numbers differ all the way to 27, where what he takes as no. 27 I divide into no. 26 and 27.

44. For this term, cf. my n. 37, above.

eloquence is not exhausted. (17) One's body does not get weary. (18) One's memory does not fail. (19) One's mind is not afflicted. (20) One's throat does not grow slack. (21) One's speech is clear and comprehensible. (22) Guarding oneself, one is not stirred up. (23) Solicitous for another's mind, one does not anger the other person. (24) One instills belief in the opponent's mind. (25) One pursues a path that proceeds without enmity or rivalry. (26) One gains widespread words and verses of praise and fame in the cardinal and intermediate directions. (27) One becomes reckoned, gets resounding words in the world, "the great teacher, the great teacher."

/ tadyathā kāmopabhogī maṇi-mukti-vaiḍūryādi*ra*citair harṣakaṭakakeyūrādibhir ābharaṇair atyarthaṃ[45] bhāsate / tapati virocayate / evam eva vādy ebhiḥ saptaviṃśatyānuśaṃsaiḥ pratyarpitena pañcavidhena vādālaṃkārenātyarthaṃ bhāsate tapati virocayate / tasmād vādālaṃkāra·ity ucyate / ayam ucyate vādālaṃkāraḥ /

[The meaning of 'ornament' (*alaṃkāra*)]. For example, one enjoying pleasures shines, blazes, illumines even more with such adornments as necklace, wrist and arm bracelets that are studded with gems, pearls, lapis lazuli, and so on. Likewise, the first speaker (*vādin*) shines, blazes, illumines even more with the five kinds of debate ornaments that are fastened with the twenty-seven benefits. Therefore, one calls them 'debate ornaments'.

/ vādanigrahaḥ katamaḥ / sa trividho draṣṭavyaḥ kathātyāgaḥ kathāsādaḥ kathādoṣaś ca /

V. POINTS OF DEFEAT IN THE DEBATE

What are the points of defeat in the debate (*vādanigraha*)? There are three kinds: A. Surrender of the discussion, B. Collapse of the discussion, C. Faults of the discussion.

/kathātyāgaḥ katamaḥ / iha vādī trayodaśākārayā vāgvijñaptyā prativādinaṃ vijñapayan kathāṃ parityajati / trayodaśākāra-vāgvijñaptiḥ katamā / tadyathā; asādhu mama; sādhu vā tava; asupariksitaṃ mama; supariksitam vā tava; ayuktam mama; yuktam vā tava; asahitaṃ mama; sahitaṃ vā tava; nigṛhīto madvādaḥ

45. I am pleased to give up my MS reading *abhyartha* in favor of the reading *atyartha* presented by Pa and followed by Ya, here and soon below.

pratiṣṭhito vā yuṣmadvāda; etāvad me 'tra pratibhāti; uttare[46] vā punaḥ saṃcintya vakṣyāmi; alam astv etavān na punaḥ kathāṃ kariṣyāmīti / ananyā trayodaśākarayā vāgvijñaptyā prativādinaṃ vijñapayan viprakṛtāṃ kathāṃ parityajati / tasyāś ca parityāgāj jito bhavati / parājitaḥ parāpṛṣṭīkṛto nigṛhītaḥ tasmāt kathātyāgo nigrahasthānam ity ucyate /

A. What is surrender of the discussion (*kathātyāga*)? Here the first speaker informs the respondent by thirteen kinds of vocal candor that oneself surrenders the discussion. What are the thirteen kinds of vocal candor (*vāgvijñapti*)? As follows: 1. "Mine is not good." 2. "Yours is good."3. "Mine was not well-considered." 4. "Yours was well considered." 5. "Mine is not cogent." 6. "Yours is cogent." 7. "Mine is incoherent." 8. "Yours is coherent." 9. "My side has been defeated." 10. "Your side has been well-established." 11. "This is all that occurs to me in this case." 12. "After some more thinking, I shall resume the discussion later on." 13. "Let so much suffice! I shall not further discuss the matter." Informing the respondent with these thirteen kinds of vocal candor, one abandons the thwarted discussion. Having abandoned it, one is defeated, one's logic overcome. Retreating, one is beaten. Therefore, the surrender of the discussion is called 'points of defeat' (*nigrahasthāna*).

/ kathāsādaḥ katamaḥ / yathāpi tad vādī parāvādinābhibhūtaḥ anyenānyaṃ pratisarati / bahirdhā kathām upanayati / kopaṃ ca dveṣaṃ ca mānaṃ ca mrakṣaṃ cāghātaṃ cākṣāntiṃ cāpratyayaṃ ca prāviṣkaroti / tūṣṇīmbhūto vā bhavati / madgubhūtaḥ srastaskandhaḥ adhomukhaḥ pradhyāna-paramaḥ / niṣpratibhānaḥ/

B. What is collapse of the discussion (*kathāsāda*)? As follows: That first speaker, having been overcome by the respondent [acts in these ways], 1. By means of another (matter) shifts ground; 2. Brings up irrelevant matters; 3-9. Manifests anger, haterd, pride, dissimulation, aggression, lack of forbearance, a bad situation; 10. Becomes speechless; 11. Is upset; 12. Droops shoulders and lowers face; 13. Occupies oneself with subtle reflection, one's resourcefulness gone.

---

46. Pa, then Ya: *uttari*; but cf. Edgerton, BHS Dirctionary, s.v. showing that the Pa-Ya term means 'further,' 'beyond'. My reading of the MS, namely, *uttare*, is the locative of *uttara*, and here means 'later on'.

/ kathaṃ anyenānyaṃ pratisarati / pūrvikāṃ pratijñām utsṛjyānyam ālambate / pūrvakaṃ hetum udāharaṇaṃ sārūpyaṃ vairūpyaṃ pratyakṣam anumāṇam āptāgamam utsṛjyānyam āptāgamam ālambate /

B-1. How does one, by means of another (matter), shift ground? Having given up one's former thesis, one espouses another. Having given up the former reason, example, similarity, dissimilarity, direct perception, inference, lineage of the masters, one espouses another lineage of masters.

/ kathaṃ bahirdhā-kathām upanayati / viprakṛtāṃ kathāy*ās* utsṛjya yānnakathā pānakathā rājakathā / corakathā vīthīkathā veśyākathā ity evambhāgīyāḥ kathāḥ viprakṛtāyāḥ kathāyā bahirdhā-kathety ucyate / tām upanayati / atikramyottara-vādaṃ/

B-2. How does one bring up irrelevant matters? Having given up one's offensive discussion, whatever the discussion of food, of drink, of the king, of thieves, of shops, of prostitutes; and any discussion of like category after the offensive discussion—these are the "irrelevant matters". One brings up the (irrelevant matters), namely, a topic that is extraneous.

/ kathaṃ kopaṃ prāviṣkaroti / pāruṣyāsabhya[47]-vādena prativādinam avasādayati /

B-3. How does one manifest anger? With words that are harsh and unfit for an assembly, one assails the respondent.

/ kathaṃ dveṣaṃ prāviṣkaroti / pratikartavyatā-vādena prativādinaṃ abhiyojayati/

B-4. How does one manifest hatred? One threatens the respondent by saying oneself will get even (with that person).

/ kathaṃ mānaṃ prāviṣkaroti / hīnajātigotrakulādi-vādena prativādinaṃ paṃsayati /

B-5. How does one display pride? One mocks the respondent by referring to that person's low lineage, clan, family, etc.

/ kathaṃ mrakṣaṃ prāviṣkaroti/praticchāditaduścaritodvādana-vādena prativādinaṃ codayati /

B-6. How does one express dissimulation? One petitions the respondent by speaking in a raised voice that conceals one's own bad conduct.

---

47. I am pleased to give up my MS reading *asatya* in favor of the reading by Pa, followed by Ya, of *asabhya*.

/ katham āghātaṃ prāviṣkaroti / vadhaka-pratyarthika-pratyamitra-vādena prativādinam ākṣipati /

B-7. How does one express aggression? One challenges the respondent by calling that person a murderer, or an adversary, or an enemy.

/ katham akṣāntiṃ prāviṣkaroti / vairiṇ*opādāna*[48]-vādena prativādinaṃ tarjayati /

B-8. Hoes does one express lack of forbearance? One threatens the respondent with words that adopt enmity.

/ katham apratyayaṃ prāviṣkaroti / bhinnacāritra-vādena prativādinaṃ pratikṣipati /

B-9. How does one express a bad situation? One chides the respondent with words that the course of action has been shattered.

/ kathaṃ tūṣṇīmbhūto bhavati / vākkarma-saṃkocataḥ /

B-10. How does one become silent? By withdrawing from acts of speech.

/ kathaṃ madgubhūto[49] bhavati / manaskarmasaṃkocataḥ /

B-11. How does one become inattentive? By withdrawing from (volitional) acts of mind.

/ kathaṃ srastaskandho bhavaty adhomukhaḥ / kāyākarmadhairya-saṃkocataḥ /

B-12. How does one lower one's shoulders and have a lowered face? By withdrawing from acts of body and courage.

---

48. Pa, repeated by Ya, has a different reading, *vaira-niryātana,* but *niryātana* has a basic meaning of 'giving back'—not what Asaṅga would say here, nor does their solution go with the Tibetan translation for the verbal part, namely, *gzuṅ ba.* But my reading of the MS was: *vairiṇa-padana-*; and I found in the Lokesh Chandra, *Tibetan-Sanskrit Dictionary,* among the entries for *gzuṅ ba,* the reading *upādāna,* which fits; and my reading of the initial word, *vairiṇa,* yields a perfectly good Sanskrit word.

49. There is no problem of text reading here. It is a matter of meaning. The usual reference works, such as the Monier-Williams Sanskrit-English Dictionary, do not help, while Edgerton's BHS Dictionary was approaching, but still does not help here. The Tibetan translation departs from the usual literal-type rendition, presenting a paraphrase: *yul yul por gyur pa.* The term *yul* means the objective world; but for *yul po* I had to resort to the 3-vol. Tibetan-Chinese Dictionary called *Bod rgya tshig mdzod chen mo,* which in Vol. 3, p. 2590 defines *yul po* as *sems ston lhaṅ lhaṅ* "deserted of mind, a clear sound". As applied to the present case, it means that the objective realm has been deserted by mind, and that the respondent's voice is heard just as a steady drone.

/ kathaṃ pradhyānaparamo bhavati niṣpratibhānaḥ / pratibhāna-saṃkocataḥ /

B-13. How does one get preoccupied with subtle reflection, one's resourcefulness gone? By withdrawing from resourcefulness.

/ ity ebhis trayodaśabhir ākāraiḥ kathāsādo veditavyaḥ / dvābhyāṃ pūrvakābhyāṃ vikṣepapratipattitaḥ saptabhir madhyair mithyā-pratipattitaḥ / caturbhiḥ paścimaiḥ apratipattitaḥ / ayam ucyate kathāsādaḥ nigrahasthānam/

By these thirteen aspects one may recognize the collapse of the discussion. The first two (1-2) are through distraction; the middle seven (3-9) are through deviant (or, perverse) action; the last four (10-13) are through inaction. This is called 'collapse of the discussion', as points of defeat.

/ kathādoṣaḥ katamaḥ/ navabhir doṣai raktā[50] kathā / kathādoṣa ity ucyate / navadoṣāḥ katame tadyathā ākulaṃ vacanaṃ; saṃrabdham; agamakam; amitam; anarthayuktam; akālena; asthiram; adīptam; aprabaddhaṃ ca vacanam /

C. What are the faults of the discussion (*kathādoṣa*)? The discussion is discolored with nine faults, called 'faults of the discussion'. What are the nine faults? As follows: The discussion 1. has confused language; 2. is violent; 3. is incomprehensible; 4. is inordinate; 5. is fallacious; 6. is mistimed; 7. oscillates; 8. is purblind; 9. is faltering.

/ ākulaṃ vacanaṃ katamat / yad adhikāram utsṛjya vicitrakathā-pratānam /

C-1. What is confused (*ākula*) language? Having given up the authorized topic (*adhikāra*), to have a prolixity (*pratāna*) of variegated discussion.

/ saṃrabdham vacanaṃ katamat / yat kopoddhataṃ dravod-dhataṃ ca /

C-2. What is violent (*saṃrabdha*) language? That which is exaggerated in fury and that which is exaggerated in sport.

/ agamakaṃ vacanaṃ katamat / yad dharmato 'rthataś ca parṣadvādibhyām agṛhītam /

50. Pa. followed by Ya: *duṣṭā*; but *raktā* is what I saw in the MS and it agrees with the Tib. tr. *chags pa*.

C-3. What is incomprehensible (*agamaka*) language? That which cannot be understood by one's retinue and the respondent from the standpoint of doctrine (*dharma*) and its meaning (*artha*).

/ amitaṃ vacanaṃ katamat / yad adhikaṃ punar uktārthaṃ nyūnārthaṃ ca /

C-4. What is inordinate (*amita*) language? Whose expressed meaning is excessive or whose meaning is deficient.

/ anarthayuktam vacanaṃ katamat / tad daśākāram draṣṭavyam / nirarthakam; apārthakam; yuktibhinnaṃ; sādhyasamam; aticchalām asaṃhitaṃ ca; arthānupalabdhitaḥ; asambaddhārthatas; anekāntikataḥ; sādhanasyāpi sādhyatas; ayoniśo sādhyasarvavādānugamataś ca /

C-5. What is fallacious (*anarthayukta*) language? It is of ten aspects, to wit: (1) meaningless (*nirarthaka*), because (6) not observing meaning (*arthānupalabdhi*); (2) departed from meaning (*apārthaka*), because (7) not connected in meaning (*asambaddhartha*); (3) unsound of reason (*yuktibhinna*), because (8) uncertain (*anekāntika*); (4) identical with the thesis (*sādhyasama*), because (9) the thesis is also within the proving (*sādhanasyāpi sādhya*); (5) equivocal (*aticchalā*) and irrelevant (*asaṃhita*), because (10) pursuing all debate of the thesis in an improper manner (*ayoniśo sādhyasarvavādānugama*).

/ akalena vacanaṃ katamat / yad pūrvaṃ vaktavyaṃ paścād abhihitaṃ / paścād vaktavyaṃ pūrvam abhihitam/

C-6. What is mistimed (*akalena*) language? What should have been said earlier is said later; what should have been said later is said earlier.

/ asthiraṃ vacanaṃ katamat / yat pratijñāyā avajñātam *avajñaya*[51] pratijñātam atitvaramāṇatayā ca /[52] avyaktam/

C-7. What is oscillating (*asthira*) language? Any one that shows contempt for the thesis; and after rejecting it, agrees with it. And (the position of the language) is undetermined (*avyakta*), due to the excessive haste [of the oscillating].

---

51. Ya claims this word should be entered here. He is right, per Tib. *bor ba las.*
52. Now Ya repeats Pa's phrase *atitūrṇāparāmṛṣṭaṃ*, where *atitūrṇa-* means the same as the *atitvara-* of the preceding phrase; and *aparāmṛṣṭa* neither accords with the Tibetan text nor helps the definition. And neither Pa nor Ya gave what I saw in the MS, *avyaktam*, agreeing with the Tib. *mi gsal ba.*

/ adīptaṃ vacanaṃ katamat / yac chando[53]-lakṣaṇena *viruddham/* apūrvavacanottaravihitaṃ[54] / *saṃskṛtabhāṣaṇenārabhya prākṛtabhāṣaṇena paryavasitaṃ prākṛtabhāṣaṇenārabhya saṃskṛtabhāṣaṇena paryavasitam* /[55]

C-8. What is purblind (*adīpta*) language? What is prohibited by the definition of word order (*chando-lakṣaṇa*), e.g. replying to what was not asked; having started with the Sanskrit language, to end up with a vernacular; or having started with a vernacular, to end up with the Sanskrit language.

/ aprabaddhaṃ vacanaṃ katamat / yad antarādhiṣṭhitavicchinnaṃ vākpratibhānavicchinnaṃ /

C-9. What is faltering (*aprabaddha*) language? What interrupts control in the middle, and interrupts the eloquence of words.

/ navabhiṛ doṣai raktā kathā / iyam ucyate / ayam ucyate kathādoṣaḥ nigrahasthānaṃ /

What is referred to as the language discolored by those nine faults is called 'faults of the discussion'.

The foregoing is points of defeat in the debate.

/vādaniḥsaraṇaṃ katamat / trividhayā parīkṣayā suparīkṣya vādasyākaraṇato vā karaṇato vā / vādaniḥsaraṇam ity ucyate / trividhā parīkṣā katamā / guṇadoṣaparīkṣā parṣatparīkṣā kauśalyaparīkṣā ca /

VI. DECISION WHETHER TO UNDERTAKE THE DEBATE

The undertaking or not undertaking of the debate, when one carefully considers by three kinds of consideration, is called 'decision whether to undertake the debate'. What are the three kinds of consideration? Consideration of the merits and demerits; consideration of the assembly; consideration of the skill.

/ guṇadoṣaparīkṣā katamā / yathāpi / tad vādī vādārambhī evaṃ pratyavekṣate /[56] *sacet* iyam *me* vādakriyā ātmavyābādhāya saṃvartate paravyābādhāyobhayavyābādhāya / dṛṣṭadhārmikasyāvadyasya prasavāya sāmparāyikasya / dṛṣṭadharma-sāmparāyikasya / taj-

53. The term *chandas* is being employed here in a special meaning of Buddhist Sanskrit as 'word order'.

54. The expression *uttaravihitam* is here employed in Buddhist Sanskrit as 'making response'.

55. My portion in italics differs somewhat from the solution in Pa, mostly followed by Ya; but the solution here given exactly goes with the Tibetan translation.

56. Pa and Ya start this paragraph slightly differently from my presentation.

jātasya[57] caitasikasya duḥkhadaurmanasya / śastrādāna-daṇḍādāna-kalaha-bhaṇḍana-vigraha-vivādānāṃ śāṭhya*vadana*[58]-nikṛtimṛṣā-vādānām / anekavidhānāṃ pāpakānām akuśalānāṃ dharmāṇām utpattaye / nātmahitāya na parahitāya na bahujanahitāya na bahujanasukhāya na lokānukampāya nārthāya hitāya sukhāya devamanuṣyāṇām / sacet sa evaṃ pratyavekṣamāṇo jānīyād/ iyam me vādakriyā ātmavyābādhāya saṃvartate vistareṇa yāvan nārthāya hitāya sukhāya devamanuṣyāṇām / tena vādinā pratisaṃkhyāya vādo na kartavyaḥ / sacet punaḥ sa evaṃ pratyavekṣamāṇo jānīyād iyaṃ me vādakriyā nātmavyābādhāya vistareṇa yāvad arthāya hitāya sukhāya devamanuṣyāṇāṃ/ tena vādinā pratisaṃkhyāya vādaḥ karaṇīyaḥ / idaṃ prathamaṃ vādaniḥsaraṇaṃ / yad uta / akaraṇato vā karaṇato vā /

A. What is consideration of the merits and demerits (*guṇadoṣa*)? As follows: That debater, formulating a debate, carefully considers in this manner: whether my debating would be harmful to myself, harmful to others, harmful to both; whether incurring blame in the present time, future time, or both present and future time; and arising therefrom, the mental natures sorrow and dissatisfaction, the taking up of a weapon, the taking up of a staff, strife, fault picking, schism, contention, deceitful words, harm and lies, and many kinds of sinful, unvirtuous natures. And one reviews in his mind whether there would be a disservice to oneself, a disservice to the other, a disservice to many persons, a displeasure to many persons, a failure of compassion toward the world, against the aim, benefit, and happiness of gods and men. And if one has in this manner carefully considered, and realizes, if I were to inaugurate it, it would be harmful to myself, and so on, down to, against the aim, benefit, and happiness of gods and men—that debater, having carefully considered, should not undertake the debate. But, if, after carefully considering in this manner, were I to undertake the debate, realizes that it would not be harmful to himself, and so on, down to, it would be the aim, benefit, and happiness of gods and men, that one, having so considered, should inaugurate it. This is the first decision whether to undertake the debate, that is, either not undertaking it or undertaking it.

57. Pa and Ya: *tajjasya*.

58. Pa and Ya: *vancana*. My reading agrees with the Tibetan reading: *tshig*.

/ parṣatparīkṣā katamā / yathāpi tad vādī evaṃ pratyavekṣate / kiṃ tv iyaṃ parṣad abhiniviṣṭā vā 'nabhiniviṣṭā vā / sabhyā vā 'sabhyā vā / kuśalā vā 'kuśalā vā / sacet sa evaṃ pratyavekṣamāṇo *jānīyād* iyaṃ parṣad anabhiniviṣṭā na 'bhiniviṣṭā 'sabhyā na sabhyā 'kuśalā na kuśalā tena vādinā pratisaṃkhyāya tasyāṃ parṣadi kathā na karaṇīyā / sacet sa evaṃ pratyavekṣamāṇo *jānīyād* iyaṃ parṣad abhiniviṣṭā nānabhiniviṣṭā sabhyā nāsabhyā kuśalā nākuśalā tena vādinā pratisaṃkhyāya tasyāṃ parṣadi kathā karaṇīyā / idaṃ dvitīyaṃ vādaniḥsaraṇaṃ yad utākaraṇato vā karaṇato vā/

B. What is consideration of the assembly (*parṣat*)? As follows: The 'first speaker' carefully considers, is it that this assembly is of fixed mind, or of open mind, a good assembly or a bad assembly, expert or amateur? If, having so considered, he realizes that it is not of open mind, i.e. is of fixed mind; is not a good assembly, i.e. is a bad assembly; is not expert, i.e. is amateur, then that surveyor, having carefully considered, should not undertake a discussion to that assembly. If, upon considering, he realizes that this assembly is open-minded, not of fixed mind; is a good assembly, not a bad assembly; expert, not amateur—then that 'first speaker', having carefully considered, should undertake a discussion to that assembly. This is, namely, the second decision whether to undertake the debate, that is, either not undertaking it or undertaking it.

/ kauśalyaparīkṣā katamā yathāpi tad vādī ātmani kauśalyam upaparīkṣate / kiṃ tu kuśalo 'haṃ vādasya vādādhikaraṇasya vādādhiṣṭhānasya vādālaṃkārasya vaādanigrahasya āhosvid akuśalo vā / kiṃ tu pratibalo 'ham sva*siddhāntaṃ*[59] sthāpayituṃ nigrahasthānād vimuktaḥ paravādaṃ ca nigṛhītum / sacet sa evaṃ pratyavekṣamāno jānīyād akuśalo 'ham na pratibalaḥ / tena vādinā pratisaṃkhyāya prativādinam kathā na karaṇīyā / sacet sa evaṃ pratyavekṣamāno jānīyāt kuśalo 'haṃ nākuśalaḥ pratibalo 'haṃ nāpratibalaḥ tena vādinā pratisaṃkhyāya prativādinaṃ kathā karaṇīyā / ity ucyate tṛtīyaṃ vādaniḥsaraṇaṃ yad utākaraṇato vā karaṇato vā / ayam ucyate vādaniḥsaraṇam/

C. What is the consideration of skill (*kauśalya*)? As follows: The 'first speaker' carefully considers whether he/she is skilled, (thinking:) Am I skilled in the setting of the debate, in the foundation of the debate, in the ornaments of the debate, in the points of defeat

59. Pa, followed by Ya: *svavadam.*

in the debate; or am I not skilled (in them)? Am I capable of establishing my own theory-system (*siddhānta*); and freed from the points of defeat in the debate, (capable) of defeating the opposing position? If upon so considering, one realizes that one is not skilled, an amateur; is not a match for it, i.e. unequal to the task—then that 'first speaker', having carefully considered, should not undertake a discussion to the 'respondent'. If, upon considering, one realizes that one is skilled, not an amateur; that one is a match for it, i.e. not unequal (to the task), then that 'first speaker', having carefully considered, should undertake a discussion to the 'respondent'. This is, namely, the third decision whether to undertake the debate, that is, either not undertaking or undertaking it.

The foregoing is called 'decision whether to undertake the debate'.

/vāde bahukarā dharmāḥ katame / trayo dharmā vāde bahukarā veditavyaḥ svaparasamayajñatā / vaiśāradyaṃ pratibhānaṃ ca / kasmād ime trayo dharmā vāde bahukarā ity ucyante / yathāpi vādī svaparasamayajñatayā sarvatra vastuni kathāṃ karoti / vaiśāradyena sarvasyāṃ parṣadi kathāṃ karoti / pratibhānena sarvatrābhihite uttaraṃ prayacchati / tasmād ime trayo dharmā vāde bahukarā ity ucyante / ime ucyante vāde bahukarā dharmāḥ /

VII. ATTRIBUTES OF MUCH UTILITY IN THE DEBATE

What are the attributes (*dharma*) of much utility (*bahukara*) in the debate? Three attributes are of much utility in the debate: (1) Knowledge of one's own and the other's context (*svaparasamayajñatā*), (2) Confidence (*vaiśāradya*), (3) Resourcefulness (*pratibhāna*). Why are these three attributes said to be of much utility? It is this way: (1) The first speaker, by knowing one's own and the other's context, is able to make a discourse on all given matters. (2) By confidence one is able to deliver a discourse to all groups. (3) By resourcefulness one is able to offer reply to everyone who addresses [with challenge of response]. Therefore, these three attributes are said to be of much utility. The foregoing are the attributes of much utility in the debate.

/ uddhānaṃ /

/ vādo 'dhikaraṇaṃ tasya tadadhiṣṭhānaṃ eva ca /
/ bhūṣaṇaṃ nigrahas tasya *niśritir*[60] bahukarakāḥ //

Summation verse:

The debate and its setting, its foundation;
its ornaments and points of defeat; undertaking it, and
what are of much utility for it.[61]

[Finished is *Asaṅga's Rules of Debate*].

60. The MS reading *nisṛti*, seen by Pa, by Ya, and myself, is obviously wrong, since it means 'disappearance'. But then Pa, also Ya, gave the correction *niḥsṛti*, which does not fit, since it means 'departure'. My solution of *niśriti* does fit, since it means something like 'going to with support', so 'undertaking' it. But this is a rare form of the root *ni-śri*, and so easily became corrupted into *nisṛti*.

61. May I say that the above work completely supersedes my old essay (n. 3, above). Still, I have nothing to apologize for that essay, which is among my earliest.

INTRODUCTION TO DHARMAKĪRTI'S *Nyāyabindu* AND KAMALAŚĪLA, *Nyāyabindupūrvapakṣasaṃkṣipti*

It appears that Dharmakīrti flourished in the middle of the 7th century of India, and Kamalaśīla in the middle of the 8th century of Tibet, where he had moved along with his teacher Śāntarakṣita. Dharmakīrti's greatest text is his *Pramāṇavārttika,* the Sanskrit for which (now available) was not yet available at the time Stcherbatsky wrote his well-known two-volume work *Buddhist Logic* (Leningrad, circa 1930). In his day, Dharmakīrti's *Nyāyabindu* and Dharmottara's commentary on it were available in edited Sanskrit, and Stcherbatsky devoted half his volume two for a rendition into English of this text and commentary along with many notes. Rendering just the *Nyāyabindu,* I translated from the Sanskrit of Chowkhamba Sanskrit Series, 1954. I followed Stcherbatsky's paragraph numbers and his inclusions, while finding his own English translation tantamount to a foreign language. By the Sanskrit alongside, it should be easy for the reader to compare my renditions with the Sanskrit.

Then I added Kamalaśīla's treatise, providing what this author accepts as the opponents envisaged by Dharmakīrti's formulations in the *Nyāyabindu.* (This contrasts with both Dharmottara's and Vinītadeva's commentaries, which were not especially concerned with opponents.) Since I translated this from Tibetan, I have included this text from the Peking Tibetan canon. Kamalaśīla is well-known to modern Buddhist scholarship for his extensive commentary on Śāntarakṣita's *Tattvasaṃgraha,* which is available in Sanskrit, Tibetan, and an English translation. He also wrote three important works each called *Bhāvanākrama.*

Dharmakīrti's *Nyāyabindu* is of course an introduction to the topic, providing the main ideas in a sort of condensed form. Various of these ideas will be amplified in other texts of this Vol. One of my Millennium.

DHARMAKĪRTI'S *Nyāyabindu*

I. PRATYAKṢA (DIRECT PERCEPTION)

1. The success of all human aims is preceded by right cognition. Therefore, this (cognition) is here taught.	samyagjñānapūrvikā sarvapuruṣārthasiddhir iti tad vyutpādyate /
2. Right cognition is twofold:	dvividhaṃ samyagjñānam /
3. Direct perception and inference.	pratyakṣam anumānaṃ ca /
4. Among them, direct perception is free from constructive thought and is non-delusory.	tatra kalpanāpoḍham abhrāntam pratyakṣam/
5. Constructive thought is the cognitive dawning of an image able to coalesce with verbalism.	abhilāpasaṃsargayogyapratibhāsa-pratītiḥ kalpanā/
6. Cognition free from such (constructive thought), when not subject to disturbances such as the eye-caul, whirling motion, embarking in a boat, and agitation is direct perception.	tayā rahitaṃ timirāśubhramaṇanauyānasaṃkṣobhādyanāhitavibhramaṃ jñānaṃ pratyakṣam/
7. It is fourfold—	tac caturvidham /
8. (1) Sense-organ cognition.	indriyajñānam /
9. (2) Mental perception (which) is engendered by the immediately preceding condition, to wit, the cooperating sense-organ cognition as an object that immediately follows its own (partite) sense object.	svaviṣayānantaraviṣayasaha-kāriṇendriya-jñānena samanantarapratyayena janitaṃ tan manovijñānam /
10. (3) Introspection (which) is of every thought and mental.	sarvacittacaittānām ātmasaṃvedanam /
11. And (4) yogin's cognition (which is) born of the vivid	bhūtārthabhāvanāprakarṣaparyantajaṃ yogijñānam ceti /

fulfilment from contemplating the true end.	
12. Its object is the individual character.	tasya viṣayaḥ svalakṣaṇam /
13. The individual character of whatever object-entity is the difference of cognitive image due to nearness and remoteness (of that entity)	yasyārthasya saṃnidhānāsaṃnidhānābhyāṃ jñānapratibhāsabhedas tat svalakṣaṇam /
14. That alone is absolute existence.	tad eva paramārthasat /
15. Because it is a given thing, to wit, has a character capable of purposive activity.	arthakriyāsāmarthyalakṣaṇatvād vastunaḥ /
16. Different from it is the generality character.	anyat sāmānyalakṣaṇam /
17. This is the object of inference.	so 'numānasya viṣayaḥ /
18-19. And indeed the direct-perception cognition is an authority-result, because it has the form of the object-entity's cognitive dawning.	tad eva ca pratyakṣaṃ jñānaṃ pramāṇaphalam arthapratītirūpatvāt /
20. Its authority is the likeness to the object-entity.	arthasārūpyam asya pramāṇam/
21. By dint of this, there is success of the object-entity's cognitive dawning.	tadvaśād arthapratītisiddher iti /

II. SVĀRTHĀNUMĀNA (INFERENCE FOR ONESELF)

1. Inference is twofold—	anumānaṃ dvidhā /
2. for oneself and for others.	svārtham parārthaṃ ca /
3. Among them, the inference for oneself is the cognition, in regard to the inferable, from evidence having three modes.	tatra svārthaṃ trirūpāl liṅgād yad anumeye jñānaṃ tad anumānam /
4. Here also, the establishment of the authority as a	pramāṇaphalavyavasthātrāpi pratyakṣavat /

result is the same as in the case of direct perception.	
5. Besides, it is certain that the triple mode of evidence is (1) only its existence in the inferable; or	trairūpyaṃ punaḥ liṅgasyanumeye sattvam eva /
6. (2) its existence only in similar locuses (sapakṣa); or	sapakṣa eva sattvam /
7. (3) only its absence in dissimilar locuses (asapakṣa).	asapakṣe cāsattvam eva niścitaṃ/
8. The inferable is here the factual base whose distinction it is desired to cognize.	anumeyo 'tra jijñāsitaviśeṣo dharmī /
9. A similar locus is an object-entity which is similar through the generality of the thesis feature.	sādhyadharmasāmānyena samāno 'rthaḥ sapakṣaḥ /
10. A dissimilar locus is not a similar locus, namely, others than it, opposed to it, or its absence.	na sapakṣo 'sapakṣaḥ tato 'nyas tadviruddhas tadabhavaś ceti /
11. And the three modes have only three evidences.	trirūpāṇi ca trīṇy eva ca liṅgāni/
12. (1) nonapprehension, (2) individual presence, and (3) result.	anupalabdhiḥ svabhāvakārye ceti /
13. Among them, nonapprehension is, e.g. on some particular place there is no pot, because, while characters are met for (its) being apprehended, there is nonapprehension.	tatrānupalabdhir yathā na pradeśaviśeṣe kvacid ghaṭa upalabdhilakṣaṇaprāptasyānupalabdher iti /
14. "Characters met for being apprehended" means there is a distinct individual presence, and the totality of all other conditions for apprehension.	upalabdhilakṣaṇaprāptir upalambhapratyayāntara-sākalyaṃ svabhāvaviśeṣaś ca /

15. Individual presence only occurs to direct perception, given the other conditions for apprehension.	yah svabhāvah satsv anyeṣ-ūpalambhapratyayeṣu yat pratyakṣa eva bhavati sa svabhāva /
16. Individual presence is a reason when the thesis feature has a presence that amounts to the (concrete) existence of itself.	svabhāvaḥ svasattāmātra-bhāvini sādhyadharme hetuḥ /
17. as e.g. "This is a tree, because it is an Aśoka."	yathā vṛkṣo 'yaṃ śiṃśapātvād iti/
18. Result is, e.g. "Here is a fire, because there is smoke."	kāryaṃ yathāgnir atra dhūmād iti /
19. Among them, two (individual presence and result) prove a given thing, and one (nonapprehension) is a reason for exclusion.	atra dvau vastusādhanau / ekaḥ pratiṣedhahetuḥ /
20. Thus, (one) entity can comprehend (another) entity when there is a relation with (its) individual presence;	svabhāvapratibandhe hi saty artho 'rtham gamayet /
21. because for an entity unrelated to that (other) there is no assurance of not mistaking it.	tadapratibaddhasya tad-avyabhi-cāraniyamābhāvāt /
22-23. The relation is of evidence for the thesis entity, either because of identity with the thesis entity as a given thing, or else because of arising from the thesis entity (as a given thing).	sa ca pratibandhaḥ sādhye 'rthe liṅgasya vastutas tādātmyāt sādhyārthād utpatteś ca /
24. Because when an entity is not the individual presence of that (other), or does not arise from it, there is no related individual presence.	atatsvabhāvasyātadutpatteś ca tatrāpratibaddhasvabhāvatvāt /

25. Thus, these two, the identity with it and the arising from it, are only individual presence and result; and only through these two is there proof of a given thing.	te ca tādātmyatadutpattī svabhāvakāryayor eveti tābhyām eva vastusiddhiḥ /
26. Also, proof of an exclusion is due only to non-apprehension, as was stated (previously);	pratiṣedhasiddhir api yathoktāyā evānupalabdheḥ /
27. because when a given thing is present, there is no possibility of that (non-apprehension).	sati vastuni tasyā asambhavāt /
28. And because otherwise, when there are the things inaccessible by place, time, and individual presence, while characters are met for (their) being apprehended—there would be no assurance whether their absence was due to (temporary) suspension of one's own direct perception.	anyathā cānupalabhilakṣaṇaprāpteṣu deśakālasvabhāvaviprakṛṣṭeṣv ātmapratyakṣanivṛtter abhāvaniścayābhāvāt /
29. Suspension of the reasoner's past or present direct perception whose memory motivation is not confused, proves the convention of absence;	amūḍhasmṛtisaṃskārasyātītasya vartamānasya ca pratipattṛpratyakṣasya nivṛttir abhāvavyavahārasādhanī /
30. because by that (suspension) alone is there assurance of absence.	tasyā evābhāvaniścayāt /
31. And that (non-apprehension) is of eleven kinds by difference of formulation.	sā ca prayogabhedād ekādaśaprakārā /
32. (1) Non-apprehension of individual presence is, e.g., "There is no smoke here,	svabhāvānupalabdhir yathā / nātra dhūma upalabdhilakṣaṇaprāptasyānupalabdher iti /

because while conditions are met for (its) being apprehended, there is no apprehension (of smoke)."

33. (2) Non-apprehension of result is, e.g., "There are here no material causes that are capable and unimpeded for smoke, because there is no smoke."

kāryānupalabdhir yathā / nehāpratibaddhasāmarthyāni dhūmakāraṇāni santi dhūmābhāvāt /

34. (3) Non-apprehension of pervader is, e.g., "There is here no Aśoka tree, because there are no trees."

vyāpakānupalabdhir yathā / nātra śiṃśapā vṛkṣābhāvād iti /

35. (4) Apprehension opposing an individual presence is, e.g., "Here there is no contact with cold, because there is a fire."

svabhāvaviruddhopalabdhir yathā / nātra śītasparśo 'gner iti/

36. (5) Apprehension of opposing result is, e.g., "Here there is no contact with cold, because there is smoke."

viruddhakāryopalabdhir yathā/ nātra śītasparśo dhūmād iti /

37. (6) Apprehension with pervasion opposed is, e.g., "Destruction is not a constant presence belonging to an ongoing thing even though it was originated, because it (the destruction) depends upon a different cause."

viruddhavyāptopalabdhir yathā/ na dhruvabhāvī bhūtasyāpi bhāvasya vināśo hetvantarāpekṣaṇād iti /

38. (7) Apprehension opposing a result is, e.g., "Here there are no material causes capable and unimpeded for cold, because there is a fire."

kāryaviruddhopalabdhir yathā/ nehāpratibaddhasāmarthyāni śītakāraṇāni santy agner iti /

39. (8) Apprehension opposing a pervader is, e.g., "Here there is no touching

vyāpakāviruddhopalabdhir yathā/ nātra tuṣārasparśo 'gner iti /

of any cold thing, because there is a fire."

40. (9) Non-apprehension of material causes is, e.g., "Here there is no smoke, because there is no fire."

kāraṇānupalabdhir yathā / nātra dhūmo 'gnyabhāvād iti /

41. (10) Apprehension opposing a material cause is, e.g., "He has no distinction such as (cold-caused) erect hair, etc., because nearby is the distinction of scorching heat."

kāraṇaviruddhopalabdhir yathā / nāsya romaharṣādiviseśaḥ saṃnihitadahanaviśeṣatvād iti /

42. (11) Apprehension of result opposing a material cause, is, e.g., "This place does not have a person possessing distinctions such as (cold-caused) erect hair, because there is smoke."

kāraṇaviruddhakāryopalabdhir yathā / na romaharṣādiviśeṣayuktapuruṣavān ayaṃ pradeśo dhūmād iti /

43. All the ten formulations of non-apprehension beginning with non-apprehension of result (nos. 2-11) may be included in the non-apprehension of individual presence (no. 1);

ime sarve kāryānupalabdhyādayo daśānupalabdhiprayogāḥ svabhāvānupalabdhau saṃgraham upayānti /

44. i.e. indirectly—although there is a difference of formulation—by affirmation and exclusion of some other entity.

pāramparyeṇārthāntaravidhipratiṣedhābhyāṃ prayogabhede 'pi /

45. By repeated consideration of the formulations, thus the rulings-out will come to dawn upon oneself as well. Hence, also, the mention of formulations of that (non-apprehension) are in the 'inference for oneself'.

prayogadarśaṇābhyāsāt svayam apy evaṃ vyavacchedapratītir bhavatīti svārthe 'py anumāne 'syāḥ prayoganirdeśaḥ /

46. And in all those cases, in

sarvatra cāsyām abhāvavyava-

regard to non-apprehension as the conventional proof of absence, whether the exclusion is stated by apprehension opposing individual presence, etc., or stated by non-apprehension of material cause, etc., the apprehension and the non-apprehension should be understood for those cases while characters are met for (their) being apprehended,—

hārasādhanyām anupalabdhau yeṣāṃ svabhāvaviruddhādīnām upalabdhyā kāraṇādīnām anupalabdhyā ca pratiṣedha uktas teṣām upalabdhilakṣaṇa-prāptānām evopalabdhir anupalabdhiś ca veditavyā /

47. because there is no proof of the presence of opposition, result, and material cause in other cases.

anyeṣāṃ virodhakāryakāraṇa-bhāvāsiddheḥ /

48. The non-apprehension of an inaccessible object, having the character of suspending direct perception and inference, is a cause for doubt, because there is no proof of the absence of an entity when the two authorities (i.e. direct perception and inference) are suspended.

viprakṛṣṭaviṣayānupalabdhiḥ pratyakṣānumānanivṛttilakṣaṇā saṃśayahetuḥ pramāṇanivṛttāv apy arthābhāvāsiddher iti /

III. PARĀRTHĀNUMĀNA (INFERENCE FOR OTHERS)

1. Inference for others is the communication of the evidence with three modes,

trirūpaliṅgākhyānaṃ parār-thānumānam /

2. when there is the material cause by way of a metaphoric transfer of the result.

kāraṇe kāryopacārāt /

3-4. It is twofold, by difference of formulation—

tad dvividham prayogabhedāt/

5.	feature concordance and feature discordance.	sādharmyavad vaidharmyavac ceti /
6-7.	Actually, there is no difference between the two, except for the difference of formulation.	nānayor arthataḥ kaścid bhedo 'nyatra prayogabhedāt /
8.	Among these, the feature concordance is as follows:	tatra sādharmyavad /
9.	while conditions are met for apprehending, and one proves that a conventional object is nonexistent. For example, some other illustration (is made), viz., horns on a rabbit, etc.; and a jar is not apprehended in a particular spot, while characters are met for apprehending it.	yad upalabdhilakṣaṇaprāptaṃ san nopalabhyate so 'sadvyavahāraviṣayaḥ siddhaḥ / yathānyaḥ kaścid dṛṣṭaḥ śaśaviṣāṇādiḥ / nopalabhyate ca kvacit pradeśaviśeṣa upalabdhilakṣaṇaprāpto ghaṭa iti /
10.	Likewise, the formulation of individual-presence reason:	tathāsvabhāvahetoḥ prayogaḥ /
11.	(1) "Everything that exists is impermanent; for example, a pot." This is the formulation of a bare ('pure') individual-presence reason.	yat sat tat sarvam anityam yathā ghaṭādir iti / śuddhasya svabhāvahetoḥ prayogaḥ /
12.	(2) "Whatever has origination, is impermanent." This is the formulation of individual presence with difference of a feature existent in the individual presence.	yad utpattimat tad anityam iti / svabhāvabhūtadharmabhedena svabhāvasya prayogaḥ /
13.	(3) "Whatever is a product, is impermanent," with difference of an extra factor.	yat kṛtakaṃ tad anityam ity upādhibhedena /
14.	A product is a presence that is contingent on the	apekṣitaparavyāpāro hi bhāvaḥ svabhāvaniṣpattau kṛtaka iti /

function of something else for the consummation of the individual presence.	
15. To be viewed the same way are such expressions as 'having differentiation by difference of condition.'	evaṃ pratyayabhedabheditvādayo draṣṭavyāḥ /
16. Sound as 'existent,' as 'having origination,' or as 'a product' indicates the 'locus feature' (*pakṣadharma*).	sann utpattimān kṛtako vā śabda iti pakṣadharmopadarśanam /
17. All those (three) proving features, according to their own authorities, are to be understood as having proved the connection of the proving feature solely to the thesis feature;	sarva ete sādhanadharmā yathāsvaṃ pramāṇaiḥ siddhasādhanadharmamātrānubandha eva sādhyadharme 'vagantavyāḥ/
18. (1) because (just) it (the proving-feature) is the individual presence of that (thesis feature);	tatsvabhāvatvāt
19. (2) because it is the reason for the individual presence;	svabhāvasya ca hetutvāt /
20. (3) because actually it is the identity of these two;	vastutas tayos tādātmyāt
21. (4) because there would be no individual presence of that (proving) if the one (the thesis feature) were not generated when the other (the proving feature) has been fulfilled;	tanniṣpattāv aniṣpannasya tatsvabhāvatvābhāvād
22. (5) and because there would be the possibility of a mistake.	vyabhicārasambhavāc ca /
23. The formulation of result-reason is: "Wherever there is smoke, there is fire, for example, as in the kitchen;	kāryahetur api prayogaḥ / yatra dhūmas tatrāgnir yathā mahānasādāv asti ceha dhūma iti /

and here also there is smoke."

24. And here the result-reason should be mentioned when the material cause is the thesis, and (this) only when the presence of result and the material cause is proved (or, established).

ihāpi siddha eva / kāryakāraṇabhāve kāraṇe sādhye kāryahetur vaktavyaḥ /

25. The method with feature discordance is: When characters are met for apprehending something, it might be apprehended, e.g. a particular blue, etc. In this case, while conditions are met for apprehending it, there is no apprehension of the pot. So the formulation of non-apprehension.

vaidharmyavataḥ prayogo yat sat upalabdhilakṣaṇaprāptaṃ tad upalabhyata eva / yathā nīlādiviśeṣaḥ / na caivam ihopalabdhilakṣaṇaprāptasya sat upalabdhir ghaṭasyety anupalabdhiprayogaḥ /

26. This is the formulation of individual-presence reason: An actuality does not exist when it is absent or impermanent; it does not have an origin, nor is a product. But sound exists, has an origin, or is a product.

asaty anityatve nāsti sattvam utpattimattvaṃ kṛtakatvaṃ vā/ asaṃś ca śabda utpattimān kṛtako veti svabhavahetoḥ prayogaḥ /

27. This is the formulation of result-reason: In the absence of fire, there would be no smoke. But there is (smoke).

asatv agnau na bhavaty eva dhūmo 'tra cāstītī kāryahetoḥ prayogaḥ /

28-29. Indeed, when there is a formulation by feature concordance, one understands a feature discordance by way of meaning; for if it

sādharmyeṇāpi hi prayoge 'rthād vaidharmyagatir iti / asati tasmin sādhyena hetonvayābhāvāt /

were not so, there would be no similar presence of the reason with the thesis.

30-31. Likewise, one understands similar presence by a feature discordance; for if it were not so, there would be no proof that in the absence of the thesis there is no reason.

tathā vaidharmyeṇāpy anvayagatiḥ / asati tasmin sādhyābhāve hetvabhāvasyāsiddheḥ /

32. For when there is no connection with an individual presence, in the event of suspending one (of those two), assuredly there is suspension of the other one.

na hi svabhāvapratibandhe saty ekasya nivṛttāv aparasya niyamena nivṛttiḥ /

33. And in all cases, there two kinds, as was stated: the character of identity with that, or the character of arising from that.

sa ca dviprakāraḥ / sarvasya tādātmyalakṣaṇas tadutpattilakṣaṇas cety uktam /

34. Therefore, when suspension (of a thesis or of proving) is mentioned, the connection (or, relation) must be revealed. Accordingly, the mention of a suspension just shows a suggested connection. And the pointing to a connection, is precisely the statement of similar presence. Thus, by a single utterance entailing similar presence or entailing dissimilar absence, there is shown existence or non-existence going with evidence (*liṅga*) of a similar locus or dissimilar

tena hi nivṛttiṃ kathayatā pratibandho darśanīyaḥ / tasmān nivṛttivacanam ākṣiptapratibandhopadarśanam eva bhavati / yac ca pratibandhopadarśanam tad evānvayavacanam ity ekenāpi vakyenānvayamukhena vyatirekamukhena vā prayuktena sapakṣāsapakṣayor liṅgasya sadasattvakhyāpanaṃ kṛtaṃ bhavatīti nāvaśyavākyadvayaprayogaḥ /

locus. Therefore it is not indispensable to mention both formulations.	
35. Also, in the event of non-apprehension, when conditions are met for apprehending something, it might be apprehended, as was stated. Because of the dawning (to the mind), "Such a thing is non-existent while it is not being apprehended," there is proof of the similar presence.	anupalabdhāv api yat sad upalabdhilakṣaṇaprāptaṃ tad upalabhyata evety ukte 'nupalabhyamānaṃ tādṛśam asad iti pratīter anvayasiddhiḥ/
36. When there are either of these two formulations, it is not indispensable to mention the locus (*pakṣa*).	dvayor apy anayoḥ prayoge 'vaśyaṃ pakṣanirdeśaḥ /
37. When there is a formulation having feature concordance, given that characters are met for apprehending something and it is not apprehended here, it is a conventional object that is non-existent. It having been mentioned, "A pot is not apprehended here, although characters are met for apprehending it," by dint of that, one says, "Here there is no pot."	yasmāt sādharmyavat prayoge 'pi yad upalabdhilakṣaṇaprāptaṃ san nopalabhyate so 'sadvyavahāraviṣayaḥ / nopalabhyate cātropalabdhilakṣaṇaprāpto ghaṭa ity ukte sāmarthyād eva neha ghaṭa iti bhavati /
38. Likewise, when there is a formulation having feature discordance, given that characters are met for apprehending what is an existent conventional object, it might be apprehended.	tathā vaidharmyavat prayoge 'pi yaḥ sadvyavahāraviṣaya upalabdhilakṣaṇaprāptaḥ sa upalabhyata eva na tathātra tādṛṣo ghaṭa upalabhyata ity ukte sāmarthyād eva neha sadvyavahāraviṣaya iti bhavati /

It having been mentioned, "Here though, such a pot is not apprehended," by dint of that, one says, "Not here is the conventional object that is existent."	
39. Well, then, what is it to be called a 'locus' (*pakṣa*)?	kīdṛśaḥ punaḥ pakṣa iti nirdeśyaḥ /
40. A *pakṣa* ('locus') is what is accepted by oneself just by its own form and is not contradicted.	svarūpeṇaiva svayam iṣṭo 'nirākṛta pakṣa iti /
41-42. We claim that 'by its own form' means 'by what is the thesis.' We claim that 'just by its own form' means 'by what is the thesis' and not 'the proving (of it)'.	svarūpeṇeti sādhyatveneṣṭaḥ / svarūpeṇaiveti sādhyatveneṣṭo na sādhanatvenāpi /
43. For example, suppose the thesis is "Sound is impermanent." A (given) reason, to wit, "It is visible," is indeed not a proof for sound and so (itself) is a thesis (i.e. needs to be proved). Since it is named (by some) as a proving, it is not here claimed as a thesis.	yathā śabdasyānityatve sādhye cākṣuṣatvaṃ hetuḥ / śabde 'siddhatvāt sādhyaṃ na punas tad iha sādhyatvenaiveṣṭaṃ sādhanatvenāpy abhidhānāt /
44-45. 'Oneself' means the disputant, who on this occasion sets forth the proving.	svayam iti vādinā yas tadā sādhanam āha /
46. Then, suppose someone taking a stand on a treatise states a proving, and the author of the treatise has admitted several features in the factual base. We state that the feature which on	etena yady api kvacic chastre sthitaḥ sādhanam āha / tac chāstrakāreṇa tasmin dharmiṇy anekadharmābhyupagame 'pi yas tadā tena vādinā dharmaḥ svayaṃ sādhayitum iṣṭaḥ sa eva sādhyo netara ity uktaṃ

the given occasion the disputant himself has claimed for himself to prove, just that is the thesis, not any other (feature).	bhavati/
47-48. The term 'accepted' (in the definition of *pakṣa*) means for which sake (i.e. one's own) a proving is announced in the dispute, i.e. for it a proof is accepted. Even if it is not expressed in (so many) words, the thesis (is accepted)—because it is the context of the dispute.	iṣṭa iti yatrārthe vivādena sādhanam upanyastaṃ tasya siddhim icchatāṃ so 'nukto 'pi vacanena sādhyas tad adhikaraṇatvād vivādasya /
49. For example, (the respondent's claim) "The eye, etc. are for the sake of others, because they are composites, like beds, chairs, and other implements." While it is not explicitly stated here that they are for the sake of oneself. (That is, the respondent was aiming his claim against the first speaker's acceptance).	yathā parārthāś cakṣurādayaḥ saṃghātatvāc chayanāsanādyaṅgavad iti / atrātmārthā ity anuktāv apy ātmārthatānenoktamātram eva sādhyam ity uktaṃ bhavati /
50. The term 'not contradicted' means an addition to the definition (of *pakṣa*) so as also to demonstrate that the (respondent's) point, held to prove it is not a *pakṣa*, i.e. it is contradicted (if such be the case) by perception, by inference, by general usage, or by its own words.	anirākṛta iti / etallakṣaṇayoge 'pi yaḥ sādhayitum iṣṭo 'py arthaḥ pratyakṣānumānapratītisvavacanair nirākriyate na sa pakṣa iti pradarśanārtham /

51. Among those, contradicted by direct perception is, e.g. "Sound is inaudible."

tatra prayakṣanirakṛto yathā aśrāvaṇaḥ śabda iti/

52. Contradicted by inference is, e.g. "Sound (or a pot) is permanent."

anumānanirākṛto yathā nityaḥ śabda iti /

53. Contradicted by general usage is, e.g., "'Having a hare' (*śaśin*) is not the moon."

pratītinirākṛto yathā acandraḥ śaśīti /

54. Contradicted by its own words is, e.g., "Inference is not an authority."

svavacananirakṛto yathā nānumānaṃ pramāṇaṃ /

55. Thus the four fallacies of locus (*pakṣa*) are contradicted.

iti catvāraḥ pakṣābhāṣā nirākṛtā bhavanti /

56. A thesis is the reverse of (a) something already proved, (b) something not proved but deemed as proving, (c) what the first speaker himself has not held to prove on the given occasion, (d) what is merely stated, (e) what is contradicted. Thus the unassailable definition of *pakṣa* (we have) shown: the *pakṣa* which the first speaker holds and accepts just by its true form, and which is not contradicted.

siddhasyāsiddhasyāpi sādhanatvenābhimatasya svayaṃ vādinā tadā sādhayitum aniṣṭasyoktamātrasya nirākṛtasya ca viparyayeṇa sādhyas tenaiva svarūpeṇābhimato vādina iṣṭo 'nirākṛtaḥ pakṣa iti pakṣalakṣaṇam anavadyaṃ darśitaṃ / bhavati /

57-58. It was stated already that inference for others is an expression of the three-moded evidence. Now, when among the three modes even one is not stated, there is a fallacy of proving, as there is when they being stated there is

trirūpaliṅgākhyānaṃ parārthānumānam ity uktam / tatra trayāṇāṃ rūpāṇām ekasyāpi rūpasyānuktau sādhanābhāsāḥ uktāv apy asiddhau saṃdehe vā / pratipādyapratipādakayor/

non-proof or doubt for both the hearer and the speaker.

59. When there is non-proof or doubt of the one mode, namely relation with the factual base, there is the 'unproved' fallacy of reason.

ekasya rūpasya dharmīsaṃbandhasyāsiddhau saṃdehe cāsiddho hetvābhāsaḥ /

60. For example, when the thesis is "Sound is impermanent," (the reason) "because it is visible" is unproved for both (the hearer and the speaker).

yathā anityaḥ śabda iti sādhye cākṣuṣatvam ubhayāsiddham /

61. When the thesis is "Trees have thinking," (with the reason) "because they die when all the bark is stripped off," it is unproved to the (Buddhist) opponent, because he holds that death (for one with thinking) is defined as cessation of perception, sense organs, and life (-motivation, *āyuḥsaṃskāra*), and (that such a death) does not occur among trees.

cetanās tarava iti sādhye sarvatvagapaharaṇe maraṇaṃ pratibādyasiddhaṃ vijñānendriyāyurnirodhalakṣaṇasya maraṇasyānenābhyupagamāt tasya ca taruṣv asaṃbhavāt /

62. The thesis of the Sāṃkhya, "Pleasure and other (feelings) are without thinking," (with the reasons) "because they have an origin" or "because they are transient"—is unproved to the first speaker himself (i.e. is inconsistent with the Sāṃkhya system itself).

acetanāḥ sukhādaya iti sādhya utpattimattvam anityaṃ vā sāṃkhyasya svayaṃ vādino 'siddham /

63. When there is doubt regarding (the reason) itself or its location, it is unproved.

tathā svayaṃ tadāśrayaṇasya vā saṃdehe 'siddhaḥ /

64. For example, (as to the reason itself) when considering a proof of fire, and (a reason is advanced) "There is an assemblage of elements" while a doubt prevails whether it is a mode of vapour, etc.—it is unproved (because) doubted.

yathā vāṣpādibhāvena saṃdigyamāno bhūtasaṃghāto 'gnisiddhāv upadiśyamānaḥ saṃdigdhāsiddhaḥ /

65-66. For example (as to the location), "There is a peacock in this mountain-cavern, because there are peacock-like cries." There could be a mistake regarding the place from which the cries issue.

yatheha nikuñje mayūraḥ kekāyitād iti / tadāpātadeśavibhrame /

67. When there is no proof of the factual base, (the reason) is also unproved. For example, when there is the thesis "The self is omnipresent" and (the reason) "Its attributes are apprehended everywhere."

dharmyasiddhāv apy asiddho yathā sarvagata ātmeti sādhye sarvatropalabhamānaguṇatvam/

68. When another mode (of evidence)—its absence in the dissimilar locus—is unproved, there is the 'uncertainty' fallacy of the reason.

tathaikasya rūpasyāsapakṣe 'sattvasyāsiddhāv anaikāntiko hetvābhāsaḥ /

69. For example, when the thesis feature is the permanence, etc. of sound, and (the reason is advanced) "because the sanction etc.

yathā śabdasyānityatvādike dharme sādhye prameyatvādiko dharmaḥ sapakṣavipakṣayoḥ / sarvatraikadeśe vā vartamānas/

feature occurs in all of, or in one place of the similar and contrary locuses."

70. Likewise, when there is doubt of precisely this mode (of evidence), there is indeed the 'uncertainty'.

tathāsyaiva rūpasya saṃdehe 'py anaikāntika eva /

71. For example, when there is the thesis) that a certain person who wishes to speak is non-omniscient, or is subject to lust and other defilements, and (the reason is advanced) "He has such features as speech-faculty," the reverse in contrary cases is dubious. (i.e. the omniscience and freedom from lust in a mute person is dubious).

yathā 'sarvajñaḥ kaścid vivakṣitaḥ puruṣo rāgādimān veti sādhye vaktṛtvādiko dharmaḥ saṃdigdhavipakṣavyāvṛttikaḥ /

72. Again (for the thesis) "An omniscient speaker is not apprehended," a dubious reason is given "because he is an object which cannot be witnessed by oneself." Thus, to derive the reverse of speaking etc. from the reverse of non-omniscience, is dubious, because there is no opposition between the faculty of speech and omniscience.

sarvajño vaktā nopalabhyate iti/ evaṃ prakārasyānupalambhasyādṛśyātmaviṣayatvena saṃdehe hetutvāt /asarvajñaviparyayād vaktṛtvāder vyāvṛttiḥ saṃdigdhā /vaktṛtvasarvajñatvayor virodhābhāvāc ca /

73. The dissimilar absence "Whoever is omniscient, is not a speaker," cannot be proved when witness is lacking, because of doubt.

yaḥ sarvajñaḥ sa vaktā na bhavatīty adarśane 'pi vyatireko na sidhyati / saṃdehāt /

74. Opposition between entities is of two kinds—

dvividho hi padārthānāṃ virodhaḥ /

75-76. (1) Opposition in the situation where one given thing continues as long as its material cause is not deficient and disappears with the presence of another given thing, for example, the sensations of heat and cold.

avikalakāraṇasya bhavato 'nyabhāvaḥ / abhāvād virodhagatiḥ /śītoṣṇasparśavat/

77. (2) Opposition by reason of the established character of mutual exclusion, as between presence and absence.

parasparaparihārasthitalakṣaṇatayā yā [bhāvā]bhāvavat /

78. Now, these two kinds of opposition do not occur between the speech faculty and omniscience.

sa ca dvividho 'pi virodho vaktṛtvasarvajñatvayor na sambhavati /

79-80. Even if there has not been apprehension of their unapposed manner, there is no comprehension of absence (of one,) in the event of presence of the other), because there is no proof of the presence of a material cause and of its result between such defilements as lust and such forms of expression as speech.

na cāviruddhavidher anupalabdhāv apy abhāvagatiḥ / rāgādīṇāṃ vacanādeś ca kāryakāraṇabhāvāsiddheḥ /

81-82. There is no suspension of speech, etc. when there is suspension of the material cause of some other entity. Speech, etc. (if presented as a mode of evidence) would be an uncertainty and whose dissimilar absence (in the event of

arthāntarasya vā kāraṇasya nivṛttau na vacanāder nivṛttir iti saṃdigdhavyatireko 'naikāntiko vacanādiḥ /

omniscience and extinction of lust) is dubious.

83. When there is proof of the reverse of two modes (of the three-moded evidence) there is the 'opposing' (reason).

dvayo rūpayor viparyayasiddhau viruddhaḥ /

84-86. What are the two? Its existence in the similar locus. For example, when the thesis is permanence, the state-of-being-a-product or state-of-being-due-to-effort is a fallacy of reason that is 'opposing' (i.e. respectively opposes the individual presence reason and the result reason).

kayor dvayoḥ sapakṣe sattvasyāsapakṣe cāsattvasya yathā kṛtakatvaṃ prayatnānantarīyakatvaṃ ca nityatve sādhye viruddho hetvābhāsaḥ /

87-88. These two prove the reverse because of their nonexistence in the similar locus and their existence in the dissimilar locus. Each is 'opposing' because proving the reverse (or opposite) of the thesis.

anayoḥ sapakṣe 'sattvam asapakṣe ca sattvam iti viparyayasiddhiḥ / etau ca sādhyaviparyayasādhanād viruddhau /

89. Is there not a third 'opposing' (reason) that rejects what is accepted (by the first speaker)?

[nanu] ca tṛtīyo 'pīṣtavighātakṛd viruddhaḥ /

90. For example, (for the thesis) "Eyesight and other senses are for the sake of others," (the reason) "be cause they are composites like beds, chairs, and other implements".

yathā parārthās cakṣurādayaḥ saṃghātatvāc chayanāśanādy. aṅgavad iti/

91-92. It is (indeed) an opposing (reason), because proving the reverse of what is accepted (by the

tad iṣṭāsaṃhatapārārthyaviparyayasādhanād viruddhaḥ sa iha kasmān noktaḥ / anayor evāntarbhāvāt/

first speaker) which is the noncontiguous dependence on others (*pārārthya*). Then, why is it not mentioned here (as a third variety)? Because it is included in the two others.

93-94. This one is not differentiated from the two, because (exactly like them) it is proving the reverse of the thesis. (Furthermore, there is no difference at all between 'accepted' and 'stated' (as in the other two) as regards the thesis.

na hy ayam ābhyāṃ sādhyaviparyaya-sādhanatvena bhidyate / na hīṣṭoktayoḥ sādhyatvena kaścid viśeṣaḥ iti/

95. When there is no proof of one of the two modes (of evidence), and doubt of the other one, there is uncertainty (of the reason).

dyavo rūpayor ekasyā siddhāv aparasya ca saṃdehe naikāntikaḥ /

96. For example, "Someone is free from lust, or is omniscient, because he is a speaker." In this case, the dissimilar absence is unproved, the similar presence doubtful.

yathā vītarāgaḥ kaścit sarvajño vā vaktṛtvād iti / vyatireko 'trāsiddhaḥ / saṃdigdho 'nvayaḥ/

97 Due to the inaccessibility of omniscience and freedom from lust, the actuality or nonactuality of speech, etc., among them, is doubtful.

sarvajñavītarāgayor viprakarṣād vacanādes tatra sattvam asattvaṃ vā saṃdigdham

98-99. When there is doubt regarding those two modes (of evidence), there is uncertainty (of the reason). For example, "The living body possesses (an eternal)

anayor eva dvayo rūpayoḥ saṃdehe 'naikāntikaḥ / sātmakaṃ jīvaccharīraṃ prāṇādimattvād ti /

self, because it has breath, etc."

100-101. Now, given the class possessing (an eternal) self, and the class lacking (an eternal) self, there is no other class wherein is located breath and the like. Because everything is comprised within the occurrence or the ruling out of a self.

na hi sātmakanirātmakābhyām anyo rāśir asti / yatra prāṇādir vartate / ātmano vṛttivyavacchedābhyāṃ sarvasaṃgrahāt /

102-103. Besides, there is no certainty of the occurrence in one of these two (classes), because there is no proof of breath, etc, when determining by way of (an eternal) self or by way of a non-(eternal) self.

nāpy anayor ekatra vṛttiniścayaḥ/ sātmakatvena nirātmakatvena vā prasiddhe prāṇāder asiddhiḥ /

104-106. Hence, breath, etc. has connection with a living body. Since there is no proof (of breath) by exclusion from all (given things) that have a self or that lack a self, it is not dissimilarly absent in those two. Nor is it similarly present therein, because there is no proof that it is in one self.

tasmaj jīvaccharīrasaṃbandhī prāṇādiḥ / sātmakād anātmakāc ca sarvasmād vyāvṛttatvenāsiddheḥ / tabhyāṃ na vyatiricyate na tatrānveti / ekātmany apy asiddheḥ /

107- 110. On the other hand, there is no certainty of missing a similar presence or a dissimilar absence of it (the breath, etc.) through having a self or through lacking a self, because the certainty that one is missing has necessary connection with missing of the other;

nāpi sātmakān nirātmakāc ca tasyānvayavyatirekayor abhāvaniścayaḥ / ekābhāvaniścayāsyāparābhāvanāntarīyakatvāt / anvayavyatirekayor anyonya-vyavacchedarūpatvāt / ata evānvayavyatirekayoḥ saṃdehād anaikāntikaḥ / sādhyetarayor ato niścayābhāvāt /

and because it forms a mutual ruling out of similar presence and dissimilar absence. Hence, there is uncertainty through doubt about the similar presence and dissimilar absence, because there is no certainty from it (breath, etc.) of the thesis and of the other one (i.e. the opposing reason).

111. Thus there are three fallacies of the reason—the unproved, the opposing, and the uncertain. (They are produced) according to circumstances when from among the three modes (of evidence), any one of them, or any pair of them, is unproved or dubious.

evaṃ trayāṇāṃ rūpāṇām ekaikasya dvayor dvayor vā rūpayor asiddhau saṃdehe ca yathāyogam asiddhaviruddhānaikāntikās trayo hetvābhāsāḥ /

112-113. The 'opposing non-mistake' has been stated (formerly) as a cause of doubt. Why is it not stated here? Because it is not possible in the object of inference.

viruddhāvyabhicāry api saṃśayahetur uktaḥ / sa iha kasmān noktaḥ / anumānaviṣaye 'saṃbhavāt /

114-115. For there is no possibility of an opposing factor of result, individual presence, and non-apprehension as their definitions have been stated; and there is no other 'non-mistake'.

na hi saṃbhavo 'sti kāryasvabhāvayor uktalakṣaṇayor anupalambhasya ca viruddhatāyāḥ / na cānyo 'vyabhicārī /

116. Therefore, the 'opposing non-mistake' has been explained (by Dignaga), during analyses of its meaning by resort to the inference which is founded on the *agama*, as a fault of

tasmād avastudarśanabalapravṛttam āgamāśrayam anumānam āśritya tadarthavicāreṣu viruddhāvyabhicārī sādhanadoṣa uktaḥ /

proving, i.e. as not proceeding on the strength of observing given things (i.e. the first kind of inference);	
117-118. Because it is possible for authors of treatises to ascribe individual presence by delusion regarding entities—of course its reverse is not possible, regarding apprehensions that are results of self, which are based on given things (vastu) as they are really established.	śāstrakārāṇām artheṣu bhrāntyā viparītasya svabhāvopasaṃhārasambhavāt / na hy asya sambhavo yathāvasthitavastusthitiṣv ātmakāryeṣūpalambheṣu /
119. Here is an example: "Whatever is connected simultaneously by its own connections with objects situated in all places, is omnipresent, e.g. like space. A global[1] also is connected simultaneously by its own connections with objects situated in all places."	tatrodāharaṇaṃ yat sarvadeśāvasthitaiḥ svasambandhibhiḥ sambadhyate tat sarvagataṃ yathākāśam abhisambadhyate sarvadeśāvasthitaiḥ svasambandhibhir yugapat sāmānyam iti/
120. The state of individual presence residing in its place is connected as only individual presence of that connection. The formulation of individual presence reason is, "For wherein something is not, it does not pervade that place by itself."	tatsambandhisvabhāvamātrānubandhinī taddeśasaṃnihitasvabhāvatā / na hi yo yatra nāsti sa tad deśam ātmanā vyāpnotīti svabhāvahetuprayogaḥ /

1. The rendition 'global' is for *sāmānya*. This term occurs three times in Dharmottara's commentary *(Sanskrit* text of Banaras, 1954, p. 88) and in no case was ever expanded to *sāmānyalakṣaṇa*. One may conclude that this *sāmānya* is not the object of inference *(anumāna)*, but is the object of mental perception *(mānasa-pratyakṣa)*, for which Dignāga, in his comments on PS-Prat, writes *sāmānya-gocaram* (global scope) as its object (see in this Vol. One, Part II, Analysis, P-Vin-Bu, 22b-4).

121. The second formulation is as follows: When characters are met for apprehending something somewhere and it is not apprehended, it is not therein. For example, in a certain place there is no pot. And a global, although conditions are met for apprehending it, is not apprehended in the intervals of visibility (of external characters). This formulation of non-apprehension, and individual presence, since they are proving entities mutually opposed, generate doubt (when) in a single place.

dvitīyo 'pi prayogo yad upalabdhilakṣaṇaprāptaṃ san nopalabhyate na tat tatrāsti / tadyathā kvacid avidyamāno ghaṭaḥ / nopalabhyate copalabdhilakṣaṇaprāptaṃ sāmānyaṃ vyaktyantarāleṣv iti / ayam anupalambhaprayogaḥ svabhāvas ca parasparaviruddhā rthasadhanād ekatra saṃśayaṃ janayataḥ /

122. The reason with its three modes has been explained. With that much, there is cognitive dawning of the *artha* (i.e. the meaning). Hence, the example is by no means a separate member of the proving (process). Therefore, its definition is not mentioned separately, because it is a thing already understood.

trirūpo hetur uktaḥ / tāvataivārthapratītir iti na pṛthagdṛṣṭānto nāma sādhanāvayavaḥ kaścit / tena nāsya lakṣaṇaṃ pṛthag ucyate / gatārthatvāt /

123. The mode of a reason has been explained without a difference (*bheda*) as the existence only in the similar locus and exclusion everywhere in the dissimilar locus. Furthermore, there have been explained with distinction (*viśeṣa*) two things to be demon-

hetoḥ sapakṣa eva sattvam asapakṣāc ca sarvato vyāvṛtto rūpam uktam abhedena punar viśeṣeṇa kāryasvabhāvayor janma tanmātrānubandhau darśanīyāv uktau / tac ca darśayatā yatra dhūmas tatrāgnir asaty agnau na kvacid dhūmo yathā mahānasetarayoḥ / yatra kṛtakatvaṃ tatrānit-

strated—for result an origin, and for individual presence a connection just with it. Then, to demonstrate these: (for result) "Whatever there is smoke, there is fire; and where there is no fire, there is no smoke; for example, like the kitchen, or like the other case (e.g. the lake)." (for individual presence) "Wherever there is a product, there is impermanence; and where there is no impermanence, there is no product; for example, like a pot, or else like space." For, not otherwise is it possible to demonstrate according to their stated aspects the existence in the similar case and nonexistence in the dissimilar locus, to wit: the assurance that the result of it (the origin) belongs to the evidence of result; and that the pervasion by individual presence belongs to the evidence of individual presence. When this significance is demonstrated, the example is indeed demonstrated, because its nature amounts to no more than just that.

yatvam anityatvābhāve kṛtakatvāsambhavo yathā ghaṭākāśayor iti darśanīyam / na hy anyathā sapakṣavipakṣayoḥ sadasattve yathoktaprakāre śakye darśayitum / tatkāryatāniyamaḥ kāryaliṅgasya svabhāvaliṅgasya ca svabhāvena vyāptiḥ / asmiṃs cārthe darśite darśita eva dṛṣṭānto bhavati / etāvanmātrarūpatvāt tasyeti /

124-125. Fallacious examples also thereby become rejected. For example, "Sound is permanent, be-

etenaiva dṛṣṭāntadoṣa api nirastā bhavanti / yathā nityaḥ śabdo 'mūrtatvāt / karmavat paramāṇuvad ghaṭavad iti /

cause it is incorporeal, like an action (*karma*), like an atom, and like a pot." Thus, they (the examples, respectively) miss the thesis feature ('permanent'), the proving feature ('incorporeal'), or both.

sādhyasādhana-dharmobhayavikalās /

126. Likewise, there is a dubious thesis feature, and so on. Some illustrations: "This person has lust and other defilements" (dubious thesis), "because he has speech, like a man of the street." "This person has a mortal nature," "because he has lust and other defilements" (dubious proving), "like a man of the streets." "This person is non-omniscient, because he has lust and other defilements, like a man of the streets" (both thesis and proving are dubious).

tathā saṃdigdhasādhya-dharmādayaś ca / yathā rāgādimān ayaṃ vacanād rathyāpuruṣavat / maraṇadharmo 'yaṃ puruṣo rāgādimattvād rathyāpuruṣavat / asarvajño 'yaṃ rāgādimatvād rathyāpuruṣavad iti /

127. (It might be that) there is absence of similar presence, or (that) similar presence is not properly demonstrated, (respectively): (1) for example, "Whoever is a speaker, he is subject to lust and other defilements, like the given person (*iṣṭapuruṣa*)." (2) for example, "Sound is impermanent, because it is a product, like a pot."

ananvayo 'pradarśitānvayaś ca / yathā yo vaktā sa rāgādimān iṣṭapuruṣavat / anityaḥ śabdaḥ kṛtakatvād ghaṭavad iti /

128. Likewise, there is the reversed similar presence. For example, "Whatever is impermanent, is a product." (The proper order

tathā viparītānvayaḥ / yad anityaṃ tat kṛtam /

is: Whatever is a product, is impermanent; cf. Buddhist axiom, "All *saṃskāras* are impermanent.")

129. The foregoing are by way of feature concordance.

iti sādharmyeṇa /

130. Also, by way of feature discordance, there are the examples, like an atom, like an action, like space, which do not have the (stipulated) dissimilar absence for the thesis, etc.

vaidharmyeṇāpi paramāṇuvat karmavad ākāśavad iti sādhyādyavyatirekiṇaḥ /

131. Likewise, there is the dissimilar absence etc. in the case of the dubious thesis. For example, "Kapila, and so on, are not omniscient or are not experts, because they do not know how to demonstrate in a superior way the authority which is the evidence of omniscience and expertness being present." Here is an illustration of feature discordance: "Whoever is omniscient or is an expert is an instructor of Jyotiṣ (astronomy or astrology), like Ṛṣabha, Vardhamāna, and others." In this illustration, there is dubious dissimilar absence of the non-omniscience and non-expertise being thesis features.

tathā saṃdigdhasādhya-vyatirekādayaḥ / yathā 'sarvajñāḥ kapilādayo 'nāptā vā / avidyamāna-sarvajñatāp-tatāliṅgabhṛta-pramāṇātiśa-yaśāsanatvād iti / atra vaidharmyodāharaṇaṃ yaḥ sarvajña āpto vā sa jyotirjñānādi-kam upadiṣṭavān / tadyathā / ṛṣabhavardhamānādir iti / tatrāsarvajñatānāptatayoḥ sād-hyadharmayoḥ saṃdigdho vyatirekaḥ /

132. A dubious dissimilar absence of proving is as follows: "A brahmin versed in the three Vedas should not accept the words of some person (wishing to

saṃdigdhasādhanavyatirekaḥ / yathā na trayī-vidā-brāhmaṇena grāhyavacanaḥ kaścit puruṣo rāgādimattvād iti / atra vaidharmyodāharaṇam / ye grāhyavacanā na te rāgādi-

speak), because (this person) has lust and other defilements." Here is the illustration of feature discordance: "The ones whose words should be accepted are free from lust and other defilements, like Gautama and other authors of Dharmaśāstra (legal codes). But that Gautama and those others are excluded from lust and other defilements—the proving feature—is dubious.

maṇtas tadyathā gautamādayo dharmaśāstrāṇāṃ praṇetāra iti gautamādibhyo rāgādimattvasya sādhanadharmasya vyāvṛttiḥ saṃdigdhā /

133. Dubious dissimilar absence of both, is as follows: For example, "Kapila and the others are not free from lusts, because they are addicted to acquisition and avarice." Here is an example by way of feature discordance: "Whoever is free from lusts does not have acquisition or avarice, like Ṛṣabha and so on." But that Ṛṣabha and so on are both free from lusts and free from addiction to acquisition and avarice, respectively the thesis feature and the proving feature, is a dubious dissimilar absence.

saṃdigdhobhayavyatirekaḥ yathā 'vītarāgāḥ kapilādayaḥ parigrahāgrahayogād iti / atra vaidharmyeṇodāharaṇam/ yo vītarāgo na tasya parigrahāgraho yathā ṛṣabhāder iti/ ṛṣabhāder avītarāgatvaparigrahāgrahayogayoḥ sādhyasādhanadharmayoḥ saṃdigdho vyatirekaḥ /

134. The lack of dissimilar absence is as follows: For example, "He is not free from lusts, because he is a speaker." Here is an

avyatireko yathā 'vītarāgo vaktṛtvāt / vaidharmyodaharaṇaṃ yatra vītarāgatvaṃ nāsti sa vaktā yathopalakhaṇḍa iti / yady apy upalakhaṇḍād

example by way of feature discordance: "In whatever there is freedom from lusts, it does not speak, like a piece of rock." Even if there is dissimilar absence of both in the piece of rock (It has neither lust nor speech), nevertheless, that all who are free from lust are not speakers, is not a proof of dissimilar absence in the sense of pervasion, and so there is no dissimilar absence.

ubhayaṃ vyāvṛttayā sarvo vītarāgo na vakteti vyāptyā vyatirekāsiddher avyatirekaḥ /

135-136. Improper demonstration of dissimilar absence, is as follows: For example, "Sound is impermanent, because it is a product, like space." Also as feature discordance there is the reversed dissimilar absence, as follows: For example, "Whatever is a product, is permanent."

apradarśitavyatireko yathā anityaḥ śabdaḥ kṛtakatvād ākāśavad iti / vaidharmyeṇāpi viparīta-vyatireko yathā yad akṛtakaṃ tan nityaṃ bhavatīti/

137. Those fallacious examples are not capable of demonstration with assurance the generalizing character of the reason, to wit, its existence only in the similar locus and indeed its nonexistence everywhere in the dissimilar locus; and also not capable of demonstrating with assurance the definition of distinctions. Therefore, their rejection is to be understood

na hy ebhir dṛṣṭāntābhāsair hetoḥ sāmānyalakṣaṇaṃ sapakṣa eva sattvaṃ vipakṣe ca sarvatrāsattvaṃ eva niścayena śakyaṃ darśayituṃ viśeṣa-lakṣaṇaṃ vā / tad arthāpattyaiṣāṃ nirāso veditavyaḥ /

by implication from the circumstance.	
138-139. Refutation is the expression of the deficiency and other (fallacies). Refutation means exposing whatever are the faults of proving, such as deficiency, etc. set forth above, because it prevents the success of the position espoused by the respondent (i.e. the opponent).	dūṣaṇā nyūnatāyuktiḥ / ye pūrvaṃ nyūnatādayaḥ sādhanadoṣā uktās teṣām udbhāvanaṃ dūṣaṇam / tena pareṣṭārthasiddhipratibandhāt/
140. Fallacies of refutation are sophistries (*jāti*).	dūṣaṇābhāsās tu jātayaḥ /
141. Sophistic rejoinders disclose nonexisting faults.	abhūtadoṣodbhāvanāni jātyuttarāṇīti

[Finished is the *Nyāyabindu*].

KAMALAŚĪLA'S *Nyāyabindupūrvapakṣasaṃkṣipti* (NB-PPS)

bcom ldan 'das ṅag gi dbaṅ phyug la phyag 'tshal lo /
I bow with homage to the Bhagavat Vāgīśvara (Lord of Speech).

I. ADVERSARIES OF DIRECT PERCEPTION (NB, CHAPTER)

/ log par rtog pa ni rnam pa bzhi ste / graṅs la log par rtog pa daṅ / raṅ gi ṅo bo la log par rtog pa daṅ / spyod yul la log par rtog pa daṅ / 'bras bu la log par rtog pa'o /

There are four kinds of wayward constructive thought (*mithyāvikalpa*): (1) of count, (2) of individual nature, (3) of sense object, (4) of result.

/ de la graṅs la log par rtog pa ni / 'di lta ste / phur bu pa rnams ni mṅon sum gcig pu kho na tshad ma yin gyi / gzhan ni ma yin no zhes zer ro / graṅs can pa rnams ni mṅon sum daṅ / rjes su dpag pa daṅ / sgra las byuṅ ba daṅ tshad ma gsum kho na'o zhes zer ro / rigs pa can rnams ni mṅon sum daṅ / rjes su dpag pa daṅ / dpe daṅ /

sgra las byuṅ ba daṅ / tshad ma bzhi kho na'o zhes zer ro / rgyal dpog pa rnams ni mṅon sum daṅ / rjes su dpag pa daṅ / dpe daṅ / sgra las byuṅ ba daṅ / don gyis go ba daṅ / dṅos po med pa zhes bya ba daṅ / tshad ma drug kho na'o zhes zer ro / tsa ra ka la sogs pa ni rigs pa daṅ / mi dmigs pa daṅ / srid pa daṅ / zhes grags pa daṅ / sñam du sems pa zhes bya ba tshad ma gzhan dag kyaṅ yod do zhes zer ro /

(1) Wayward constructive thought of count (on NB, Prat, 2-3): The Bārhaspatya-ṣ (= Cārvākas) hold that only direct-perception is an authority, and that there is no other one. The Sāṃkhya hold precisely three authorities—direct perception, inference, and testimony. The Naiyāyikas hold direct perception, inference, analogy, and testimony. The Jaiminīya (T. rgyal dpog pa rnams) claim there are six authorities: direct perception, inference, analogy, testimony, implication from a circumstance (*arthāpatti*), and absence. Caraka [author of a medical text], etc., opine that there are other authorities, such as reasoning [about the three aims of life] (*yukti*), nonapprehension (*anupalabdhi*), origination (*sambhava*), tradition (*aitihya*), and identification (T. sñam du sems pa, S. *itimanya).

/ de la raṅ gi ṅo bo la log par rtog pa ni / 'di lta ste / rigs pa can rnams ni mṅon sum thams cad ṅes pa'i bdag ñid yin pa'i phyir / rnam par rtog pa daṅ bcas pa kho na'o zhes zer ro / rgyal dpog pa rnams ni gtod par byed pa'i śes pa skad cig ma daṅ po kho na rnam par rtog pa med par skye la / de'i 'og rol gyi mṅon sum thams cad ni rtog pa daṅ bcas pa ñid do zhes zer ro /

(2) Wayward constructive thought of individual nature (on NB-Prat, 4-11): The Naiyāyika claim that since all direct perceptions amount to certainty, they are indeed accompanied by constructive thought (*vikalpa*). The Jaiminīya claim that only the first moment of fixed awareness is free from constructive thought, and that thereafter all direct perceptions are attended with constructive thought.

/ de bzhin du gzhan dag ni duṅ la ser por śes pa la sogs pa 'khrul pa yaṅ tshad ma ñid yin par 'dod do / de bzhin du bye brag pa la sogs pa ni rnam par śes pa'i ṅo bo ma yin pa ñid de / dbaṅ po daṅ / don brel pa yin par brjod do / kha cig ni bdag daṅ yid 'brel pa'i 'o bo yin par brjod do / gzhan dag ni mṅon sum rna ba la sogs pa'i dhaṅ po 'jug pa'i ṅo bo yin brjod do /

Likewise, other's claim that such delusions (*bhrānti*) as the cognition of yellow in the conchshell are an authority. Likewise, the Vaiśeṣika, and others, say that *vijñāna* (perception, what understands, etc.) has no individual nature, and that the sense-organ and its object unite. Some assert an individual nature which unites self and mind. Other assert an entrance nature of direct perception in the sense-organs of ear, etc.

/ de bzhin du rna ma phug la sogs pa ni yid kyi zhes bya ba'i mṅon sum tshad mar rigs pa ma yin te / sṅar mṅon sum gyi gzuṅ ba las yul gzhan ma yin na de gzuṅ zin pa 'dzin pa'i phyir tshad ma ma yin pa kho na'o / yul don gzhan ñid yin na ni 'di raṅ dbaṅ du 'jug pa'i phyir daṅ don thams cad yul yin pa'i phyir / 'ga' yaṅ loṅ ba la sogs pa'i dṅos por mi 'gyur ro zhes zer ro /

·Likewise, Aviddhakarṇa, etc. assert that a direct perception of the mental (*manas*) kind is not valid as an authority, since if there is not another object than what direct perception previously grasped, it (i.e. that direct perception) grasps what was already grasped; and if the object were a different object, since it would enter independently and since all objects could be the sensory object (*viṣaya*)—would it not be an (object) entity for a blind man, and so on?

/ bye brag tu smra ba la sogs pa ni raṅ rig pa'i mṅon sum yaṅ rigs pa ma yin te /bdag ñid la byed pa 'gal ba'i phyir ro zhes zer ro / rgyal dpog pa rnams na re skyes bu thams cad ni 'dod chags la sogs pa daṅ ma rig pas 'khrul pa yin to / 'gro ba 'di lta bu ma yin pa ni 'ga' yaṅ med do / thams cad la dbaṅ pos mi soṅ ba'i don mthoṅ ba'i thabs med pa'i phyir la mnon sum la sogs pa'i tshad mas grub pa'i rnal 'byor pa dag kyaṅ med de / de'i phyir dbaṅ pos mi soṅ ba'i don mthoṅ ba mi srid pas rnal 'byor pa'i śes pa med pa kho na'o zhes zer ro /

The Vaiśeṣika, and others, assert that an introspective direct perception (*svasaṃvedana-pratyakṣa*) is not valid, since it conflicts with the self as agent. The Jaiminīya say that all persons are deluded by lust, etc. and by nescience (*avidyā*), and that there is no living being at all that is not this way; and also because none of them have any method for viewing entities that fail to come into their senses, there are no *yogīs* who succeed [in a magical sense] by the authority of direct perception, etc. And consequently, with no possibility of viewing entities (*artha*) that are not received by sense-organs, there is surely no *yogī* cognition.

/ de la yul la log par rtog pa ni 'di lta ste / rigs pa can la sogs pa na re spyi' dṅos por gyur pa yaṅ yod pa'i phyir la / de yaṅ mṅon sum gyis yoṅs su bcad par bya ba yin phyir te / de'i phyir mṅon sum ni spy'i mtshan ñid kyi yul çan yaṅ yin no / de bzhin du bdag la sogs pa raṅ gi mtshan ñid kyi ṅo bo yaṅ rjes su dpag pa'i tshad mas yoṅs su gcad par bya-ba ñid yin pa'i phyir / rjes su dpag pa yaṅ de'i yul can gyi tshad ma yin par rigs so zhes zer ro /

(3) Wayward constructive thought of an object (*viṣaya*) (on NB, Prat, 12-17): The Naiyāyika, etc. say that since there is not only a presence of 'generality' (*sāmānya*) but also that it must be distinguished by a direct perception—it follows that the direct perception is the subjective cognition (*viṣayin*) of the 'generality character'. And likewise, since the self, etc. have the nature of an individual character (*svalakṣaṇa*)—which is to be determined by the authority of inference—it follows that inference is valid as the authority for its subjective cognition.

/ de la 'bras bu la log par rtog pa ni 'di lta ste / rgyal dpog pa la sogs pa na re / 'jig rten na bsgrub par bya ba daṅ sgrub pa dag ni pha tshun tha dad pa'i bdag ñid du grags pa'i phyir / 'bras bu ni tshad ma las don gzhan du gyur pa kho nas yin par rigs te / dgra sta ñid chad pa ma yin no / de lta bas na de kho na ñid 'di ni rnam pa bzhir yoṅs su rdzogs pa yin te / 'di lta ste / 'jal par byed pa daṅ gzhal bya daṅ tshad ma daṅ rtogs pa'o / 'di la 'jal par byed pa ni skyes bu yin no / gzhal bya ni gzugs la sogs pa'i yul yin no / tshad ma ni dbaṅ po la sogs pa yin no / rtogs pa ni don yoṅs su chod pa yin no / gaṅ gi tshe śes pa kho na tshad ma yin pa de'i tshe yaṅ / śes pa phyi ma ni 'bras bu yin la / sna ma ni tshad ma yin te / spyi la sogs pa'i khyad par gyi śes pa gaṅ yin pa ni tshad ma yin no / rdzas la sogs pa'i khyad par can gyi śes pa gaṅ yin pa de ni 'bras bu yin no zhes zer te /

(4) Wayward constructive thought of result (*kārya*) (on NB-Prat, 18-21): The Jaiminīya, etc. say that since in the world the thesis and the method of proof are recognized to be mutually different, it is valid that the result would be in reality a different entity than the authority (= the means), e.g. the axe is not cut. Hence, this reality is fulfilled as four kinds, to wit, *pramātṛ* (authorizer), *prameya* (authorized), *pramāṇa* (authority, i.e. means), *pramiti* (resultative authority). Of these, the 'authorizer' is a person. The 'authorized' is the form, etc. object. The 'authority' (i.e. means) is the sense-organ, etc. The 'resultative authority' is the decision about the meaning (*artha*). At whatever time a cognition (*jñāna*) is the only authority, at that time each successive cognition is the result, and the preceding one is the authority. Thus, whatever is the specialized cognition of a 'generality', etc., it is the authority; and whatever is the specialized cognition of a substance (*dravya*), etc., it is the result (*kārya*).

/ gzhan dag de ltar mṅon sum la log par rtog pa rnam pa maṅ po zhig yod pas de dag dgag par tshad ma' i mtshan ñid ji lta ba bzhin 'di byas so / 'di ni bcom ldan 'das kyaṅ bzhed pa kho na yin te/ ji skad du / dge sloṅ dag go mkhas rnams kyis / bsreg bcad bdar bas gser bzhin du / yoṅs su brtags nas ṅa yi bka' / blaṅ bar bya yi gus phyir min / zhes gsuṅs pa lta bu'o /

(Kamalaśīla further comments)

Besides, there are many other wayward constructive thoughts regarding direct perception, so he (i.e. Dharmakīrti in NB) has written in accordance with the characteristic of authority in order to refute them. And precisely as the Lord (*bhagavat*) has maintained when he said:

Monks, just as experts examine gold by heating, cutting, and rubbing, so is my teaching to be accepted, but not out of respect (for me).	tāpāc chedāc ca nikaṣāt suvarṇam iva paṇḍitaiḥ / parīkṣya bhikṣavo grāhyaṃ madvaco na tu gauravāt //

/ 'dis ni mṅon sum daṅ rjes su dpag pa' i mtshan ñid rnam pa gñis kho na zhal gyi bzhes pa yin te / dpe la sogs pas yoṅs su brtag par zhal gyis bzhes pa'i phyir ro / mṅon sum gyi dpe ni bsreg pa daṅ chos mthun par bstan pa'i phyir ro / rjes su dpag pa' i ni bdar ba daṅ chos mthun par bstan pa'i phyir ro / phan tshun du mi 'gal ba ni gcad pa daṅ chos mthun par yoṅs su brtag par gsuṅs te / de yaṅ rjes su dpag pa kho na yin no'/

This passage verbally directs only to the two kinds of characters of direct perception and inference, because it verbally direct the examining by examples. (a) Because it teaches the example of direct perception as concordant with 'heating'. (b) Because it teaches (the example) of inference as concordant with rubbing. To avoid inconsistency, (the passage) states the examination concordant with cutting; and this is also only [of] inference.

/ 'di ltar don ni rnam pa gsum ste / mṅon sum daṅ / lcog tu gyur pa daṅ / śin tu lcog tu gyur pa'o / de la bka'i don mṅon sum la ni sreg pas gser bzhin du mṅon sum gyis brtags yin no / don lkog tu gyur pa la bdar ba bzhin du rjes su dpag pas brtags pa yin no / de ñid kyi don śin tu lkog tu gyur pa la ni gcad pas gser bzhin du phan tshun mi 'gal ba'i sgo nas brtag pa yin te / de ltar yoṅs su dag pa'i luṅ la ni yul lkog tu gyur kyaṅ / rtog pa daṅ ldan pa tshad ma yin par yid ches pa rnams 'jug pa'i phyir ro /

Accordingly, the meaning is of three kinds: 'direct perception' (*pratyakṣa*), 'beyond sight' (*parokṣa*), and 'further beyond sight' (*atyanta-parokṣa*). Among them, the scriptural meaning regarding direct perception is the examination by direct perception in the manner of gold by heating, The meaning regarding the 'beyond sight' is the examination by inference in the manner of rubbing. Its meaning regarding the 'further beyond sight' is the examination by way of avoiding inconsistency in the manner of gold by cutting. Accordingly, in regard to the pure scripture, even though its domain is beyond sight, it is the authority for one using discursive thought, because it is understood by the trustworthy ones.

/ chos mṅon pa las mig gi rnam par śes pa daṅ ldan pas / sṅon po śes kyi sṅon po'o sñam du ni ma yin no zhes bya ba daṅ / don la don du śes kyi don la chos su 'du śes pa ma yin no zhes gsuṅs te / sṅon po śes pa daṅ don la don du śes kyi zhes bya ba 'di gñis kyis ni yul phyin ci ma log par bstan pa'i phyir / ma 'khrul pa ñid bśad pa yin no / sṅon po'o sñam du ni ma yin no zhes bya ba daṅ / chos su 'du śes pa ni ma yin no zhes bya ba 'di gñis kyis ni miṅ daṅ 'brel pa'i don 'dzin pa spaṅs pa'i phyir rtog pa daṅ bral ba ñid bśad pa yin te / de ñid las mig la sogs pa'i rnam par śes pa ṅes par rtog pa daṅ / rjes su dran pa'i rnam par rtog pas / rnam par mi rtog pa ñid du yaṅ brjod la mig la sogs pa'i rnam par śes pa'i tshogs gzugs la sogs pa'i skye mched kyi raṅ gi mtshan ñid kyi yul can yin par yaṅ bstan to /

According to the Abhidharma, when one is using eye-perception and one perceives blue, one does not [necessarily] think "It is blue." And when one perceives an entity as an entity, one does not [necessarily] have the idea that the entity has a [certain] feature (dharma). And it explains that there is no delusion of object in either case of perceiving blue or perceiving an entity as an entity. That explains the nondelusive (situation). It explains the freedom from constructive thought (*kalpanā*) by avoiding the grasping of an entity along with a name, since there are both cases: no thinking "It is blue" and no idea of it as having a feature (*dharma*). From the same source (i.e. Abhidharma), certainty reflection and reflection of remembrance *(anusmṛti)* declare the perceptions of eye, etc., to be without constructive thought and teach that the set of perceptions of eye, etc. are the subjective cognition (*viṣayin)* for the 'individual characters' (*svalakṣaṇa*) of the sense bases of form, etc.

/ mdo las kyaṅ / 'du byed thams cad skad cig ma / mi gnas bya ba ga la yod / 'di dag 'byuṅ ba de ñid ni / bya ba de ñid byed par brjod / ces gsuṅs te /

Also, the *Sūtra* states:

All the constructions (*saṃskāra*) are momentary. Whence the continuous	kṣaṇikāh sarvasaṃskārā asthirāṇāṃ kutaḥ kriyā /

activity (*kriyā*) of transient things? Their existence is precisely the continuous activity as well as the doing it.	bhūtir yeṣāṃ kriyā saiva kārakaṃ saiva cocyate //

/ 'dis ni byed pa po daṅ las la sogs pa'i dṅos po yaṅ dag pa bkag pas bya ba la sogs pa thams cad kyi khoṅs su 'dus pa spaṅs pa'i phyir / bya ba'i mtshan ñid kyi 'bras bu don gzhan du gyur pa bkag pa yin no /

This passage rightly denies a materiality (T. *dṅos po;* S. *vastu, bhāva, dravya*) of an agent, of *karma* [which includes *kriyā*], and so on. So it obviates the centering of any continuous activities. Therefore, it denies that the result of the continuous-activity characteristic amounts to a different entity.

II. ADVERSARIES OF INFERENCE FOR ONESELF (NB, CHAPTER)

/rjes su dpag pa la yaṅ log par rtogs pa snaṅ ste / 'di lta ste / [b]rda [for text, rda-] sprod pa rnams ni rjes su dpag pa tshad ma ma yin te / 'khrul pa srid pa'i phyir ro zhes zer ro /

(On NB-Sva, 3:) Morever, there is a wayward constructive thought toward inference (*anumāna*), to wit, the Vaiyākaraṇa [Grammarians] (T. brda-sprod-pa, possibly =ṅo sprod-pa) claim that inference is not an authority, because of the possibility of error.

/ snod kyi rje na re ni gzhan du mi 'thad pa'i no bo gcig pu kho na gtan tshigs kyi rtogs par byed pa ñid kyi yan lag yin gyi /phyogs kyi chos la sogs pa'i mtshan ñid kyi tshul gsum pa ni ma yin no /'di ltar sṅo bsaṅs yin te de'i bu yin pa'i phyir /de'i bu snaṅ ba bzhin no zhes bya ba'i gtan tshigs 'di la tshul gsum pa yod kyaṅ gzhan du mi 'thad pa ñid kyi yan lag med pa'i phyir rtogs par byed pa ñid ma yin no / tshul gsum pa med kyaṅ gzhan du mi 'thad pa daṅ ldan pa tsam kho nas gtan tshigs rtogs par byed pa yin pa yaṅ mthoṅ ste / 'di lta ste /dṅos po daṅ dṅos po med pa ni ji ltar yaṅ yod pa'i bdag ñid dag yin /ji ltar yaṅ dmigs pa'i bya ba yin pa'i phyir ro zhes bya ba lta bu'o / 'di la chos mthun pa daṅ chos mi mthun pa'i dpe dag med de / dṅos po thams cad kyi tshogs dṅos po daṅ / dṅos po med pa phyogs su byas pa'i phyir ro / de dag la ma gtogs pa gzhan med pa'i phyir gaṅ zhig dpe ñid yin par 'gyur /phyogs kyi chos kyaṅ gzhan du mi 'thad pa ñid kho na'i khoṅs su 'dus pa'i phyir ro /de ltar na rtags ni tshul gcig pa kha na yin par rigs kyi tshul gsum pa ñid ni ma yin pa'i rigs so zhes zer ro /

(On NB-Sva, 3-7:) Pātrasvāmin avers that only the single form which if otherwise would be invalid is the member that supplies understanding of the reasoning. Not the three modes among characteristics that include the locus-feature (*pakṣa-dharma*), to wit: "He is dark [the thesis], because he is the son of that one [the reason], like (another) son of that one appears [the example]." (He says that) while this reasoning exhibits the three modes, it lacks the member of being invalid otherwise and so does not supply understanding (of the reasoning). Furthermore, even in the absence of the three modes, but having the (member of) being invalid if otherwise, one arrives at understanding of the reasoning, to wit: "Presence and absence somehow have a reality because (somehow) they are apprehended." Here there are no feature-concordant or feature-discordant examples, because it takes the locus (*pakṣa*) "presence and absence" as the set of all entities; and because there is nothing apart from those; and because whatever be the example, the locus-feature is only the inner nature (*antarbhāva*) of being invalid if otherwise. Accordingly, he avers that the evidence (*liṅga*) is the principle of only a single character (*ekalakṣaṇa*), and not the principle of the three modes.

/ gzhan dag ni phyogs kyi chos ñid daṅ / mthun pa'i phyogs la yod pa ñid daṅ / mi mthun pa'i phyogs la med pa ñid daṅ / gnod pa med pa'i yul can ñid daṅ /rjod par 'dod pa'i graṅs gcig pa can ñid daṅ / ses pa ñid ces bya ba mtshan ñid drug pa kho na'o zhes zer ro /

Others claim that there are in fact six characters, to wit: 1. *pakṣadharmatā* (which is a locus feature), 2. *sapakṣatva* (which has a locus), 3. *avipakṣatva* (which does not lack a locus) [which are the three we espouse], plus 4. *abādhitvaviṣayatva* (which does not cancel the thesis—on behalf of another authority), 5. Tib. rjod par 'dod pa'i graṅs gcig pa can ñid (is the solitariness of the espoused utterance—i.e. no opposing evidence) [which are the two more espoused by the Naiyāyika] 6. *jñātatva* (which is known).

/ graṅs can pa rnams na re rjes su dpag pa ni 'brel pa gcig las lhag ma grub pa yin no / lhag ma grub pa ni 'dir ñe bar btags pa'i sgo nas rtags śes pa kho na yin te / rjes su dpag par 'dod kyi / rjes su dpag par bya ba śes pa ni ma yin no zhes zer ro /

The Sāṃkhya claims that there is inference which proves an *a posteriori* (*śeṣavat*) from a single relation (*saṃyoga*). That this is an inference where the a *posteriori* is just the cognition of evidence by what is pointed out in this case. And that this is not a cognition of an inferable (*anumeya*).

/ slob dpon dbyig gñen yaṅ med na mi 'byuṅ ba'i don mthoṅ ba ni de'i rig pa'i rjes su dpag pa yin no zhes zer te / 'di yaṅ rjes su dpag pa ni rtags śes pa kho na yin la / rjes su dpag par bya ba śes pa ni 'bras bu yin par 'dod de /

Ācārya Vasubandhu holds that upon noticing the nonoccurrence of an entity when it is absent, one has an inference which envisages this. In this case, the claim is that this inference is only the cognition of the evidence, while the cognition of an inferable is (its) result.

/ phyir rgol ba 'di thams cad ni 'bras bu tshad ma las don gzhan kho na yin par yan 'dod pa ñid /

All these adversaries claim that the result is surely a different thing from the authority (*pramāṇa*).

/ bye brag pa la sogs pa ni yaṅ dag par ma grub pa yaṅ gtan tshigs su ñe bar rtog par byed de / 'di lta ste / bdag ni thams cad na yod pa yin te / thams cad na yon tan dmigs pa'i phyir ro zhes bya ba la sogs pa lta bu'o /

The Vaiśeṣika, etc., engage in an imagination that even what is not rightly proven is a reasoning [a 'syllogism']; for example, "I exist in everything, because I visualize the qualities in everything;" and so on.

/ rgyal dpog pa la sogs pa ni mi mthun pa'i phyogs la yod pa yaṅ gtan tshigs su ñe bar brten te / 'di lta ste / sgra ni rtag pa ste / gzhal bya yin pa'i phyir ro zhes bya ba daṅ / de bzhin du rjod par 'dod pa'i skyes bu 'ga' zhig thams cad mkhyen pa ma yin te / gzhal bya daṅ / śes bya daṅ / dṅos po daṅ / yod pa'i phyir ro zhes bya ba la sogs pa lta bu'o / de rnam par geod pa'i phyir ṅes par gzuṅ ba yin no /

The Jaiminīya, etc., rely upon a reasoning using the dissimilar locus (*asapakṣa*); for example, "Sound is permanent, because it is a *prameya* (an object of *pramāṇa*)" Likewise, "Whatever persons wish to express themselves are not omniscient, because (they are) a *prameya* (object of *pramāṇa*), knowables (*jñeya*), beings present (*bhāva*), and/or real things (sat)." So as to analyze those, (Dharmakīrti) apprehends (them) with certainty.

/ graṅs can pa la sogs pa ni gtan tshigs 'gal bar mthoṅ bzhin du yaṅ śin tu ṅo mtshar che ba'i ma rig pas blo gros phyin ci log tu gyur pas mi 'gal ba bzhin du rtogs par byed de / 'di lta ste / mig la sogs pa ni gzhan gyi don yin te / bsags pa yin pa'i phyir / ma cha daṅ stan la sogs pa'i yan lag bzhim no zhes bya ba la sogs pa lta bu'o / de rnam par gcod pa'i phyir / mi mthun pa'i phyogs la med smos so /

The Sāṃkhya, etc., when faced with a violation of the reasoning by an astonishing nescience with intellect gone awry, understand it as though there were no (such) violation, saying, for example, "The eye, etc., is the object of another, because it is a composite," [Sāṃkhya-kārikā, 17:] "like the members of beds, chairs, etc." So as to analyze that, (Dharmakīrti) mentions its lack of a dissimilar locus.

/ gaṅ dag raṅ gi phyogs grub par bya ba phyir / mi mthun pa'i phyogs gcig la yod pa la yaṅ gtan tshigs su gtogs par byed de / 'di lta ste / sgra ni rtag pa ste / brtsal ma thag tu 'byuṅ ba yin pa'i phyir ro zhes bya ba la sogs pa lta bu de rnam par gcad pa'i phyir ṅes par gzuṅ ba yin no / gñi gar yaṅ khyad par can gyi gnas su ṅes par gzuṅ ba ni brtsal ma thag tu 'byuñ ba la sogs pa mthun pa'i phyogs gcig la yod pa yaṅ mi rtag pa ñid la sogs pa'i sgrub pa ñid du 'gal ba med do zhes bya bar rab tu bstan pa'i phyir ro/

Since whichever are to be proven of our side [of the debate] are in a single dissimilar locus, and pertain to the reasoning [sequence]; as follows: "Sound is permanent, because it arises immediately upon the striking [of the drum];" and other similar reasonings. So as to analyze such [assertions], (Dharmakīrti) takes hold of them with certainty. Furthermore, his taking hold of them with certainty is the distinguishing of the two cases [their side and our side], because he shows that the incidence immediately upon striking, etc. pertains to a single similar locus; and because there is no contradiction to the proving of impermanence, and so on.

/ tshul gsum pa dṅos kyi tshul du yod kyaṅ ji srid du rtogs par ma gyur pa de srid du de las bsgrub par bya ba rtogs par mi 'gyur ro zhes bya bar rab tu bstan pa'i phyir / ṅes pa zhes bya ba smos pa yin te / de bzhin du dper brjod pa yaṅ 'di ñid las ston par 'gyur ro /

So as to show that given the three modes as the primary modes, as long as one does not uderstand them, so long will one not understand what is to be proven—he (Dharmakīrti) says "It is certain." Accordingly, the example (*udāharaṇa*) is shown by this very (statement).

/ rjes su dpag par bya ba chos daṅ chos can gyi spyi yin pa'i phyir / de ma grub pa de la rtags yod pa rtag tu ma grub pa kho na'o/ 'on te sgrub na ni bsgrub par bya ba sṅa ñid nas grub pa'i phyir / rtags kyi rjes su 'braṅ ba don med do zhes bya ba'i klan ka yoṅs su spaṅs pa'i phyir / 'di las rjes su dpag par bya ba ni 'dir zhes bya ba la sogs pa bśad do /

(On NB-Sva, 8:) Since the inferable is the generalization of feature and factual base, when it is not proved, given evidence for it, it is just never proved. However, if it is proven, it is proved from the formerly 'to be proved' [requiring evidence]. So one avoids the blame of asserting that there is no sense to follow the evidence; and so he (Dharmakīrti) explains the inferable from this by the word 'here' (*atra*), and so on.

/ grańs can pa la sogs pa gań dag bsgrub par bya ba'i chose dań mi dra ba yań phyogs dań mthun pa ñid du rtogs par byed de / 'di lta ste / mal cha dań stan la sogs pa'i yan lag bzhin no zhes bya ba lasogspaltabuste/de'iphyir mthun ba'i phyogs bye brag tu bśad do/

(On NB-Sva, 9:) The Sāṃkhya, etc., are made to understand that a difference with the feature (*dharma*) to be proven amounts to a similarity with the locus; as follows "like the members of beds, seats etc." Therefore, they explain the similar locus in various ways.

/ rigs pa can la sogs pa gań dag med pa'i ṅo bo mi mthun pa'i phyogs yin par mi 'dod de / med pa'i ṅo bo las 'ga' yań ldog par mi ruń ba'i phyir ro / de'i phyir 'dus ma byas med par smra ba byas pa'i phyir mi rtag go zhes bya bar sgrub par byed pa rnams kyi gtan tshigs ma ṅes pa yin no zhes zer ba de dag la mi mthun pa'i phyogs bye brag tu bśad do /

(On NB-Sva, 10:) the Naiyāyikas, etc., deny the dissimilar locus of a nonexistent nature, for the reason that it is invalid to revert at all from a nonexistent nature. Therefore, they hold that there is no certainty of a reasoning of proofs such as "It is impermanent because of denying that it is unconstructed (*asaṃskṛta*);" and they explain the dissimilar locus in various ways.

/ kha cig rjes su dpag pa'i rab tu dbye ba dań / rań gi ṅo bo gzhan du brjod de / 'di lta ste / rigs pa can rnams na re / de sṅon du 'gro ba'i rjes su dpag pa ni rnam pa gsum ste / sṅa ma dań ldan pa dań / lhag ma dań ldan pa dań / spyir mthoń ba'i rjes su dpag pa'o zhes zer ro / bye brag pa rnaṃs ni rtags las byuń ba ni 'di'i 'di zhes bya ba ste / 'bras bu dan / rgyu dan / 'brel pa dań / don gcig la ldan pa dan 'gal ba'o zhes zer ro / ser skya pa la sogs pa ni rjes su dpag pa rnam pa gñis te / spyir mthoń ba dań / khyad par du mthoń ba'o zhes zer ro / de'i phyir 'di dag gi log par rtogs pa bsal pa'i phyir rtags kyi rab tu phye ba brjod do /

(On NB-Sva, 11-12:) Some express differently the variety and the individual nature of inference. Thus the Naiyāyika claims that the prior [i.e not requiring a prior direct perception] inference is of three kinds to wit, *pūrvavat* [anticipating a result], *śeṣavat* [rsasoning about] what happened), or *sāmānyatodṛṣṭa* [the seen explained by general rules]. The Vaiśeṣika claims that the expression arising from evidence, to wit, "This is of that" is in conflict with having a result, a cause, a relation, and a single entity (*ekārtha*). The Kapila, etc. claim that there are two kinds of inference. e.g. *sāmānyato dṛṣṭa* [the seen by a generality] and *viśeṣato dṛṣta* [the seen by a distinction]. Consequently, these have deviant thought. In order to dispel them, he (Dharmakīrti) expresses the good analysis of the evidence (*liṅga*).

/ rgyal dpog pa la sogs pa ni thams cad mkhyen pa la sogs pa dmigs pa'i rig byar ma gyur pa yaṅ raṅ gi dmigs pa log pa tsam gyi sgo nas 'gog par byed de / de'i phyir mi dmigs pa bye brag tu bśad do /

(On NB-Sva, 13:) The Jaiminīya, etc. are unable to clearly realize omniscience and other objects (*ālambana*), and they refute only by way of their own deviant objects. Therefore, he (Dharmakīrti) explains 'non-apprehension' (*anupalabdhi*) in various ways.

/ gnas ma'i bu'i sde pa la sogs pa ni mi rtag pa la sogs pa phyis 'byuṅ ba yaṅ byas pa la sogs pa'i raṅ bzhin yin par brjod de / de bsal ba'i phyir raṅ bzhin gyi gtan tshigs kyi yul bśad do /.

(On NB-Sva, 14-17:) The Vātsiputriya, etc. set forth that impermanent things later reoccur, and that there is an individual nature for the various constructed things. To dispel this, he (Dharmakīrti) describes the object (*viṣaya*) which is the reasoning of the individual nature.

/ brda sprod pa la sogs pa me ma yin pa brgya byin kyi spyi bo la sogs pa las kyaṅ du ba 'byuṅ ba mthoṅ nas / me la sogs pa 'grub par bya ba sogs pa 'bras bu'i rtags 'khrul ba smra ste / de'i phyir 'bras bu'i gtan tshigs brjod do /

(On NB-Sva, 18:) The Vaiyākaraṇa (grammarians), etc., having observed smoke arising from the crown of Viṣṇu (the statue), which lacks fire, mistakenly assess the evidence (*liṅga*) for the result, namely, that fire, etc. is provable. For that reason, he (Dharmakīrti) tells the reasoning of the result.

/ graṅs can pa rnams ni dṅos po rnams kyi 'brel pa rnam pa bdun brjod de / 'di lta ste / bdag daṅ bdag gir 'brel pa ni lhas byin daṅ rta lta bu'o / raṅ bzhin daṅ [?] 'brel pa ni 'jim pa daṅ bum pa lta bu'o / rgyu daṅ rgyu can du 'brel pa ni rdza mkhan daṅ bum pa lta bu'o bu'o / rgyu daṅ 'bras bur 'brel pa ni sa bon daṅ myu gu lta bu'o / pha daṅ ma lta bu 'brel pa ni yal ga daṅ śiṅ ljon pa lta bu'o / lhan cig spyod pa'i 'brel pa ni dur ba daṅ khyo śugs lta bu'o / dgra zla'i 'brel pa ni bya rog daṅ 'ug pa lta bu'o zhes zer ro /

(On NB-Sva, 19-25:) The Sāṃkhya, etc., say that there are seven kinds of relation (*saṃyoga*) of *bhāva* (modes of being, presences, concrete entities), as follows:

1. relation of self and of what belongs to self, like Devadatta and his horse.

2. relation of own being, like clay and the pot.

3. relation of cause (**nimitta*) and cause-possessing (**naimittika*), like the potter and the pot.

4. relation of cause and effect. like the seed and the sprout.

5. relation as though father and mother, like the branch and the tree.

6. relation of companions (*sahacārī*), like the inseparable husband and wife (said of certain birds).

7. relation of enemies, like the crow and the owl (as in a story of their traditional quarreling).

/ rigs pa can la sogs pa ni rnam pa lṅar brjos de / 'byor pa'i mtshan ñid kyi 'brel pa ni du ba daṅ me lta bu'o / ldan pa'i mtshan ñid kyi 'brel pa ni de ñid daṅ gzugs lta bu'o / 'phrod pa'i 'du ba'i mtshan ñid kyi 'brel pa ni de ñid daṅ gzugs daṅ ldan pa ñid lta bu'o / 'du ba'i ldan pa'i mtshan ñid kyi 'brel pa ni / dper na de ñid daṅ du ba yod pa'i gzugs la sogs pa lta bu'o' ldan pa'i 'phrod pa'i 'du ba'i mtshan ñid kyi 'brel pa ni / dper na me de ñid daṅ du ba la yod pa'i gzugs la sogs pa'i daṅ ldan pa ñid lta bu'o zhes zer ro /

The Naiyāyika, etc., speak of five kinds:

1. The character relation of 'inherence' (*samavāya*) [being in the same place], like smoke and fire.

2. The character relation of containment, like that same fire and its form.

3. The character relation of relevant gathering, like that very (fire) and the contained state of form.

4. The character relation, containment of gathering, for example, that very (fire) and the form of existent smoke.

5. The character relation, relevant gathering of containment, for example, that very fire and the state of containing the form, which exists in the smoke.

/ de dag gi gzhuṅ lugs ni 'brel pa de dag kho nas 'brel pa'i gtan tshigs ni rtogs par byed pa yin no zhes bya ba yin te / de bsal ba'i phyir 'brel pa gñis brjod do /

Those schools [the Sāṁkhya and the Naiyāyika] assert that one understands the reasoning of a relation only by way of those [stated] relations. So as to dispel those, he (Dharmakīrti) tells the two kinds of relation [identity with it, and arising from it.].

/ *sprod pa pa [for spyod pa pa]rnams ni da ltar thams cad mkhyen pa la sogs pa mi dmigs pa'i phyir / ma 'oṅs pa'i dus na yaṅ de'i sgo nas de med par śes te / de bsal ba'i phyir mi dmigs pa brjod do /

/ rgyal dpog pa la sogs pa gaṅ dag raṅ gi dmigs pa la sogs pa rgyu ma yin pa daṅ / khyab par byed pa ma yin pa daṅ / ' bras bu ma yin pa'i bkag pa daṅ / tshig la sogs pa dṅos su daṅ rgyud pas kyaṅ mi 'gal ba bsgrub pa'i sgo nas thams cad mkhyen pa la sogs pa'gog par smra ste / de dag gi de rigs pa ma yin no zhes bya bar bstan pa'i phyir daṅ/ 'jig pa rgyu daṅ bcas par smra ba dgag pa'i phyir / mi dmigs pa'i rab tu dbye ba brjod do /

(On NB-Sva, 26-45, Kamalaśāla has only these two paragraphs:) The Mīmāṃsaka say that since nowadays omniscient persons are not apprehended, one may know for the future as well that they will consequently not be (apprehended). In order to reject this (position), he (Dharmakīrti) explains nonapprehension (*anupalabdhi*).

The Jaiminīya refute any noncause (*rgyu ma yin*) for any individual apprehension, any nonpervader (for it), any nonresult (for it), and by way of proving that words as given things and as derivatives are not in contradiction, they speak in opposition to omniscience. So as to show that they have a false principle, so as to refute those who say impermanence needs a cause, he (Dharmakīrti) speaks, well analyzing the nonapprehension.

/ dgag pa'i gtan tshigs kyi sbyor ba'i dbye ba rnam pa maṅ po zhig yod kyaṅ me la sogs pa me ñid la sogs pa gzhan las dgag pa 'grub pa ma yin gyi / 'on kyaṅ raṅ bzhin mi dmigs kho nas yin no zhes bya bar bstan pa'i phyir / khoṅs su 'du ba 'thad pa daṅ bcas pa brjod de / 'thad pa ni thams cad la zhes bya ba la sogs pas bstan to /

(On NB-Sva, 46-47:) While there are many differences of formulation of the reasoning in terms of negation, and given no proof of negation for fire, and so on when by way of a different fire-state, and so on—still, in order to show it is just nonapprehension of an individual presence, he (Dharmakīrti) points to the inner gathering along with validity, and shows the validity in all cases.

/ bskal pa'i yul zhes bya ba la sogs pa ni / pha rol pos rab tu sbyar ba'i mi dmigs pa la nus pa med par bstan pa yin no /

(On NB-Sva, 48:) In the case of the inaccessible object (*viprakṛṣṭa-viṣaya*), he (Dharmakīrti) shows that there is no use for a 'nonapprehension,' which is the opponent's formulation.

/ rjes su dpag pa 'di'i mtshan ñid ni / bcom ldan 'das rjes su dpag pa'i rten gyi rtags ston par mdzad pa ñid kyis gsuṅs te / 'di la rtags ni bsgrub par bya ba med ba mi 'byuṅ bar ṅes pa yin na / rjes su dpag pa'i śes pa'i rgyu yin te / de yaṅ dge slon dag kun 'byuṅ ba'i chos can gaṅ ci yaṅ ruṅ ba de thams cad ni 'gog pa'i chos can yin no zhes de skad du bsgrub par bya bas /

(Kamalaśīla further comments)

The definition of this inference was told by the Bhagavat who pointed to evidence (*liṅga*) as the basis of an inference. Here, the evidence is the certainty of necessary connection (*avinābhava*) with what is to be proven; and is the reason (*hetu*) which cognizes the inference. Furthermore, he taught, "Monks, whatever the nature-holders (*dharmin*) that arise, they are all nature-holders that cease." [He refers to the celebrated verse:

Whatever natures arise by cause,	ye dharmā hetuprabhavā
their cause the Tathāgata declares	hetun teṣāṃ tathāgato āha· /
and also their cessation. So	teṣāṃ ca yo nirodho
speaking is the great ascetic.	evaṃvādī mahśramaṇaḥ //]

/ gtan tshigs la khyab par ston par mdzad pas / gsal ba kho nar rab tu bstan pa yin no / rtags de yaṅ raṅ bzhin daṅ / 'bras bu daṅ / mi dmigs pa'i bdag ñid rnam pa gsum du yaṅ bstan pa kho na ste / de la dge sloṅ dag kun 'byuṅ ba'i chos can gaṅ ci yaṅ ruṅ zhes bya ba 'dis ni raṅ bzhin zhes bya ba'i gtan tshigs bśad do /

When he taught the pervasion in the reasoning, he taught it just clearly. And he taught that the evidence is threefold as individual presence (*svabhāva*), result (*kārya*), and nonapprehension (*anupalabdhi*). Here he taught the reasoning called 'individual presence' by saying, "Monks, whatever the nature-holders that arise." [That is, "*dharma*-holders that arise" are the presence (*bhāva*)—e.g. a given or named tree, a *dharma*-holder, of the 'individual' (*sva*)—e.g. treeness (=the class of trees)].

/ 'bras bu zhes bya ba yaṅ du ba las ni mer śes te / chu skyar las ni chu yin no / byaṅ chub sems dpa' blo ldan gyi / rigs ni mtshan ma rnams las śes / zhes bya ba 'dis bstan pa kho na yin no /

As to the (logical) result, he surely taught that one is aware of fire from smoke, water from rain-clouds, and that one is aware of the principles of a wise Bodhisattva from his marks.

/ mi dmigs pa tsam tshad ma ñid yin par spoṅ bar mdzad pas / mi dmigs pa'i khyad par zhes bya ba yaṅ bstan pa kho na ste / ji skad du / dge sloṅ dag gaṅ zag gis gaṅ zag la tshod ma 'dzin cig / gaṅ zag la tshad kyaṅ ma 'dzin cig / dge sloṅ dag gaṅ zag gis gaṅ zag la tshod 'dzin pa ni ñams par 'gyur te / gaṅ zag gi tshod ni ṅa 'am ṅa daṅ 'dra ba yod pa gaṅ yin pas gzuṅ bar bya'o zhes gsuṅs pa lta bu'o / 'dis ni ṅo bo ñid kyis bskal pa'i don dag la mi dmigs pa tsam tshad ma ñid yin pa spoṅ bar mdzad pas / mi dmigs pa kho na tshad ma yin gyi / gzhan ni ma yin no zhes bstan par 'gyur ro /

He (the Buddha) taught a rejection of mere nonapprehension as an authority; and surely taught distinctions of nonapprehension when he spoke thus: "Monks, a person should not place authority in a person, and should not uphold it in a person. Monks, the person who places authority in a person loses. A person's authority should be taken in my [Dharma] or in what agrees with my [Dharma]." [Cf. *Mahāvyutpatti*, nos. 7028 and 7029, *mā pudgalaḥ pudgalaṃ pramiṇetu; pudgale vā mā pramāṇam udgṛhṇātu*]. [Hence, also, final resort in *dharma* amounts to nonapprehenion of *pudgala*]. Thereby he taught to reject the authority of mere nonapprehension in the case of entities that are inaccessible by nature. Thus he taught that there is a nonapprehension which is an authority (i.e. authority of *dharma*), while the other one (i.e. the inaccessible kind of nonapprehension) is not.

III. ADVERSARIES OF INFERENCE FOR OTHERS (NB, CHAPTER 3)

/ rigs pa can la sogs pa ni gzhan gyi don gyi rjes su dpag pa tshig yan lag lṅa pa yin te / yan lag lṅa ni / dam bca' ba daṅ / gtan tshigs daṅ / dpe daṅ / ñe bar sbyar ba daṅ / mjug bsdu ba rnams so zhes zer ro / raṅ gi sde pa kha cig kyaṅ / gzhan gyi don gyi rjes su dpag pa ni / tshig yan lag gsum pa yin te / yan lag gsum ni / dam bca' ba daṅ / gtan tshigs daṅ / dpe rnams so zhes bya bar rtogs so / gzhan dag ni sṅar bśad pa'i yan lag lṅa po kho na ltar 'dod de / de dag dgag par 'di'i ran gi ṅo bo bstan to /

(On NB-Par, 1-2:) The Naiyāyikas, etc. claim there are five member-terms in Inference for Others. The members are 1. (pledged) thesis (*pratijñā*), 2. reason (*hetu*), 3. example (*dṛṣṭānta*), 4. application (*upayoga*), 5. conclusion (*nigamana*). Some insider Buddhists imagine that there are three-member terms for Inference for Others, to wit, (pledged) thesis, reason, and example. Other accept in accordance with precisely the five members previously mentioned. For refuting them, he (Dharmakīrti) teaches their individual forms (*svarūpa*).

/ rtog ge pa gzhan thams cad ni 'di ltar re zhig chos mthun pa daṅ / chos mthun pa daṅ / chos mi mthun pa dan ldan pa'i tshig sbyor ba gaṅ yin pa 'di tsam zhig tshul yin no / de lta ma yin na chos mthun pa tsam zhig sbyar bas kyaṅ / ji ltar chos mi mthun pa rtogs par 'gyur / chos mi mthun pa tsam zhig sbyar na yaṅ chos mthun pa rtogs par ga la 'gyur / de lta bas na gñi ga rtogs par bya ba'i phyir gñi ga brjod par bya dgos so zhes bya bar rtogs so / de bsal ba'i phyir de ni rnam pa gñis te zhes bya ba la sogs pa rab tu dbye ba brjod do / de la sbyor ba gcig gi yaṅ nus pa ñe bar bstan pa'i phyir / dper brjod pa bsñad do /

(On NB-Par, 3-9:) All other logicians (*tārkika*) have a method tantamount to what is herein give: they claim a formulation (*prayoga*) of word that has feature-concordance (*sādharmya*) and feature-discordance (*vaidharmya*). [And they add:] Were it not so, with formulating merely a feature-concordance, how would one understand a feature-discordance? Again, if one formulated merely a feature-discordance, how would one understand a feature-concordance? [And they conclude:] Accordingly, since one should understand both, one may comprehend the stipulation to expound both. So as to reject this, he (Dharmakīrti) expounds the two with good analysis. But here, to show the usefulness as well of a single formulation, he adds illustrations (*udāharaṇa*).

/ bye brag pa la sogs pa ni skye ba daṅ ldan pa thams cad la 'brel pa la sogs pa khyad par sgra rnams 'jug pa'i rgyu mtshan tha dad pa kho na yod par ñe bar rtog ciṅ / sgra tsam tha dad pa'i sgo nas don tha dad par rtogs te / de dag gi gzhuṅ lugs dgag pa'i phyir / raṅ bzhin gyi gtan tshigs rnam pa 'di gsum car gyi yaṅ lag par rtog pa bsal ba'i phyir / sṅar bśad pa kho na'i yul ñe bar bstan par sgrub pa'i chos de dag thams cad ni zhes bya ba la sogs pa smos so /

(On NB-Par, 10-24:) The Vaiśeṣika, etc., imagine that there are different reasons for understanding the words that differentiate the relations in all (entities) that have arising, and understand a difference of meaning by way of the differences of the words themselves. So as to refute their school, and so as to dispel the deviant reflection about the three kinds of reasoning, beginning with the individual-presence one, he (Dharmakīrti), while setting forth precisely the object (*viṣaya*) previously explained, refers to all these proving (*sādhana*) features.

/ sbyor ba gcig la yaṅ tshul gsum pa'i rtags bsgrub pa'i nus pa yod pa kho na'o zhes bya bar bstan pa'i phyir / chos mthun pas kyaṅ zhes bya ba la sogs pa tshul ñe bar brjod do /

(On NB-Par, 25-33:) So as to teach that there is indeed a usefulness in proving the evidence with the three modes even be there a single formulation, he sets forth the method with (just) feature-concordance (*sādharmya*).

/ raṅ gi sde pa gaṅ dag ñe bar sbyar ba daṅ / mjug bsdu ba dag ni zlos pa yin pa'i phyir ma bstan pa la yaṅ ṅag na phyogs go ci ste ston par mi byed sñam ste sems pa de dag la sbyor ba 'di gñi ga la yaṅ phyogs bstan par ṅes pa med de zhes bya ba la sogs pa smos so /

(On NB-Par, 34-38:) Certain insider (i.e. Buddhist) groups, adopting the *upayoga* and *nigamana* [4th and 5th 'syllogism' members], whether not showing them, or else voieing them, think "Why a locus? We need not show it." He (Dharmakīrti) states, "It is not indispensable to have the two formulations [4th and 5th members] of these thinkers and also show the locus."

/ gzhan dag bsgrub par bya ba ma yin pa yaṅ bsgrub par bya ba ñid du bzuṅ nas/ de'i sgo nas gtan tshigs kyi skyon rjod par byed de / de dag gsal ba'i phyir phyogs kyi mtshan ñid bśad do /

(On NB-Par, 39-56:) Some others, while lacking a thing to prove, take on a 'provable' and by way of it bespeak fault of reasoning. So as to expose them, he (Dharmakīrti) presents the definition of locus (*pakṣa*).

/ rigs pa can la sogs pa ni dam bca' ni bsgrub par bya ba bstan pa yin no zhes phyogs kyi msthan ñid kha na ma tho ba daṅ bcas par ñe bar ston to / de bzhin du raṅ gi sde pa kha cig gis kyaṅ mtshan ñid yoṅs su ma dag par ñe bar bstan te / de skad du slob dpon dbyig gñen gyis mam par dpyad par 'dod pa'i don phyogs yin no zhes bśad do /

When the Naiyāyika, etc. say that their (pledged) thesis (*pratijñā*) expresses what is to be proved, he indicates that their definition of locus is fallacious. Likewise, certain insider Buddhists have portrayed the definition in an impure manner. So speaking, the *ācārya* Vasubandhu explained the locus as the preferred object while pondering.

/ nam mkha'i gos can rnams ni phyogs kyi phyogs gcig la yod pa yaṅ gtan tshigs yin par rtogs te / dper na śiṅ rnams ni sems can yin te / nub mo ñal pa'i phyir ro zhes zer ba lta bu'o / de dag gis ñal ba 'dab ma 'khums pa la sogs pa tsam gyi mtshan ñid yin par rjod par 'dod mod kyi / 'on kyaṅ 'di ni phyogs su byas pa'i śiṅ thams cad la ma grub ste / de śiṅ tin-ti-ḳa la sogs pa kho na la mthoṅ ba'i phyir ro / de rnam par gcad par go rims bzhin du rjes su dpag par bya ba la yod pa daṅ / ṅes par gzuṅ ba smos te / yul khyad par can du ṅes par gzuṅ ba ni 'dod pa'i don rtogs par bya ba'i phyir ro / de lta ma yin na bśad ma thag pa'i don rtogs par mi 'gyur ro /

The Digambara (Jains) understand that there is a reasoning in the case of a locus among locuses. For example, they claim that trees are sentient beings because they sleep at night. They point to the characteristic amounting to the sleeping leaves that are unopened. However, this is not proved for all trees that are made into the locus, because it is a fact just for a group of trees like the Tamarind (*tintika*). For their decision, they insist that there is an inferable according to the sequence and which is accepted in certainty—because the acceptance of a distinction in an object in certainty is to be understood as the preferred object. If it were not so, there would be no understanding of the object immediately upon being explained.

/ bye brag pa la sogs pa ni / rjes su dpag par bya ba kho na la yod pa thun moṅ ma yin pa ma ṅes pa yaṅ dṅos su gtan tshigs yin par khas len te / dper na gson po'i lus ni bdag daṅ bcas pa yin te / srog la sogs pa daṅ ldan pa'i phyir zhes zer ba lta bu'o / de bzlog pa'i phyir mthun pa'i phyogs la yod pa brjod do /

The Vaiśeṣika, etc., take the position that as long as there is an inferable, even if there is no certainty of being unshared (*asādhāraṇa*), there is a reason in a material sense; for example, "A living body is accompanied with a self, because it is possessed of life." In order to disprove this, he (Dharmakīrti) refers to the existence of a concordant locus.

/ phyogs kyi mtshan ñid 'di rnam pa gñi ga yaṅ ha caṅ khyab ches pa'i ñes pa yod la / de dag la gtan tshigs daṅ dpe ma grub pa smra ba yaṅ yod pa'i phyir te / de'i phyir yaṅ phyogs kyi mtshan ñid bstan to /

Both of them (i.e. the Digambara and the Vaiśeṣika) have a definition of locus (*pakṣa*) exhibiting an extreme fault of overpervasion, because they mention a reason and an example that are [each] unproven. Therefore, he (Dharmakīrti) again teaches the definition of a locus.

/ graṅs can pa rnams ni rgol ba daṅ phyir rgol ba dag la ma grub pa yaṅ bsgrub par bya ba ñid du bston te / dper na mig la sogs pa ni gzhan gyi don yin no zhes zer ba lta bu'o / gzhan gyi don ni spyi yin pas de'i phyir raṅ gi ṅo bo zhes bya ba smos so / kho na zhes bya ba ni ha caṅ yaṅ khyab ches pa'i ñes pa bsal ba'i phyir ro /

(On NB-Par, 57-82:) when the Sāṃkhya teach what is to be proved, it is unproven both to the first speaker and his respondent. For example, they assert that the eye (and other organs) are for the sake of others. They claim that "for the sake of others" is a generality, and so it is called 'individual nature', He (Dharmakīrti) saying "Indeed," then refutes the extreme fault of over-pervasion.

/ graṅs can pa la sogs pa ni rgol ba mi 'dod kyaṅ bla ste / bstan bcos byed pa'i 'dod pa thams cad bsgrub par bya ba kho ba yiṅ no zhes bya bar rtogs te / de'i sgo nas byas pa ñid la sogs pa yaṅ dag pa'i sgrub pa la yaṅ 'gal brjod par byed de / de daṅ 'dra bar chos can sgra la nam mkha'i yon tan yaṅ med par sgrub pa'i phyir / bye brag pa la sogs pa'i gtan tshigs ni 'gal ba yin no zhes zer ba lta bu ste / de'i phyir bdag ces bya ba smos so /

The Sāṃkhya, etc. understand that it is better to not believe the opponent, and that the only things to prove are all the beliefs of [their] treatises. Thereby, they speak in contradiction to the genuine proof for what has happened, and so on; because of proving that the feature-base (*dharmin*) sound—in a similar case is not a quality of space (*ākāśa*). They claim that the reasoning of the Vaiśeṣika and others is contradicted; and so they assert that there is a 'Self' (*ātman*).

/ graṅs can pa la sogs pa na re tshig tu smras pa kho na bsgrub par bya ba yin gyi ma smras pa ni ma yin no zhes zer zhes grag ste / de'i phyir 'dod pa zhes bya ba smos so /

It is reported that the Sāṁkhya and others assert that just by speaking there is something to prove; but there is not such if one does not speak. Therefore, they call it a 'belief' (Tib. *'dod pa*).

/ rgyal dpog pa rnams ni raṅ rig pa'i mṅon sum du rab tu grub pa blo daṅ bde ba la sogs pa yaṅ mṅon sum ma yin pa ñid du rab tu śes te / de dag gi dam bca' ba ni sgra mñan par bya ba ma yin pa ñid du dam 'cha' ba de bzhin du / mṅon sum gyi gnod pa yin no zhes bstan pa'i phyir/ 'gal ba daṅ po brjod do / de dag ñid sgra rtags pa ñid du śes la / graṅs can pa la sogs pa gsal bar smra ba rnams kyaṅ rtags pa ñid du gsal ba kho nar khas len pas / de'i phyir rjes su dpag pas gnod pa bsal to /

The Jaiminīya 'know well' that there is no intellect that proves the introspective direct perception (*svasaṃvedana-pratyakṣa*) or that there is any direct perception of pleasure, etc. Since their (pledged) thesis (*pratijñā*) is not an audible sound, and since, like their (pledged) thesis, they show opposition to direct perception, they express the initial contradiction. They consider the sound as the evidence, and hold that while the Sāṃkhya and others speak clearly, they only clarify what is the evidence. On that account, he (Dharmakīrti) refutes the opposition to inference.

/brda sprod pa pa kha cig sgra bzaṅ po kho na rjod par byed pa yin gyi mi bzaṅ ba ni ma yin no zhes zer ba ni dṅos po thams cad sgra thams cad kyi brjod par bya ba ñid du ruṅ bar 'dod pa tsam gyi rjes su byed pa skye bo gnag rji mo yan chad la grags pa 'dor bar byed pa ste / de'i phyir grags pas bsal ba bsal to /

Certain Vaiyākaraṇa (Grammarians) assert that they recite only good words, so there are no bad ones; that is to say, every entity is feasibly expressible by some word, and a person does act in accordance with such a belief. Then (Dharma)Kīrti rejects this as a 'boner' (*āgopāla*).Therefore, (Dharma) Kīrti refutes and refutes.

/'jig rten rgyaṅ 'phan pa rnams ni gzhan dag la raṅ gi rjod par 'dod pa'i don lkog tu gyur pa / tshig rtags de med na mi 'byuṅ ba'i sgo nas rjes su dpog par byed kyaṅ / rjes su dpag pa tshad ma ma yin no zhes bya bar rab tu śes te / de'i phyir raṅ gi tshig daṅ 'gal ba brjod do /

The Lokāyata, although inferring by way of the necessary connection (*avinābhāva*) of verbal evidence, whose object that is beyond sight (*parokṣa*) [i.e. a form of inference] is believed in by their own expressions to others, still 'well know' that inference is not an authority.

/ rigs pa can rnams ni gtan tshigs ltar snaṅ ba rnams kyi mtshan ñid ni 'khrul pa daṅ bcas pa daṅ 'gal ba daṅ / skabs daṅ mtshuṅs pa daṅ / dus las 'das pa ni gtan tshigs ltar snaṅ ba dag yin no zhes gzhan du 'chad par byed de / de la 'khrul pa daṅ bcas pa ma ṅes pa yin te / dper na sgra ni rtag pa ste / lus can ma yin pa'i phyir ro zhes bya ba lta bu'o / grub pa'i mtha' khas blaṅs pas / de daṅ 'gal bar byed pa ni 'gal ba ste / dper na bye brag pa ṇa re rdul phra rab dag ni lus can ma yin pa'i phyir rtsom par byed pa ma yin no zhes zer ba lta bu'o / gaṅ gi phyir skabs bsams pa de gtan la dbab pa'i phyir / bstan pa ni skabs daṅ mtshuṅs pa ste / dper na bdag ni rtag pa ste lus las gzhan yin pa'i phyir ro zhes bya ba lta bu'o / bsgrub par bya ba daṅ khyad par med pa ni bsgrub par bya ba yin pa'i phyir bsgrub par bya ba daṅ mtshuṅs te / dper na sgra ni rtag pa ste / lus can ma yin pa'i phyir blo lta bu zhes bya ba lta bu daṅ / gzhan dag na re rdzas yin te / lus las 'oṅ ba daṅ ldan pa'i phyir ro zhes dper rjod par byed pa lta bu'o / dus 'das nas bstan pa ni dus las 'das pa ste / dper na sgra ni mi rtag pa ste bum pa bzhin no zhes smras na dris pa daṅ byas pa'i phyir ro zhes gtan tshigs smra ba lta bu'o zhes zer ro /

(On NB-Par, 83-121:) The Naiyāyika explain otherwise the characteristics of the fallacies of reasons, as delusive (*sa-bhrānti*), contradictory (*viruddha*), equal to the locus (**pakṣasama*), the same as the thesis (*sādhyasama*), and disregarding of time (*kālātīta*). As to those fallacies of reasons, they assert: 1. the delusive (usually called *sa-vyabhicāra*) is uncertain; for example, "Sound is eternal, because it is incorporeal." 2. The contradictory opposes a tenet of the theory-system (*siddhānta*); for example, the Vaiśeṣika claim that since fine dust particles are incorporeal they do not operate. 3. The tantamount to a locus (apparently the *satpratipakṣa-hetu*) is a teaching (or doctrine), because founded on a contemplation of the locus; for example, "The self is eternal, because it is other than the body." 4. The one same as the thesis (presumably the *asiddha-hetu*) is indeed the same as the thesis because it is what is to be proved; for example, "Sound is eternal, because it is incorporeal, like intelligence (*buddhi*)." Others say it is a substance, in illustration saying, "because it issues from the body." 5. The disregarding of time is shown by avoiding time; for example, saying, "Sound is impermanent, like a pot," and after being asked, gives a reason (i.e. did not give a reason at the time of stating the thesis).

/ bye brag pa rnams na re ston pa ma yin pa ni rab tu ma grub pa daṅ / med pa daṅ / the tshom za ba'o zhes zer te/ gaṅ la rtags daṅ rtags can dag 'brel par ma grub pa de la ma grub pa yin no / 'brel pa med pa ni med pa ste / dper na rva can yin pa'i phyir rta'o zhes bya ba lta bu'o / rva can yin pa'i phyir ba laṅ ṅo zhes bya ba lta bu ni the tshom za ba yin no zhes zer ro /

The Vaiśeṣika claim that the 'undemonstrated' is the unfounded (*asiddha*), the absent (**abhūtva*), and the doubtful (*saṃdigdha*). The unfounded one is in whatever case that the evidence and evidence-possessor do not succeed to relation. The absent one is the lack of a relation; for example, "It is a horse, because it has horns." The dubious one is, for example, "It is a cow, because it has horns."

/ de dag dag pa'i phyir daṅ gzhan gyis rab tu sbyar ba'i gtan tshigs rnams kyis ma grub pa ñid la sogs pa'i skyon rjod pa'i phyir gtan tshigs ltar snaṅ ba dag bstan to /

So as to purify those (theories), and so as to bespeak the faults of what is unproven by reasons offered by (still) others, he (Dharmakīrti) points out the fallacies of reasons.

/ śiṅ dag la sems yod pa yin no zhes bya ba ni nam mkḥa'i gos can rnams kyis dam 'cha' ba yin no / bde ba la sogs pa la sems med do zhes bya ba ni graṅs can pa rnams kyi yin no / bdag ni thams cad na yod pa yin no zhes bya ba ni rigs pa can rnams kyi yin no / sgra ni rtag pa'o zhes bya ba ni sprod [text: spyod] pa pa rnams kyi yin no / skyes bu thams cad thams cad mkhyen pa ñid ma yin par dam 'cha' ba ni rgyal dpog pa rnams kyi yin no / raṅ gi sde pa kha cig kyaṅ 'dod pa la gnod pa byed pa zhes bya ba 'gal ba gzhan yaṅ yod de zhes brjod par byed de / de dgag pa'i phyir 'dod pa la gnod pa byed pa 'gal ba gsum pa ma yin nam zhes bya ba la sogs pa smos so /

That trees are sentient is a thesis presented by the Digambara. That pleasure, etc. is nonsentient is (a thesis) of the Sāṃkhya. That the self is present in all, goes with the Naiyāyika. That sound is eternal belongs to the Mīmāṃsaka. The thesis that no person is omniscient is the Jaiminīya's. Some Buddhist insiders claim there is a further fallacy called "nullification (*bādhaka*) of the claim." In order to refute this, he (Dharmakīrti) raises the question of whether there are not three fallacies that nullify the claim.

/ rigs pa can rnams na re / gson po'i lus ni bdag daṅ bcas pa yin te / srog sogs pa daṅ ldan pa'i phyir ro zhes zer ro /

The Naiyāyika assert that a living body is attended with a self, because it is possessed of life (*jīva, prāṇa*).

/ raṅ gi sde pa kha cig ni dṅos po'i stobs kyis zhugs pa'i rjes su dpag pa la yaṅ 'gal ba mi 'khrul ba can zhes bya ba ma ṅes pa'i gtan tshigs yod do zhes brjod de / de la dper rjod pa ni dper na sgra mi rtag pa ste byas pa'i phyir bum pa lta bu'o zhes byas pa la gaṅ gi tshe gzhan zhig gis brgal te / sgra ni rtag pa ste mñan par bya ba yin pa'i phyir sgra ñid lta bu'o zhes smras pa de'i tshe sbyor ba sṅa ma ma ṅes pa yin no zhes zer ro zhes grag ste / de dgag pa'i phyir / 'gal ba mi 'khrul pa can yaṅ zhes bya ba la sogs pa smos so /

Some Buddhist insiders, speak about an uncertain reason, and the 'refutation without mistake' in the inference (variety) 'aroused by dint of a present thing'. It is reported that at the time they give the illustration "For example, sound is impermanent, because it is created, like a pot," someone else takes them to task. Then, at that time the other person says, "Sound is eternal, because it is audible, like sound," and claims that the former formulation is uncertain. In order to refute that (other person), he (Dharmakīrti) presents the refutation without mistake.

/ pe lu ka na re spyi ni thams cad yod pa yin te / gsal ba dag daṅ de dag gis stoṅ pa thams cad na yod pa'i phyir ro zhes zer ro / pe'i tha ra na re de ni gsal ba thams cad na yod pa yin gyi / bar [?] gyi yul la yod pa ni ma yin no zhes zer ro /

A Pailuka claims that the generality is [in] everything, because it is in everything that is bright as well as in everything devoid of those (colors). A Paiṭhara claims that it is in everything that is bright, and not present in an object that is dark.

/ rigs pa can la sogs pa ni mtshan ñid gsum pa'i gtan tshigs las ma gtogs pa dpe zhes bya ba sgrub pa'i yan lag yod do zhes zer te / de bsal ba'i phyir / mtshan ñid gsum zhes bya ba la sogs pa smos so / gzhan gyi rab tu sbyar ba'i dpe kha cig kyaṅ skyon can ñid du brjod pa'i phyir / dpe ltar snaṅ ba ñe bar bkod do /

(On NB-Par, 122-141:) The Naiyāyika, etc. claim there is a member of the proof, to wit, an example that is outside the reasoning of the three modes. In order to confure them, he (Dharmakīrti) mentions the three modes. So as to describe certain examples of others as faulty, he organizes the fallacies of example.

/ bye brag pa la sogs pa'i ltar na rdul phra rab rnams ni rtag pa yaṅ yin la lus can yaṅ yin te / lus can ni rdzas thams cad na yod pa ma yin pa'i mtshan ñid yin no / las ni lus can yaṅ ma yin la mi rtag pa yaṅ ma yin no / bum pa ni mi rtag pa yaṅ yin la lus can yaṅ yin no /

According to the Vaiśeṣika, etc., the fine dust particles (or 'atoms') are eternal and corporeal. 'Corporeal' is a characteristic present in all substances. 'Karman' is neither corporeal nor impermanent. The pot is both impermanent and corporeal.

/ ser skya la sogs pa ni 'dod chags daṅ ldan pa yin te smra ba'i phyir lam po che'i mi bzhin no zhes bya ba ni rgyal dpog pa rnams kyi sbyor ba yin no / bye brag pa la sogs pa na re / sgra mi rtag pa ste byas pa'i phyir bum pa bzhin no zhes zer ro / de dag ñid rjes su 'gro ba rab tu bstan pa'i gtan tshigs kyaṅ rab tu sbyor ba byed do / ser skya la sogs pa thams cad mkhyen pa ma yin no zhes bya ba la sogs pa ni nam mkha'i gos can rnams kyi sbyor ba yin no / gsum rigs pa'i bram zes ni mi 'ga' zhig gis rjod par 'dod pa'i tshig gzuṅ bar mi byed ste zhes bya ba la sogs pa ni bram ze rnams kyi sbyor ba yin no / ser skya la sogs pa ni 'dod chags daṅ bral ba ma yin no zhes bya ba la sogs pa ni nam mkha'i gos can rnams kyi yin no / smra ba'i phyir 'dod chags daṅ bral ba ma yin no zhes bya ba la sogs pa ni sprod [text: spyod] pa pa rnams kyi yin no / sgra ni mi rtag pa ste byas pa'i phyir ro zhes bya ba la sogs pa ni rigs pa can gyi yin no /

The Kāpila, etc. say that one possesses passion, because he speaks, like a traveller does—which is (also) a formulation of the Jaiminīyas. The Vaiśeṣika claim that sound is impermanent, because it is constructed, like a pot—their formulation with a reason shows *anvaya* (presence in similar cases). The Kāpila, etc. when saying there is no omniscience agree with the Digambara. The Trikulabrahmaṇa, who says he refrains from accepting the claim word expressed by a certain man, has the formulation of the Brahmins. The Kāpila, etc. who insist that there is no freedon from passion, and so on, have the position of the Digambara. The Mīmāṃsaka claim, "They are not free from passion, because they speak." The Naiyāyika assert, "Sound is impermanent, because it is a product."

/ de la ltag ma chod rnams kyi dper brjod pa phyogs tsam zhig brjod par bya ste /

(Kamalaśīla further comments:)

Here I shall express just a locus (*pakṣa*) which illustrates the sophistries (*jāti*).

/ dper na mi rtag pa ñid la sogs pa bsgrub par byas pa ñid daṅ brtsal ma thag tu 'byuṅ ba la sogs pa yaṅ dag par sbyar kyaṅ ltag ma chod smra bas brgal ba khyod kyi gtan tshigs 'di ci bsgrub par bya ba daṅ phrad nas sgrub par byed dam 'on te ma phrad nas / gal te phrad nas yin na ni de'i tshe bsgrub par bya ba daṅ khyad par med par 'gyur te / kluṅ gi chu rgya mtsho daṅ phrad pa bzhin no /

For example, given that impermanence, etc. have been proven and right after the effort have been properly formulated. Does your reasoning (*hetu*), which takes on the task to express sophistry, encounter the thesis (*sādhya*) and prove it, or does it not encounter it? If it encounters it, at that time it would be distinguished from the thesis, like the stream which meets the ocean.

/ gzhan yaṅ 'di bsgrub par bya ba grub zin pa daṅ lhan cig phrad par 'gyur ram / ma grub pa daṅ phrad / re zhig ma grub pa daṅ ni ma yin te / ri boṅ gi rva bzhin med pa'i phyir ro / bsgrub par bya ba grub zin na yaṅ 'di gaṅ gi gtan tshigs yin par 'gyur / de'i phyir phrad pa'i phyogs ni rigs pa ma yin no / yaṅ ma phrad ces bya ba'i phyogs kyaṅ ma yin te / gtan tshigs ma phrad pa rnams daṅ khyad par med pa'i phyir ro zhes bya ba lta bu yin no /

Moreover, have you finished proving the thesis, after encountering it, or have not proved the thesis, after encountering it? For the interval it is not proved, it is not [true], because like the horn of the horned rabbit, it does not exist [as a genuine thesis]. And if you have finished proving, what is the [announced] reason (*hetu*) for this? Therefore, the locus (*pakṣa*) encountered is not valid. And the locus of said nonencounter does not exist, because the reason is not distinguished from the nonencountered ones.

/ 'di ni phrad pa daṅ ma phrad pa mtshuṅs pa zhes bya ba'i rtag chod yin te / rigs pa med pas gtan tshigs sun 'byin pa'i phyir ro / gaṅ la phrad pa daṅ ma phrad pa yod par chos mthun pa tsam gyis gtan tshigs kyi mtshan ñid daṅ ldan pa yaṅ gtan tshigs ma yin par 'gyur ro zhes bya ba 'di la rigs pa ci zhig yod / chu daṅ 'byuṅ ba ñid la sogs par chos mthun pa'i phyir mes mi sreg pa ni ma yin no / bsgrub par bya ba yaṅ ri boṅ gi rva bzhin du śin tu ma grub pa ñid ma yin no /

The sophistry "encountering and nonencountering are the same" is without principle, since it is a disgrace of a reason. What principle is there in this remark that in whatever there is encountering and nonencountering, there is the characteristic of a reason by just the feature-concordance, even though no reason [is furnished]! And there is still no [reason] with "not burnt by fire" due to the feature-concordance that it arises along with water. So the thesis, like the horn of a rabbit, stays unproven and (therefore) nonexistent.

/ 'o na ci zhe na / ṅes pa ma skyes pa'i phyir ro / khyod kyi sun 'byin pa la yaṅ klan ka 'di thams cad mtshuṅs pas sun 'byin pa ma yin pa ñid do / de lta bas na 'dri ba log pa de lta bu dag la mtha' med pas / de dag gi mtshan ñid logs śig tu brjod par mi bya ste / tshad ma'i mtshan ñid ji skad bśad pa ṅes par gzuṅ ba kho nas de dag bsal ba ñid do sñam du bsams pa yin no /

Well then, what is it? Since certainty has not arisen. Your 'refutation' is not really a refutation because it amounts to all these blameworthy remarks. That being the case, and since there is no limit to such wayward questions, I need not travel along by-roads to depict their characteristics. Having embraced the certainty of the definition of authority (*pramāṇa*) as it was explained [by Dharmakīrti], I have given thought to confute those [selected wrong views].

/ rigs pa'i thigs pa'i phyogs sṅa ma mdor bsdus pa / slob dpon maṅ du thos pa ka-ma-la-śī-las mdzad pa rdzogs so /

The *Nyāyabindupūrvapakṣasaṃkṣipti* has been finished by the *ācārya* who heard much, Kamalaśīla.

Antarvyāptisamarthana of RATNĀKARAŚĀNTI

INTRODUCTION

A number of years ago (1985) I published a translation of this text by the 11th century author Ratnākaraśānti (referred to in Tibet as Śānti-pā).[1] Rather than simply reproduce my previous translation, I have decided to enclose the Sanskrit[2] by paragraphs along with my translation. The reason for this is that while on the whole the earlier edition is dependable, there were a few important spots where the Tibetan translation suggested modifications (to be indicated in the Sanskrit text by italics), while the Tibetan itself had some obvious corruptions.[3] J.Kajiyama published a Japanese translation of the Sanskrit text; and his views are mentioned in Mimaki's work dealing with Ratnakīrti's *Sthīrasiddhidūṣaṇa*, where Mimaki in the introduction discusses certain passages from Ratnākaraśānti's *antarvyāpti* (inner pervasion) treatise.[4] This is because Ratnakīrti is held to be Ratnākaraśānti's teacher in Buddhist logic, and because this Japanese circle has considered the possibility that Ratnakīrti, even though being himself an apparent partisan of 'outer pervasion', may have prepared for Ratnākaraśānti's explicit formulation of the 'inner pervasion' position. The relevant passage of the *Antarvyāpti* work is as follows:[5]

1. A. Wayman, "Ratnākaraśānti's Antarvyāptisamarthana," Journal of the Asiatic Society, Vol. XXVII, No. 2, 1985, pp. 31-44. This printing omitted one page between its pages 32 and 33, which included the beginning of the translation iitself. I typed this omission, made copies thereof, and enclosed a copy when I gave an offprint to scholars.
2. The Sanskrit edition by Haraprasad Shastri was the sixth of his valuable *Six Buddhist Nyāya Tracts* (Calcutta: Asiatic Society, 1910), pp. 103-114.
3. I employ the Tibetan version in PTT Vol. 138, p. 104-3-6 to 106-4-4.
4. Katsumi Mimaki, La refutation bouddhique de la permanence des choses (Paris, 1976), pp. 51-4.
5. Shastri edn. (n. 2, above), p. 112.

> kevalaṃ jaḍadhiyām eve niyamena dṛṣṭāntasāpekṣaḥ sādhanaprayogaḥ paritoṣāya jāyate / teṣām evānugrahārtham ācāryo dṛṣṭāntam upādatte / yat sat tat kṣaṇikaṃ yathā ghaṭa iti / paṭumatayas tu naivaṃ dṛṣṭāntam apekṣante /
> The syllogism of *sādhana* with reliance on an example is brought up just by obligation for pleasing those of dull mind.[6] In order to assist them the *ācārya* points to an example (to wit), "what exists is momentary, like a pot." Those of sharp mind do not depend on an example.

The Ratnakīrti connection was made in the light of his saying near the outset of his *Kṣaṇabhaṅgasiddhi, yat sat tat kṣaṇikam, yathā ghaṭaḥ,* so Kajiyama came to believe that Ratnakīrti might be the *ācārya* mentioned. While granting this as a possibility, I may mention that my reading in Buddhist logic literature led me to conclude that when the author of a citation is given simply as '*ācārya*' (e.g. as in the *Tattvasaṃgraha* of Śāntarakṣita and Kamalaśīla), the reference is to Dignāga.

I suppose that Ratnākaraśānti was replying to someone who had taken the theory of 'inner pervasion' to task. That someone may well be the author Muktākalaśa who criticizes *antarvyāpti* in his *Kṣaṇabhaṅgasiddhivivaraṇa,* a commentary on Dharmottara's *Kṣaṇabhaṅgasiddhi.* I have noticed in the Tibetan Tanjur version of the Muktākalaśa treatise a discussion critical of "inner pervasion," charging that it vitiates the *anvaya* kind of pervasion, and making these remarks in the context of 'sequence' (*krama*) and 'simultaneity' (*yaugapadya*), the very context with which Śānti-pā starts his own treatise. Muktākalaśa says in part: "This fallacy (*doṣa*) is the theory of inner pervasion. Their theory lacks a valid *anvaya.*"[7] Muktākalaśa may indeed have been arguing against the Jaina *antarvyāpti* position, as found in a work *Nyāyāvatāra* that has been attributed to Siddhasena Divakara—an attribution which Dhaky argues against.[8] This Jain

---

6. Madeleine Biardeau, "Le rôle de l'exemple dans l'inférence indienne," *Journal Asiatique,* 1957, pp. 235-6, cites Vātsyāyana on distinguishing the example in general by the *dṛṣṭānta,* which has a pedagogical role implicating specialists and ordinary persons, from the word *udāharaṇa,* the example in the syllogism and related to the thesis (*sādhya*).
7. Muktākalaśa in PTT, Vol. 138, p. 85-3-3, ff. for the *vyāpti* discussion, the cited remark at 85-4-1: skyon 'di ni naṅ gi khyab pa smra ba la yod do / de dag gi smra ba ni rigs pa'i rjes su 'gro ba ma yin te /
8. Cf. M.A. Dhaky, "The Date and Authorship of *Nyāyāvatāra,*" in *Nirgrantha* (Ahmedabad, 1st issue, 1995). He rather assigns the authorship to a different Siddhasena known as Siddharṣi.

text may have the earliest use of the term, anyway after the time of Dignāga.

Dharmakīrti is of course not attributed a belief in the *antarvyāpti* theory. Nevertheless, he does not mention a *dṛṣṭānta* in his summary verse in the *Pramānavārttika*, last verse of the PS chapter:

> anumānāśrayo liṅgam avinābhāvalakṣaṇam /
> vyāptipradarśanād dhetoḥ sādhyenoktaś ca tat sphuṭam //
> The basis of the inference is the evidence (*liṅga*) with the characters of necessary connection through the reason (*hetu*) that reveals the pervasion (*vyāpti*), and (the basis) was spoken clearly by a thesis (*sādhya*).

This minimal statement would suit both the *antarvyāpti* and the *bahirvyāpti* positions.

Śānti-pā feels it would suffice to find one case of valid inference where an external example is not required, so he says: "In the particular event of a *sattvahetu* there is no possibility of an external pervasion" (*sattvahetor viśeṣeṇa na bahirvyāptisambhavaḥ*). But then, what is a *sattvahetu*? It seems to deny the formulation already given: "What exists is momentary, like a pot." If we take only the words "what exists," these would satisfy the word *sattva*; but Śānti-pā writes, "It (an actuality) exists just when it is momentary." Hence, "is momentary" does not add a quality to the *sattva* as does 'red' to a pot. The *sattva* is perceived; not so according to the Nyāya-Vaiśeṣika, for whom, D.N.Shastri points out that a substance, causing its qualities, precedes them by one moment, devoid of all qualities [only] in the first moment of its existence when it cannot be comprehended.[9] But Śānti-pā writes from a different philosophical base, one in which a reason (*hetu*) can be given for a *sattva* (actuality) irrespective of qualities, disallowing a *dṛṣṭānta* which alludes to a quality-holder. This position is necessary for religious or supramundane topics. Indian religious texts are constantly making assertions and giving reasons, but rarely add examples. By 'example' is meant one that is 'popular' (*prasiddha or pratīta*), e.g. the kitchen stove. Śānti-pā made his text somewhat difficult by purposely foregoing examples.

It should be interesting to take notice of the verse in the Jain work *Nyāyāvatāra*, no. 20,[10] which mentions the expression *antarvyāpti*:

---

9. Dharmendra Nath Shastri, *Critique of Indian Realism* (Agra: Agra University, 1964), p. 20.
10. This text was edited by Satis Chandra Vidyabhusana, and published along with his English translation at Arrah (India) by The Central Jain Publishing House, 1915. M.A. Dhaky kindly furnished a copy of this to me, making it possible for me

> antarvyāptyaiva sādhyasya siddher bahirudāhṛtiḥ/
> vyarthā syāt tadasadbhāve 'py evaṃ nyāyavido viduḥ //
> Logicians have noticed that an external example would be useless (*vyartha*), since even in its absence there is proof of a thesis (*sādhya*) just by internal pervasion (*antarvyāpti*).

The author's unfortunate expression 'useless' is belied by his own use of external examples in other verses in the *Nyāyāvatāra.* Indeed, the verse discounts the example in every case. When we compare with Ratnākaraśānti's arguments, one finds no reason to believe that the latter even knew of this position of the Jain work. We rather conclude that at the time of Śānti-pa (his chief writings in early 11th century),[11] there were various texts discussing this issue, for and against.

As to translation of certain terms, I have gradually adopted renditions (discussed in my Introduction). For *dharmin,* mine is 'factual base', where is located the 'feature(s)' (*dharma*). For *vyavaccheda,* 'ruling out'. For *pratīti,* 'cognitive dawning'. For *pakṣa,* 'locus' (=place) or 'side'.

Ratnākaraśānti's brief 11th century work, herein translated into English, has many implications for the Indian logical theory of 'pervasion' (*vyāpti*) and special implications for the topic of Buddhist logic itself.

ANTARVYĀPTISAMARTHANA (SANSKRIT AND TRANSLATION)

/ iha sattvam arthakriyākāritvaṃ taditarasattvalakṣaṇāyogāt / tac ca kramayaugapadyābhyāṃ vyāptaṃ parasparavyavaccheda-lakṣaṇātvād anayoḥ / prakārāntareṇa karaṇāsambhavāt / kramayaugapadye cākṣaṇikatve na *sthaḥ* / pūrvāparakālayor avicalitaikasvabhāvasya karttṛtvākarttṛtve viruddhadharmadvayāyogāt /[12]

---

to write an article "The Nyāyāvatāra and Buddhist Logical Works by Dignāga and Ratnākaraśānti," which has appeared in *Nirgrantha* (cf. n. 8, above), 2d issue 1997, in which I cited this k. 20.

11. In the essay, Alex Wayman, "An Historical Review of Buddhist Tantras,' *Journal of Rare Buddhist Texts Research Project* (Sarnath, Varanasi: Central Institute of Higher Tibetan Studies, 1995), pp. 148-9, it was argued that Śānti-pā was about 20 years younger than the translator Rin-chen bzang-po (born 958 A.D).

12. PTT Vol. 138, p. 104-4-1.

(1) Here (in this world, or the position defended here) an actuality (*sattva*) has purposeful activity (*arthakriyākāritva*), because it is impossible for the definition of an actuality to be other than this. And this is pervaded by sequence (*krama*) or by simultaneity (*yaugapadya*), when other than there being the characteristic of their mutual ruling out (*parasparavyavaccheda-lakṣaṇatva*); and when other than there being the impossibility of being effective in a different manner. And neither of the two, sequence and simultaneity, exists without momentariness, because it is impossible that two opposed features (*viruddha-dharma*), to wit, former and later times, agency and nonagency, would have a single unaltering individual presence (*svabhāva*).[13]

/ tatra na tāvat kramaḥ kramāṇām ekaikaṃ prati pūrvāparakālayoḥ karttṛtvākarttṛtvāpatteḥ / evaṃ sarvakramābhāvāt kevalaṃ sakalakāryayaugapadyam avaśiṣyate / tatra ca sphuṭataraḥ pūrvāparakālayoḥ karttṛtvākarttṛtva-prasaṅgaḥ / viruddhe ca karttṛtvākarttṛtve ekadharmiṇi na sambhavataḥ / ekasvabhāvás ca tāvat kālam akṣaṇika iti siddha etasmin kramayaugapadyayor ayogaḥ / tad evam akṣaṇike vyāpakānupalabdhyā niṣiddhaṃ sattvaṃ kṣaṇika evā[va] tiṣṭhate iti kṣaṇikatvena vyāptaṃ / tat tena vyāptaṃ yat yatra dharmiṇi sidhyati tatra kṣaṇikatvaṃ presādhayati /[14]

(2) Now let us suppose that there is no sequence among them, giving as reason that each event of a sequence has a 'fatal logical flaw' (*āpatti*) of both agency and nonagency in former and later time. In such a case, given no sequences at all, there would remain only every simultaneity of results [which is ridiculous]. That points out clearly the absurdity of attributing both agency and nonagency in former and later time, because it is impossible for the opposed agency and nonagency to have a single factual base (*dharmin*). And should one prove that an individual presence is nonmomentary through time, it would follow that neither sequence nor simultaneity would be possible. If it were thus nonmomentary, actuality would be refuted by the nonapprehension of a pervader. It (actuality) exists just when it is momentary. Consequently, it is pervaded by momentariness. So

13. This topic is the basis of Ratnakīrti's *Kṣaṇbhaṅgasiddhi-vyatirekātmikā*, which was edited by Anantalal Thakur in *Ratnakīrti-nibandhāvaliḥ* (Patna, 1957), from which edition A.C. Senape McDermott translated it into English in an *Eleventh-Century Buddhist Logic of 'Exists'* (Dordrecht, 1970). Prof. Thakur has a second revised edition of the book (Patna, 1975) of Ratnakīrti texts.

14. PTT, p.104-4-4 (end).

in whatever factual base anything is proved as pervaded by (a pervader), therein one further proves the momentariness.

/ idam evedānīṃ vicāryate / keyaṃ (kveyaṃ) vyāptir grahītavyā dṛṣṭāntadharmiṇi sādhyadharmiṇi vā / kecid āhuḥ / dṛṣṭāntadharmiṇy eva dhūmavat / anyathā sādhana-vaiphalyaṃ syāt / ubhayadharmasiddhi(dhe)r anāntarīyakatvāt vyāptisiddheḥ / nahi mahānasasiddhāyām agnidhūmayor vyāptau punar agnisiddhaye dhūmaliṅgam anviṣyata iti / tathā hi /

> dṛṣṭānte gṛhyate vyāptir dharmayos tatra dṛṣṭayoḥ /
> hetumātrasya dṛṣṭasya vyāptiḥ pakṣe tu gamyate //
> sa ca sarvopasaṃhārāt sāmānyam avalambate /
> tasya dharmiṇi vṛttis tu pratīyetānumānataḥ //

pratyakṣadṛṣṭayor vahnidhūmayoḥ kāryakāraṇabhavasiddhau tayor vyaptisiddhir iti pratyakṣasiddhe vahnau yuktam anumāna-vaiphalyam /[15]

(3) Now just this is to be pondered: Is this pervasion to be grasped in a factual base of the (external) example (*dṛṣṭānta*) or in a factual base of the thesis (*sādhya*)? Some persons respond: "Just in a factual base of the example, e.g. 'like smoke'. Otherwise, the proving method (*sādhana*) would be fruitless, because the pervasion is proved by the necessary connection (*anāntarīyakatva*) of proving both features. Since the pervasion of fire and smoke is proved in the kitchen, for proving the fire it does not suffice to follow (just) the evidence of smoke (*dhūma-liṅga*)."

(An unlike formulation)[16] is as follows:

> The pervasion is seized in the example by the two features observed therein. But the pervasion of what is witnessed amounting to the reason (*hetu*) is understood in the locus (*pakṣa*). Since it (i.e. the pervasion) comprises everything, it takes a generality as object. Its (i.e. the generality's) role (*vṛtti*) in the factual base cognitively dawns (*pratīyeta*) by inference (*anumāna*).

Thus, when the fire and the smoke are both observed by direct perception, it proves the pervasion of the two as the proof that the

15. PTT, p. 104-5-1.
16. Tibetan version (PTT, p. 104-4-7) has 'unlike formulation' (*mi 'dra bar bkod pa*), missing in Sanskrit.

material cause and the result are present. Now, if fire is proved by direct perception (*pratyakṣa*), it is pointless to use inference.[17]

/ naivaṃ vyāptisiddheḥ prāk pramāṇāntarasiddhaṃ dharmiṇi kṣaṇikatvam / sādhanadharmam eva tu kevalam anupaśyanto viparyaye bādhakapramāṇabalāt tasya kṣaṇikatvena vyāptiṃ pratīmaḥ / tat tataḥ sādhanavaiphalyam / vaiphalyam eva, kṣaṇikatvavyāptasya sattvasya tathātvena dharmiṇi pratītau kṣaṇikatvasyāpi pratīter iti cet / na / sarvopasaṃhāravatau hi vyāptiḥ sādhyasiddher aṅgam / tad iyam anapekṣitadharmiviśeṣaṃ sādhanadharmamātram avalambate / tadyathā / yatra dhūmas tatrāgnir iti / na punar yatra mahānase dhūmas tatrāgnir iti / evam ihāpi yat sat tat kṣaṇikam iti vyāptipratītau sādhanadharmasyāpi dharmiṇi sattvaṃ nāntarbhavati / kiṃ punaḥ sādhyadharmasya / tasmāt sattvasāmānyasya sādhanadharmasya pakṣadharmatvaṃ vyāptiś caikaśaḥ pratipādya tadubhayasāmarthyāt sādhyadharmasya dharmiṇi vṛttiḥ pratīyata iti kuto 'numānavaiphalyaṃ /[18]

(4) Suppose they say: "Prior to the proof of pervasion, another authority [where the authority is direct perception] cannot prove the momentariness in the factual base. But although we observe only the *sādhana*-feature, on the other hand we cognize the pervasion in its (second) moment by dint of the annulling authority (*bādhaka-pramāṇa*).[19] It follows that (your) proving method (*sādhana*) fails. It fails because there is cognitive dawning of the momentariness when the factual base dawns by the realia (*tathātva*) of actuality (*sattva*) [e.g. kitchen smoke] pervaded by momentariness." It is not so! For the pervasion that comprises everything is a member (*aṅga*) of the proof of the thesis. Consequently, this (pervasion) supports only a *sādhana*-feature that is not contingent on a specialized factual base, namely (supports), "where there is smoke, there is fire." But does not (support) further that "where is smoke in a kitchen, there is fire." Likewise, here also, when there is cognitive dawning of the pervasion, viz., "What exists, is momentary," it is not inherent to the actuality in the factual base of a proving (*sādhana*)-feature. How

17. Biardeau (*op. cit.*), pp. 237-9, discusses the primacy of perception in certain Indian systems, notably the Pūrvamīmāṁsā. Also in Buddhist logic, with its two authorities (*pramāṇa*),direct perception (*pratyakṣa*) precedes inference (*anumāna*).

18. Tib. at PTT, p. 104-5-6.

19. Toward the end of his treatise, Śānti-pā clarifies his own use of the term *bādhaka* (annulling) to be the process called elsewhere 'course of exclusion' (*vyāvṛtti-anuvṛtti*), also 'exclusion of what is not it' (*atadvyāvṛtti*), well known as the Apoha theory of the Buddhist logicians.

much less (in one) of a thesis (*sādhya*)-feature! Hence, when the pervasion is treated one by one as the locus-feature (*pakṣa-dharma*) of a generality of reals and of a proving-feature, the role is understood as meaning the factual base of the thesis-feature by way of the capability of those two. So how could the inference fail!

/ yady evaṃ vyāptipratītāv asati dharmaṇi parāmarśe sādhyadharmiṇi vyāptigrahaṇam iti / kutaḥ / tata dṛṣṭasya sattvasya vyāptipratīteḥ / tathā mahānasadṛṣṭāgnidhūmayor vyāptigrahe dṛṣṭāntadharmiṇi vyāptigrahaṇam ucyate / na hi vyāptigrahaṇe mahānasaparāmarśo 'stīty uktaṃ / na nu vyāptipakṣadharmatvayor ekaśaḥ pratītav api yasyaiva pakṣadharmatvam avagatan tasyaiva sādhyena vyāptir avasiteti sāmarthyāt sādhyasattvākathanaṃ vaiyarthyaṃ sādhanasya / nanu na pakṣadharmatvagatiḥ / sādhyagatiḥ sādhyadharmasaṃsparśāt / nāpi vyāptipratītir eva sādhyasiddhiḥ / sāmānyālambanatayā dharmiviśeṣeṇa dharmayor anavacchedāt / anyathā *dharma*viśeṣayor vyāpti*pra*saṅgāt[20] tad ayaṃ *vyāpti*[21]-viṣayaḥ sāmarthyād iti hetunirdeśaḥ /[22]

(5) Suppose they say: "In that way there is no cognitive dawning of pervasion. There is grasping of the pervasion when there is the factual base of the thesis and there is the factual base having 'conclusion from experience' (*parāmarśa*), wherefor the cognitive dawning of a pervasion of actuality witnessed therein. There is grasping of the pervasion when there is the factual base of an example (*dṛṣṭānta*), e.g. grasping the pervasion of fire and smoke when having witnessed a kitchen. For was it not said: For grasping the pervasion, there is the 'conclusion from experience', to wit, the kitchen?" Is it not a fact that when there is cognitive dawning one by one of a locus-feature and the pervasion, and there is understood of which one it is the locus-feature, and there is ascertained the pervasion of precisely that one by way of the thesis—the assertion that the thesis stands up by capacity of the foregoing ['conclusion from experience'] is pointless for the proving method (*sādhana*)? Is it not a fact that there is no understanding of what is the locus-feature and (no) understanding of the thesis by (mere) contact with a thesis-feature? Nor is there proof of the thesis just through the cognitive

20. The two additions are according to Tibetan, PTT edn., p. 105-1-3, giving khyad par gyi chos dag gis khyab par 'gyur pa'i phyir ro /.

21. According to Tibetan (PTT edn., p. 105-1-3), khyab pa'i (yul 'dis), the edited text's *vyasta* should be corrected to *vyāpti*.

22. Tibetan at PTT edn., p. 105-1-3.

dawning of the pervasion, because this does not rule out two features, by support of a generality or by distinction of the factual base. Furthermore, because it reduces to the absurdity (*prasaṅga*) that there is pervasion by the two feature distinctions. So, one shows the reason (*hetu*) as a domain of pervasion (*vyāpti-viṣaya*) by dint of (the latter's) capacity.

/ atha hetos trairūpyapariccheda-sāmarthyāt / sādhyapratītir utpadyata ity ucyate / tarhīdānīṃ vyartho hetuḥ / svarūpaniścayena sādhyaniścayopajananāt / na hi kvacid ayattādhikaṃ liṅgasya karttavyam astīti / api ca /

> gṛhīte pakṣadharmatve sambandhe [ca] smṛte 'numānaṃ /
> bhavadbhir iṣyate tadvad antarvyāptāv apīṣyatāṃ //[23]

na hi bahirvyāptivādinām api vismatāyāṃ vyāptāv anumāna-pravṛttir asti / tatra yasyaiva pakṣadharmatvam avagataṃ tasyaiva sādhyadharmeṇa vyāptismṛteḥ kiṃ na sarvānumāna-vaiyarthyaṃ /[24]

(6) Then, as to what they say: "The intellectual dawning of the thesis emerges through the capacity of analyzing the triple mode of the reason": In this case as well the reason is pointless, since the certainty about the thesis (*sādhya*) comes forth by its own mode's certainty. For with just that much, there is nothing further for the evidence (*liṅga*) to do. Besides,

> When one accepts the locus-feature, and when the relation (*sambandha*) is remembered, you sirs claim it as the inference (*anumāna*). Likewise, admit that it is your 'inner pervasion'!

So, when the adherents of external pervasion forget the pervasion, they do not engage in inference! Here, according to him (the opponent), would not all inference be pointless for those who recognize the locus-feature, on account of their remembering the pervasion by way of the thesis-feature?

/ sādhyadharmiṇo 'parāmarśeṇa vyāpteḥ smaraṇād iti cet / sādhyadharmiṇi dṛṣṭasyaiva vyāptismaraṇe kathaṃ sādhyadharmiṇo 'parāmarśaḥ/ sāmānyālambanatvād vyāpteḥ / sādhyadharmiṇo 'navacchedād iti cet / nanu tatra dṛṣṭāsya kathaṃ tenānavacchedaḥ / tenāvacchinnasya vā asādharaṇatvāt kathaṃ vyāptiḥ /

---

23. The Tibetan translation at PTT, p. 105-1-5, translated this as a verse, which requires dropping out the *ca*, here bracketted, so to leave 16 syllables in the first and second lines. However, probably in error, Tibetan misread the term *antar-* (of the *antarvyāptāv*). The verse, evidently cited by Śānti-pā, has an importance as possibly a traditional one.

24. Tib. at PTT, p. 105-1-6.

ayogavyavacchedena viśeṣaṇān nāsādhāraṇateti cet tathāpi kiṃ na sādhyadharmo parāmṛśyate /[25]

(7) If it is as one says, "because remembering the thesis-factual base and the pervasion with 'conclusion from experience' (*parāmarśa*)," how come there is no 'conclusion from experience' of the thesis-factual base when the one who witnesses it remembers the pervasion?[26]

If it is as he says, "because there is no ruling out of the thesis-factual base, and because one focusses on the generality of pervasion," how is it not a fact that the non-ruling out by him in that place belongs to the witness? Or:

How is there pervasion of what is ruled out by one, due to being too restricted (*asādhāraṇa*)? If it is as one says, "not too restricted, because there is differentiation by 'ruling out non-connection (*ayogavyavaccheda*),"[27] why would not the thesis-factual base also be a conclusive experience?

/ yatra yatra parvate dhūmas tatra tatrāgnir yathā mahānasa iti sāmānyālambanāyāṃ vyāptau dharmiviśeṣaparāmarśasyānaṅgatvād iti cet yuktam etat sādhyadharmiṇā hy ayogavyavacchedaḥ sādhanadharmasya rūpāntaram eva pakṣadharmatvākhyaṃ / na tv ayaṃ vyāpter aṅgaṃ / tam antareṇāpi vyāpteḥ sāmānyālambanāyāḥ paricchedaparisamāpteḥ katham anyathā dṛṣṭāntadharmiṇi vyāptigrahaṇavārttāpi tadedānīṃ pakṣadharmatvāyogāt pakṣadharmatvāgrahaṇāt pakṣadharmatvagrahaṇe vā tadaiva sādhyam api sāmarthyād asiddhaṃ siddham iti sarvānumānavaiyarthya-prasaṅgaḥ / paścāt kālabhāviliṅgajñānam api ca smṛtir eva syāt na pramāṇaṃ / tasmāt vyāpter anaṅgatvāt pakṣadharmatvaṃ vyāptigrahaṇe sad api nāntarbhavatīti pṛthaggṛhītasmṛtayoḥ pakṣadharmatvavyāptyoḥ sāmarthyād anumeyagatir utpadyate iti / evam avaiyarthyaṃ sādhanānām eṣitavyam iti mānaphalatvāt / tadvat

25. Tib. at PTT, p. 105-2-1.

26. The point here seems to be that in the exemplar syllogism, starting with "On yonder hill there is fire, because (we see) smoke," is this not just as much a remembered experience as what happens in the kitchen?

27. This is one of three kinds of *vyavaccheda* which Yuichi Kajiyama discusses in a paper, "Three kinds of Affirmation and Two kinds of Negation of Buddhist Philosophy," *WZKS*, XVII, 1973, pp. 161-175, while translating Dharmakīrti's *Pramāṇavārttika*, IV, 190-192. These are among six verses classifed as 'definition of the reason' (*hetu-lakṣaṇam*). Therefore, they are a topic of Dharmakirti's *Hetubinduḥ*, Teil II, the translation and notes by Ernst Steinkellner (Wien, 1967), pp. 88-9.

pṛthagbhūtayoḥ pakṣadharmatvavyāptyoḥ sāmarthyād anumānotpattir antarvyāptāv api kiṃ neṣyate / tad iṣṭau vā kathaṃ sādhanavaiyarthyaṃ /[28]

(8) Suppose one says: "At whatever place on a mountain there is smoke, at that very place there is fire; for example, like a kitchen stove," (and adds:) "It is when the pervasion has a generality as a support, since there is no member (involved) of conclusive experience of a specialized factual base." (We respond:) That is right, since the ruling out of nonconnection is by the thesis-factual base. It is said to be a locus feature that is just another form of the proving feature. But according to you it is not an ancillary of pervasion, because even in its absence one can arrive at a determination of pervasion having a generality as support. And because how otherwise is there acceptance of pervasion in the factual base of the (external) example since at this time there is no possibility of the locus feature? Or, if one accepts the locus feature, there is the absurdity that at this time the thesis is deemed proven although perforce is unproven, so all inference is pointless. There is no authority just of memory, although it be knowledge of evidence for a later time. Therefore, since it is not an ancillary of pervasion, and the locus feature exists (only) when one accepts the pervasion, there is perforce understanding of the inferable (*anumeya*) by the accepted and the remembered that are separate and by the locus feature and the pervasion. One should not in your way claim a pointlessness of the proving method (*sādhana*) since there is the inference fruit. Likewise, why should one not admit an inner pervasion when there is perforce the occurrence of inference by the accepted and the remembered that are separate and by the locus feature and the pervasion? And, if admitted, how is the proving method pointless?

/ trairūpyagatisāmarthyād anumeyagatir iti hi tad *utpādana*[29]-śaktir eva sāmarthyam ucyate; na tu trairūpyapratīter antarbhāva iti sarvaṃ samānaṃ / na sarvaṃ samānaṃ / antarvyāptau hi vyāptiṃ prati gatyaiva pakṣadharmatvam avagatam anavagate pakṣadharmatve vyāpter apy anavagateḥ / tato vyāptipūrvake sādhanavāhye pakṣadharmavacanam anarthakam anantarvyāptau[30] / naivam bahirvyāptau bahir eva vyāptigrahaṇāt / atrāha:

---

28. Tib. at PTT, p. 105-2-8.
29. Ed. text has *upādāna* here, while the correction is due to the Tib. *bskyed pa'i*.
30. Ed. printed text omitted the *r* of *antar*.

yena tena krameṇātra prayukte sādhane sati /
avetya pakṣadharmatvaṃ paścād vyāptiḥ pratīyate //
pratyakṣa iva dṛṣṭānte tatra sety anyathā kathaṃ /
dvau dṛṣṭvā vidma iti cet; vyāpteḥ prāk dvayadṛk kathaṃ //

vyāptipakṣadharmatve hi svavākyābhyāṃ yena tena prayuktābhyāṃ sūcyete na tu sākṣāt pratīyete / vācaḥ svayam apramāṇatvāt / yadāha:

śaktasya sūcakaṃ hetur vaco 'śaktam api svayam / iti /

sucitayo 'stu tayoḥ sattve hetau prathamatare pakṣadharmatvaviṣayam eva pramāṇam abhimukhībhavatu / tena pramāṇena dharmaṇi siddhasya sattvasya paścād vyāptiḥ pramāṇāntareṇa gṛhyata iti kasya vaiyarthyam iti / pratyakṣe 'pi dṛṣṭāntadharmiṇi prathamaṃ hetur gṛhyate paścād vyāptir ity eṣa eva kramaḥ anyathā dṛṣṭāntadharmiṇi vyāptir gṛhītety etad eva na syāt / dṛṣṭāntadharmiṇy-adṛṣṭasyaiva hetor vyāptigrahaṇāt /[31]

(9) That is because when one says that the understanding of the inferable is through the capacity of understanding the triple modes, this one admits the 'capacity' as just the power of generating it (*utpādana*); but should not say, "the interiorization (*antarbhāva*) of the cognitive dawning of the triple modes is entirely the same (*sarvaṃ samānaṃ*)". It is not entirely the same, for in the event of the inner pervasion one understands the locus feature (*pakṣadharma*) precisely by understanding the pervasion itself—for when one does not understand the pervasion this one does not understand the locus feature. Therefore, it is pointless to speak of a locus feature prior to the pervasion and outside of the proving-method (*sādhana*), i.e. when it is not an inner pervasion. It is not so when the pervasion is external, because one grasps the pervasion just outside. Here one (the opponent) says:

> "By whatever the sequence here, and given a cogent proving-method when one understands the locus-feature, afterwards the pervasion cognitively dawns (*pratīyate*). Given the example in direct perception, how can it be other than that here?" (But) if this one says, "We know the two by seeing them," how does this one see the two before the pervasion?

For, by whatever cogent words in themselves the pervasion and the locus-feature are indicated, they do not cognitively dawn in imme-

31. Tib. at PTT. p. 105-3-7.

diacy because the word by itself is not an authority. This is what one said:

> The reason (*hetu*) is the indicator of capability.
> The word by itself is incapable.

Let it be among the two that are indicated! When the reason is the actuality (*sattva*) first of all, let it face the authority as just the scope of the locus-feature! It is pointless for someone to assert, about a proven actuality in a factual base by that authority, later the pervasion is grasped by a different authority. Also in the event of (your) direct perception, when there is the factual base of an example, first the reason is grasped and later the pervasion: this is the sequence. So, it should not be said, to wit: When there is the factual base of an example, the pervasion is grasped, because the pervasion is grasped through the reason even when the factual base of an example is not seen.

/yady evaṃ sādhyadharmo 'pi vyāptigrahaṇādhikaraṇe dharmiṇi grahītavya eva yathā vahnidhūmayor iti cet / na / tatra dṛṣṭasya hetor vipakṣe bādhakavṛttimātrād eva vyāptisiddheḥ / jñātaś caivaṃ na khalu vyāptigrahaṇāt prāk kṣaṇikasya kvacid api siddhir asti tasyānumeyatvāt / asiddhāyāñ ca vyāptāv anumānāpravṛtteḥ / sādhanāntarasya ca tad artham ananusaraṇāt / anusaraṇe 'py anavasthā syāt / avasthāne tāvat prayāsasya vaiyarthyāt / viparyaye vyāptibalād eva vyāptisiddher avighātāt / vahnidhūmayos tu nādṛṣṭayoḥ kāryakāraṇabhāvasiddheḥ / tatsiddhau na vipakṣe bādhakavṛttir iti dvayadarśanavyapekṣā / vahnidhūmayor vyāptisiddhiḥ sattvakṣaṇikatvayos tu naivaṃ/ yathoktanyāyena vyāptisiddheḥ / tasmāt sattvamātrasya tatra dharmiṇi siddhasya bādhakavaśād vyaptiḥ setsyatīty eṣitavyaṃ / tadvad antarvyāptāv api / te ime vyāptipakṣadharmatve svasvapramāṇavyavacchedya-sādhanavākyena[32] tu kevalaṃ sūcayitavye / na cānyataravākyena śakyam ubhayaṃ sūcayitum iti kuto 'nyataravākyavaiyarthyaṃ /

> ekasyaiva hi dharmasya kramāt trairūpyaniścayaḥ /
> vismṛtāv anumąbhāvāt tat kiṃ vyarthānumākhila // iti /

api ca saṃgrahaślokaḥ :

> bādhakāt sādhyasiddhiś ced vyartho hetvantaragrahaḥ /
> bādhakāt tadasiddhiś ced vyartho dharmyantaragrahaḥ //

32. Ed. text had *vākye na*, which is corrected to *vākyena* by the Tibetan translation.

yadi hi dharmiṇi vyāptiḥ sidhyaty[33] eva sādhyasiddhim antarbhāvayati / nanu lābha evaiṣaḥ vyāptiprasādhakād eva pramāṇāt sādhyasiddheḥ sattvahetvapāśrayaṇaprayāsasya nirasanāt / na hi vyasanam evaital liṅgāntarānusaraṇaṃ nāma / atha na vyāptisādhakāt sādhyasiddhiḥ / na tarhy-antarvyāptau hetuvaiyarthyam iti kim akāṇḍakātaratayā bahutaram āyāsam āviśasi /[34]

(10) Suppose it be said: "Accordingly, a thesis-feature (*sādhyadharma*) is indeed to be grasped when there is a factual base as receptacle for grasping the pervasion, like smoke and fire." (We reply:) No, because it is a proof of pervasion through just the role (*vṛtti*) of annulment (*bādhaka*), given the opposing side (*vipakṣa*) to the reason that is seen therein. Accordingly, you should know what is meant is that there is no proof at all at a moment prior to grasping the pervasion, because it must be inferred; and because when the pervasion is not proved, there is no engagement with inference. (Also) because for a different proving-method (*sādhana*) one does not pursue that aim: because even if one would pursue (that aim,), there would be no opportunity (*avasthā*); and because even if there were an opportunity, with no more than that, the effort is fruitless; and because in the opposite case there is no annulling the proof of pervasion with no more than the force of pervasion. (Also) because when the smoke and the fire are not witnessed, there is no proof of the presence of a material cause and effect. Were there proof of it, there would be no role for the annulling in the opposing side (*vipakṣa*). Thus in dependence on witnessing the two, there is proof of pervasion of smoke by fire; but not so of the actuality (*sattva*) and the moment (*kṣaṇa*), because there is proof of pervasion by the previously expressed rule (*nyāya*). Therefore, one should agree that the pervasion is proved (*setsyati*) by dint of the annulling of the actuality-only proven in a factual base there. Likewise, where there is inner pervasion. Now those, the pervasion and the locus-feature, are solely to be indicated by expression (*vākyena*) of the proving-method, ruling out their respective authority. And not by another expression is one able to indicate the two. Well, then, how is it that another expression is pointless?

> For the ascertainment of the triple-modes in sequence belongs to a single feature. Since there is no inference in the event of forgetfulness, that is always how inference is pointless.

33. For ed. text *sidhyanty*.
34. Tibetan at PTT, p. 105-5-2.

Moreover, a summary verse:

> If a thesis could be proved by way of an annulling, there would be no use to take up another reason. If it could not be proved by way of an annulling, there would be no use to take up another factual base.

For, should the pervasion be proved in the factual base, and one includes it in the proof of the thesis, is this not a profit? Because the thesis is proved precisely by the authority which proves the pervasion; and because one avoids attempting a recourse to the 'reason of an actuality' (*sattva-hetu*). Following that course, there is no 'addiction' (*vyasana*) called 'chasing another evidence'. However, if the thesis-proof is not by way of proving the pervasion, in that event, there not being inner pervasion, (we call it) 'pointlessness of the reason'. So why do you suffer the pain of hostility when there is no opportunity (to refute us)?

/ dvayaṃ hi bhavataḥ sādhyaṃ dṛṣṭāntadharmiṇi vṛttiḥ sādhyadharmiṇi ca / yathākramaṃ vyāptipakṣadharmatvayoḥ siddhyarthaṃ / na nu yadā pratiniyate dharmiṇi vivādaḥ tad bahirbhūte ca dharmiṇi vyāptigrahaṇaṃ tadānīṃ bhaved vaiyarthyaṃ / yadā tu vastumātre vivādaḥ tadā sarvavastuṣu hetor vṛttis tvayā 'pi sādhyā mayā 'pi ceti katamasmin dharmaṇi hetor vṛttisādhanaṃ mama vyarthaṃ bhaviṣyati / katham idānīṃ bahirvyāptir vivādādhikaraṇaṃ bhūta evānyatam asmin vyāptisādhanāt / tāvan mātralakṣaṇatvāñ ca sādhyadharminaḥ / bādhakaṃ pramāṇaṃ pravarttamānam antargatam api dharmiṇaṃ bahiṣkarotīti cet etad eva kathaṃ bādhakena pravarttamānenaiva tasmin sādhyasādhanāt / sādhyasaṃśayopagame sādhyadharmiṇi lakṣaṇopagamād iti cet ayuktam etat / bādhakamātrāt na sādhyasiddhir ity asmin pakṣe dharmyantaraparigrahavaiyarthyābhidhānāt / bādhakāt sādhyasiddhir ity asmiṃs tu pakṣe sādhanavaiyarthyam āpāditaṃ / tasmād bādhakamātreṇa sādhyāsiddhau na kvacit sandehanivṛttiḥ / sandehānivṛttau na sādhyāsiddhau na kvacit sandehanivṛttiḥ / sandehānivṛttau na bahiṣkaraṇam abahiṣkṛtaś[35] ca sādhyadharmy eveti /[36]

35. For *bahiṣ-* and *abahiṣ-*, the ed. Sanskrit text had *vahiṣ-* and *avahiṣ*.
36. Tibetan at PTT, p. 106-1-1.

(11) According to you, sirs, there are two theses: 1. occurring in the factual base of the example; 2. occurring in the factual base of the thesis—in that order, so as to prove the pervasion of the locus-feature. Moreoever, (according to you, sirs), were there a dispute (*vivāda)* at the time when the factual base is particularly determined (*pratiniyate*), then at that time when the factual base be external, a grasping of the pervasion would be pointless. But at the time there is a dispute regarding just a given thing, at that time the role of a reason regarding all given things would have to be proven by yourself as well as by me; so in regard to which factual base will my reason's proving-method of role (*vṛtti*) turn out pointless? What in this situation is the external pervasion? Suppose one says: "It externalizes the ground of dispute, be it either from the proving-method of pervasion or from the extent-character of the thesis-factual base; and (externalizes) the current annulling authority, also the interior factual base." (We ask:) How must that happen? Suppose this one replies: "in this situation, by the current annulling, from the proving-method of the thesis: or in the event of the thesis-factual base experiencing doubt of the thesis; or in the event of the thesis, from experiencing the character." (We respond:) That is not right, because by definition (the formulation) "There is no proof of a thesis by just annulling" is the pointlessness, given the locus for accepting another factual base; and because (the formulation) "There is proof of a thesis by annulling" is an announcement of pointlessness, given this locus of the proving-method (*sādhana*). Therefore, when the proof of the thesis is just by annulling, there is no end at all to doubt. As long as doubt is not ended, there is no externalization. And when not externalized, there is just the thesis-factual base—we say.

/ tatra vyāptir antarvyāptir eva nedānīm bahirvyāpter vārttā 'pi / tad iyam bahirvyāptir amusmin pakṣe kathaṃ bhavati yadi pratiniyate dharmiṇi vivādaḥ / tadbahirbhūte ca dharmiṇi vyāptigrahaṇaṃ bhavati / tatra ca duruddharaḥ dharmyantaraparigrahavaiyarthyadoṣaḥ / bādhakamātreṇa tu sādhyasiddhau hetv-antaram eva vyarthaṃ / api ca sattvahetor viśeṣeṇa na bahirvyāptisambhavaḥ /

> asiddhe dharmiṇaḥ sattve vivādānavatārataḥ /
> tatrāsiddhasya ca vyāptigrahaṇe sādhyadharmiṇi //
> vyāptigrahaḥ kathaṃ na syād dṛṣṭānte 'pi na vā bhavet //

yatra hi dharmiṇi dṛṣṭasya hetor vyāptiḥ pratīyate tatra tasya vyāptigrahaṇam ākhyāyate / dṛṣṭañ ca sādhyadharmiṇi sattvam anyathā vimatyayogād iti katham nāntarvyāptiḥ /[37]

(12) So therein the pervasion is just internal pervasion; not in this situation does external pervasion operate. Well, then, how does this external pervasion behave when there is yonder locus? If there is a dispute regarding the factual base that is determined, and (if) there is a grasping of pervasion in the factual base that is exterior to it (i.e. the locus)—here it is difficult to avoid the fault of pointlessness of accepting the different factual base, for when the proof of the thesis is merely by annulling, precisely a different reason is pointless. Accordingly:

> When there is an actuality (*sattva*) of a factual base, it is unproven because not subject to dispute. In that case, (it is) when there is grasping of pervasion and when there is the thesis-factual base—to wit, of what is unproven.
> Why would there not be a grasp of pervasion even when there is no example (*dṛṣṭānta*)?

For wherever the pervasion of a reason witnessed in a factual base cognitively dawns, in that place the grasping of its pervasion is declared. Given an actuality witnessed in a thesis-factual base—because it is not possible to disagree otherwise[38]—why is there not internal pervasion?

/ tathāpi sādhanavaiyarthyaniṣedhāya bahir eva gṛhṇīm iti cet tat kim idānīṃ tvadicchānurodhāt dharmiṇi hetor darśanam adarśanam astu / darśanaviśeṣe vā bahir eva vyāptigrahaṇavyavasthāstu / ubhayatra dṛṣṭasya vyāptigrahaṇe 'py asti bahirvyāptibhāga iti cet / nanu kim artham iyān bhāgo yatnena saṃrakṣyate / mābhūt hetuvaiyarthyam iti cet / nanu yadi bādhakavṛttimātreṇa vyāptigrahaṇādhikaraṇe dharmiṇi sādhyasiddheḥ sādhanavaiyarthyam antarvyāptau tad etad bahirvyāptāv api tulyaṃ / tasmād vyasanamātraṃ bahirvyāptigrahaṇe viśeṣeṇa sattve hetau kevalaṃ jaḍadhiyām eva niyamena dṛṣṭāntasapekṣaḥ sādhanaprayogaḥ paritoṣāya jāyate / teṣām evānugrahārtham ācāryo dṛṣṭāntam upādatte / yat sat tat kṣaṇikaṃ yathā ghaṭa iti / paṭumatayas tu naivaṃ

37. Tibetan at PTT, p. 106-1-6.

38. Śānti-pā seems here to make the point that people, after all, could not disagree on anything if they were not able to agree on something, called the 'actuality' (*sattva*).

dṛṣṭāntam apekṣante /

> tasmād dṛṣṭantar*akt*[39] ebhyo ghaṭaṃ dṛṣṭāntam abravīt /
> tathā māneṣv avaiyarthād antarvyāptāv apīṣyatām //

ity antaraślokaḥ /[40]

(13) Suppose you say, "Accordingly, we accept precisely the external one for opposing a pointlessness of the proving-method." Then, for obliging your claim in this situation, may there be your sight of the reason in the factual base— [so far] (your) nonsight! Or in the particular event of seeing (it), may there be your decision to grasp the pervasion just as 'external'! Suppose you say, "There is a portion (*bhaga*) of external pervasion even in grasping the pervasion of the witnessed in both places." Then why do you not watch zealously this much portion! Suppose you say, "Let there not be a pointlessness of the reason." Well, according to (the theory of) internal pervasion the pointlessness of the proving-method is of a proof of thesis in a factual base whose ground for accepting the pervasion is just by the role of the annulling. If that is the way it is according to (the theory of) external pervasion, it is the same (for both of us). Therefore, it is only an 'addiction' to accept as an external pervasion in the particular situation when the reason is an actuality. The syllogism *sādhana* with reliance on an example is brought up just by obligation for pleasing those of dull mind. In order to assist them the *ācārya* (master) points to an example (to wit), "What exists is momentary, like a pot." Those of sharp mind do not depend on an example. A medial verse:

> Therefore, he told the example 'pot' for those who crave an example. May one accept internal pervasion, since that way it is not pointless to have authorities (*māna* = *pramāṇa*).

/ katham idānīm anumeye sattvam eva sapakṣa eva sattvam asapakṣe vāsattvam eva niścitam iti hetos trirūpyam avagantavyam /

> matau sapakṣāsapakṣau sādhyadharmayutāyutau /
> sattvāsattve tatra hetos te grāhye yatra tatra vā //

sādhyadharmayuktaḥ sarvaḥ sāmānyena sapakṣaḥ; atadyuktaś

39. The ed. Sanskrit text had *rokte* (as though *ra* + ukte). The Tibetan *chags rnams,* at PTT, p. 106-2-2 (end), supports the better reading.
40. Tibetan at PTT, p. 106-2-3.

cāsapakṣa iti / tasmin sapakṣa eva sattvam asapakṣe cāsattvam eva yathākramam anvayavyatirekau tau punar yatra tatra vā dharmiṇi grahītavyau yatra śakyau grahītum /[41]

(14) How in this situation may one understand the triple-modes of the reason as certain when the inferable has just a similar locus toward just an actuality or has a dissimilar locus toward just a nonactuality?

> The actuality or nonactuality there of the reason is (respectively) claimed to be accepted where is the similar locus, or there is the dissimilar locus; where it is accompanied by the thesis-feature, or there it is unaccompanied (by the thesis-feature).[42]

That means: All accompanied by a thesis-feature are of similar locus in the sense of generality; and unaccompanied by it are of dissimilar locus. The actuality is just in the similar locus, the nonactuality just in the dissimilar locus. In the given order they are the *anvaya* (presence in similar case) or *vyatireka* (absence in dissimilar case). Furthermore, where or there they be, to be grasped in a feature base (*dharmin*), therein they are capable to be grasped.

/ tad iha sattvasya sarvato 'kṣaṇikād vyāvṛttau bādhakabalāt siddhāyāṃ yat sat tat kṣaṇikam eveti anvayaḥ sādhyadharmiṇy avagṛhyate / tatra dṛṣṭasya hetor vyāptigrahaṇāt dharmy-antarāsambhavāt / sambhave 'pi tad-anusaraṇavaiyarthyāt / yady evam asādhāraṇo nāma katham anaikāntika uktaḥ /

> asādhāraṇatāṃ hetudoṣam mūḍhavyapekṣayā //
> abravīd agrahād vyāpti(te)r naivaṃ sarvopasaṃhṛtau //

uktam etaj jaḍadhiyo dharmy-antara eva vyāptigrahaṇaṃ pratipannāḥ / tad abhimānāpekṣayā 'sādhāraṇam anaikāntikam āha śrāvaṇatvaṃ dṛṣṭāntābhāvāt / sādhyadharmiṇi ca vyāptir aniṣṭer agṛhītāyāṃ vyāptau sandigdhobhayatayā 'niścayakaratvāt / athavā asādhāraṇataiva śrāvaṇatvasya mūḍhābhmānopakalpita / dṛṣṭaiva hi śabdavyaktidharmiṇī vivādādhikaraṇāt / anyathā dharmy-asiddhiprasaṅgāñ ca / dṛṣṭādṛṣṭaśabdavyaktisādhāraṇañ ca

41. Tibetan at PTT, p. 106-2-6.

42. The purport of this particular verse and subsequent amplification seems to be the position of the *antarvyāpti* defenders, since there is no statement alluding to the opponent for such viewpoints.

śrāvaṇatvaṃ hetuḥ / dhūmasāmānyavat / tataḥ sarvopasaṃhāravat yāḥ vyāpteḥ sambhavāt sattvādivad aduṣṭam[43] eva sādhanaṃ śrāvaṇatvākhyaṃ / kramayaugapadyānupalambha eva cātra bādhakaṃ pramāṇaṃ / śrotrajñānajanakatvam eva hi śrāvaṇatvaṃ / tasmān mūḍhavyapekṣayā 'sādhāraṇatvāt / asādhāraṇasya sarvopasaṃhārāyogāt / sādhyatvāt / asādhāraṇasya sarvopasaṃhārāyogāt / sādhyadharmiṇi vyāptirpratītāv eva sādhyapratīteḥ sādhanavaiphalyaṃ syād eva / tan mābhūd vaiphalyam iti naiva vyāptir grahītavyā / tasyām agṛhītāyāṃ sandigdhobhayatayā syād anaikāntikatvaṃ / sarvopasaṃhāreṇa tu vyāptigrahaṇe yathoktanyāyena sādhana-vaiphalyābhāvāt / aduṣṭaṃ sattvādi sādhanam eveti veditavyam / tad evam ubhayathā mūḍhajanāpekṣayā 'sādhāraṇam anaikāntikam uktam /[44]

(15) Therefore, when here the exclusion (*vyāvṛtti*), proved by dint of annulling, is of nonmomentariness on all sides of the actuality (*sattva*), one says: "Whatever exists is momentary." The *anvaya* (presence in similar case) is apprehended in the thesis-factual base; because one apprehends the pervasion of the reason that is witnessed therein; because there is no possibility of a different factual base, and even if it were possible, it would be pointless to pursue it. If thus it is 'too restricted' (*asādhāraṇa*) why is it called 'uncertain (evidence)'?

> Because of the deluded resort to a fault of reason, i.e. to the too restricted, he declared: "through non-apprehension of the pervasion, when not all is encompassed that way."

Saying that, he declared that those of dull minds engage the apprehension of pervasion in just another factual base by conceited resort to it, and so he stated the 'too restricted' kind of uncertain (evidence); because there is no example for the audibility; because there is no claim that the pervasion is in the thesis-factual base; and because when the pervasion is not apprehended, there is uncertainty by double doubt. Besides, the too restricted state of the audible is an imagination of deluded conceit; because it is a ground for quarrel that there are two factual bases—the witnessed (one) and the clarity of word; moreover, because it entails nonproof of the

43. For ed. text *adṛṣṭa*; correction per Tibetan at PTT, p. 106-4-2, *skyon med pa*.
44. Tibetan at PTT, p. 106-4-2. The Sanskrit appears to have a sentence lacking in Tibetan.

factual base. And there is the unrestricted (evidence)' (*sādhāraṇa*), e.g. the witnessed and the unwitnessed, and the clarity of word, like the generality of smoke as the cause for audibility. Then, because of the possibility of pervasion that encompasses all, there is no fault in saying that the proving method is audible in the manner of an actuality,. etc. In this situation, the non-apprehension of sequence and simultaneity is the annulling authority; and generation of the hearing cognition is the audibility. Therefore, the proving-method might be (*syād eva*) pointless; because too restricted by deluded resort; because of impossibility to encompass all of the too restricted; and because there is cognitive dawning of the thesis when there is cognitive dawning of the pervasion in the thesis-factual base. One would not grasp the pervasion just by saying, "May it not be pointless!" There would be uncertainty by double doubt of not apprehending it. Since the proving-method is free from pointlessness by way of the aforementioned rule, by encompassing all when there is apprehension of pervasion, one should understand that precisely it is the faultless proving-method in the manner of an actuality, etc. Accordingly is stated the too-restricted kind of uncertainty in both ways, by resort of deluded persons.

/ *sādhanañ*[45] caitad bahirvyāptivādinām apí yadi hi mūḍhamatāpekṣā na syāt syād eva śrāvaṇatvam aduṣṭo hetuḥ / sattvādivan niyataśabdeṣu hi vivāde śabdāntaraṃ syāt / dṛṣṭāntaḥ sarvaśabdeṣu vigatau bādhakaṃ pramāṇaṃ pravarttamānaṃ adṛṣṭāntam api tatraikaṃ dṛṣṭānta*yutīti*[46] katham asādhāraṇam anaikāntikaṃ veti /

(16) And that proving-method (*sādhana*) also belongs to followers of external pervasion, if it were not by resort to deluded opinion; and if it were the faultless cause for audibility. For when there is a quarrel regarding the words that are determined, like an actuality, etc., there would be a different word, to wit, the 'example', in the sense of deviation (*vigatau*) in all words. Even though the annulling authority proceeds without an example, therein is a unit. When an example is added, is how there is the too-restricted kind of uncertainty.[47]

---

45. Ed. text has *samānañ*, corrected by Tibetan *sgrub par byed pa*, at PTT, p. 106-4-1.
46. For ed. text *yatīti*.
47. Finally, Śānti-pā blames the example for one of the two kinds of uncertainty of the reason, the one called 'too-restricted' (*asādhāraṇa*). Thus he charges that the very example which is ordinarily thought to clarify, turns out to be a limitation

antarvyāptisamarthanaṃ samāptam iti //
kṛtir iyaṃ ratnākaraśāntipādānām iti //
The *Antarvyāptisamarthanam* thus concludes. Its author is Ratnākaraśānti (or Śānti-pā).[48]

Granted that there are some matters brought up by Śānti-pā that are not sufficiently clarified, either in this author's own exposition, or in the rather few explanatory notes of the translator. In my Millennium, Vol. Two, I expect again to treat the problem of pervasion (*vyāpti*), hopefully to further clarify some of these issues.

---

on understanding, perhaps substituting the example for the 'actuality', or forgetting the original 'factual base' (*dharmin*) in favor of the one occupied by the example. The term *vigatau* as the locative of *vigati* appears to have the grammatical locative of the Dhātupāṭhas, employed for definition, in the sense of deviation—as the Tibetan suggests (p. 106-4-3): *log par rtog pa* (deviant reflection').

48. There has been modern work on various facets of this author's writing. Padmanabh S. Jaini edited his *Sāratamā*, a Pañjikā on the *Aṣṭasāhasrikā Prajñāpāramitā*; Michael Hahn studied a part of his *Chandoratnākara*, "On the Pratyaya Rules of Ratnākaraśānti," *Journal of the Oriental Institute*, XXX, 1-2, Sept.-Dec. 1980, pp. 61-77; I worked through his commentary on the *Sarvarahasyatantra* for my translation of this text, which appeared in *Acta Indologica*, 1984 issue (Naritasan Shinshoji, Japan); and so on, suggesting Śānti-pā's voluminous writings in both tantric and nontantric Buddhism.

PART II

THE DIGNĀGA-DHARMAKĪRTI SYSTEM

INTRODUCTION TO THE DIGNĀGA-DHARMAKĪRTI SYSTEM BY THE 'ELEVENS'

This section is devoted to exposing five sets of eleven verses each, namely, the first eleven verses in the Pratyakṣa chapter of Dignāga's PS; and the first eleven verses in each of the four chapters of Dharmakīrti's PV, i.e. PV-Sid, PV-Prat, PV-Sva, and PV-Par. In the following part of this section entitled "PS, Prat, first eleven verses" I explain how the number 'eleven' is arrived at. Having found this to be the case for the first section in Dignāga's work I took this as a numerical suggestion to translate, for introductory purposes, the first eleven verses in each of PV's chapters. I compared these sets of PV, leaving out PV-Sid, with the three chapters of P-Vin in terms of their outlines as depicted in the present work. This leads to the intriguing observation that the first eleven verses of PV-Par seem to cover the outline of P-Vin-Par except for the last part on 'examples' which occupy a separate chapter in PS on 'example' (*dṛṣṭānta*) and its fallacies. The observation of the contents in these sets of eleven verses immediately supports the Sanskrit-text order of chapters in PV. This is because the first chapter of the Sanskrit text is the *Pramāṇasiddhi*, whose first eleven verses distinguish between *pramāṇa* and non-*pramāṇa*, the most introductory of topics; while the first chapter in the PV, Tibetan version in the Tanjur, is the *Svārthānumāna*, whose first eleven verses are devoted to the advanced topic of the three kinds of reason (*hetu*). Another result involving particularly the PV-Par verses in comparison with my P-Vin-Par analysis, and with the Parārthānumāna treatment in the text translated from Tibetan (*Guided Tour*) in the present work, is that in all likelihood Dharmakīrti kept Dignāga's exposition of PS-Par and the 'fallacies' pretty much intact; and that it was in Pratyakṣa and Svārthānumāna that Dharmakīrti made some advances beyond the Dignāga system. Consistent with this observation is the fact that Dharmakīrti wrote a *Svavṛtti* (self-commentary) on PV-Sva.

PS, PRAT
FIRST ELEVEN VERSES

Below, I shall show how to determine the first eleven verses of Dignāga's PS, Prat. Here he makes some important points that became characteristic of Buddhist logic thereafter. He maintains only two kinds of *pramāṇa,* which I render 'authority'. These two he names 'direct perception' (*pratyakṣa*) and 'inference' (*anumāna*). He maintains that they are 'authorities' because they are authorized by their two objects, the *prameya,* which I therefore render 'sanction(s)', and which therefore precede the 'authorities'. The *prameya* are the two characters (*lakṣaṇa*), not here named, but which are the individual (*sva-*) and the generality (*sāmānya-*) characters. The two authorities do not lack these introducing characters. Besides, by rejecting memory as an authority, Dignāga anticipates the stress on authority's being 'new', i.e. not previously there. There are four kinds of 'direct perception', namely, sense perception by the five senses, mind perception, introspection, and yogin's perception. In verse 3 he first describes the five-senses kind, and his remark can be stated this way: from a valid particular (*bheda*) (e.g. a single sense organ) it is not valid to make a generality (*sāmānya*) (e.g. a factual base for multiple features). Mental perception is like the outer senses in that it can entertain objects in the manner of a sense organ and yet be without constructive thought. In the case of introspection, Dignāga uses the term *svasaṃvitti,* while the standard form in later times is *svasaṃvedana.* This introspection has as its object any interior given thing, thus even constructive thought is admitted as an object for introspection (which itself is devoid of constructive thought); the object is here called an 'image' (*ākāra*). Asserting that the yogin's vision of the object is unmixed with the guru's instruction, agrees with the previous rejection of memory as an authority; such guru instruction is ordinarily in the form of remembered precepts. This does not constitute a downgrading of such traditional lore; rather a regarding of it as a sanction, *prameya,* rather than a *pramāṇa.* Hence, sentences of Dharma, as distinguished types of constructive thought, are appropriate objects of introspection.

Then Dignāga points out that perception is a semblance in various ways, and scholars have written articles in clarification.

The implication that the *prameya* precedes the *pramāṇa* is behind the insistence that 'authority' is a result (*kārya*) and that it is attended with (i.e. introduced by) a function (*vyāpāra*). This function when attending *pratyakṣa* would be the purposive activity (*arthakriyā*) of the individual character (*svalakṣaṇa*); while the attending *anumāna* would be the constructive thought 'wishing to speak'. This introducing function (the *vyāpāra*) is the only instrument—it is instrumental to the result called *pramāṇa*. It should be observed that Hindu and Jain opponents of the Buddhist logicians preferred an instrumental value for *pramana*; and we should recognize this to appreciate their positions, just as we should recognize the usage of the term by the Buddhist logicians to appreciate their positions. For example, 'impermanence' (*anityatā*) is not an 'authority' in Buddhism, for it is a 'sanction' (*prameya*), a function that helps toward 'authority' (*pramāṇa*).

Dignāga's insistence (in k.11) that a sense object is experienced by only one cognition, seems consistent with the general Indian theory of the sense-organ as a power to cognize the particular object. Hence, there is no 'old' cognition that cognizes a former as well as a present object. So Dignāga states in k.10 that there are two forms of cognition—the new cognition of an object, and that cognition which is influenced by memory.

Establishing the Beginning of Dignāga's *Pramāṇasamuccaya*

My study of a remarkable Tibetan work on logic, that by Bu-ston, editor of the Kanjur and Tanjur, namely his extensive commentary (the *Ṭīk*) on Dharmakīrti's *Pramāṇaviniścaya,* has led me to reevaluate Masaaki Hattori's solution in *Perception* about the Tibetan *kārikā* in the *Pratyakṣa* chapter of Dignāga's celebrated *PS.* Hattori's work represents a great step forward in the study of Buddhist logic, for which see my review. Therefore, the corrections to be set forth below are not meant to detract from his work, which should continue to be very helpful in these matters. Hattori (*Perception,* pp. 17-18) gives reasons for deciding that the two *kārikā* texts of *PS* in the Tanjur are not independent of the two translations of Dignāga's own *Vṛtti,* but were in fact extracted from the *PSV.* A compelling reason for making an adjustment, as Hattori acknowledges, is that in the Tanjur texts of the *kārikā* two sections of the *Pratyakṣa* chapter fail to have integral numbers of the verses but have extra half-verses. He decided that a certain set of two seven-syllable segments (= one-half Sanskrit *śloka*) was just part of the *Vṛtti* and not actually verse in the first section, and besides decided to amend this very set to drop a negative syllable—which he carefully tried to justify in his notes (*Perception*, p. 100). At the outset we should agree with Hattori that it is justified to drop somewhere a half-verse to make integral numbers. However, what is questionable is whether he picked the right half-verse to drop.

Now, of Hattori's solution to end up with 12 verses in the first section is due to his inclusion as *kārikā* no. 1 the introductory salutation verse. But this verse is for the entire work, not just the *Pratyakṣa* chapter. Besides, in the *PV* itself, the initial two introductory verses are put at the beginning of the Sanskrit text which presents the *Pramāṇasiddhi* as first chapter. They are also put at the beginning of the Tibetan version following a tradition that puts the *Svārthānumāna* chapter first. Hence, those two introductory verses are independent of the *PV* chapters. In the case of Bu-ston's *Ṭīk* on *PVin*, first this Tibetan author writes a brief commentary on the title and salutation verse; and proceeds to a separately entitled commentary on the *PVin* itself. Finally, Louis de La Vallée Poussin was undoubtedly correct in his edited Sanskrit text of Candrakīrti's commentary on Nāgārjuna's *Madhyamakakārikā* to start Chapter One with the verse *na svato* . . ., which is not the salutation verse. Therefore, in my numbering of the *Pratyakṣa* Chapter of *PS*, first section, I omit the initial salutation. Hence, the integral number of verses in the *Pratyakṣa* chapter, first section, is 11.

Then we notice that Bu-ston cites the whole verse (my number 7) of four seven-syllable lines from which Hattori decided to drop the second half from the *kārikā* text; and furthermore Bu-ston cites this with the double-negative line, which Hattori insists we should amend by omitting one negative. Bu-ston also cites what appears to be a half-*kārikā* that Hattori admits: his k. 4cd (*Perception*, p. 26, for the translation). But examining this supposed half-verse we observe even in Hattori's translation the initial Tibetan word *der* (= Skt. *tatra*) rendered "there" and bracketted "in the above-cited Abhidharma passages." Thus it is clear that this particular set of two seven-syllable lines is just part of the *Vṛtti*, since it refers to the immediately previous *Vrtti* mention of abhidharma positions, and does not refer to the previous *kārikā* or half-*kārikā*. It follows that once we agree with

Hattori that a certain half-*kārikā* should be dropped so that the total verses of the section will be of integral number, it follows that it is this set of two seven-syllables that should be dropped from the *kārikā* text and not the one that Hattori picked. My own solution of which half-*kārikā* to drop improves rather strikingly the verse numbering of Dignāga's *Pratyakṣa,* first section. Thus, Dignāga's verse about *pratyakṣābhāsa* is in my solution given its own verse number (no. 6); whereas in Hattori's numbering, it is 7cd-8ab, as though Dignāga had allotted half the verse to one *kārikā* and the second half to the next *kārikā.*

The foregoing sets the stage for citing the entire text of Tibetan verses of *PS-Prat,* first section, in the way that Bu-ston cited them in Vol. Ya of his collected works, with indication of the respective place (e.g. 'fol. 18b') in this commentary, *P-Vin-Bu,* my signal for this native Tibetan commentary, the *Pramāṇaviniścaya-ṭīk.* Any part of the Tibetan not cited by him will be taken from the 'Kanakavarman' version in the Tibetan Tanjur and be bracketed in my edition of these 11 verses, as follows:

> Dignāga's PS, Pratyakṣa chapter, Sec. 1; Tibetan kārikā edited by A. Wayman, with folio references to P-Vin-Bu; and English translation.

1. / mṅon sum daṅ ni rjes su dpag /
/ tshad ma'o mtshan ñid gñis gźal bya /
/ de la rab sbyor phyir tshad ma /
/ gźan ni yod pa ma yin no // (fol. 18b)

There are two authorities (*pramāṇa*)—direct perception (*pratyakṣa*) and inference (*anumāna*). The sanction (*prameya*) is two characters (*lakṣaṇa*). In the sense of being enjoined, they are authorities. There are no other (authorities).

2. / yaṅ yaṅ śes pa'aṅ ma yin te /
/ thug pa med 'gyur dran sogs bźin / (fol. 18b)
/ miṅ daṅ rigs sogs sbyor ba yi /
/ rtog pa daṅ bral mṅon sum mo // (fol. 22a)

Nor are (authorities) those like memory, and so forth, that repeatedly cognize and reduce to an endless series (*anavasthā-prasaṅga*). Direct perception is free from constructive thought (*kalpanā*) which adds a name, class, etc.

3. / thun moṅ min pa'i rgyu yi phyir /
/ de yi tha sñad dbaṅ pos byas / (fol. 23a)
/ du ma'i ṅo bo'i chos can ni /
/ dbaṅ po las rtogs srid ma yin // (fol. 35a)

Its name (viz. *pratyakṣa* = direct[ed] perception) is called by a sense organ (*akṣa*) because of the unshared causes (viz., *prati*= 'each one'). A factual base (*dharmin*) for multiple natures can in no case be understood from a (single) sense-organ.

4. / raṅ raṅ rig bya tha sñad kyis /
/ bstan min ṅo bo dbaṅ po'i yul / (fol. 35b)
/ yid kyaṅ don daṅ [chags la sogs /
/ raṅ rig rtog pa med pa yin] // (fol. 39a)

The nature in the range of a sense is to be individually experienced, and cannot be (verbally) designated. Also, the mental (sense) having the object-entity (*artha*) as well as self-intuition (*svasaṃvitti*) of passion (*rāga*), etc., are without constructive thought.

5. / rnal 'byor rnams kyi bla mas bstan /
/ ma 'dres pa yi don tsam mthoṅ / (fol. 55b)
/ rtog pa' aṅ raṅ rig ñid du 'dod /
/ don la ma yin der rtog phyir // (fol. 42b)

(Also), the yogins' vision of just the object unmixed with the guru's instruction. Even constructive thought is admitted for self-intuition because the constructive thought there is not toward an (external) object.

6. / 'khrul daṅ kun rdzob yod śes daṅ /
/ rjes dpag rjes du dpag las byuṅ /
/ dran daṅ mṅon 'dod ces bya 'o /
/ mṅon sum ltar snan rab rib bcas // (fol. 59b)

Semblance of perception is (of the varieties) (a) delusive cognition, (b) cognition of conventional existence, (c) (the set, viz.) inference, derived from inference, derived from memory, derived from belief; (d) along with sensory affliction.

7. / bya daṅ bcas pa rtogs pa'i pa'i phyir /
/ 'bras bu ñid yin 'jal byed la /
/ tshad ma ñid du 'dogs pa ste /
/ bya ba med pa'aṅ ma yin no // (fol. 60b)

Since one realizes it is attended with (in fact, introduced by) function (*vyāpāra*), the authority (*pramāṇa*) is just a result (*kārya*); and one calls it an 'authority' when it does not lack the (introducing) function.

8. / yaṅ na raṅ rig 'bras bu yin /
/ de yi ṅo bo las don ṅes / (fol. 70b)
/ yul gyi snaṅ ba ñid de 'di'i /
/ tshad ma de yis' jal bar byed // (fol. 70b)

Furthermore, the introspection here is a result, for from the nature of that [result] is certainty (*niścaya*) of the object-entity (*artha*). That very appearance of the object is judged by its authority.

9. / gaṅ tshe snaṅ ba de gźal bya /
/ tshad ma daṅ de'i 'bras bu ni /
/ 'dzin rnam rig pa'o de yi phyir /
/ de gsum tha dad du ma byas // (fol. 72a-b)

At the time the sanction (*prameya*) is apparent, by reason of it, there are three, to wit, the authority, the result of that [sanction], and the apprehending intuition. But one should not take those as different.

10. / yul śes pa daṅ de śes pa'i /
/ dbye bas blo yi tshul gñis ñid / (fol. 78b)
/ [dus phyis dran pa las kyaṅ ṅo /
/ gaṅ phyir ma myoṅ bar 'di med'] //

There are two forms of cognition by distinction of (a) cognition of a sense object, and (b) that cognition—(respectively) because of memory at a subsequent time; and because there is no (memory) in the absence of the already-experienced.

11. / [śes pa gźan gyis ñams myoṅ na /
/ thug med de la'aṅ dran pa ste /
/ de ltar yul gźan dag la 'pho /
/ med 'gyur de yaṅ 'dod pa'o] //

If it were experienced by a different cognition, there would be memory in an endless series. Accordingly, there is no shift (of a cognition) to other objects, but this is held [in some quarters].

PV-SID

FIRST ELEVEN VERSES

Bu-ston cites this chapter for his extremely brief work explaining the title *Pramāṇaviniścaya*, and his citations are within the first eleven verses. Since *PV-Sid* is not represented by a chapter in P-Vin, Bu-ston's choices agree that most elementary statement of the system is in PV-Sid, and precisely in these verses. The basic exposition found here is the discrimination between 'authority' (*pramāṇa*) and non-authority. But one should also observe that the matters dealt with here are topics of dispute, and that the further discussions become very detailed, with fine distinctions.

We have previously met with the discussion of *pramāṇa* as of two kinds—direct perception (*pratyakṣa*) and inference (*anumāna*). These are faculties. But *PV-Sid* uses the term *pramāṇa* also for the 'authoritative person', i.e. the Buddha, who "*is* the authority" (*pramāṇabhūta*). Then verse 8a, b, c, "There is no eternal authority . . ." consistent with a celebrated passage of Buddhist literature, "Whether Tathāgatas arise or not ... " Since the knowable affects the knowing, the impermanence of the knowable disallows an eternal authority.

Verse 9cd stipulates that an authority be "helped," since the authority is in the Dignāga-Dharmakīrti system a result (*kārya*) and the object-function is taken as "helping." Impermanence is not helped, so it is not possibly an authority; but as an appropriate meditative object in Buddhism, impermanence can help.

Dharmakīrti insists that the perception of an individual character (*svalakṣaṇa*) must precede the inference of a generality character (*sāmānyalakṣaṇa*). This is implied in *PV-Sid,* verse 1, first stating, "Authority is a non-deceptive cognition"; then alluding to two scopes of non-deception, "Non-deception is the rule of purposive activity (*arthakriyā*) and is also in speech in that it reveals intention." Then inference is a kind of discursive thought (*kalpanā*) that is non-deceptive. But there are also fallacies of inference, as were already detailed by Dignāga (e.g. in *PS,* Jātiparīkṣā chapter), so inference is not always an authority, i.e. non-deceptive. This recalls the term *samyagdṛṣṭi* ('right views') as a member of the Eightfold Noble Path of Buddhism, while *dṛṣṭi* often connotes false views. Thus, the Buddhist insistence that some 'views' are right ones, leads to a theory that some 'inferences' are valid ones, namely 'non-deceptive'. This non-deception is found in "speech in that it reveals intention". Here again, it should be acknowledged that much speech does not reveal intention. So here it is a certain kind of speech that is referred to, namely, that kind which does reveal intention.

Now comes a delicate distinction, since Dharmakīrti has the task of disallowing as authority any derivative cognition that "apprehends what was already apprehended", while allowing for an authoritative discrimination to validate the Buddhist path of rejecting the bad and accepting the good. Starting with verse 4d, Dharmakīrti makes it difficult for a translator by intending some remarks to go with the adversaries and some to go with the Buddhist logicians themselves. For 4d-5a, Sastri's Sanskrit edition (his nos. 6d-7a) provides a heading "Mīmāṃsakamatakhaṇḍanam" (opposition by Mīmāṃsaka position). It is true that the statement "the comprehension of the true form (*svarūpa*) is from oneself" is a position of the Vedānta (the 'later Mīmāṃsā') which holds that one can realize the true form by a process of 'annulling' (*bādha*) within oneself; but those who take the authoritativeness by conventional language would probably be the realists, the Nyāya-Vaiśeṣika. The Buddhist logician's position is in 5bc (Sastri Skt., no. 7bc) with the line, "A śāstra averts delusion." This is because a *śāstra* ('religious treatise', here meaning a good one) has the better kind of inference directed thereto, apparently the only kind of inference that helps avert delusion.

PV-Sid, 1-11, Sanskrit and English

1. pramāṇam avisaṃvādi jñānam arthakriyāsthitiḥ /
   avisaṃvādanaṃ śābde 'py abhiprāyanivedanāt //
   Authority is a non-deceptive cognition. Non-deception is the rule of purposive activity, and is also in speech in that it reveals intention.
2. vaktṛvyāpāraviṣayo yo 'rtho buddhau prakāśate /
   prāmāṇyaṃ tatra śabdasya nārthatattvanibandhanam //
   The sense object whose function goes with a speaker is the object-entity which appears in cognition. In that (cognition) the authoritativeness of the communication [as heard] is independent of the object-entity's reality.
3. gṛhītagrahaṇān neṣṭaṃ sāṃvṛtaṃ dhīpramāṇatā /
   pravṛttes tatpradhānatvāt heyopādeyavastuni //
   Because it apprehends what was already apprehended, a derivative convention is not claimed (as authority). There

is authority of a (discriminating) cognition when a given thing is to be rejected or accepted, because it (the discriminating cognition) is the main thing for the function;

4abc. viṣayākārabhedāc ca dhiyo 'dhigamabhedataḥ /
bhāvād evāsya tadbhāve;
because the separate understandings of cognition are due to the separate images of sense objects; and because there is presence of those (understandings) just when there is presence of those (separate images).

4d-5c. svarūpasya svato gatiḥ //
prāmāṇyaṃ vyavahāreṇa śāstraṃ mohanivartanam /
ajñātārthaprakāśo vā;
(Some say:) the comprehension of the true form (*svarūpa*) is from oneself; (or say:) authoritativeness is by conventional language (*vyavahāra*); (we say:) a *śāstra* averts delusion; besides, (an authority) reveals the unknown object-entity.

5d-6b. svarūpādhigateḥ param //
prāptaṃ sāmānyavijñānam avijñāte svalakṣaṇe /
(Some say:) After comprehension of the true form, perception of generality (*sāmānya*) is met with, even when an individual character (*svalakṣaṇa*) has not been perceived.

6cd-7. yaj jñānamity abhiprāyāt svalakṣaṇavicārataḥ //
tadvat pramāṇaṃ bhagavāt abhūtavinivṛttaye /
bhūtoktiḥ sādhanāpekṣā tato yuktā pramāṇatā //
(We say:) Because having the intention, "Which cognition?;" and because examining the individual character. The authority having those [two] is the Bhagavat. To reject the (challenge), "He is not (such an authority)" there is the saying (by the master Dignāga), "He is (the authority)." The authoritativeness relies on a means of proof (*sādhana*) and then is valid.

8. nityaṃ pramāṇaṃ naivāsti prāmāṇyād vastusadgateḥ /
jñeyānityatayā tasyā adhrauvyāt kramajanmanām//
There is no eternal authority, because authoritativeness comprehends the existence of a given thing (*vastu*); because there is no constancy of that [comprehension] due to the impermanence of the knowable; and [no constancy] of those born in sequence.

9ab. nityād utpattiviśleṣād apekṣāyā ayogataḥ /
Because it is not valid that there is arising from the permanent, and because it is not fit (for the permanent) to be dependent.

9cd. kathaścin nopakāryatvāt anitye 'py apramāṇatā //
Because it is not helped at all, impermanence (the non-eternal) is also not an authority.

10. sthitvā pravṛttiḥ saṃsthānaviśeṣārthakriyādiṣu /
iṣṭasiddhiḥ asiddhir va dṛṣṭānte saṃśayo 'thavā //
(The lord which you infer) when there is a going ahead after stopping, claimed as proved in terms of distinct shapes and purposive activity, is unproved in the example or doubtful.

11. siddhaṃ yādṛg adhiṣṭhātṛbhāvābhāvānuvṛttimat /
sanniveśādi tad yuktaṃ tasmād yad anumīyate //
Of whatever sort is the proven shape, etc., patterned after the presence or absence of a Supreme Disposer (*adhiṣṭhātṛ*), one may infer from that just what is valid.

PV-PRAT

FIRST ELEVEN VERSES

Dharmakīrti begins by insisting that measures (*māna*), i.e., authorities, require something to measure, and that these objects when capable of purposeful activity (*arthakriyā*) are the proper object of direct perception (*pratyakṣa*), and when incapable of purposeful activity are the proper object of inference (*anumāna*). But then, how about perception that is afflicted, e.g. the eye seeing 'hairs' that are not really there. Dignāga's Pratyakṣa chap, 1st section, verse 6, had already mentioned 'sensory affliction' as a kind of 'semblance of perception' (*pratyakṣābhāsa*). This 'semblance of perception' is not direct perception' (*pratyakṣa*). These sensory afflictions are declared 'unpurposeful' (*anartha*). How so? The reason given that there is no conviction (*adhimokṣa*) in their purposefulness rests upon conventional or worldly agreement. But then are they an appropriate object for inference? Later, this will be denied, because the 'hairs' are themselves a non-object. But the sentence, "There is the sensory affliction 'hairs'" is a generality fit for an object of inference.

And reasons are given for the non-shared, or non-overlapping assignment of the two authorities; because the objects are similar (general) or dissimilar (individual) respectively, object (*viṣaya*) or non-object of word, without a third possibility (*Vṛtti: na rāśy-antaram*). Verse 3 mentions that the object of perception is real in the absolute sense, while the object of inference is real in a conventional sense.

In theoretical arguments with opponents over 'capacity' (śakti), verses 4-5 shows the invalidity of a universal denial of capacity, since seeds have it to engender shoots, and so on. Dignāga and Dharmakīrti do not deny the capacity that is conventionally claimed, since this is the 'function' (*vyāpāra*) or the purposeful activity. But capacity should not be claimed for everywhere, since the generality character (*sāmānyalakṣaṇa*) lacks it.

Verse 6 is aimed against the Nyāya-Vaiśeṣika or Realist school. The *Vṛtti* and *Bhāṣya* explain that the 'jar' is the *avayavi dravya*; 'raising' is the *kriyā* or *karma*; 'counting' is the *guṇa*; 'global' is the *sāmānya* resident in *dravya, guṇa,* and *karman.* The 'etc.' takes in such realistic categories as *saṃyoga* (relation) and *vibhāga* (disconnection). Dharmakīrti challenges the realistic assignment of these categories as real external objects. He insists that the realist categories in fact were made up in mental functions of subsumption (*samaya*) and variegation (*ābhoga*).

Verse 11 sums up the difference between direct perception and inference for establishing a given thing (*vastu*). Not by assigning a name, and so on, and telling the name to someone else, is it established: Only by focussing a sense faculty upon the object; and this direct perception is a result, made possible by the given thing.

By comparing with the analysis of *P-Vin-Prat* in Vol. One of the present work, it will be observed that the first 11 verses of PV-Prat deal somewhat with all four main topics, namely, with 'A. Establishment of Pratyakṣa as an authority' 'B. The varieties of Pratyakṣa—by treating the objects of *mānasa-pratyakṣa* in verses 6-10', 'C. Semblance of perception', and 'D. Authority as a result'.

PV-Prat, 1-11, Sanskrit and English

1. mānaṃ dvividhaṃ meyadvaividhyāt śaktyaśaktitaḥ /
   arthakriyāyāṃ keśādir nārtho 'narthādhimokṣataḥ //
   There are two measures (= authorities) because there are two objects—capable or incapable of purposeful activity. The 'hairs', and other (sensory afflictions) are unpurposeful, since there is no conviction in their purposeness.
2. sadṛśāsadṛśatvāc ca viṣayāviṣayatvataḥ /
   śabdasyānyanimittānāṃ bhāve dhīsadasattvataḥ /

Because (the objects are) similar (= general) or dissimilar (=individual), respectively object of word and not object of word; and because for discrimination they are existent or non-existent, given a presence of other sign-causes (*nimitta*).

3. arthakriyāsamartham yat tad atra paramārthasat /
anyat saṃvṛtisat proktaṃ te svasāmānyalakṣaṇe //
The one capable of purposeful activity is here said to be the *paramārthasat* (existent in the absolute sense), the other one said to be *saṃvṛtisat* (existent in the conventional sense). They are two, respectively the individual character (*svalakṣaṇa*) and the generality character (*sāmānyalakṣaṇa*).

4. aśaktaṃ sarvam iti ced bījāder aṅkurādiṣu /
dṛṣṭā śaktiḥ matā sā cet saṃvṛtyā 'stu yathā tathā //
If all capacity is denied, (we respond) one sees the capacity of seeds and so forth toward shoots and so forth. If it is claimed in the conventional sense, let it be like that!

5. sāsti sarvatra ced buddher nānvayavyatirekayoḥ /
sāmānyalakṣaṇe 'dṛṣṭeḥ cakṣūrūpādibuddhivat //
If it (i.e., the capacity) is (claimed to be) everywhere, (we respond) when cognition (*buddhi*) has not observed *anvaya* (presence in similar cases) and *vyatireka* (absence in dissimilar cases), it (i.e. the capacity) is not in the generality character, e.g. when the cognition is for the (pair) eye and form, etc.

6. etena samayābhogādyantaraṅgānurodhataḥ /
ghaṭotkṣepaṇasāmānyasaṃkhyādiṣu dhiyo gataḥ//
Cognitions in terms of raising a jar, global counting, etc. are explained pursuant to mental functions ("inner members") of subsumption (*samaya*) and variegation (*ābhoga*), and so on.

7. keśādayo na sāmānyam anarthābhiniveśataḥ /
jñeyatvena grahād doṣo nābhāveṣu prasajyate //
The 'hairs,' and other (sensory inventions) are not the global, since there is no object to attach to.
One might be wrong in apprehending a given knowable, but is not at fault in the cases of [external] non-existences.

8abc. teṣām api tathābhāva 'pratiṣedhāt sphuṭābhatā /
jñānarūpatayārthatvāt /

And when there is their presence that way, it is a clear appearance not to be denied, because there is an object-entity (*artha*) by way of a knowledge-form (*jñāna-rūpatā*).

8d-9ab. keśādīti matiḥ punaḥ //
sāmānyaviṣayā keśapratibhāsam anarthakam /
The notion, "There are hairs", and so on, has (i.e. involves) a global scope, while the appearance of 'hairs' lacks an external object.

9cd-10a. jñānarūpatayārthatve sāmānye cet prasajyate //
tatheṣṭatvād adoṣaḥ
When there is a global object-entity by way of a knowledge-form, is it wrong? There is no fault, because it is accepted that way.

10bcd. artharūpatvena samānatā /
sarvatra samarūpatvāt tadvyāvṛttisamāśrayāt //
There is a sameness by way of the form of the object-entity, because of the same form everywhere, and because based on its exclusion (of anything different).

11. tad avastv adhidheyatvāt sāphalyād akṣasaṃhateḥ /
nāmādivacane vaktṛśrotṛvācyānubandhani //
It is not a given thing (*vastu*) by virtue of being denotable, when pronouncing the name, etc. and when there is the communication (*vācyānubandha*) between the speaker and the listener, (but) by virtue of the result-state of sense focus (*akṣasaṃhati*).

PV-SVA
FIRST ELEVEN VERSES

Svārthānumāna is devoted to the rules for the 'first speaker', who is supposed to be skilled in the 'three reasons' and the 'three modes of evidence' and to be versed in the fallacies. The three kinds of reason (*hetu*) are result (*kārya*), individual presence (*svabhāva*), and non-apprehension (*anupalabdhi*). The three modes of evidence (*liṅga*) are *pakṣadharma*—to be discussed next, the *anvaya* (presence in similar cases), and the *vyatireka* (absence in dissimilar cases). Verse 1 introduces the term 'necessary connection' (*avinābhāva*): it means that the three kinds of reason, whichever one happens to be involved, have necessary connection to the *pakṣadharma*. According to this Buddhist logic, whichever the reason, there should be the three modes of evidence. The three kinds of reason are fully treated in Dharmakīrti's *Hetubindu*, while the three modes of evidence are exposed in both *Svārthānumāna* and *Parārthānumāna.*

Kitagawa clearly explains the *pakṣadharma.* In the formulation, "Sound is non-eternal,'' sound is the *dharmin* ('factual base'), and referred to by the word *pakṣa* ('the locus'). Non-eternality is the *dharma* ('feature') and referred to as the *sādhya* ('the thesis'). Tson-kha-pa's *Guided Tour* uses the terminology *sādhyadharma* ('thesis feature'), meaning in the present verse 1 the *aṃśa* ('part') that pervades the *pakṣa.* Hence, the term *pakṣadharma* means "feature that logically pervades the locus."

When verse 1 mentions fallacies (*ābhāsa*) of the reason (*hetu*) it excludes the three kinds because they are stipulated as requiring the 'necessary connection'. Hence, when this 'necessary connection' (*avinābhāva*) fails, there are fallacies of the reason. 'Necessary connection' is illustrated by the statement that wherever is smoke, at that place is fire; *A* being there, *B* must be there.

The rest of the eleven verses deals with the three kinds of reason. In the present work, the reader is directed to the *Nyāyabindu* (NB) in my translation, of some elementary exposition of the three. Here, verses 2-4 deal with the three kinds, with technicalities of definition. Then verses 5-11 deal with fallacies, or their possibility, which when explicit go mainly with the 'result' kind of reason.

It is important in this system to notice that fallacies expressed in terms of the reason may be expressed in terms of 'modes of evidence' (often referred to as the 'pervasion', *vyāpti*). Thus, the *Vṛtti* on *Svārthānumāna,* v.15, says that according to Dignāga, the three 'dissimilar locuses' (*vipakṣa*) are called 'nonactual (*asiddha*), the dissimilar case of the *pakṣadharma*; 'contrary' (*viruddha-viparītārtha*), the dissimilar locus of the *anvaya* (kind of pervasion); and 'uncertain' (*anaikāntika—vyabhicārin*), the dissimilar locus of the *vyatireka* (kind of pervasion). Here, the 'three modes' (*trirūpa* or *trairūpya*) of evidence (*liṅga*) are much-studied topics. According to Kitagawa's article, Dignāga's category of *asiddha* applied to the *pakṣadharma,* is tantamount to non-*liṅga*, devoid of evidence; while the other two dissimilar locuses the 'opposed' and the 'uncertain' give rise to nine groups of evidence, which Kitagawa has explained there. The present Vol. One exposes the nine in the analysis of P-Vin-Par-Bu.

In terms of my Vol. One, Analysis of P-Vin, the eleven verses are all on the three kinds of reason, although there is a brief allusion to the *pakṣadharma,* the first of the three modes of evidence. It may well be the case that in the development of this system of Buddhist logic, fallacies were first expressed in terms of the reason (*hetu*), and that inconvenient complexities arose that led to the more neat exposition in terms of the 'modes of evidence'. In this light it may be assumed that Dharmakīrti in these eleven verses stresses the older theory, even pre-Dignāga.

PV-Sva, 1-11, Sanskrit and English

1. pakṣadharmas tadaṃśena vyāpto hetuḥ tridhaiva saḥ /
avinābhāvaniyamād hetvābhāsās tato 'pare //
Given a *pakṣadharma* (= *dharmidharma*), the reason (*hetu*), pervaded by its part (*aṃśa*) (= that *dharma*), is of three kinds (result, individual presence, and non-apprehension) through certainty of necessary connection (*avinābhāva*). The fallacies (*ābhāsa*) of reason are other than those (three).

2. kāryaṃ svabhāvair yāvadbhir avinābhāvi kāraṇe /
hetuḥ svabhāve bhāvo 'pi bhāvamātrānurodhini //
Given a material cause, the result (*kārya*) has necessary connection with as many individual presences (*svabhāva*) as there are. There is a reason that is a presence (*bhāva*) when an individual presence (*svabhāva*) complies with just that presence.

3. apravṛttiḥ pramāṇānām apravṛttiphalā 'sati /
asajjñānaphalā kācid dhetubhedavyapekṣayā //
Non-application (*apravṛtti*=non-apprehension) among authorities (*pramāṇa*) has a fruit of non-application when there is a non-existent (*asat*). After one has relied on separate reasons (with apprehension), it is any one with cognitive fruit of a non-existent.

4. viruddhakāryayoḥ siddhir asiddhir hetubhāvayoḥ /
dṛśyātmanor abhāvārthānupalabdhiś caturvidhā //
There are four non-apprehensions of absent objects (*abhavārtha*), namely, proof of (1) a contrary (*viruddha*) and (2) a (contrary) result (*kārya*); disproof of (3) a cause (*hetu*) and of (4) a (self-)presence that are feasibly seen.

5. tadviruddhanimittasya yopalabdhiḥ prayujyate /
nimittayor viruddhatvābhāve sā vyabhicāriṇī //
Any apprehension that formulates a contrary sign-cause (*nimitta*) of some (result) in the absence of opposition to the two sign-causes (that are negatable and opposed), is possessed of error.

6. iṣṭaṃ viruddhakārye 'pi deśakālādyapekṣaṇam /
anyathā vyabhicāri syāt bhasmevāsītasādhane //
Moreover, a claimed dependence on place, time, etc. even in the case of a contrary result, would be erroneous, like ashes to prove non-cold.

7. hetunā yaḥ samagreṇa kāryotpādo 'numīyate /
arthāntarānapekṣatvāt sa svabhāvo 'nuvarṇitaḥ /
The arising of result inferred from a group-reason, is said to be an individual presence, because of non-dependence on another object-entity.

8. samagrīphalasaktīnāṃ pariṇāmānubandhani /
anaikāntikatā kārye pratibandhasya sambhavāt //
There is uncertainty (*anaikāntikatā*) when a result is related to succcessive change (*pariṇāma*) of capacities that are the fruit of a group (*sāmagrī*), because of the possibility of an intervention.

9. ekasāmagryadhīnasya rūpāde rasato gatiḥ /
hetudharmānumānena dhūmendhanavikāravat //
A comprehension from taste (as associative condition) of the form, etc. (sense object) that is based on a single group, is by an inference from a feature (*dharma*) of the cause, like (inferring) a change of fuel from smoke.

10. śaktipravṛttyā na vinā rasaḥ saivānyakāraṇam /
ityatītaikakālānāṃ gatis tatkāryaliṅgajā //
Without the occurrence of a capacity, there is no taste; and this (in turn) is the material cause of another. The comprehension of individual past times in that manner arises from the evidence of that result.

11. hetunā yo 'samagreṇa kāryotpādo 'numīyate /
tac cheṣavad asāmarthād dehād rāgānumānavat //
The arising of result inferred from a cause which has the wrong group is like inferring lust from (the senses and cognition of) the body which is (by itself) incapable (of it)—thus with *a posteriori* reasoning.

PV-PAR

FIRST ELEVEN VERSES

In Verse 1, Dharmakīrti shows the requirement of validating the 'first speaker' in Svārthānumāna in preparation for Parārthānumāna. Then come arguments over *āgama* with opponents who deny the applicability of inference, while it is the Dignāga-Dharmakīrti position that *āgama* (the received scripture) is in the scope of inference. A consistent scripture is in Pāli in the Anguttara-Nikāya (Book of Threes), the Kesamutti-sutta addressed to the Kālāmas, in my translation:

> "Kālāmas, do not be swayed by the Vedic tradition, what has been handed down, legends, mastery of the *piṭakas,* the reasons of logic, reasons of the state, considerations of imagery, delight in speculative views, form of what might be, an ascetic."

Among the powerful answers that Dharmakīrti gives to the adversary, that of verse 6 is especially telling. We could paraphrase the point of this view in this manner: The *āgama* after all, does not explain itself. Do you, sir, have a *present-day* understanding of it? If so, why not admit that understanding in other persons as well; and that is what we call "inferring the *āgama*".

A discussion of the *āgama* had occurred in later verses of the PV-Sva chapter, and in its *Svavṛtti,* pointed out by Malvaniya in the Introduction to the Sanskrit edition of that chapter and Dharmakīrti's *Svavṛtti.* There Dharmakīrti had anticipated and answered the arguments of the opponent as are alluded to in *PV-Par,* first eleven verses. One verse (*PV-Sva,* 216, Sastri's ed.; 218 Malvaniya's) shows how *āgama* is subjected to the two authorities of this system:

> pratyakṣeṇānumānena dvinidhenāpy abādhanam /
> dṛṣṭādṛṣṭārthayor asyāvisaṃvādas tadarthayoḥ //
> When there is no conflict by either direct perception or inference with its (i.e., *āgama*'s) two topics, the visible and invisible entities, (*āgama*) is without deception for the topic (in question).

Here, verse 2 is the challenge by the opponent who does not accept that *āgama* is in the scope of inference. The verse 3 opponent is identified by the *Vṛtti* as the Sāṃkhya speaker.

One may notice about these verses that while dealing with the *āgama* issue, Dharmakirti brings up other elements of the system. I compared my analysis of P-Vin-Par in this Vol. One, with these findings: The first topic of P-Vin-Par is 'A. Theory-systems and śāstras'. The first five verses here appear to go with this topic. The next topic is 'B. Examination of *pakṣa*'. Under this, the subtopic '(1) Definition of *pakṣa*' appears to agree with verses six and seven. The subtopic '(2) Examination of *sāmānya*' appears to agree with verse eight (which mentions *sāmānya*). Since '(3) Varieties of *pakṣadharma*' mentions that the variegation of the *pakṣadharma* is mainly through fallacies of the reason, and verse nine specifically includes this, it is proper to assign this verse, as well as verse ten which appears to continue the topic. The next topic of P-Vin-Par is 'C. Communication of the evidence' and verse eleven appears to agree. That leaves no verse among the eleven to go with the fourth main topic of P-Vin-Par, namely, 'D. Example and fallacious example'. Such agreement of this set of eleven verses with the structure of a chapter in another work of Dharmakīrti's indicates to me the orderliness of his mind; and that while sometimes the verses of PV do not seem to follow from the preceding one or ones, there is a careful method or arrangement going on.

PV-Par, 1-11, Sanskrit and English

1. parasya pratipādyatvāt adṛṣṭo'pi svayam paraiḥ /
   dṛṣṭasādhanam ity eke tatkṣepāyātmadṛgvacaḥ //
   Some assert that in order to instruct another person, even though (the means of proof) was not observed by oneself, the means of proof may be observed by others. To dismiss that (fallacious position), there is the injunction "witness by oneself" (i.e. validation of the 'first speaker').
2. anumāviṣaye neṣṭaṃ parīkṣitaparigrahāt /
   vācaḥ prāmāṇyam asmin hi nānumānaṃ pravartate //
   (The adversary says:) Because it is an embrace (*parigraha*) of what (the seers) previously observed, we deny that the authoritative statement is in the object-scope (*viṣaya*) of inference. For inference does not operate therein.
3. bādhanāyāgamasyokteḥ sādhanasya paraṃ prati /
   so 'pramāṇaṃ tadā 'siddham tat siddham akhilaṃ tataḥ //
   (The adversary says:) It would replace the *āgama* means

of proof, as though the authoritativeness were entirely proven at that time (of inference) while not (in fact) proven.

4. tad āgamavataḥ siddhaṃ yadi kasya ka āgamaḥ /
bādhyamānaḥ pramāṇena sa siddhaḥ katham āgamaḥ //
(We say:) If it were proven (simply) by having an *āgama*, whose and what is the *āgama*? If it can be replaced by an authority, how is the *āgama* proved?

5. tadviruddhābhyupagamas tenaiva ca kathaṃ bhavet /
tadanyopagame tasya tyāgāṃgasyāpramāṇatā //
And how can a thesis (*abhyupagama* = *pratijñā*) which opposes it, occur just by virtue of that (i.e., *āgama*)? And if the thesis is different from it, there is no authority for the (syllogism) member of rejection.

6. tat kasmāt sādhanam noktaṃ svapratītir yad udbhavā /
yuktyā yam āgamo grāhyaḥ parasyāpi ca sā na kim //
Why would not that means of proof be expressed which is one's own cognitive dawning (*pratīti*) coming forth? By whatever principle one may apprehend the *āgama*, why would not it (i.e. the principle) belong also to the other person (who infers the *āgama*)?

7. prākṛtasya sataḥ prāg yaiḥ pratipattyakṣasambhavau /
sādhanaiḥ sādhanāny arthaśaktijñāne 'sya tāny alam //
By whatever previous means of proof there are both the understanding and the sense activity of ordinary (= hither looking) existence, those means of proof suffice for this (ordinary existence) in the sense of knowing the capacity of the object-entity.

8. vicchinnānugamā ye 'pi sāmānyenāpy agocarāḥ /
sādhyasādhanacintāsti na teṣv artheṣu kācana //
And when not only are those relations (*anugama*= *sambandha*) broken apart, but also have no scope by way of generality, there is not toward the object-entities any pondering of the thesis (*sādhya*) or of the means of proof (*sādhana*).

9. puṃsām abhiprāyavaśāt tattvātattvavyavasthitau /
lupto hetutadābhāsau tasya vastvasamāśrayāt //
When reality and unreality are established among men by dint of their purpose (*abhiprāya*), it (the purpose) is lost to the reason and its fallacy, because there is no foundation of a given thing (*vastu*) for that (purpose).

10. sann artho jñānasāpekṣo nāsan jñāne na sādhakaḥ /
sato 'pi vastvasaṃśliṣṭā 'saṃgatyā sadṛśi gatiḥ //
An object-entity (*artha*) when given, presupposes a cognition (*jñāna*); when not given, does not prove (anything) to cognition. Even the understanding (*gati*) of one that exists, when the understanding is not related to a given thing (*vastu*), is tantamount to non-understanding.

11. liṅgaṃ svabhāvaḥ kāryaṃ vā dṛśyādarśanam eva va /
sambaddhaṃ vastutas siddhaṃ tad asiddhaṃ kim ātmanaḥ /
Evidence (*liṅga*) is an individual presence (*svabhāva*), a result (*kārya*), or just a non-view of the visible (= non-apprehension, *anupalabdhi*). Since relation is proved via a given thing (*vastu*), why is it not proved to yourself?

ANALYSIS OF P-VIN-BU

INTRODUCTION

The importance of Dharmakīrti's *Pramāṇaviniścaya* stems from Dharmottara's statement, concurred in by Bu-ston, that it is a kind of commentary on Dignāga's PS.[1] It follows that the numerous PV verses employed by Dharmakīrti to construct P-Vin *kārikā* were those that would most readily accord with the PS. It is therefore properly assumed that Dharmakīrti's PV preceded his P-Vin. Bu-ston's native Tibetan *P-Vin-Ṭīk* (hereafter; P-Vin-Bu) ["Collected Works", Vol. Ya] brings out the sense in which P-Vin can be taken as a commentary on PS, namely—or probably—a commentary on the first parts of the PS chapters, that is to say, the parts in which Dignāga presents his own system before attempting to refute rival systems. Dharmakīrti's final verse in P-Vin-Par clarifies this, since the opponent is the 'insider' (e.g. Īśvarasena), while the 'outsider' opponents are simply stated as not understanding the Buddhist logician's position. In P-Vin-Bu this feature appears especially in the commentary on P-Vin-Prat, where Bu-ston correlates this chapter with the PS-Prat, 1st section, consisting of 11 verses in my count, for which I edited the Tibetan and provided English translation in Part II of this Vol. One. Thereafter in PS-Prat, Dignāga assails various opponent positions; but P-Vin-Bu does not correlate this portion with P-Vin-Prat.

1. See Bu-ston, *History of Buddhism*, I, tr. from the Tibetan by E. Obermiller (Heidelberg, 1931), p. 45: 'The Pramāṇa-viniścaya', says the Kashmirian Pandit Jñānaśrī, 'is not to be regarded as a commentary on the *Pramāṇasamuccaya;* nevertheless, I shall elucidate its theory'. The teacher Dharmottara, on the contrary says that it is a commentary on the work in question, and this opinion is to be regarded as correct." Furthermore, Bu-ston, in his brief commentary on the title '*Pramāṇaviniścaya*'—just preceding his P-Vin-Bu (*Tshad ma rnam par ṅes pa'i ṭīk tshig don rab gsal*)—states (f. 3b-2): "The *Pramāṇa-sūtra* is the *samuccaya* (compendium); having analyzed its principal meanings, and having taken it as a foundation, there is the *Pramāṇaviniścaya* (ascertainment of authority)."

The point of making the analysis that follows is to expose as much as possible the main details of the system, while restraining the bulk of material. I took as the main data the corpus of PV verses employed for P-Vin, and additionally employed by P-Vin-Bu, as subsumed in the organizational plans of P-Vin's three chapters, devoted respectively to Pratyakṣa (Prat), Svārthānumāna (Sva), and Parārthānumāna (Par). The first two chapters have fine analyses by Vetter (P-Vin-I) and Steinkellner (P-Vin-II), respectively;[2] while the third, and somewhat larger chapter (P-Vin-Par) has no such modern analysis. Steinkellner's Index[3] has enabled me to work through this third chapter along the lines of P-Vin-Prat and P-Vin-Sva. I also extracted from P-Vin-Bu every noticed citation of Dignāga's works, as well as any other verse citation (such as those from PV-Bh).[4] Then I added a bare minimum of supporting material, whether it be from Dharmakirti's or from Bu-ston's comments, but I generally disregarded Bu-ston's use of the two commentaries in the Tibetan Tanjur on P-Vin—by Dharmottara and Jñānaśrībhadra. The included material of this Analysis is meant to indicate how the Dignāga and Dharmakīrti systems were studied via the *Pramāṇa-viniścaya.* It appeared to me, though, that if I were to include more material throughout to support the corpus of verses, it would have expanded this section with diminished profit. My object was to expose the correlation of Dignāga's works with Dharmakīrti's formulations by way of inclusion within the structural parts of P-Vin-Prat, P-Vin-Sva, and P-Vin-Par; and for this purpose the verses themselves suffice, because it appears that much of the misunderstanding of the Dignāga-Dharmakīrti system involves the difficulty of assigning inclusion, e.g. what goes under 'introspective perception' in contrast with what goes under 'mental perception'.[5] By 'structural parts'

---

2. Tilmann Vetter, *Dharmakīrti's Pramāṇaviniścayaḥ;* 1. Kapitel: Pratyakṣam (Wien, 1966); Ernst Steinkellner, *Dharmakīrti's Pramāṇaviniścayaḥ;* Zweites Kapitel: Svārthānumānam (Wien, 1973).
3. Ernst Steinkellner, *Verse-Index of Dharmakīrti's Works (Tibetan Versions)* (Wien, 1977).
4. I did not include some verses, apparently of Indian opponents, and taken from the *Tattvasaṃgraha* of Śāntarakṣita and Kamalaśīla, which is available to the Tibetans in their Tanjur.
5. For example, see Masatoshi Nagatomi's article "*Mānasa-Pratyakṣa*: a Conundrum in the Buddhist *Pramāṇa* system," in *Sanskrit and Indian Studies; Essays in Honour of Daniel H.H. Ingalls,* ed. by M. Nagatomi, *et al.* (Dordrecht, 1980), pp. 243-260. No wonder he finds it a conundrum! He says (p. 256), "PV, Book III, vss. 239-248 is devoted specifically to elucidating the object-cognizing (aspect of) *mānasa*

I mean the following structures for my analysis of the three chapters:

I. Pratyakṣa (Direct Perception)
  A. Establishment of Pratyakṣa as an authority
  B. Varieties of Pratyaksa
    (1) Outer sense perception
    (2) Mental perception
    (3) Introspective perception
    (4) Yogin's perception
  C. Semblance of perception
  D. Authority as a result

II. Svārthānumāna (Inference for Oneself)
  A. The two kinds of inference
  B. About evidence (*liṅga*)
  C. The three kinds of evidence
    (1) Non-apprehension
    (2) Individual presence
    (3) Result
  D. Logical connection

III. Parārthānumāna (Inference for Others)
  A. Theory-systems and śāstras
  B. Examination of *pakṣa*
    (1) Definition of *pakṣa* (locus)
    (2) Examination of *sāmānya* (generality)
    (3) Varieties of *pakṣadharma* (locus feature)
  C. Communication of the evidence
  D. Example and fallacious example

---

pratyakṣa". So far he is correct; cf. the edition of *Pramāṇavārttika* by Dwarikadas Shastri, p. 172, which heads these vss. with the caption "*Mānasapratyakṣam*". But then Nagatomi says (p. 257), "... we now turn to PV, III, vss. 249-267, the section which has traditionally been understood as elucidating the 'self-awareness' of pleasure and so forth as a second type of *mānasa-pratyakṣa*". But how can he be correct about this? The same Shastri edition of PV, p. 175 heads these vss. with the caption "*Svasaṃvedanapratyakṣam*". The respective sections headed by the two captions are consistent with the material in P-Vin, Analysis of I. Pratyaksa, B. Varieties of pratyakṣa, (2) Mental perception, and (3) Introspective perception. It is clear that the material about feelings, and so on, is credited to the third kind of *pratyakṣa* called *svasaṃvedana*, not to the second kind called *mānasa*. Dignāga makes the same distinction in his PS, 1st section, vs. 4 (my count) (cf. the preceding part II, "Introduction to the Dignāga-Dharmakīrti system by the 'elevens'"; and cf. Dignāga's commentary on the same vs. in this Vol. One Analysis, Pratyakṣa, Varieties, (2) Mental perception.

I initially combed P-Vin-Bu for quotations, easily locating the original Sanskrit for the PV ones by means of Steinkellner's *Index*. When PV verses were identified with P-Vin *kārikā*, I have translated them, along with certain P-Vin *kārikā* that were not identifiable with PV verses. These P-Vin (=Pramāṇa-Viniścaya) *kārikā*-s are herein numbered separately and each continuously in Dharmakīrti's three chapters designated P-Vin-Prat, P-Vin-Sva, and P-Vin-Par, with the designations followed by 'k'.— the abbreviation for *kārikā*. They are often identified with PV verses; if not, both Vetter (for P-Vin-Prat) and Steinkellner (for P-Vin-Sva) deserve special appreciation for often determining the Sanskrit from other texts, mainly other Dharmakīrti works. Yet there remained a number of Tibetan *kārikā*-s in both the Prat and Sva chapters for which no Sanskrit was determined. I have translated both those sets of *kārikā* in the given order, including the ones just available in Tibetan. In the case of P-Vin-Par, all the numbered *kārikā*-s were identified with PV Sanskrit verses (using Steinkellner's *Index*), except for the first one, the last one, and a few others in between, which of course I also translated from the Tibetan versions. These P-Vin *kārikā*-s should not be confused with other *kārikā*-s referred to, mainly in citations of Dignāga.

The corpus of PV verses from the entire P-Vin plus those cited by Bu-ston, which I also translated, amounts to circa 192 verses, as the following tabulation should clarify:

	Citations in P-Vin	*Citations in P-Vin-Bu*
PV-Sid	11-16, 18-19, 24	1, 2a-c, 3ab, 4d-5c, 82, 94, 196ab
PV-Prat	3ab, 57-58, 81-83, 124-127ab, 145, 174, 243, 247, 249cd, 251, 277-279, 282, 285, 306-308, 330cd-332, 350b-d, 351-362, 364-366	2 (in part), 53d-55ab, 63a-64c, 133, 239, 286a,d, 287, 309

	Citations in P-Vin	*Citations in P-Vin-Bu*
PV-Sva	2ab, 4d, 6-7, 9, 13-15, 17, 24-26ab, 29, 31-33, 35-38, 40-42, 60-63, 187-191, 193, 195-196, 203, 207-208, 210, 224, 317-329]	50, 57cd, 60-61, 80-81ab, 84-87, 169, 214, 216, 227ab
PV-Par	10, 14-15, 17, 27, 29, 46-59 63-64, 75, 84-86, 91-92, 128-129, 133-135, 184-188, 190-195, 197-198, 202-204, 223-236, 244, 265-270, 273-279	110cd, 260

The numbers of verses in PV editions sometimes diverge due to the inclusion, or not, of the initial bowing verses in the count. I believe my numbers agree throughout with those of Steinkellner's *Index*.

Of course, Dharmakīrti employed more verses of PV to construct various P-Vin *kārikā* and for purposes of his prose comments on P-Vin. Even so, it is clear that certain portions of PV were favoured for writing of P-Vin. PV-Sid was employed for only a few verses. After the 360-s, PV-Prat is not obviously employed, although in PV it runs to verse 541. PV-Sva is well represented in the first of 100 verses; then passing to the latter 100-s and early 200-s, it skips to a block in the 300s (i.e. 317-329), toward end of the chapter. PV-Par is well represented throughout in P-Vin. P-Vin-Bu on P-Vin-Prat and P-Vin-Sva was liberal in citing PV, but on P-Vin-Par Bu-ston had few PV citations of his own, possibly because Dharmakīrti had himself cited so many in this large chapter.

The already published texts and studies of P-Vin-Prat and -Sva mentioned above (P-Vin-I and P-Vin-II) enabled me to see the 'interim verses' (*antara-śloka*) and 'summary verses' (*saṃgraha-śloka*) for those two chapters of P-Vin. For finding the same kinds of verses in P-Vin-Par, I employed a modern edition of P-Vin (Tibetan version).[6] It is notable that both PS and P-Vin employ this terminol-

6. Separate printing of *Tshad ma rnam par ṅes pa* (Delhi Karmapae Chodhey, 1976).

ogy of verses. As I have observed their function in P-Vin, the 'interim verses', amounting sometimes to a long series of verses, appear to give new material in a self-explanatory manner not requiring commentary. The 'summary verses' occur singly or at most have several verses; and appear to summarize preceding or following material, and thus can conclude or head subsections. In contrast, the kinds of verses that are provided Dharmakīrti P-Vin commentary, especially on individual hemistichs or on smaller portions of a *kārikā*, are not called either 'interim verses' or summary verses.[7]

While observing the quotations in P-Vin-Bu, I also tried to find all the PS and PSV citations, but these were more elusive, as, besides mentioning Dignāga as source and "the *ācārya* said", Bu-ston cited PS and Dignāga's self-commentary (PSV), namely, "of the *sūtra*" (since PS is called the *Pramāṇa-sūtra*) and "from the *Samuccaya*" (from the title *Pramāṇasamuccaya*). For locating the PS citations, there are the helpful *Perception* by Hattori[8] including edited Tibetan for both translations of the PSV, Pratyakṣa chapter, and *Dignāga* by Kitagawa[9] including edited Tibetan for both translations, first half only, of the PSV's *Svārthānumāna, Parārthānumāna, Dṛṣṭānta-dṛṣṭāntābhāsa* (omitting the Apoha chapter). Besides, I looked at the Tanjur edition of the 'Kanakavarman' translation of PS and PSV. With these various aids, most of the citations were rather quickly located. Then observing where Bu-ston had cited these verses or part-verses of PS-Prat, it turned out that these were all contained within the P-Vin-Bu on P-Vin-Prat. Furthermore, except for one citation, they were all in the Tanjur order of the verses. This permits a conclusion: that Dharmakīrti probably patterned his discussion of P-Vin-Prat after Dignāga's PS-Prat and PSV-Prat, 1st section.

Since P-Vin has only three chapters, devoted like the *Nyāyabindu* (NB) to Pratyakṣa, Svārthānumāna, and Parārthānumāna, it follows that a correlation with Dignāga's PS must subsume within those three chapters materials to which PS devotes six chapters. That is,

7. Various theories about the 'interim verses' and 'summary verses' are given in Katsumi Mimaki, "Sur le role de l'antarasloka ou du samgrahasloka," in *Indianisme et Bouddhisme;* Mélanges offerts a Mgr Étienne Lamotte (Louvain, 1980), pp. 233-244.

8. Masaaki Hattori, *Dignāga, on Perception,* (Harvard University Press, 1968).

9. Hidenori Kitagawa, *A Study of Indian Classical Logic—Dignāga's System* (Tokyo, 1965).

besides three chapters named the same as those of P-Vin, the quotations in P-Vin and P-Vin-Bu clarify that chapter 5 on *Apoha* was mainly incorporated in P-Vin-Sva, and that both chapter 4, *Dṛṣṭānta-dṛṣṭāntābhāsa,* and chapter 6, *Jāti-parīkṣā,* were incorporated in P-Vin-Par.

Dharmakīrti's P-Vin is written in the same style as Dignāga's PSV, mixed verses and prose. Hattori is certainly on good grounds to have claimed that the independent texts of PS *kārikā* in the Tibetan Tanjur are in fact extracted from the two translations of Dignāga's PS commentary (the 'V-version' and the 'K-version').[10] The fact that Dignāga's PS commentary is essential for understanding many of the PS verses suggests that Dignāga wrote a unified text of prose and verse. Dharmakīrti appears to have imitated this in P-Vin.

It remains to say a few words about the author of P-Vin-Bu, Bu-ston. Living from 1290-1364 A.D., he gave the definitive form to the previously translated texts into the Tibetan language—the Kanjur (translation of the revealed scriptures), and Tanjur (translation of the exegetical and miscellaneous works). The author of many works in the fields of Tantra and non-tantra, he especially excelled in survey-type treatises, such as the work translated by E. Obermiller as *History of Buddhism* (T. *Chos 'byuṅ*).[11] His large commentary on the *Pramāṇaviniścaya* is a kind of treasure, because it preserves one of the two traditions of Buddhist logic study in Tibet—that of the P-Vin combined with Dignāga; while the prevalent study thereafter was through the *Pramāṇavārttika,* introduced by the 'Seven Books' treatises which is the other tradition.

As to my use of Bu-don's own words (which undoubtedly incorporated remarks from the lineage he follows), while I consulted his commentary throughout to draw out the numerous citations herein enclosed, I sparingly employed his own comments in portrayal of P-Vin-Prat-Bu and of P-Vin-Sva-Bu; then used them to greater extent when based on P-Vin-Par-Bu, especially near the end with Bu-don's treatment of "Example and Fallacious Example."

10. Hattori, *Dignāga, on Perception,* p. 17.

11. For more information about Bu-ston, see D.S. Ruegg, *The Life of Bu-ston Rin po che with the Tibetan text of the Bu-ston rNam thar* (Rome, 1966).

RE BU-STON'S INITIAL COMMENTS

Bu-ston's great commentary on P-Vin (P-Vin-Bu), 4b-2, cites PV-Sva, 214:

> sambaddhānuguṇopāyam puruṣārthābhidhāyakam /
> parīkṣādhikṛtaṃ vākyam ato' nadhikṛtam param //
> The means which is cogent and consistent is the reference (*vākya*) defining human purpose pursuant to inspection, hence not pursuant to something else.

The discussion continues through citation, P-Vin-Bu, 6a, of PV-Sid, 5b:

> śāstraṃ mohanivartanam
> A treatise (*śāstra*) averts delusion.

'Human purpose' is heaven (*svarga*) or liberation (*apavarga*). How do the references embodied in a treatise serve such a purpose, since the treatises are composed by constructive thought (*kalpanā*) subject to delusion? Asaṅga in the *Yogācārabhūmi* mentions two kinds of treatises, nine in all. The meaningful, eliminative-of-suffering, and devoted-to-accomplishment treatises are the three that avert delusion. The meaningless, erroneous, perverse, hard-hearted, devoted-to-worldly-learning, and devoted-to-polemics treatises are the six which the PV verse calls 'something else' (*param*). The kind of treatise that averts delusion is the one clarifying what one should reject and what accept (*heyopādeya* of PV-Sva, 217), as P-Vin-Bu, 6a-4, mentions. As to the 'inspection,' to avoid or eliminate doubt, Kamalaśīla's '*Pūrvapakṣa*' work translated in this vol. One and Tsoṅ-kha-pa's *Guided Tour* also in this Part II, set forth three ways, by the similes of testing gold.

I. PRATYAKṢA (DIRECT PERCEPTION)

A. Establishment of Pratyakṣa as an authority
B. Varieties of Pratyakṣa
  (1) Outer sense perception
  (2) Mental perception
  (3) Introspective perception
  (4) Yogin's perception
C. Semblance of perception
D. Authority as a result

A. Establishment of Pratyakṣa as an Authority

P-Vin-Prat (Vetter, p. 30, n. 3-4), k. 1:

> pratyakṣam anumānaṃ ca pramāṇe 'ntarbhāvād eva /
> apratyakṣasya sambhandhād anyataḥ pratipattitaḥ //
> Direct perception (*pratyakṣa*) and inference (*anumāna*) are only to be included in authority (*pramāṇa*—because of (personal) observation of no direct perception other than in conjunction with (i.e. in the category of authority).

P-Vin-Bu, 8a cites PV-Sid, 1:

> pramāṇam avisaṃvādi jñānam arthakriyāsthitiḥ /
> avisaṃvādanaṃ śabde 'py abhiprāyanivedanāt //
> Authority is a non-deceptive cognition. Non-deception is the rule of purposive activity (*arthakriyā*), and is also in speech in that it reveals intention.

Also, PV-Sid, 5c, and 3ab:

> ajñātārthaprakāśo vā /
> Besides, (authority) reveals the (previously) unknown object-entity.
> gṛhītagrahaṇān neṣṭaṃ sāṃvṛtaṃ dhīpramāṇatā /
> The derivative of convention is not claimed (as authority) since it apprehends what was already apprehended. There is authority of cognition.

P-Vin-Bu, 8a-7, on the 'non-deceptive cognition':

> "What produces certainty that the two—perception and inference—have a non-deceptive character? As to the authority of inference (*anumāna-pramāṇa*), due to the certainty in the single alternative of sanction (*prameya*) by way of evidence (*liṅga*) certain of 'necessary connection' (*avinābhāva*), the certainty that it is an 'authority' by itself. As to perception (*pratyakṣa*), the perception of an appearing purposive activity, and (the perception) that is habitual, has the certainty that it is an authority by itself."

Bu-ston goes on to clarify the 'habitual perception' (*goms pa'i mṅon sum*) as subject to various conditions—that cognition is not affected by sleep, etc., that sense-organs are sound, the sense object is close, there are no concomitant discordant appearances—in such case perception experiences its object, with certainty that the object is real. These two forms of perception were much discussed; and Bu-ston (9a-2) mentions that Dharmottara denied the status of 'authority' for the second kind of perception, while Devendrabuddhi, Śākyabuddhi, and 'Rgyan' (PV-Bh) admitted it as an 'authority.' Of course, there was no disagreement about the authority when there was an 'appearing purposive activity.' The discussions were carried on in particular with the terminology 'non-apprehension' (*anupalabdhi*), one of the three reasons (*hetu*), as well as with the terminology 'feasibly seen' (*dṛśya*) and 'not feasibly seen' (*adṛśya*) (PV-Par, 108).

P-Vin-Bu, 9a-5, cites PV-Sid, 4d-5b:

> . . . svarūpasya svato gatiḥ /
> prāmāṇyaṃ vyavahāreṇa śāstraṃ mohanivartanam /
> (Some say:) the comprehension of the true form is from oneself; (or say:) authoritativeness is by way of conventional speech. (We say:) (there is) a *śāstra* (which) averts delusion.

This gives Bu-ston the opportunity to mention rival theories about the number or kind of 'authorities'. Here we need to bear in mind that the Dignāga-Dharmakīrti system insists on two, and only two authorities—perception and inference. Any others are held to be varieties of these two, or perhaps their objects.

P-Vin-Bu, 10b-6, Bu-ston's first citation from Dignāga, PS-Sva, 5ab (K-version):

> āpta-vākyāvisaṃvāda-sāmānyād anumānatā /
> When the state of inference is from a generality (consisting) of the non-deceptive references of the master, . . .

P-Vin-Bu, 10b-6, Bu-ston shows that PV-Sva, 216, uses Dignāga's words:

> āptavādāvisaṃvādasāmānyād anumānatā /
> buddher agatyābhihitā **parokṣe* 'py asya gocare //
> When the state of inference is from a generality (consisting) of the non-deceptive references of the master, it (the state of inference) is defined (by Dignāga) in the sense of one's

domain beyond (the 'out of bounds,'=*atyantaparokṣa*) to which the intellect (*buddhi*) cannot go.

P-Vin-Bu, 10b-7, Bu-ston, then shows that there is no inconsistency in PV- Prat, 53d:

> meyam tv ekaṃ svalakṣaṇam /
> The individual character is a single sanction.

As I understand Bu-ston's remark, the meaning of the word 'single' is that the 'individual character' is not unique. Of course, this system sets forth two sanctions—the individual character' (*svalakṣaṇa*) and the 'generality character' (*sāmānyalakṣaṇa*).

P-Vin-Bu, 11b, cites PV-Prat, 63a-64b:

> na pratyakṣaparokṣābhyāṃ meyasyānyasya sambhavaḥ /
> tasmāt prameyadvitvena pramāṇadvitvam iṣyate //
> tryekasaṃkhyānirāso vā prameyadvayadarśanāt /
> There is no possible other sanction than *pratyakṣa*'s and *parokṣa's*. Therefore, by reason of two sanctions, we claim there are two authorities. In view of the pair of sanctions, we exclude the count of three or one.

This passage continues the position stressed by Dignāga that the two authorities are results, with the suggestion here that they are results of their respective objects, the individual and the generality character. Besides, inference (*anumāna*) is here called *parokṣa* ('beyond the senses'). When inference's object is the 'non-deceptive' scripture, it is a special kind called *atyantaparokṣa* ('further beyond the senses'), as alluded to above (P-Vin-Bu, 10b-6).

P-Vin-Bu, 12b, cites PV-Sid, 2a-c:

> vaktṛvyāpāraviṣayo yo 'rtho buddhāu prakāśate /
> prāmāṇyaṃ tatra śabdasya
> The sense object with function of 'speaker,' which object-entity manifests to the cognition (of the hearer), is the authorizing there of the speech.

The *Vṛtti* and *Bhāṣya* agree that 'speaker' means the speaker's intention (*vivakṣā*). *Bhāṣya* explains authorizing as the function (*vyāpāra*), which, according to Dignāga, PS-Prat, 1st, (my number) 7, accompanies (in fact, introduces) authority. It follows that the term 'authorizing' (*prāmāṇya*) means 'accompaniment of authority'.

P-Vin-Bu, 13b, going with P-Vin-Prat (Vetter, p. 34.8-14), deals with two kinds of 'non-apprehension': (1) when it is right to apprehend, as conventionally recognized, and one says, "It is there," thus with delusion. (2) when something does not appear, and so is conventionally denied. The P-Vin example is of the father. When a woman is pregnant, one is deluded to deny there is a generator (= a father). But when a family has no children, a 'father' is conventionally denied. Both kinds are in the purview of logic. They appear to be alluded to by Bu-ston, P-Vin-Bu, 9a-4, as a passage of PV-SV (on PV-Sva, 3; Gnoli, p. 5.2-6):

> evam anayor anupalabdhyoḥ svaviparyayahetvabhāvabhāvābhyāṃ sadvyavahārapratiṣedhaphalatvaṃ tulyaṃ / ekatra saṃsāyād anyatra viparyayāt / tatrādyā sadvyavahāraniṣedhopayogāt pramāṇam uktā / na tu vyatirekadarśanādāv upayujyate / saṃśayāt / dvitīyā tv atra pramāṇaṃ niścayaphalatvāt /
>
> Accordingly, as to these two non-apprehensions, there is equivalent exclusion-result of a conventional remark about existence, through absence and presence of its own and the opposite reason, in one case through doubt, and in the other case through the opposite (i.e. certainty). Among them, the first (non-apprehension) is said to be an authority because appropriate for exclusion of a conventional remark about existence, but is not appropriate for viewing, etc. the *vyatireka* (absence in dissimilar cases), because there is doubt. The second one is here an authority because of being the certainty result.

P-Vin-Prat (Vetter, p. 34, n. 2), k. 2:

> pramāṇetarasāmānyasthiter anyadhiyāṃ gataḥ /
> pramāṇāntarasadbhāvaḥ pratiṣedhāc ca kasyacit // 2 /
> And the real presence of another authority due to the exclusion of anything [renders] understood another cognition having the rule of the authority and some other *sāmānya.*

The *kārikā* seems to allude to the situation of a shift to a different one among the two kinds of *pramāṇa* by exclusion of the former one.

P-Vin-Bu, 18b, cites PS-Prat, 1st, (my numbers) 1-2b:

> pratyakṣam anumānaṃ ca pramāne lakṣanaḍvayam /
> prameyaṃ tasya saṃdhāne [*prame] na pramāṇāntaram /

> There are two authorities—direct perception and inference. The sanction is two characters. In the sense of enjoining it, there are two authorities. There are no other authorities.

P-Vin-Bu, 19a, cites PS-Prat, 1st, Dignāga's commentary on (my no.) 7:

> "The resultant cognition arises bearing the image (*ākāra*) of the sense object (*viṣaya*) and is understood to be attended with (in fact, introduced by) function (vyāpāra). In consideration of that, it is called 'authority'."

And cites PS-Prat, 1st Dignāga's commentary on (my no.) 8:

> "Whatever the image of an external thing (*artha*), white, non-white, and so forth, that appears in cognition, this (cognition) is judged to be attended with the object that is of such-and-such a nature."

Bu-ston cites those two passages in opposition to a theory that there is (perception) authority even without the image of the sense object (= the *nirākāra* theory). The opponent's theory appears to be presented in P-Vin-Prat (Vetter, p. 38, n. 1), k. 3:

> arthasyāsambhave 'bhāvāt pratyakṣe 'pi pramāṇatā /
> pratibaddhasvabhāvasya taddhetutve samaṃ dvayam // 3 /
> (Opponent:) Even when perception lacks an object-entity, it is an authority by way of absence.
> (Dharmakīrti's response:) Since the reason for that goes with an implicated individual presence, both (authorities) would be the same!

P-Vin-Prat (Vetter, p. 38.10) immediately after this verse states: "Besides, perception is an authority since it is without deception regarding the object-entity." P-Vin-Bu, 20a, cites PS-Prat, 3rd (Examination of the Nyāya theory), Dignāga's commentary on k.1:

> "There is no possibility of the (external) object itself being delusive, because the delusive object is (just) the mental object."

Bu-ston, 20b-1, goes on to say that Dignāga holds that there is no delusion belonging to the external object that has a function in practical life.

P-Vin-Bu, 21a, cites PS-Prat, 1st, Dignāga's commentary on (my no.) 4ab:

> viśeṣaṇam *atra paramatāpekṣaṃ, sarve tv avikalpakā eva
> "The distinction here (of perception from what is not perception) is in consideration of others' theory, but all (four kinds of perception) are devoid of constructive thought."

PVBh, 252.24 replaces **atra* with *lakṣaṇe*, probably meaning "in definition"; so "The distinction in definition . . ." P-Vin-Prat (Vetter, p. 40.2), gives Dharmakīrti's well-known definition, *pratyakṣaṃ kalpanāpoḍham abhrāntam* (Perception is devoid of constructive thought and is without delusion); so the further distinction *abhrānta* (without delusion) is added to Dignāga's definition. P-Vin-Bu, 21a-4, ff. goes with P-Vin-Prat (Vetter, p. 40. 3-5) about 'semblance of perception' (*pratyakṣābhāsa*), indicating that Dharmakīrti added the *abhrānta* to differentiate 'semblance of perception' from 'perception'. For the list of these semblances cf. below, P-Vin-Bu, 59b, and Tsoṅ-kha-pa's *Guided Tour.* P-Vin-Bu, 22a, cites PS-Prat, 1st, (my no.) 2cd:

> Direct perception is free from constructive thought (*kalpanā*). It (*kalpanā*) adds a name (*nāma*), class (*jāti*), etc.

P-Vin-Bu, 22a, cites from PS-Prat, 1st, Dignāga's commentary on (my no.) 3ab, this Abhidharma passage:

> cakṣur-vijñāna-samaṅgī nīlaṃ vijānāti no tu nīlam iti /
> arthe 'rtha-saṃjñi, na tv arthe dharma-saṃjñi /
> One equipped with eye-perception perceives blue, but does not think (with the eye-perception), "It is blue." In respect to an object-entity (*artha*), he has the idea, "It is an object-entity," but does not, in respect to the object-entity, have the idea, "It is a feature (*dharma*)."

And cites from Dignāga's commentary on the same 3ab, this Abhidharma passage:

> āyatana-svalakṣaṇaṃ praty ete svalakṣaṇa-viṣayā na dravya-svalakṣaṇaṃ prati
> These (sense perceptions) have individual characters as their sense objects, toward (each) (outer) sense-base individual character, not toward a material (i.e. composite) individual character.

These outer sense bases are five in number, going with the five outer-directed senses, 'form' for the eye, 'sound' for the ear, etc. Thus, an 'individual character' is not allowed for a gross object, but rather for the partite aspects, namely, the visible, the audible, the touchable, and so on. Dignāga takes this as an Abhidharma tenet preceding his system.

P-Vin-Bu, 22b-4, cites PS-Prat, 1st, what I take to be part of Dignāga's commentary on 3ab, but which Hattori decides was a half-*kārikā* of PS-Prat, 1st section:

> tatrānekārthajanyatvāt svārthe sāmānyagocaram
> There (i.e. in that Abhidharma passage), since (mind-perception) is engendered by multiple external entities, it has a global (*sāmānya*) scope in the sense of its own object-entity.

And also cites the immediate continuation of Dignāga's commentary:

> aneka-dravyotpadyatvāt tat svāyatane sāmānya-gocaram ity ucyate, na tu bhinneṣv abheda-kalpanāt / [Skt. from Hattori, *Dignāga*, p. 90].
> Since (mind perception) is aroused by many substances, it is said, in regard to its own (sense) base that it has a global scope, but not toward particular (things) because without constructive thought (*kalpanā*) of particularity.

The point here is that the *svalakṣaṇa* object of *mānasa-pratyakṣa* is labelled a 'global scope' (*sāmānya-gocaram*). The denial that this 'global scope' is the object of 'constructive thought' is consistent with the tenets of Dignāga-Dharmakīrti that lead to a conclusion about the role of the old Buddhist term *mano-vijñāna,* the perception based on the sixth sense-organ, the *mano-indriya.* This term *mano-vijñāna* apprently had a double function, (a) to perceive in the mind the mental forms of the five other senses; (b) to perceive the realm of *dharmas.* A conclusion is unavoidable that the (a) function led to the Buddhist logic term *manasa-pratyakṣa*; while the (b) function, according to Dharmakīrti, *Nyāyabindu* (opening section on *pratyakṣa*), led to the term *svasaṃvedanapratyakṣa,* since it perceives the set of thought and mentals (*citta-caitta*) which is also called the *dharma-realm.*

P-Vin-Bu, 22b-4 (end), cites PS-Prat, 2nd (Examination of the *Vādavidhi* definition), k. 3:

/ gaṅ zhig snaṅ ba de las min /
/ lṅa po bsags la dmigs pa'i phyir /
/ gaṅ las de ni don dam pa /
/ de la tha sñad du ma byas / zhes bśad do /
Any representation (in mind perception) is not from them (i.e. the five partite, or atomic, sense objects), because the consciousness-support (*ālambana*) is an aggregation of the five. That which is its (i.e. the representation's) cause is absolute-existence (*don dam pa*) (i.e. the atoms), but (the representation) is not made up of those (atoms), even conventionally.

P-Vin-Bu, 22b-5, cites 'by Dignāga;' in fact, the citation is *Ālambanaparīkṣā,* lcd:

> They (the atoms) do not appear therein. So its (i.e. the representation's) sense object (*viṣaya*) is not the atoms, like a sense-organ (has objects).

P-Vin-Bu, 22b-6, mentions the theory that the mind of a young child is free from all constructive thought, and promptly goes into the reasons for rejecting this theory, claiming that baby behaviour can only be explained by accepting influences from previous lives. Dharmakīrti, P-Vin-Prat (Vetter, p. 42.2-3) says that the 'mind-based perception' (*manovijñāna*) possesses (or, holds) constructive thought; and whether this is inconsistent with Dignāga's passage presented and discussed above, will have to be considered. In accordance with old Buddhist theories, Dharmakīrti, P-Vin-Prat (Vetter, p. 42.4) mentions that it (the mind-based perception) is affected by the habit-energy (*vāsanā*) of constructive thought, independent of approaching an efficacious object-entity—thus placing the cause in past lives.

P-Vin-Bu, 23a-1 cites Śāntarakṣita's *Tattvasaṃgraha,* k. 1215:

> atītabhavanāmārthabhāvanāvāsanānvayāt /
> sadyojāto 'pi yadyogād itikarttavyatāpaṭuḥ //
> As a result of obeying the habit-energy of (repeatedly) cultivating the meaning of words in past lives, even one newly born, by union with this (habit-energy), has the know-how to do something 'thus'.

To compare with Dignāga, it seems the way to show consistency with Dharmakīrti's P-Vin statement, is to conclude that the old Buddhist category called mind-based perception' (*mano-vijñāna*) is what is attributed possession of constructive thought (*kalpanā*); and so Dignāga replaced this with another term *mānasa-pratyakṣa*, not attributed constructive thought, even though having an object called *sāmānya-gocaram*. This may be why, in the PS passage cited above (P-Vin-Bu, 22b-4), it was necessary in the translation to add "mind perception" in parentheses: Dignāga did not literally state it.

B. Varieties of Pratyakṣa

P-Vin-Prat (Vetter, p. 40, reconstructed), k. 4:

> pratyakṣaṃ kalpanāpoḍham abhrāntam abhilāpinī /
> pratītiḥ kalpanārthasya sāmarthyena samudbhavāt // 4 /
> Direct Perception is free from constructive thought (*kalpanā*) and is nondeluded (*abhrānta*). Discourse with recognition is due to the generation by force of the meaning of constructive thought.

P-Vin-Bu, 23a-2, begins treating the standard four kinds of *pratyakṣa*—that of the outer-directed senses, of mind, of introspection, and of the yogin. Since these all are described as free from constructive thought (*kalpanā*), they involve difficult matters. P-Vin-Bu, 23ā-5, cites PV-Prat, 133:

> manaso yugapadvṛtteḥ savikalpāvikalpayoḥ /
> vimūḍho laghuvṛtter vā tayor aikyaṃ vyavasyati //
> A dull person, (considering) whether the mind, with its constructive thought and lack of constructive thought, has simultaneous modification or quick modification, decides that the two are one.

For example, note the following passages on *yoga-kṣema*, moved here from two later positions because of the applicability here.

P-Vin-Bu, 41a-4, cites as though from *Hetubindu*, but apparently in a paraphrase (cf. Steinkellner, p. 34. 26-30):

> "Because the later moments of *pratyakṣa* are (like) 'acquisition' (*yoga*) and 'security' (*kṣema*) that are not distinguished (tha dad pa med pa)".

P-Vin-Bu, 38b-1, cites *Hetubindu* (Steinkellner's reconstructed Sanskrit, 35.14-16):

> tato 'pi vikalpād vastuny eva tadadhyavasāyena pravṛtteḥ, pravṛttau vikalpasya pratyakṣenābhinnayogakṣematvāt /

> It is a result of a constructive thought, because engaging in a given thing (*vastu*) by clinging to it; and because, there being the engagement, there is acquisition and security (*yoga-kṣema*) not dissociating direct perception (*pratyakṣa*) and constructive thought (*vikalpa*).

Here the *dvandva* compound *yogakṣema* appears to allot 'acquisition' to 'direct perception' and 'security' to 'constructive thought.' Since in this system 'direct perception' apprehends the previously not experienced, its object can be construed as an 'acquisition'. The 'security' would then be the constructive thought (*vikalpa*) in the role of Dignāga's comment, cited below, "the image of experience" (*anubhavākāra*) derived from the speech community. The 'image' could be among the objects of 'mental perception'—devoid of constructive thought—as long as it is a particularity (*bheda*), because as long as the objects of 'mental perception' are disparate there is no 'generality character' (*sāmānyalakṣaṇa*). The above HB passage suggests that it is by reason of clinging to "the image of experience" serving as a 'given thing' (*vastu*)—hence object of 'mental perception'—that one cannot dissociate direct perception from constructive thought.

(1) *Outer Sense Perception*

Bu-ston, in the course of rejecting the decision of the 'dull person,' cites (23a-7) PS- Prat, 1st, (my no.) 3ab, about outer sense perception:

> asādhāraṇahetutvād akṣais tad vyapadiśyate /
> Its name (viz. '*pratyakṣa*') is designated by a sense-organ (*akṣa*) because of the non-overlapping causes (viz., *prati* = 'each one').

P-Vin-Prat (Vetter, p. 42), k.5-6, deals with lack of constructive thought of this sense perception:

> athopayoge 'pi punaḥ smārtaṃ śabdānuyojanam /
> akṣadhīr yady apekṣeta so 'rtho vyavahito bhavet //5/
> Besides, if sense cognition were dependent on reminiscence bound to a word, even for application to an object-entity, this object-entity would be screened from view.
>
> yaḥ prāg ajanako buddher upayogāviśeṣataḥ /
> sa paścād api tena syād arthāpāye 'pi netradhīḥ //6/

And it would follow that, although previously there was no generation of a cognition due to no distinction of application (to an object-entity), it (the reminiscence) would later become eye-cognition even in the absence of the object-entity.

P-Vin-Prat, k. 7-8, use PV-Prat, k. 145, 174:

viśeṣaṇaṃ viśeṣyas ca sambandhaṃ laukikīṃ sthitim/
gṛhītvā saṅkalayyaitat tathā pratyeti nānyathā // 145 /
When someone takes the distinction(i.e. *jāti,* etc.) and the distinguishable (i.e. *dravya,* etc.) (as earlier and later), (takes) (their) relation (i.e. *samavāya,* etc.) and the worldly rule, and treats them together, so does he come to understand (the realist opponent), not otherwise.

saṃketasmaraṇopāyaṃ dṛṣṭasaṃkalanātmakam /
pūrvāparaparāmarśaśūnye taccākṣuṣe katham // 174 /
How can there be a means of recalling signals (*saṃketa*), (a means) that treats together what is seen, in the eye faculty which is void of positing earlier and later?

P-Vin-Prat (Vetter. p. 46—no Sanskrit), k. 9:

/ de ni rtog pas bslad na yaṅ /
/'dod pas ldog daṅ ñe ba'yi /
/ don la blo ni ltos med 'gyur /
/'di ñid kyis gzhan min zhe na /
When one is corrupted by constructive thought, and affected by desire, and has no attention of (sense) cognition to a nearby entity, is there nothing else by this one?

P-Vin-Prat (Vetter, p. 46, 48—no Sanskrit), k. 10:

/de dbaṅ spyod yul ma yin phyir/
/ med daṅ tha dad med pa la 'aṅ /
/ reg pa las kyan blo der 'gyur /
/ gal te reg de rdzas yin no /
Since a sense-organ is not its objective domain, also in regard to the absent and to the nondistinct, a (constructive) cognition may occur from contact thereto. (Indeed.) if one can touch it, it is material.

P-Vin-Prat (Vetter, p. 48—no Sanskrit), k.11-12:

/ ma yin 'di ni bum pa zhes /

/ śes la kha dog snaṅ phyir ro /
/ gaṅ zhig yod la gaṅ mthoṅ ba /
/ de mthoṅ ba las de yi sgra / (11)
/ dran rigs de rtogs med na ni /
/ sgra yi khyad par ji ltar dran /
/ de ma dran na de daṅ don /
/ bsres nas rig pa de ji ltar / (12)
While knowing this pot is absent, its colour still shines. Given something existent, which one sees; after the seeing—there is its sound. (11)
When there is no understanding that a memory is correct, how remember a distinction of sound? When not remembering something, having mixed up that thing and (another) entity, how is there a knowing? (12)

P-Vin-Prat, k.13-14, use PV-Prat, 124-125:

saṃhṛtya sarvataś cintaṃ stimitenāntarātmanā /
sthito 'pi cakṣuṣā rūpam īkṣate sākṣajā matiḥ // 124 /
When thought is drawn together from all sides and fixed with a motionless inner nature, (one recognizes that) the mind views form by means of the eye, to wit, is born from the sense-organ (without constructive thought).

punar vikalpayan kiṃcid āsīn me kalpanedṛśī /
iti vetti na pūrvokāvasthāyām indriyād gatau // 125 /
Then, again engaging in a bit of constructive thought, one recognizes, "Such was my constructive thought." (And recognizes that) it is not in the sense of understanding through sense organ of the previously mentioned (Prat, 124) situation.

P-Vin-Bu, 35a-b, cites (with slight differences from both Tanjur versions) PS-Prat, 1st (my no.) 3cd-4ab:

dharmiṇo 'neka-rūpasya nendriyāt sarvathā gatiḥ /
svasaṃvedyam anirdeśyaṃ rūpam indriya-gocaraḥ //
A factual base (*dharmin*) for multiple forms can in no case be understood from a (single) sense-organ. The form in the range of a sense is to be introspected, and cannot be (verbally) designated.

P-Vin-Prat (Vetter, p. 54), k. 15:

śabdenāvyāpṛtākṣasya buddhāv apratibhāsanāt /
arthasya dṛṣṭāv iva tad anirdeśyasya vedakam //

In the manner when one 'sees' an object-entity by word, so one understands the non-functional sense organ to-lack the designatable, since there is no appearance to cognition.

P-Vin-Prat, k.16, uses PV-Prat, 126:

> ekatra dṛṣṭo bhedo hi kvacin nānyatra dṛśyate /
> na tasmād bhinnam asty anyat sāmānyaṃ buddhyabhedataḥ /
> For a particular observed in one place is never observed in another place. There is no other generality partitioned off from that, since it has no particularization of cognition.

P-Vin-Prat (Vetter, p. 58—no Sanskrit), k.17ab:

> / de la gzhan la blo daṅ ni /
> / sgra 'jug phyir na mi rtogs min /
> There is no lack of understanding for engaging a sound, while the (sense) cognition is on something different.

P-Vin-Prat, k. 17cd, uses PV-Prat, 127ab:

> tasmād viśeṣaviṣayā sarvaivendriyajā matiḥ /
> Therefore, every cognition born from a sense-organ has a distinct thing as a sense object.

P-Vin-Prat (Vetter, p. 58), k. 18:

> taddṛṣṭāv eva dṛṣṭeṣu saṃvitsāmarthyabhāvinaḥ /
> smaraṇād abhilāṣeṇa vyavahāraḥ pravartate //
> Conventional speech proceeds by belief through memory arisen from the effectiveness of experience in visible things, when there was sight of them.

(2) *Mental Perception*

P-Vin-Bu, 39a-4, attributes to the Buddha ('Bhagavat') the remark, "The cognition cognizing form is of two kinds—that based on sense-organs (*indriya*) and that based on the mind (*manas*)." Bu-ston declares the meanings of this remark to be in PS (my no. 4cd) and Dignāga's commentary thereon:

> mānasaṃ cārtha(ṃ) rāgādi-svasaṃvittir akalpikā / (4cd) /
> Also the mental (sense) having the object-entity (*artha*) and self-intuition of passion (*rāga*), etc., are without constructive thought.

> mānasam api rūpādi-viṣayālambanam avikalpakam anubhavākārapravṛttam /
> Also the mental (sense) with a consciousness-support (*ālambana*)—from the sense object of form, etc., promoted by the image of experience—is without constructive thought.

For the two Sanskrit passages, see the references in Hattori, *Perception*, Notes, pp. 92-93, where it was not noticed that to make sense of the first passage, all one has to do is insert the omitted *anusvāra* (the dot often lost from Sanskrit manuscripts) after the word *artha.*

The Buddhist logician's theory of 'mental perception' drew various criticisms from opponents.

P-Vin-Bu, 39a-5, 6 inroduces a PV verse as showing the challenge by Aviddhakarṇa (T. Rnam phug pa), namely, PV-Prat, 239:

> pūrvānudbhūtagrahaṇe mānasyāpramāṇatā /
> adṛṣṭagrahaṇe 'ndhāder api syād arthadarśanam //
> (If) when one apprehends the previously experienced, his mind has no authority, then when one apprehends the not-yet-seen, there would be viṣion of the object-entity even by the blind, etc.

P-Vin-Prat, k. 19a-c, uses PV-Prat, 243, reply to Aviddhakarṇa:

> tasmād indriyavijñānāntarapratyayodbhavam /
> mano 'nyam eva gṛhnāti viṣayaṃ nāndhadṛk tataḥ //
> Therefore, the mind, arising by condition right after sense perception, apperceives indeed another object; hence it is not a view by the blind.

P-Vin-Prat, k. 20, uses PV-Prat, 247:

> bhinnakālaṃ kathaṃ grāhyam iti ced grāhyatām viduḥ /
> hetutvam eva yuktijñā jñānākārārpaṇakṣamam //
> (Opponent:) How can one apprehend a particular time? (Response:) Those knowing the principle, would know the apprehensible state and the causal state (*hetutva*) capable of focussing upon the cognitive image.

Dharmakīrti classifies this as an 'interim verse' (*antaraśloka*).

P-Vin-Bu, 40b-6, as a citation of '*ācārya* Dignāga':

> / tshad mar źal gyis bźes pa'i phyir yul gźan 'dsin pa yin gyi /
> raṅ gyi yid kyis brtags pa'am bzuṅ ba 'dsin pa ma yin nam/

(Opponent:) "Should we not apprehend a different sense object (*viṣaya*) to admit as authority (*pramāṇa*), be it examined by one's own mind, or the apprehension of the already apprehended?"

Bu-ston goes on to denounce this theory of 'authority' since the Dignāga-Dharmakīrti system does not accept as 'authority' an apprehension of the already apprehended.

P-Vin-Bu, 42a-5, cites *Rgyan mdzad*, i.e. PV-Bh-Prat, p. 305.4, the verse no. 443:

> idam ityādi yaj jñānam abhyāsāt purataḥ sthite /
> sākṣātkaraṇatas tat tu pratyakṣaṃ mānasaṃ mataṃ //
> When, as a result of habitual practice, (the object) is situated in front, whatever the cognition 'this' and so on, since it is a direct realization, we claim it to be 'mental perception.'

(3) ***Introspective Perception***

P-Vin-Bu, f. 42b-3, cites 'own commentary' (*raṅ 'grel*) what is in fact Dignāga's own comment on PS-Prat, 1st section (my no.) 4cd:

> / 'dod chags daṅ / źe sdaṅ daṅ / gti mug daṅ / bde ba daṅ duḥkha la sogs pa ni / dbaṅ po la mi ltos pa'i phyir raṅ rig pa'i mṅon sum mo /

The Sanskrit for this is in PV-Bh, p. 305, cited as the words of the '*mūlācārya*':

> rāgadveṣamohasukhaduḥkhādiṣu svasamvedanam indriyānapekṣatvāt.
> Introspective (perception) is toward lust, hatred, and delusion; pleasure and pain, etc., because independent of sense organs.

However, the Tibetan of PV-Bh, in the PTT edition, p. 142-2-6, 7, agrees with the Sanskrit text edited by Sāṅkrityāyana that immediately after the above-cited Sanskrit occurs the words *mānasaṃ pratyakṣam*, as though this author—Prajñākāragupta—takes the passage as indicating Svasaṃvedana (introspection) toward passion, etc. and that there is Mānasa-pratyakṣa through independence of sense-organs, i.e., denying that the 'mental perception' is a sixth sense. Prajñākāragupta seems misrepresented, since the Dignāga statement that follows below shows that it is the Svasaṃvedana that is independent of external sense-organs.

P-Vin-Bu, 42b-4, cites PS-Prat, 1st, (my no.) 5cd (Sanskrit available) and Dignāga's own comment (Skt. not available):

> kalpanāpi svasaṃvittāv iṣṭā nārthe vikalpanāt /
> Even constructive thought is admitted as (object for) self-intuition (=introspection), because the constructive thought (there) is not toward an [external] object. (5cd). "When toward an (external) object, like lust, and so forth, it is not a direct perception, because it is not an introspection; (thus) there is no fault." (Comment).

P-Vin-Bu, 42b, cites PV-Prat, 287:

> śabdārthagrāhi yad yatra taj jñānaṃ tatra kalpanā /
> svarūpaṃ ca na śabdārthas tatrādhyakṣam ato 'khilam //
> Whatever the cognition and wherever is its apprehension of auditory object, therein is the constructive thought. But there is no auditory object in its own form, since therein all belongs to direct perception.

P-Vin-Prat, k. 21ab (Vetter, p. 62):

> / gzhan la brten min bdag ñid phyir /
> / bde sogs rnams la brda nus min /
> Because [in that case] oneself lacks dependence on another, there is no capability of words for pleasure, etc.

P-Vin-Prat, k. 21cd, uses PV-Prat, 249cd:

> teṣām ataḥ svasaṃvittir nābhijalpānuṣaṅginī /
> Therefore, the self-intuition of those is not in conjunction with words.

P-Vin-Prat, k. 22, uses PV-Prat, 251:

> tadatadrūpiṇo bhāvās tadatadrūpahetujāḥ /
> tat sukhādi kim ajñānaṃ vijñānābhinnahetujan //
> The on-going things with form of this and not this, are born from causes with form of this and not this. Why is this pleasure, etc. the ignorance born from a cause not distinct from perception?

P-Vin-Prat, k. 23, uses PV-Prat, 270 (but Tibetan does not exactly correspond):

> tasyāviśeṣe bāhyasya bhāvanātāratamyataḥ /
> tāratamyaś ca buddhau syān na prītiparitāpayoḥ //

> When there is no difference of the external, due to a distinction of deep meditation; and a distinction in Buddhi (cognition) would not be of joy and sorrow.

The foregoing, k. 23, appears to be part of an argument with the Sāṃkhya.

P-Vin-Bu, 44a, turns to the rejection of the categories of objective reality espoused by the Nyāya-Vaiśeṣika, as in a half-verse; / rdzas daṅ yon tan las daṅ spyi / bye brag 'du ba rnam pa drug / "There are six kinds: *dravya, guṇa, karman, sāmānya, viśeṣa,* and *samavāya.*"

P-Vin-Bu, f. 48a-b, cites for rejection purposes verses about the Sāṃkhya evolutes attributed to Īśvarakṛṣṇa as the author of the *Sāṃkhya-kārikā.* Thus, k. XXII:

> / raṅ bźin las chen de las ṅa rgyal te /
> / de las tshogs ni rnam pa bcu drug go /
> / bcu drug po ni de dag rnams las kyaṅ /
> / lṅa po rnams las 'byuṅ ba chen po lṅa //
> prakṛter mahaṃs tato 'haṅkāras tasmād gaṇaś ca ṣoḍaśakaḥ /
> tasmād api ṣoḍaśakāt pañcabhyaḥ pañcabhūtāni //
> k. xxii. From Prakṛti is Mahat (=Buddhi); from this, is Ahaṃkāra (creation of "I"); from this the aggregate of sixteen. From five among the sixteen, are the five gross elements.

or, k. XXI:

> / skyes bu mthoṅ ba'i don du daṅ /
> / de bźin gtso bo 'ga' źig don /
> / źa loṅ bźin du gñis ka'i yaṅ /
> / 'brel pa de yis 'khor ba bya /
> puruṣasya darśanārthaṃ kaivalyārthaṃ tathā pradhānasya/
> paṅgv-andhavad ubhayor api saṃyogas tatkṛtaḥ sargaḥ //
> k. xxi. The association of the two, like a lame person and a blind person, is for viewing the Puruṣa (=the consciousness side) and for detachment of primal matter (=Prakṛti). Also, the evolution [from Prakṛti] proceeds from this association.

P-Vin-Prat, k. 24ab (Vetter, p. 66):

> / myaṅ phyir sems pa de raṅ bzhin /
> / ma yin myoṅ ba min phyir ro /
> There is no individual presence of a thinking-volition resulting from experience, because it does not experience.

P-Vin-Bu, 52a-5 (cf. Vetter, p. 70.4); "It would be a contradiction for these to be simultaneous in a single (cognition)." And P-Vin-Bu now cites the view of Jñānaśrī: It would be a contradiction for these to be simultaneous in a single external thing (phyi'i bdag ñid gcig la gcig car 'gal). This commentator took "a single (one)" as the external entity rather than the cognition.

P-Vin-Prat, k. 24cd (Vetter, p. 70):

> / de yi raṅ bzhin las ldog pa'i /
> / blo ni rtogs pa med phyir ro //
> And because the cognition contrary to its individual presence does not understand.

P-Vin-Prat, k. 25ab uses PV-Prat, 227 ab:

> saṃsargād avibhāgaś ced ayogolakavahnivat /
> (Opponent:) By a mixture when there would be no separation, like an iron ball and fire.

P-Vin-Prat, k. 25cd, uses PV-Prat 277cd:

> bhedābhedavyavasthaivam ucchinnā sarvavastuṣu
> (Response:) Were that so, then in all given things the establishment of particularity and non-particularily would be lost (i.e. impossible).

P-Vin-Prat, k. 26-27, use PV-Prat 278-279:

> abhinnavedanasyaikye yan naivaṃ tad vibhedavat /
> sidhyed asādhanatve 'sya na siddhaṃ bhedasādhanam // 278/
> bhinnābhaḥ sitaduḥkhādir abhinno buddhivedane /
> abhinnābhe vibhinne ced bhedābhedau kim āśrayau // 279 /
> When there is a unity (*aikya*) for someone who does not recognize the partitioned, whatever is not so, is like a variety. When there is no proof for him which one might prove, there is no proof of a particularity (*bheda*) proved. (k. 26) When white, pain, etc. appear distinct while not distinct, then cognition and recognition, appearing not distinct, are at varience. What are the two bases that the particular and the nonparticular have? (k. 27)

Those two verses are described by Dharmakīrti as 'summary verses' (*saṃgraha-śloka*).

(4) *Yogin's Perception*

P-Vin-Prat, k. 28 (Vetter, p. 72):

/ 'jigs sogs bzhin du bsgoms pa yi /
/ stobs kyis gsal bar snaṅ gyur pa'i /
/ śes gaṅ slu ba can min pa /
/ rtog med de ni mṅon sum mo //
By dint of contemplating such things as 'fear', the awareness comes to shine brightly, with no deception. That lack of constructive thought is a perception (*pratyakṣa*).

P-Vin-Bu, 55b, cites PS-Prat, 1st, (my no.) 5ab:

yoginām gurunirdeśāvyatibhinnārthamātradṛk /
(Also,) the yogins' vision of just the object unmixed with the guru's instruction.

P-Vin-Prat, k. 29 uses PV-Prat, 282:

kāmaśokabhayonmādacaurasvapnādyupaplutāḥ /
abhūtān api paśyanti purato 'vasthitān iva // 282 /
Persons intoxicated by lust, sorrow, fear; assailed by thieves, dreams, and so on, see things as though present in front, although unreal.

P-Vin-Prat, k. 30 (Vetter, p. 74):

/ bslad pa ji bzhin gus pas ni /
/ sgrub pa rab tu mthoṅ phyir ro /
/ lkog gyur rtogs pa'i 'du śes la /
/ de lta'i 'jug pa ma mthoṅ phyir //
One should be devoted just as is the affliction, because one envisages the attainment. The idea that understands becomes secretive, because one does not envisage the onset.

P-Vin-Prat, k. 31 uses PV-Prat 285:

tasmād bhūtam abhūtaṃ vā yad yad evābhibhavyate /
bhāvanāpariniṣpattau tat sphuṭākalpadhīphalam / 285 /
Hence, whatever one contemplates in front, whether real or unreal, that, upon fulfilment of the contemplation, is a result consisting of a clear and non-constructing cognition (*dhī*).

Those are three interim verses (*antara-śloka*).

P-Vin-Bu, 57a, cites PV-Prat, 286a,c (Skt.) = 286bc (Tib.):

tad bhāvaṇājam, pramāṇaṃ saṃvādi yat, pratyakṣam iṣṭam /
Whatever authority is not deceptive, that we hold to be direct perception born of contemplation.

P-Vin-Prat, k. 32, uses PV-Prat, 283:

na vikalpānubaddhasyāsti sphuṭārthāvabhāsitā /
svapne 'pi smaryate smārttaṃ na ca tat tādṛgarthavat /
There is no vivid appearance of the object for (cognition) bound to constructive thought. Even though one remembers in a dream, the memory does not convey such a (vivid) object.

P-Vin-Bu, 57, mentioning that even when a memory is proved to be fallacious, it is in fact memory, so cannot be annulled by a principle, Bu-ston then cites a half-verse as though from PV (Tib. *Rnam 'grel*), but which could not be traced through Steinkellner's *Index*:

/ gnod byed rigs pa dam pa ni /
/ med na ñams myoṅ spaṅ bya min /
"The illustrious principle of *bādhaka* (annulment) is: when there is no experience, there is nothing to eliminate."

On a hunch since Tib. *Rnam 'grel* can also refer to Skt. *Svavṛtti* in the special case of Dharmakirti's own commentary on PV-Sva, I also surveyed this *Svavṛtti* for the passage, but without success.

P-Vin-Bu, 58a, cites the *Sarvajña-siddhi-(kārikā)* (by Kalyāṇarakṣita):

/ gaṅ gaṅ gnas skabs gźan dag tu /
/ khyad par du ni rab 'jug pa /
/ de de śin tu dri ma med /
/srid de gser la sogs pa bźin //
Whatever be the other states (*avasthā*) to which one ascends in distinguished manner, those are the immaculate worlds, like gold and other (precious articles).

That citation concludes the discussion of Yogi-pratyakṣa.

C. Semblance of Perception

P-Vin-Bu, 58a-7, beginning of discussion of 'semblance of perception' (*pratyakṣābhāsa*), with the argument over whether dream cognition has constructive thought (*kalpanā*).Bu-ston concludes that according to this *ācārya* (? Dignāga) dream cognition lacks *kalpanā*, but is not a *pratyakṣa* because deluded (*bhrānta*).

P-Vin-Prat, k. 33 (Vetter, p. 76):

/ rnam rtog dṅos mi snaṅ phyir daṅ /
/ ñe bar bslad pa slu ba'i phyir /
/ mṅon sum ltar snaṅ . . .
= vikalpo 'vastunirbhāsād visaṃvādād upaplavaḥ /
pratyakṣābhaḥ [= ābhāsaḥ] . . .
/ . . . dbaṇ skyes kyaṅ/
/ gzhan las de khyad med phyir ro //
Constructive thought is an affliction, because it lacks the appearance of given things, and because it deceives. Also, Semblance of Perception arises from sense-organs, because it is not distinguished from other [persons' sense-organs].

P-Vin-Bu, 59b, cites PS-Prat, 1st, (my no.) 6:

bhrānti-saṃvṛtisaj-jñānam anumānānumānikam /
smārtābhilāṣikaṃ ceti pratyakṣābhaṃ satairmiram //
Semblance of perception is (of the varieties) (a) delusive cognition, (b) cognition of conventional existence, (c) (the set, viz.) inference, derived from inference, derived from memory, derived from belief: (d) along with sensory affliction.

P-Vin-Bu, 60a-5, introduces a Dignāga comment, saying:

"The *Pramāṇasamuccaya*, after developing the definition of *pratyakṣa* (i.e. in 1st sect.), elsewhere (i.e. in 2nd sect.) in the phase of examining the *Vādavidhi* (k.3, and comm.) explains the sense cognitions as two apprehensions, to wit, it is absurd to take the eye, and so forth, as (exhibiting) sense objects (as they are), since however the objective things are, they (eye, etc.) are the cause for (those things) appearing elsewhere, altering as sense objects, because the atoms of eye, etc. are the cause both for the 'double moon' (sense affliction) and for the perception of blue, etc. appearances."

P-Vin-Bu, 60a-7, cites PS-Prat, 2d, k. 3, the Dignāga comment:

cakṣurādinām apy ālambanatva-prasaṅgaḥ te 'pi paramārthato 'nyathā vidyamānā nīlādy-ābhāsasya dvi-candrādy-ābhāsasya ca jñānasya kāraṇī-bhavanti.
It is absurd that they, as the object supports of eye, etc. become the cause of cognition with the blue, etc., double moon, etc. semblances since they are otherwise in the absolute sense.

P-Vin-Bu, 60b-2, mentions that PS, while refuting wayward constructive thought, sets forth six kinds of constructive thought (*kalpanā*); and that PV, while explaining PS, mentions (i.e. reduces them to) three kinds of *kalpanā*, namely, involved either with (1) signal-support (*saṃketasaṃśraya*), (2) superimposition (*samāropa*), or (3) sense-transcendence (*parokṣa*); with non-constructive thought (*akalpanā*) as no. 4. But that here, the discussion is in terms of just 'constructive thought' and 'non-constructive thought' as two. Hattori (*Perception*, p. 83) says that for Dignāga, *kalpanā* means associating a name with a thing, and has for this purpose five categories, *nāman, jāti, guṇa, kriyā*, and *dravya*.

D. Authority as a Result

P-Vin-Bu, 60b, cites PS-Prat, 1st, (my no.) 7, Skt. available for first half; Hattori rejects the second half as a *kārikā* portion:

> savyāpāra-pratītatvāt pramāṇaṃ phalam eva sat /
> . . .
> Since one realizes it to be attended with (in fact, introduced by) function (*vyāpāra*), the authority is just a result (*kārya*); and one calls it an 'authority' (*pramāṇa*) when it does not lack (the introducing) function.

P-Vin-Prat (Vetter, p. 78, n. 3), k. 34:

> arthena ghaṭayaty enaṃ na hi muktvārtharūpatām /
> tasmāt prameyādhigateḥ pramāṇaṃ meyarūpatā //
> This connects the presented form of the external entity—which is unavoidable—with the external entity. Therefore, the authority for understanding the sanction [= the objective entity] (involves) the presented form of the sanction.

The intention here is to insist that both kinds of sanction—the individual character (*svalakṣaṇa*) and the generality character (*sāmānyalakṣaṇa*)—require presented forms (*rūpatā*) for the authority of two kinds, respectively, direct perception and inference.

P-Vin-Bu, 63a-5, cites a half *kārikā*, which seems not to be in *PV*:

> / ṅes par rtogs pa med pa'i phyir /
> / legs par rnam par gzhag pa yin /
> Because it has no certainty understanding, (yet) is a superb constancy (**samyag-vyavasthāna*).

Bu-ston's attendant discussion clarifies that the reference is to a sense-organ, e.g. the eye, which cannot decide (i.e. understand) that something is blue and not yellow, yet direct perception (*pratyaksa*) depends on such an organ to render such a judgment (i.e. understanding).

P-Vin-Prat, k. 35-37, use PV-Prat, 306-308:

> tasmāt prameyādhigateḥ sādhanaṃ meyarūpatā /
> sādhane 'nyatra tatkarmasambandho na prasidhyate // 306 /
> Hence, the proof for realizing the sanction (*prameya*) is the true form of the inferable. Should the proof be otherwise, the connection of its activity would not be proved.
>
> sā ca tasyātmabhūtaiva tena nārthāntaraṃ phalam /
> dadhānaṃ tac ca tām ātmany arthādhigamanātmanā // 307 /
> Besides, that (realization) is the 'embodiment' of it (the sanction). Hence, the result is not another object. The carrying it (the true form of the object) in itself by being the realization of the object,—
>
> savyāpāram ivābhāti vyāpāreṇa svakarmaṇi /
> tadvaśāt tadvyavasthānād akārakam api svayam // 308 //
> appears as though attended with function by a function in the sense of its own action; because, by virtue of it (true form of the inferable) by itself, without an agent, there is establishment of it (the realization).

Those three are interim verses.

P-Vin-Bu, 64a, cites PV-Prat, 309:

> yathā phalasya hetūnāṃ sadṛśātmatayodbhavāt /
> heturūpagraho loke 'kriyāvattve 'pi kathyate //
> Just as in the world the apprehension of the form of a cause is told after the occurrence of similarity of causes to the fruit, so also when there is no possession of activity.

P-Vin-Prat (Vetter, p. 86), k.38:

> nānyo 'nubhāvyo buddhyāsti tasyā nānubhavo paraḥ /
> grāhyagrāhakavaidhuryāt svayaṃ saiva prakāśate //
> (So,) there is no other thing to be experienced by the cognition, and it has no further experience, due to the deprivation of apprehended and apprehending. Indeed, that (i.e. the cognition, and the cognisable) appears by itself.

P-Vin-Bu, 69a-4, in the discussion going with the above verse (P-Vin-Prat, k. 38), gives the heading "showing that introspection is a result when there is no external entity" (*phyi don med pa la raṅ rig 'bras bur bstan*). This has two subsections, "refuting intuition of the other as a fruitional authority" (*gźan rig tshad 'bras dgag*) and "establishing introspection as a fruitional authority" (*raṅ rig tshad 'bras gźag pa*). The verse agrees with these two subsections. To explain 'appears by itself,' Bu-ston says (69a-7), "Just as a lamp shines by itself, so a cognition 'shines' (appears) by itself." Thus, 'appears by itself' does not mean 'comes into existence by itself.' but rather 'is self-illumining.' This establishes 'introspection.' The first part of the verse denies intuition of an external object. Hence the two conditions for 'introspection' are negative and positive.

P-Vin-Prat, k. 39-40, use PV-Prat, 330c-332b:

> avedyavedākārā yathā bhrāntair nirīkṣyate // 330cd /
> vibhaktalakṣaṇagrāhyagrahakākāraviplavā /
> tathākrtavyavastheyaṃ keśādijñānabhedavat // 331 /
> yadā tadā na saṃcodyagrāhyagrāhakalakṣaṇā / 332ab /
> So has this establishment been made as it was seen by deluded persons, (establishment) affected by the images of apprehended and apprehending when their characters are divided, without the image of knowable and knowing—like the separate cognition of hair (i.e. the sense affliction type), etc. That is the time when it does not have the impelling character of apprehendable and apprehending.

Those verse lines, k. 39-40, are interim verses.

P-Vin-Prat, k. 41ab, uses PV-Prat, 332cd:

> tad anyasaṃvido 'bhāvāt svasaṃvit phalam iṣyate //
> Since it is not another's intuition, we claim that self-intuition (= introspection) is a result.

P-Vin-Bu, 70b, cites PS-Prat, 1st (my no.) 8, in parts, with comments:

> svasaṃvittiḥ phalaṃ vātra (k. 8a)
> Furthermore, the introspection here is a result.

"That explanation of the meaning is the first examination of the result" (źes pa'i don 'chad pa 'bras bu'i rtog pa daṅ po yin no).

> tad-rūpo hy arthaniścayaḥ (k. 8b)
> For its nature is certainty of the object.

For the comment, Bu-ston cites Dignāga's commentary (K-version):

> / gaṅ gi tshe śes pa yul daṅ bcas pa don yin pa de'i tshe de daṅ rjes su mthun pa'i raṅ rig pa 'dod pa' am mi 'dod pa'i don rtogs par byed do /
> At the time the cognized is an external object (*artha*) serving as a sense object (*viṣaya*), at that time an introspection conforming to that (cognition) would understand the object, either accepting or not accepting it.

Bu-ston adds (70b-6): "This explanation (by Dignāga) is the second examination of the result ('bras bu'i rtog pa gñis pa); (so) here (I need) not explain it."

Then Dignāga's introductory remark to k. 8cd: "At the time one authorizes only the external object (*artha*), at that time:—" (gaṅ gi tshe phyi rol gyi don 'ba' źig gźal byar byed pa de'i tshe ni)—

> / yul gyi sñan ba nid de 'di'i /
> / tshad ma de yis 'jal bar byed / (k. 8cd)
> That very appearance of the sense object by which one authorizes, is the authorizing (**prāmāṇyam*) of this.

Bu-ston adds (70b-7): "This explanation (by Dignāga) teaching that introspection is a result even when it is toward an existing external object [in the form of a cognition as object] is the third examination of the result" (ces pa'i bśad pa phyi rol gyi don yod pa la yan raṅ rig 'bras bur ston pa 'bras bu'i rtog pa gsum pa). [Since elsewhere Dignāga had denied introspection to have an external object, this present statement implies that when Dignāga ascribed feelings to introspection, these feelings (whether liking, disliking, etc.) would be toward the mental form of external objects as are presumably the object of *mānasa-pratyakṣa*.]

[Introduction to P-Vin-Prat (Vetter, p. 88, 90)]: There appears no Tibetan for k. 41cd or Tibetan for k. 42a. Vetter, p. 90, n. 7, claims that these three Tibetan verse phrases have been incorporated in the prose (namely, after k. 41ab). But since the verse 42 is ascribed three Tibetan seven-syllable lines, b, c, d; and the line is the same as the 41b-line, except for the last syllable, '*dod* in 41b, and *bśad* in 42d, it is necessary to reject Vetter's conclusion here. Since *bśad* is a standard commentarial syllable in Tibetan, it is now clear that his 42d is part of the commentary on the *kārikā*-s (including the Sanskrit phrase *svasaṃvedanaṃ phalam* /), and that his 42bc is actually 41cd. Therefore, since I must respect Vetter's following numbering of *karikā*-s, I shall regard k.42 as nonexistent.

P-Vin-Prat, k. *41cd, 43-44, use PV-Prat, 350c-d; 351-352:

> uktaṃ-svabhāvacintāyāṃ tādātmyād arthasaṃvidaḥ // 350c-d /
> tathāvabhāsamānasya tādṛśo 'nyadṛśo 'pi vā /
> jñānasya hetur artho 'pīty arthasyeṣṭā prameyatā // 351 /
> yathākathaṃcit tasyārtharūpaṃ muktvābhāsinaḥ /
> arthagrahaḥ kathaṃ satyaṃ na jāne 'ham apīdṛśam // 352 /
> It is said: When one ponders the individual presence (*svabhāva*), because its nature amounts to intuiting the object-whether the cause, the object, is similar or not similar to the cognition-mind so appearing, the state of a sanction is claimed for the object. (Someone says:) Well, in the absence of any object-form for that (cognition) when it appears, how is there apprehension of an object? (Another replies:) Right! But I don't know it like that.

Those are interim verses. The PV-Bh says that the question is posed by the Sautrāntika and that the reply is made by the Yogācārin.

P-Vin-Bu, 71B-3, 4, 5, summarizing Dharmakīrti's comments on those verses:

> / 'di ltar phyi rol gyi don gyi tshul la don ni gzhal bya / gzuṅ ba'i rnam pa tshad ma / don rig pa 'bras bu / rnam par śes pa smra ba la bdag ñid gzhal bya / 'dzin pa'i rnam pa tshad ma / raṅ rig pa 'bras bu yin la / 'dir ni don gyi tshul gñis pa don gzhal bya / gzuṅ ba'i rnam pa tshad ma / raṅ rig pa 'bras bu yin no bstan pa yin no /
> "This way: in the manner of external object, the object is the sanction (*prameya*); the aspect of apprehending (*grahaṇākāra*) is the authority; intuition of the object (*artha-saṃvid*) is the result. In terms of perception (*vijñāna*), the personal, is the sanction; the aspect of apprehending is the authority; introspection is the result. Here, in both manners of object, the object is the sanction; the aspect of apprehending is the authority; and introspection is the result."

P-Vin-Prat, k. 45, uses PV-Prat, 353:

> avibhāgo 'pi buddhyātmā viparyāsitadarśanaiḥ /
> grāhyagrāhakasaṃvittibhedavān iva lakṣyate // 353 /
> While the personal cognition is impartite, by inverted views it

is characterized as though having particulars as the apprehendable (i.e. the object), the apprehending (i.e. the aspect), and the intuition (i.e. the result).

P-Vin-Bu, 72a, cites PS-Prat, 1st (my no.) 9 (Skt. corrected from Hattori, p. 107):

yad ābhāsaṃ prameyaṃ tat pramāṇa(ṃ) phalati punaḥ /
grāhakākārasaṃvittī trayaṃ nātaḥ pṛthakkṛtam //
At the time the sanction is apparent, three [particulars] result, e.g. the authority, the aspect of apprehending, and intuition. Not on that account should one take those as separate.

P-Vin-Prat, k. 46-54, use PV-Prat, 354-362:

mantrādyupaplutākṣāṇāṃ yathā mṛcchakalādayaḥ /
anyathaivāvabhāsante tadrūparahitā api // 354 /
For example, for persons whose senses are affected by incantations, etc., bits of clay, and so forth, appear as other things, though lacking the form of those (things).

tathaivādarśanāt teṣām anupaplutacakṣuṣām /
dūre yathā vā maruṣu mahān alpo 'pi dṛśyate // 355 /
For example, for those whose eyes are not (so) affected since they do not see that way, still in the distance in deserts a small thing appears big.

yathānudarśanaṃ ceyaṃ meyamānaphalasthitiḥ /
kriyate 'vidyamānāpi grāhyagrāhakasaṃvidam // 356 /
For example, (the triad) apprehendable, apprehension, and intuition (= introspection) operates even though not existing (separately); and the rule of the sanction, the authority, and the result operates for consideration.

anyathaikasya bhāvasya nānārūpāvabhāsinaḥ /
satyaḥ kathaṃ syur ākāras tadekatvasya hānitaḥ // 357 /
Otherwise, how could the images be true for a single on-going thing appearing with multiple forms, since there would be loss of its singleness and—

anyasyānyatvahāneś ca nābhedo 'rūpadarsanāt /
rūpabhedaṃ hi paśyanti dhir abhedaṃ vyavasyati // 358 //
loss of its otherness as another? (Otherwise,) there would be

no non-particularization on account of not seeing a form. For the intelligence that notices a particularization of form, decides on non-particularization.

bhāvā yena nirūpyante tad rūpaṃ nāsti tattvataḥ /
yasmād ekaṃ anekaṃ ca rūpaṃ teṣāṃ na vidyate // 359 /
That form in which on-going things are noticed, does not exist in reality; for which reason, a form, whether single or multiple, is not found among them.

sādharmyadarsanāl loke bhrāntir nāmopajayate /
atadātmani tādātmyavyavasāyena neha tat // 360 /
(Opponent:) In the world what is called 'error' (*bhrānti*) occurs from viewing a 'feature agreement' by deciding on an equivalence when there is no identity with it. Here it is not that (situation),—

adarśanāj jagaty asminn ekasyāpi tadātmanaḥ /
astīyam api yā tv antarupaplavasamudbhavā // 361 /
doṣodbhvā prakṛtyā sā vitathapratibhāsinī /
anapekṣitasādharmyadṛgādis taimirādivat // 362 /
because one does not see in this world even one (thing) identical with it. (Response:) There is also this (error), namely, one which arises through inner influence, appearing contrary by nature, having arisen from fault, and independent of noticing a 'feature agreement,' etc. to wit, like the eye-caul, and so on.

The preceding, P-Vin-Prat, k. 45-54, are all interim verses.
P-Vin-Prat (Vetter, p. 94); k. 55ab:

sahopalambhaniyamād abhedo nīlataddhiyoḥ /
There is no distinction between blue and its cognition, because it is certain that their consciousness-support is together.

P-Vin-Prat (Vetter, p.96), k.55cd:

apratyakṣopalambhasya nārthadṛṣṭiḥ prasiddhyati //
A view of the object-entity is not effectuated when there is no consciousness-support for perception (*pratyakṣa*).

P-Vin-Prat, k.56-58, use PV-Prat, 364-366:

tatrātmaviṣaye māne yathā rāgādivedanam /
iyaṃ sarvatra samyojyā meyamānaphalasthitiḥ // 364 /

> tatrāpy anubhavātmatvāt te yogyāḥ svātmasamvidi /
> iti sā yogyatā mānam ātmā meyaḥ phalaṃ svavit // 365 /
> grāhakākārasaṃkhyātā paricchedātmatātmani /
> sā yogyateti ca proktaṃ pramāṇaṃ svātmavedanam // 366 /
> This rule of sanction, authority, and result is applicable everywhere, e.g. in the case of authority where the object is oneself, according to the experiences of lust, etc.
> And because self is the experience there, those (lust, etc.) are feasible when there is intuition of oneself. Accordingly, the feasibility is the authority. When self is the sanction, introspection is a result. The feasibility mentioned as the apprehension-image in oneself—the discrimination self—is explained as the introspection authority.

Those three, P-Vin-Prat, k. 56-58, are interim verses.
P-Vin-Bu, 78b, cites PS, (my no.) 10ab:

> viṣayajñāna-tajjñāna-viśeṣāt tu dvi-rūpatā /
> There are two forms of cognition by distinction of (a) cognition of sense object, and (b) that cognition.

P-Vin-Prat, k. 59 (Vetter, p. 98, 100):

> / de phyir snaṅ don blo de dag / phyi don yod kyaṅ tha dad min /
> / des na blo ni tshul gñis pa / phyi rol ldog pa las grub 'gyur //
> So there are appearing objects and cognitions; while what be external objects, lack separation. Hence, cognition has two manners: (1) externalized, (2) reversed [into itself].

II. SVĀRTHĀNUMĀNA (INFERENCE FOR ONESELF)

A. The two kinds of inference
B. About evidence
C. The three modes of evidence
  (1) Nonapprehension
  (2) Individual presence
  (3) Result
D. Logical connection

A. The Two Kinds of Inference

For oneself (*svārtha*) and for others (*parārtha*)
P-Vin-Sva, k. 1 (Steinkellner, P-Vin, Teil I, pp. 22-25):

> anumānaṃ dvidhā, svārthaṃ trirūpāl liṅgato 'rthadṛk /
> atasmiṃs tadgraho bhrāntir api sambandhataḥ pramā //
> Inference is of two kinds. The one for one's own aim sees the object-entity by the evidence with three modes. Although there is delusion (*bhrānti*) of apprehending what is not there, it [Svārtha] is an authority by reason of connection (*sambandha*).

P-Vin-Bu, 81a-7, since the two authorities (*pratyakṣa* and *anumāna*) are results, mentions that 'inference' (*anumāna*) is a result as 'constructive thought' (*kalpanā*), which distinguishes it from 'perception' (*pratyakṣa*) defined as free from 'constructive thought.'

P-Vin-Bu, 81b-1, cites PS-Sva, k. 1 (Kitagawa, pp. 73-74):

> anumānaṃ dvidhā, svārthaṃ tri-rūpāl liṅgato 'rtha-dṛk / pūravavat phalam, arthaḥ svarūpaṃ cātulyam etayoḥ / (approximates the *kārikā*).
> Inference is of two kinds. (The kind) for oneself sees the object-entity (*artha*) by the evidence (*liṅga*) with three modes. As previously (i.e. in the case of *pratyakṣa*), it is a result, but the object-entity (i.e. generality character) and the true form (i.e. individual character), going with those two, are not equivalent.

"Two kinds" means 'inference for oneself' and 'inference for others'.

"Those two" means 'inference' and 'direct perception'.

The triple mode of evidence according to NB, II, 4, is (the *pakṣadharma*) "its presence indeed in the inferable"; or (the *anvaya*) "its presence only in similar cases"; or (the *vyatireka*) "its absence only in dissimilar cases". Each of these three is applied to each one of the three evidences (*liṅga*)—nonapprehension (*anupalabdhi*), individual presence (*svabhāva*), and result (*kārya*).

According to Bu-ston's discussion, it should be noticed that the 'constructive thought' going with inference as the 'authority' must be 'non-deceptive' (*avisaṃvādin*). According to Dharmakīrti, 'inference' is also attended with the kind of error called *bhrānti*, which is therefore not 'deceptive'; and so 'inference' can arrive at logical truth. Perception (*pratyakṣa*) lacks *bhrānti* but also lacks 'constructive thought' so cannot deal with logical truth.

P-Vin-Sva (p. 2*-3*), k. 2-6, use PV-Prat, 81-83, 57-58:

> yo hi bhāvo yathābhūtaḥ sa tādṛgliṅgacetasaḥ /
> hetus tajjā tathābhūte tasmād vastuni liṅgidhīḥ // 81 /

For, in what way an on-going thing may be, it is the cause (*hetu*) of the evidence-mentality of such sort, and from it arises, when a given thing is the same way, accordingly the cognition that bears the evidence.

liṅgaliṅgidhiyor evaṃ pāramparyeṇa vastuni /
pratibandhāt tadābhāsaśūnyayor apy avañcanam // 82 /
Thus, when there is a given thing by descent through relation to two cognitions, i.e. the evidence and evidence-bearing, that are devoid of appearance therein, also there is no deception.

tayos tadrūpaśūnyayos tadrūpādhyavasāyataḥ /
tadrūpāvañcakatva 'pi kṛtā bhrāntivyavasthitiḥ // 83 /
Even when there is no deception through the form of that (=the given, on-going thing), in the course of determining that form for the two (i.e. the evidence and the evidence-bearing cognitions) that are devoid of that form, a delusional foundation is set.

maṇipradīpaprabhayor maṇibuddhyābhidhāvataḥ /
mithyājñānāviśeṣe 'pi viśeṣo 'rthakriyāṃ prati // 57 /
yathā tathā 'yathārthatve 'py anumānatadābhayoḥ /
arthakriyānurodhena pramāṇatvaṃ vyavasthitam // 58 /
Just as for a person running forward with his gem-discrimination, by two lights of the gem-lamp, while there is no distinction of wayward cognition, there is a distinction regarding purposive activity (*arthakriyā*); so also, by those two lights of inference, while not in accordance with the external object, authority is set up with the 'complicity' (*anurodha*) of purposive activity.

P-Vin-Bu, 83a (from 82b) continues discussion of the 'gem-light' (PV-Prat, 57-58). He cites Śākyabuddhi's commentary on PV that the 'gem-light' is the evidence (*liṅga*)-result of the 'individual character' (*svalakṣaṇa*); that the 'complicity' (*anurodha* of Prat, 58) [with the purposive activity of the 'individual character'] being without memory [cf.PS-Prat, 1st, k.2] is not in conflict with inference. He also cites Dharmottara for a complicated argument that apparently disagrees with Śākyabuddhi's comment. The comments perhaps take it as too obvious to mention that the two lights of inference are the two kinds of inference, for oneself and for others.

Those verses (P-Vin-Sva, K.2-6) are interim verses (*antaraśloka*). P-Vin-Bu, 84a, cites PV-Prat, 53d-54ab:

> meyaṃ tv ekaṃ svalakṣaṇam //
> tasmād arthakriyāsiddheḥ sadasattāvicaraṇāt /
> The individual character is a single sanction according to an examination of its existence or non-existence and then proving its purposive activity.

P-Vin-Bu, 84a, cites PS-Prat, 1st, from k. 1, "The sanction is two characters (*lakṣaṇa*)," with Dignāga's commentary (V-version):

> na hi sva-sāmānya-lakṣaṇābhyām anyat prameyam asti / sva-lakṣaṇa-viṣayaṃ hi pratyakṣaṃ sāmānya-lakṣaṇa-viṣayam anumānam iti pratipādayiṣyāmaḥ /
> There is no other sanction (*prameya*) than the individual and the generality characters. For we shall find out that direct perception (*pratyakṣa*) has the object 'individual character'; and that inference (*anumāna*) has the object 'generality character'.

P-Vin-Bu, 84a- to 84b, cites PS-Sva, k. 2ab (Kitagawa, *Dignāga*, p.76, furnishes no Sanskrit):

> / raṅ gi mtshan ñid bstan bya min / yul tha dad phyir /
> The individual character cannot be announced (**anidarśana*), because it is a particular object.

and continues with citation of Dignāga's comments:

> / raṅ gi bdag ñid bźin du mṅon sum daṅ rjes su dpag pa dag gi yul tha dad pa yin no źes pa daṅ / spyi'i mtshan ñid kyi yul can ma yin pa'i rjes su dpag pa ni med do źes /
> "According to their individual nature, perception and inference have con- trasting objects," and, "There is no inference without a generality character as object".

P-Vin-Bu, 84b-3, 4, suggests the reason for Dignāga's remark that the "individual character cannot be announced" is that to announce it, or name it, is in the province of 'generality character' and constitutes a superimposition (sgro btags pa).

P-Vin-Bu, 84b, cites PV-Prat, 54cd-55ab:

> tasya svapararūpābhyāṃ gater meyadvayaṃ matam //
> ayathābhiniveśena dvitiyā bhrāntir iṣyate /
> We claim there are two sanctions by understanding its 'own' (=individual) and 'other' forms. We claim delusion (*bhrānti*, or 'error') by (or,'due to') the second one ('other'=generality character), because it clings to what is not so.

P-Vin-Bu,84b-6, cites "slob dpon gyis" (i.e. by the *ācārya*, namely Dignāga), and possibly combining passages from several places of PS-SV (for some of the words, P-Vin, II, Steinkellner's p. 3*.25, also "slob dpon gyis ni"):

> / tshad ma gñis kyi snaṅ ba don byed nus pa la 'khrul pa daṅ mi 'khrul pa can gyi gsal bar mi snaṅ ba daṅ snaṅ ba'i rnam pa tha dad pas gzuṅ don dṅos po gcig la de lta bu'i snaṅ ba tha dad de mi 'thad pa'i phyir gzuṅ don gyi dbye ba tha dad du bśad pa yin no /
> The two authorities have (respectively) a purposive activity (*arthakriyā*) appearance, and a clarity about what has delusion or non-delusion, thus a contrast of aspects (*ākāra*) of non-appearance and appearance. He explains the contrasting variety of the apprehensible object, because it is not valid that there be a contrast of such appearance for a single presence (*bhāva*) of the apprehensible object.

P-Vin-Sva (Steinkellner, p. 26, 119), k. 7:

> / tshad ma gñi ga dṅos po yi /
> / yul can snaṅ ba tha dad pas /
> / gcig la de mi 'thad pa'i phyir /
> / don gyi dbye ba bśad pa yin //
> Because there is a difference of appearance of the *viṣayin* (object-consideration) of the basic two authorities—because one is not valid [for evidence], one should explain the division of object.

P-Vin-Sva (Steinkellner, p. 4*.14-17), k. 8:

> atadrūpaparāvṛttavastumātraprasādhanāt /
> sāmānyaviṣayaṃ proktaṃ liṅgaṃ bhedāpratiṣṭhiteḥ //
> Because proving only the given thing that excludes (any) form that is not it, the evidence is declared to have a generality object, so not based on a particular one.

The verse involves the Dignāga-Dharmakīrti position that a generality and a particular object are in contrast, but adds a further point that evidence is based on a generality object and not based on a particular object.

B. About Evidence (*liṅga*)

P-Vin-Bu, 86a-4, begins treatment of the three topics of evidence. These are (1) definition of *liṅga* (T. rtags kyi mtshan ñid), (2) varieties (T. dbye ba), (3) establishing the connection of the feature (*dharma*) to the evidence (*liṅga*) (T.rtags chos kyi 'brel pa gtan la dbab pa).

(1) *Definition of Evidence*

P-Vin-Bu, f. 86b-4, speaking of a wrong generality and hence defective evidence, cites HB (Steinkellner ed., 2*.16-17):

> asādhāraṇātmanā dṛṣṭavataḥ pratyakṣeṇa yathādṛṣṭabhedaviṣayaṃ smārtaṃ liṅgavijñānam utpadyate /
> For a person who has seen with restricted direct perception (*pratyakṣa*) (a particular form), there arises the understanding (*vijñāna*) of evidence, (understanding) having as object the particular thing as it was (formerly) seen, and derived from memory.

P-Vin-Bu, f. 87a-7, in the discussion of the three 'rulings out' (*avacchedaka*), cites Smṛtijñānakīrti's *Vacanamukha:*

> / gaṅ źig raṅ gi don med ciṅ /
> / don gyis miṅ ni gsal byed pa /
> / tshig gi phrad ces bya ba ste /
> / de ldan phrad daṅ bcas pa yin //
> Any (term) that clarifies with meaning a name that by itself lacks meaning, is called "post-particle". Possessing it, (the name) is accompanied with the particle.

Of course, the particle meant is the *eva*; and the three cases are brought up now to illustrate the triple moded evidence.

P-Vin-Sva (Steinkellner, 5*.5 f) raises the question: "Given the contradiction when making the qualification with factual base (*dharmin*) elsewhere, if one does not make the qualification is there no inferable feature (*anumeya-dharma*)?" With response, "There is no (such feature), because one has made the qualification by ruling out non-connection (*ayoga*)." P-Vin-Sva (5*.10-29), k. 9-13, use PV-Par, 190-194:

ayogaṃ yogam aparair atyantāyogam eva ca /
vyavacchinatti dharmasya nipāto vyatirecakaḥ // 190 /
The particle *eva*, restriction of *dharma*, rules out (1) non-connection (*ayogam*), (2) connection with others (*yogam aparair*), (3) ultimate non-connection (*atyantāyogam* = impossibility).

viśeṣaṇaviśeṣyābhyāṃ kriyayā ca sahoditaḥ /
vivakṣāto 'prayoge 'pi tasyārtho 'yam pratīyate // 191 /
(The particle) is expressed along with (i.e. right after) the (three in respective order) 'qualifier' (*viśeṣaṇa*) (= 'feature,' *dharma*), or 'to be qualified' (*viśeṣya*) (= 'factual base,' *dharmin*), or 'possible activity' (*kriyā*). When it (i.e.the particle) is intended, even when not applied, all this meaning is understood ('cognitively dawns'), for which reason (*yatas*)—

vyavacchedaphalam vākyaṃ yataś caitro dhanurdharaḥ /
pārtho dhanurdharo nīlaṃ sarojam iti vā yathā // 192 /
an utterance is the effect of ruling out, like (1) Caitra is an archer ['indeed,' the *dharma*]; (2) Arjuna ['only,' the *dharmin*] is the archer; (3) A lotus (might be) [the activity, *kriyā*] blue.

pratiyogivyavacchedas tatrāpy artheṣu gamyate /
tathā prasiddheḥ sāmarthyād vivakṣānugamād dhvaneḥ //193/
And the counterpart to (*pratiyogin*) 'ruling out' is understood there among the meanings, to wit, by way of (1) the popularly accepted, (2) according to the capable, and (3) by following upon the wish to speak the word.

PV-M did not help for my conclusion that (1) the popularly accepted is the counterpart to *eva* interpreted as 'indeed' ("Caitra is an archer indeed."); (2) the capability is the counterpart to *eva* as 'only' ("Arjuna alone is the archer."); (3) following upon the wish to speak the word is the counterpart to *eva* as 'might be' (*bhavaty eva*) ("A lotus might be blue.") But then I found my conclusion also the interpretation of PVBh, although printed under the next verse 194. 'Counterpart' (*pratiyogin*) here seems to indicate a positive correspondence to the negative 'ruling out.'

tad ayogavyavacchedād dharmī dharmaviśeṣaṇam /
tadviśiṣṭatayā dharmo na niranvayadoṣabhāk // 194 /
Hence, through ruling out non-connection there is the

'factual base' and the 'feature'-qualifier. By reason of qualifying that (i.e. the 'factual base'), the 'feature' (*dharma*) provides no support for the fault of non-*anvaya* (*anvaya* = presence in similar cases).

The verse seems to demand that in the illustration, "Caitra is an archer indeed," 'Caitra' is the factual base (*dharmin*) qualified by the feature (*dharma*) 'archer.' Dharmakīrti implies that this ruling out of non-connection agrees with the theory of *anvaya.*

P-Vi-Sva, k. 9-13, are called 'interim verses' (*antara-śloka*).

P-Vin-Bu, 89a, cites PS-Sva, k. 8-9 (CK-versions) Kitagawa, p. 103):

> kecid dharmāntaraṃ meyaṃ liṅgasyāvyabhicārataḥ /
> sambandhaṁ kecid icchanti siddhatvād dharma-dharmiṇoḥ // k. 8 /
> Some claim one should sanction a different feature (*dharma*), because the evidence is without mistake. Some claim there is a connection because of proving both the feature and the factual base.
>
> liṅgaṃ dharme prasiddhaṃ cet kim anyat tena mīyate /
> atha dharmiṇi, tasyaiva kim arthaṃ nānumeyatā // k. 9 /
> If the evidence is proven when there is a feature, what else is sanctioned thereby? Now, when there is a factual base, why is there not an inferable of it?

(2) *Varieties of Evidence*

P-Vin-Bu, f. 89b-3. There are four varieties, stated as 'the character of opposition' (T. ldog pa'i mtshan ñid), 'the method of certitude' (T. ñes par byed tshul), 'requirement to assert an alternative' (T. logs su smod pa'i dgos pa), and fourth 'refutation of the theory that there is no [valid] opposition to absence [usually, of a reason]' (T. med pa la ldog pa med par 'dod pa dgag pa).

P-Vin-Bu, f. 90a-6 to 90b-1, in treating the fourth variety did not mention the number 'fourth':

> / ji skad du / 'gal ba las rnam par bcad par thal ba'i phyir daṅ / gtan tshigs med par 'gyur ba'i phyir ro / zhes dbaṅ phyug sde zer ro zhes grags kyaṅ phyogs sṅa ma'i gzhuṅ 'di ni kun las btus kyi ran 'grel na'aṅ yod do /
> As Īśvarasena is reported to have said: "because it would reduce to absurdity the ruling out due to contradiction; and because

there is no reason." This text of the opponent (*pūrvapakṣa*) agrees with (Dignāga's) *Samuccaya*, its self-commentary.

P-Vin-Bu, f. 90b-7 to 91a-1, on the purport of Dignāga:

> / des na / phyogs glaṅ gi dgoṅs pa ni / bsgrub bya'i chos kyis mi stoṅ na chos gzhan daṅ ldan yaṅ mi mthun phyogs min te yin na rtags mi srid par 'gyur la / 'gal ba kho la med na de ñid rnam par gcod par 'gyur ro /
> Hence, the purport of Dignāga is as follows: If there is no lack of a thesis-feature (*sādhya-dharma*), while if possessing a different feature there is no dissimilar locus (*asapakṣa*)—an evidence (*liṅga*) is impossible; and if there is no 'only' (*eva*) for the contradiction, there would be a ruling out of that [contradiction].

P-Vin-Bu, 91a, -2 cites PS-Par, k.19 (K-version):

> Being in contradiction with what is different from it, the two cannot also be 'dissimilar locus' (*asapakṣa*). Due to contradicting 'no reaction' it would reduce to absurdity the 'ruling out' (*vyavacchedaka*).

(3) *Establishing the Connection of the Feature to the Evidence*
P-Vin-Bu, f. 91a-6:

> mñan bya rjes 'gro can du thal ba daṅ / rtags tshul gñis par thal ba'i rtsod spaṅ /
> Rejecting the dispute (a) which reduces to absurdity the possessing of similar presence (*anvayin*) of the audible (*śrāvaṇa*), and (b) which reduces to absurdity two modes of evidence.

Under the second of these (b), beginning f. 92a-3, comes at f. 92a-6 the citation from NMu (Rigs pa'i sgo).

P-Vin-Sva (7*.31-32), uses NMu:

> arthāpattyā vāntareṇobhayapradarśanāt /
> Also, because showing both, for the time being, by a presumption from a circumstance [or, 'context'].

P-Vin-Bu, 92a-92b -1, cites Śākyabuddhi's comment on the NMu text:

> Given that a certain 'first speaker' and 'respondent' are already cognizant of some popular acceptance of their pervasions, and announce a proving procedure for the time being.

Also, speaking as though their two 'pervasions' are actually one, because showing both pervasions, for the time being, although a concordant formulation and a discordant formulation, by presumption from two circumstancess, i.e. according to the circumstance (*arthāt*, śugs kyis).

P-Vin-Bu, 92b-1, continuing the treatment of 'presumption from a circumstance' (*arthāpatti*), cites PS, *Dṛṣṭānta-dṛṣṭāntābhāsa-parīkṣa-pariccheda*, Dignāga's comment on chap. IV k. 5 (K-version):

/ gaṅ źig la cuṅ źig rab tu grub pa yin pa'i phyir gaṅ yaṅ ruṅ ba brjod pa yaṅ sgrub byed yin no / sgra kho na la don gñis rtogs pa'i phyir ram / gaṅ yaṅ ruṅ bas śugs kyis gñis ka bstan pa'i phyir gñis ka brjod par mi bya'o /
When something has been hardly proved, as a consequence (they) speak and prove whatever is feasible, or (they) comprehend two meanings in the sole word. One should not say there are two, because teaching two is whatever is feasible according to the circumstance (*arthāt*).

P-Vin-Bu, f. 92b-4 (In order to refute certain misconceptions in these matters, there are three sections): mi rigs par mthoṅ ba len pa blun par bṣtan / ldog pa ston pa'i tshigs 'gal / ldog pa'i don mi rigs pa daṅ gsum / (a) Taking that view that (something) is improper and showing that it is stupid. (b) Contradicting the word(s) that teach the change. (c) The impropriety of the changing entity. The discussion here, with further subdivisions, apparently treats the section of P-Vin-Sva that incorporates PV-Par, 223-228.

P-Vin-Sva (Steinkellner, 8*.15-33; 9*.1-5, k. 14-19, use PV-Par, 223-228:

nivṛttyabhāvas tu vidhir vastubhāvo 'sato 'pi san /
vastvabhāvas tu nāstīti paśya bāndhyavijṛmbhitam // 223 /
When absence of cessation is the means, also presence of a given thing exists of a non-existent. So also, observing that non-presence of a given thing does not exist, is the 'yawning of a fool.'

nivṛttir yadi tasmin na hetor vṛttiḥ kim iṣyate /
sāpi na pratiṣedho 'yaṃ nivṛttiḥ kiṃ niṣidhyate // 224 /
If there is not cessation therein, why claim an operation of the reason? And if there is not (the operation), and this exclusion were the cessation, what is denied?

> vidhānaṃ pratiṣedhañ ca muktvā śābdo 'sti nāparaḥ /
> vyavahāraḥ sa cāsatsu neti prāptātra mūkatā // 225 /
> Except for affirmation and exclusion, there is no other convention derived from speech; and since there is not, here there is obtained no speech.
>
> satāñ ca na niṣedho 'sti so 'satsu ca na vidyate /
> jagaty anena nyāyena nañarthaḥ pralayaṃ gataḥ // 226 /
> There is no negation for existent things. This one does not occur when it is non-existent. By this principle, according to the world, the non-entity has gone to dissolution.
>
> deśakālaniṣedhaś ced yathāsti sa niṣidhyate /
> na tathā na yathā so 'sti tathāpi na niṣidhyate // 227 /
> Do (you claim) there is negation of space and time? (Then,) according as it (the entity) is, not that way is it negated. And according as it is not, that way it is also not negated.
>
> tasmād āśritya sabdārthaṃ bhāvābhāvasamāśrayam /
> abāhyāśrayam atreṣṭaṃ sarvaṃ vidhiniṣedhanam // 228 /
> Therefore, when one takes recourse to the word-referent that is the common basis for presence and absence and is not an external basis—this is here claimed to be all the affirmation and negation.

It should be pointed out about the word *niṣedha* of the above verses, translated 'negation', that this term possibly means the 'entailed exclusion', *prasajya-pariṣedha,* according to Śāntarakṣita's *Tattvasaṃgraha,* Shastri ed., k. 1003, translated in my small *apoha* essay in Vol. Two of the Millennium.

P-Vin-Bu, 94a-4, cites *Rgyan mdzad,* i.e. PV-Bh-Par, p. 614, under PV-Par, k. 228, the verse no. 515:

> śabdāt tu yādṛśī buddhir naṣṭe 'naṣṭe pi tādṛśī /
> bhāvābhāvāśrayas tena śabdārtho na pramā tathā //
> Of what sort be the notion (*buddhi*) when (the referent) is lost from the word, of that sort is also (the notation) when (the referent) is not lost (from the word). Therefore, the word-referent that is the basis for presence and absence is not accordingly an authority.

P-Vin-Bu, f. 94a-5, after the citation of *Rgyan mdzad,* Bu-ston cites

Devendrabuddhi and Dharmottara on this matter of the meaning of words, and the matter is generalized to the features of bases, as in the section of P-Vin-Sva that incorporates PV-Par, 229-236.

P-Vin-Sva (Steinkellner, 9*.10-33), k. 20-27, use PV-Par, 229-236:

tābhyāṃ sa dharmī saṃbaddhaḥ khyātyabhāve 'pi tādṛśaḥ /
śabdapravṛtter astīti so 'pīṣṭo vyavahārabhāk // 229 /
Such a factual base appears related to those two even when absent. Besides, we claim that the saying, "It exists," due to word-process, is the foundation of conventional language.

anyathā syāt padārthānāṃ vidhānapratiṣedhane /
ekadharmasya sarvātmavidhānapratiṣedhanam // 230 /
anānātmatayā bhede nānāvidhiniṣedhavat /
ekadharmiṇy asaṃhāro vidhānapratiṣedhayoḥ // 231 /
230-231. Otherwise, there would be for the *padārtha*-s, when affirming or negating a single feature, the affirmation and exclusion of all individuals, due to non-multiple individuals. If they are distinct, like multiple affirmation and exclusion, there would be no inclusion of affirmation and exclusion within a single factual base (*dharmin*).

ekaṃ dharmiṇam uddiśya nānādharmasamāśrayam /
vidhāv ekasya tadbhājam ivānyeṣām upekṣakam // 232 /
niṣedhe tadviviktañ ca tadanyeṣam apekṣakam /
vyavahāram asatyārtham prakalpayati dhīr yathā // 233 /
232-233. Specifying a single factual base as the common basis of multiple features, when there is affirmation of one it is like resort to it involves equanimity toward the others; and when there is negation (of one), it is like isolation from it involves dependence on those that are other than it—according to how discrimination constructs a conventional remark with a non-existent entity.

taṃ tathaivāvikalpārthaṃ bhedāśrayam upāgatāḥ /
anādivāsanodbhūtaṃ badhante 'rthaṃ na laukikam // 234 /
The espousals annul (*bādhante*) precisely that object-entity of non-constructive thought, i.e. thusness, the base of a particular thing; but (do) not annul the mundane object, arisen from beginningless habit-energy.

tatphalo 'tatphalaś cārtho bhinna ekas tatas tataḥ /
tais tair upaplavair nītasañcayāpacayair iva // 235 /

atadvān api sambandhāt kutaścid upanīyate /
dṛṣṭiṃ bhedāśrayais te 'pi tasmād ajñātaviplavaḥ // 236 /
235-236. One sense-object is partitioned with the result thereof in one (sense organ) not the result thereon in another (sense organ). Not (really) possessing it (the sense-object), one is led through some connection (*sambandha*) to a view by the particular (sense) bases having influences ('inundations') whose increases and decreases are guided (by constructive thoughts of features and factual bases). Therefrom those (espousals) have the influence ('inundation') of misunderstanding.

The P-Vin-Sva, k.14-27, are 'interim verses'.
P-Vin-Bu, 94b-7, cites PV-Sva, 57cd:

. . .niścayaiḥ /
yan na niścīyate rūpaṃ tat teṣāṃ viṣayaḥ katham //
Since the form is not decided by certainties, how is it (= that form) their object?

P-Vin-Bu, 95a-2, cites PV-Sva, 84:

yathāpratītikathitaḥ śabdārtho 'sāv asann api /
sāmānādhikaraṇyaṃ ca vastuny asya na sambhavaḥ //
The word referent and common placement (for perception and inference) do not exist as told according to popular acceptance; indeed, there is no possibility of that (word referent or common placement) in the given thing (*vastu*).

The term *sāmānādhikaraṇyam* occus twice in PV, namely PV-Sva 84 and 132. The Tibetan equivalent is *gźi mthun ñid.* The form *gźi mthun pa,* occurring a number of times in PS, V (Apoha Chap.), Dignāga's commentary, probably equals *samānādhikaraṇa.* In Sanskrit grammar, the latter term means appositional or syntactic relationship with agreement in gender, number, etc. Dignāga's example is especially the 'blue lotus,' where 'blue' has such a syntactic relation with 'lotus'. However, such an agreement required a 'common placement'.
P-Vin-Bu, 95a-5, cites PV-Sva, 169:

nivṛtter niḥsvabhāvatvāt na sthānāsthānakalpanā /
upaplavas ca sāmānyadhiyas tenāpy adūṣanā //
Because there is no individual presence of cessation, there is no constructive thought of its possibility and impossibility; and there is influence ('inundation') of the generality intelligence. But

it (the intelligence) has no refutation on that account.

P-Vin-Bu, 96a-5, cites PV-Sva, 85-86:

dharmadharmivyavasthānaṃ bhedo 'bhedaś ca yadṛśaḥ /
asamīkṣitatattvārtho yathā loke pratīyate // 85 /
taṃ tathaiva samāśritya sādhyasādhanasaṃsthitiḥ /
paramārthāvatārāya vidvadbhir avakalpyate // 86 /
85-86. The establishment of feature and factual base; particularization and non-particularization—any of these—is the unexamined meaning of reality as popularly held in the world. Accordingly, there is formation of thesis and proving-method by recourse to precisely that (establishment of feature and factual base). It is formulated by the wise for understanding the supreme (*paramārtha*).

P-Vin-Bu, 96b-1, cites PV-Sva, 50:

yāvanto 'ṃśasamāropās tannirāse viniścayāḥ /
tāvanta eva śabdāś ca tena te bhinnagocarāḥ //
As many as be the superimpositions of parts (*aṃśa*), just so many as are also the words determined to expel them, whereby those domains are partitioned (*bhinna*, or 'particularized').

P-Vin-Bu, 96b-4, cites PV-Sva, 80-81ab:

sa ca sarvaḥ padārthānām anyonyābhāvasaṃśrayaḥ /
tenānyāpohaviṣayo vastulābhasya cāśrayaḥ //
yatrāsti vastusambandho yathoktānumitau yathā /
80-81ab. Not only does it—all of the entities (*padārtha*)—have its basis in mutual absence, but therefore also the sense-object of *anyāpoha* (exclusion of the other)—is the basis of reaching the given thing (*vastu*). In whatever there is the connection to a given thing, so is it when they are both inferred in the stated manner.

C. The Three Modes of Evidence (*liṅga*)

P-Vin-Bu, 96b-6, these are non-apprehension (*anupalabdhi*), individual presence (*svabhāva*), and result (*kārya*). Note: Sometimes these three are called three modes of reason, *hetu*; but undoubtedly the principal word for the three modes is *liṅga*.

P-Vin-Sva, k. 28 (Steinkellner, p. 40):

/ mtshan ñid de daṅ ldan pa yi /
/ gtan tshigs de ni mi dmigs daṅ /

/ bdag daṅ bras bu zhes bya gsum /
/ kho na'o //
The reason (*hetu*), accompanied with this character (*lakṣaṇa*), is precisely the three: *anupalabdhi* (nonapprehension), *svabhāva* (individual presence), and *kārya* (result).

P-Vin-Sva (Steinkellner, 10*. 14-25), Skt. (part of commentary on k. 28) from PVSV 2.19-3.3 (P-Vin-Bu, 97b-4, ff.):

svabhāvapratibandhe hi saty artho 'rthaṃ na vyabhicarati. sa ca tadātmatvāt. tadātmatve sādhyasādhanabhedābhāva iti cet. na, dharmabhedaparikalpanāt . . . tathā cāha sarva eyāyam anumānānumeyavyavahāro buddhyārūḍhena dharmadharmibhedeneti. bhedo dharmadharmitayā buddhyākārakṛto nārtho 'pi, vikalpabhedānāṃ svatantrāṇām anarthāśrayatvāt, tatkalpitaviṣayād arthapratītāv anarthapratilambha eva syāt.
When there is connection to individual presence, the entity does not mistake the entity, because it is identical with it. It being identical with it, is there no distinction of the thesis (*sādhya*) and the proving-method (*sādhana*)? Not due to the imagination of particular features (*dharma*). And he (i.e. Dignāga) speaks likewise, remarking that all this is the conventional language of inference and inferable by distinction of feature (*dharma*) and factual base (*dharmin*) in the purview of discrimination (*buddhi*). Also, the distinction (*bheda*) in terms of feature and factual base, created as an image of discrimination, is not an object-entity (*artha*), because there is no basis for an object-entity among the autonomous (*svatantra*) distinctions of constructive thought (*vikalpa*). When there is understanding of the object-entity by way of the imagined object of that (constructive thought), there can be no reach (i.e. connection) to the object-entity.

P-Vin-Bu, 98a-2, cites the *ācārya* (i.e. Dignāga) for the passage which Dharmakīrti refers to, and heads it, "to show the authority of words" (*tshig tshad mar ston pa*).

P-Vin-Sva (10*. 26-33; 11*.1-4), k. 29-31, use PV-Sva, 40-42:

sarve bhāvāḥ svabhāvena svasvabhāvavyavasthiteḥ /
svabhāvaparabhāvābhyāṃ yasmād vyāvṛttibhāginaḥ // 40 /
tasmād yato yato 'rthānāṃ vyāvṛttis tannibandhanāḥ /
jātibhedāḥ prakalpyante tadviśeṣāvagāhinaḥ // 41 /
40-41. For the reason that all on-going things by individual presence, because established in their own individual pres-

ence, partake in exclusion from other on-going things that have individual presence; for that reason, the exclusion of entities (*artha*) is from this and that. The different classes (*jāti*), based in that (exclusion), are (verbally) constructed as residing in the distinction of that.

tasmād yo yena dharmeṇa viśeṣaḥ saṃpratīyate /
na sa śakyas tato 'nyena tena bhinnā vyavasthitiḥ // 42 /
Whatever distinction is understood by a feature, it is not 'capable' by a different (feature). Fot that reason, the establishment is particular (*bhinna*).

P-Vin-Sva, k. 29-31, are 'interim verses'.

(1) *Nonapprehension (anupalabdhi)*
P-Vin-Sva (Steinkellner, 11*. 16-29), Skt. (part of commentary on k. 31) from PVSV 4.15-23 (P-Vin-Bu, 99a-7, ff.):

atrānupalabdher liṅgād asattāyām upalabdher abhāvo 'py anyayānupalabdhyā sādhya ity anavasthānād apratipattiḥ syāt. athopalabdhyabhāvo vinā 'nupalabdhyā syāt. tathā sattā 'bhāvo 'pi syāt, apārthikānupalabdhiḥ. athānyopalabdhyā 'nupalabdhisiddhir iti pratyakṣasiddhā 'nupaladhiḥ. tathānyasattayā 'sattā kiṃ na sidhyatīti. yadā punar evaṃvidhānupalabdhir evāsatām asattā, tadā siddhe 'pi viṣaye mohād viṣayiṇo 'sajjñānaśabdavyavahārān apratipadyamāno viṣayapradarśanena samaye pravartyate.
When there is nothing to prove (*asattā*) due to the evidence (*liṅga*) of non-apprehension, to say that even though there is absence of apprehension there is a thesis (*sādhya*, 'something to prove') by another non-apprehension, would be a non-ascertainment on account of 'endless series' (*anavasthāna*). Then, absence of an apprehensible would be devoid of non-apprehension; likewise, existence (of a thesis) would be absence; to wit, the non-apprehension would be meaningless. Then we say that proof of non-apprehension by another apprehension is a non-apprehension proved by a direct perception. Likewise, is there non-existence by reason of another existence? (We respond,): it is not proved. When further, precisely a non-apprehension of such kind is the non-existence of non-existents, then even when the object is proved, due to delusion of the subject whem not ascertaining the conventional langauge of words for the cognition of a non-

existent, one is occupied with a symbol for pointing out the object.

The passage is followed by an example: "It is a cow, because it is a combination of dewlap etc." [But cows are not the only creatures with dewlap.] The example goes with the difficulty of defining an object by positive characteristics.

Under this topic of 'nonapprehension' there is the case of invisible objects, such as demons, that are believed to exist, especially in certain places. P-Vin-Bu, 101b-4,ff. discusses this topic, beginning with these remarks:

> / mthu daṅ ldan pa'i mal 'byor pas sam śa za la sogs pas mi snaṅ bar byin gyis brlabs pa'i phyir 'bras bu'i dus su yang bum pa yod kyaṅ mi dmigs par 'gyur ro zhe na /mthu ldan gyi byin rlabs chos can / de'i dbaṅ gis snaṅ ruṅ bum pa yod bzhin du mi dmigs pa ma yin te / de'i dbaṅ gis yul bum pa snaṅ ruṅ daṅ dbaṅ po bum pa'i yul can du gnas pa dag las gaṅ yaṅ ruṇ ba zhig gam gñis ka gzhan du gyur pa med pa'i phyir / khyab pa yod de / de lta na byin gyis brlabs pa ñid mi 'thad pa'i phyir ro / Since demons, such as the Rākṣasa, may be invisible even to a powerful yogin, then by empowerment in fruitional time could even an existent pot not be seen? [It is said:] "The empowered factual base has the power." By dint of that, when there is a visible pot, it is not the case that it not seen. By dint of that, whether it be [called] the visible object-pot, or [called] the power place that is the objective possessor of a pot—those are not really two different cases. Consequently, there is pervasion (*vyāpti*), because in that case, the empowerment (rendering a visible pot invisible) is not valid.

[Re the attributed Sva, k. 32, Steinkellner has an unusual decision, namely, that the first two lines of k. 32 are on his p. 42 following k. 31, and concludes on p. 52 following k. 34! But then k. 35 is allowed only a half-verse found on p. 56. It is more reasonable that the supposed 2d half of k. 32 is really the first half of k. 35 And then k. 32 in its supposed first half had only one 7-syllable Tibetan line, which therefore need not be part of a verse. Since I must observe Steinkellner's later numbering of these *kārikā*, I shall regard k. 32 as nonexistent].

P-Vin-Bu, 102a-6, explains the sentence ". . .proved by a direct perception," citing the half-verse approximately PV, Par, 274ab:

"Therefore, this non-apprehension is proved by direct perception (*pratyakṣa*)," to be quoted in P-Vin-Par. Also, P-Vin-Bu, 100a-5, 6 explains, "one is occupied with a symbol": "a deluded person is occupied with conventional remarks," i.e., he confuses conventional remarks and actual objects.

P-Vin-Sva (12*.29, 31) uses PV-Sva, 4d: "There are four kinds of non-apprehension" (*anupalabdhiś caturvidhā*). P-Vin-Sva (Steinkellner, 12*.32-13*.17), Skt. (part of commentary on the supposed k. 32) from PV-SV 5.9-21 (P-Vin-Bu, 102a-7, ff.):

> yāvān kaścit pratiṣedhaḥ, sa sarvo 'nupalabdheḥ tathā hi sa dvidhā kriyeta, kasyacid vidhinā niṣedhena vā. vidhau viruddho vā vidhīyetāviruddho vā. aviruddhasya vidhau sahabhāvavirodhābhāvād apratiṣedhaḥ. viruddhasyāpy anupalabdhyabhāvena virodhā-pratipattiḥ. tathā hy aparyantakāraṇasya bhavato 'nyabhāve 'bhāvād virodhagatiḥ. sa cānupaladheḥ. anyonyopalabdhiparihārasthitalakṣaṇanatā vā virodhaḥ, nityānityatvavat. tatrāpy ekopalabdhyā 'nyānupalabdhir evocyate. anyathā 'niṣiddhopalabdher abhāvāsiddheḥ. ekasya niṣedhenānyābhavasādhane siddhaivānupalabdhiḥ, niṣedhasyānupalabdhirūpatvāt tatrāpy arthāntaraniṣedhe kāryakāraṇayor anubhayasya vā. tatrānubhayasyāpratibandhāt tadabhāve 'nyena na bhavitavyam iti kuta etat. kāryānupalabdhāv api nāvasyaṃ kāraṇāni tadvanti bhavantīti tadabhāvaḥ kutaḥ.
>
> As multiple as be the exclusion (*pratiṣedha*), it all belongs to non-apprehension. For it so amounts to twofold by affirmation or denial of anything. In the case of affirmation either the contrary or the concurrent would be affirmed. When there is affirmation of the concurrent, there is nonexclusion due to absence of 'incompatibiliity-opposition.' And when (there is affirmation) of a contrary, there is non-affirmation of opposition (as would happen) by presence of an apprehensible. For so is the understanding of opposition by absence when there is another presence of an unlimited material cause that occurs; and (when) it belongs to non-apprehension. Or opposition is the characteristic abiding in contradiction-opposition of apprehensions, like permanence and impermanence. And here it is said that there is only another non-apprehension by a single apprehension; otherwise, it would be of an undenied apprehension that is the disproof of absence. A nonappre-

hension is only proved when there is proof an another absence by denial of one, because there is the form of nonapprehension of the denied (one). And in the case of denying another object-entity, i.e. of result and material cause, or of neither. There, when there is absence of them through no connection of either, why is it not to be by another! And when there is nonapprehension of result, since there are certainly no material causes which possess it, why its absence!

P-Vin-Bu, 103a-7, while commenting on the preceding passage, refers to HB (paraphrase?):

One ought to distinguish when it appears that the denial is multiple, but one need not distinguish a denial that is non-multiple (tha dad 'gog na snaṅ ba źes khyad par bya dgos kyi ṭha mi dad pa 'gog pa la khyad par mi dgos par bśad do).

P-Vin-Bu, 102-1, names the four 'non-apprehensions' as in PV-Sva, 4: (1) *viruddha,* (2) *viruddha-kārya,* (3) *hetu,* (4) *svabhāva.* As I understand the P-Vin-Bu comments, Dharmakīrti treats these four kinds in the manner of feasible appearance to justify 'non-apprehension.' First the 'contrary' (*viruddha*) is discussed in terms of 'incompatibility opposition;' then in terms of 'contradiction opposition.' The remaining three kinds of 'non-apprehension' involve only a single apprehensible as the feasible appearance. Dharmakīrti's remaining remarks therefore apply generally to those other three kinds, affording considerable opportunity of commentarial expansion to illustrate the remaining three kinds of 'non-apprehension.' These matters are treated in this volume in the 'Guided Tour,' and previously in Dharmakīrti's *Nyāyabindu.* Dharmakīrti also has more material in P-Vin-Sva (Steinkellner, 14*, especially 13-33, with Skt. from PV-SV 5.25-6.9).

Since the discussions of non-apprehension thus diverge over the issue of two opposing apprehensions or a single apprehension which is denied, this raises the problem of distinguishing such a two from a single one. This comes out in various disputes between the Buddhist logicians and their opponents, especially the Realists, as Bu-ston puts it.

P-Vin-Bu, 106a, cites PV variant, probably from Śākyabuddhi referred to next: / *thams cad du ni* [sic. for *mi*] *sbyor ba ñid / tha dad don la tha dad med /*, going with PV-Sid, 94: *upacāro na sarvatra . . . 'bhinne bhinnārthateti cet //*

(Realist opponent:) The metaphoric transfer (*upacāra*) is not everywhere. If an entity is distinct why (pretend it is) not distinct!

P-Vin-Bu, 106a-5, comments as follows:

/ 'dir śā-kya-blos bltar ruṅ ba'i rgyu la sogs ma grub pa daṅ / bltar ruṅ ba'i 'gal ba grub pa zhes ci rigs par 'brel [read: 'grel] par 'chad pa la / chos mchog na re / de la bltar ruṅ smos pa don med de / dmigs pa bltar mi ruṅ gcad pa'i phyir zer ro / kho na re / bltar ruṅ ni dgag chos la 'dod do /

The translation of the foregoing :

Here, Śākyabuddhi explains, commenting as appropriate, that there is no proof of a cause, etc. of visibility, and that there is proof contradicting visibility. And Dharmottara claims in this case that it is meaningless to assert visibility because one may judge the vision as unfeasible. He claims that the visibility is a refutable feature.

P-Vin II (14*.34-15*.2), k. 33, uses PV-Sva, 203:

dṛśyasya darśanābhāvakāraṇāsaṃbhave sati /
bhāvasyānupalabdhasya bhāvābhāvaḥ pratīyate //
When there is no possibility of a material cause for absence of a view of the (feasibly) visible, for one who has not apprehended an on-going thing, the absence of that on-going thing is understood.

This is a 'summary verse' (*saṃgraha-śloka*).

P-Vin-Bu, 108a, cites NB:

"Although there is difference of formulation, i.e. by negations of the manner (i.e. the apprehension) of something else, indirectly, all the ten formulations of non-apprehension beginning with non-apprehension of result (nos. 2-11) may be included in the non-apprehension of individual presence (no. 1)."

P-Vin-Sva (p. 16*.5-8), k. 34, uses PV-Sva, 6:

> iṣṭaṃ viruddhakārye 'pi deśakālādyapekṣaṇam /
> anyathā vyabhicāri syād bhasmevāśītasādhane //
> Moreover, a claimed dependence on place, time, etc. even in the case of a contrary result, would be erroneous, like ashes to prove non-cold.

This k. 34 (Steinkellner's number) is an 'interim verse'. It inaugurates what in P-Vin-Bu (108b-2, f.) is a long discussion about the 'inaccessible entity' (*viprakṛṣṭa*). One reason for the lengthy discussion appears to be the religious necessity to show that some persons can become free from clinging and that some can become omniscient.

P-Vin Sva (Steinkellner, 16* 26-17*.7), Skt. (part of commentary on k. 34) from PVSV 102-2-11 (P-Vin-Bu, 109a-4, ff.):

> śāstraṃ hi pravartamānaṃ kaṃcit puruṣārthasādhanam upāyam āśritya pravartate, anyathā 'baddhapralāpasyāprāmāṇyāt. tatra ca prakaraṇe bahavo 'rthā nāvaśyaṃ nirdeśyāḥ, yathā pratyātmaniyatāh kāścana puruṣāṇāṃ cetovṛttayo 'niyatanimittabhāvinyaḥ, deśakālavyavahitā vā prakaraṇānupayogino dravyaviśeṣāḥ. na tān śāstraṃ viṣayīkaroti, na ca tathā viprakṛṣṭeṣu svasāmarthyopadhānāj jñānotpādanaśaktir asti. na cāvaśyam eṣāṃ kāryopalambho yenānumīyeran. na ca te pramāṇatrayanivṛttāv api na santīti śakyante vyavasātum.
> When a *śāstra* is being engaged, scarcely any success of human aim based on a 'means' (*upāya*) operates, because otherwise there would be no authorizing of connected (i.e. cogent) speech. And certainly in that treatise not many object-entities (*artha*) are pointed out. In illustration, there are scarcely no occurrences of definite sign-sources (*nimitta*) that are definite for every person and which modify persons' minds. And there are various substances (*dravya*) partitioned off by space and time, that are useless in a treatise; and a *śāstra* does not render them sense objects (*viṣaya*), Likewise, there is no ability to arouse cognition toward inaccessible entities, because of the near-placement (*upadhāna*) of one's own ability. And certainly (persons) would not infer by what there may be their witness of (such a) result. And they are unable to ascertain whether they are not missing the three authorities.

Karṇakagomin's *Commentary on the Pramāṇavārttikavṛtti of Dharmakīrti* (reprint of Rinsen Book Co., Kyoto, 1982) on this PV-Sva, there numbered v. 201, clarifies that by "three authorities" the text means the three kinds of reason (*hetu*), which of course are 'non-apprehension', 'individual presence', and 'result'. The passage makes salient the non-apprehension' and 'result' ones. Perhaps the *śāstra* itself intends the 'individual presence' (*svabhāva*) one.

P-Vin-Sva (Steinkellner, p. 52 [ascribed to a k. 32] (from NB; II, 27)), k. 35ab:

> [svabhāva] viprakṛṣṭeṣu . . . abhāvaniścayābhāvāt /
> While there is no assurance about the absence when things are inaccessible [by individual presence, etc.].

P-Vin-Sva (Steinkellner, p. 56), k. 35 cd:

> iṣṭo 'yam arthaḥ śakyeta jñātum so 'tiśayo yadi //
> This entity is claimed if one is able to know it as special.

P-Vin-Bu, 112b, cites entire verse PV-Sva, 224, while P-Vin-Sva, 18*.21, f. uses second half:

> girāṃ mithyātvahetūnāṃ doṣānāṃ puruṣāśrayāt /
> apauruṣeyam satyārtham iti kecit pracakṣate //
> Some persons mention a true entity without human agency through recourse to a person when words have faults that are the cause of straying (*mithyātva-hetu*).

PV-M explains "some persons" as the 'Jaiminīya'.

P-Vin-Bu, 117b, cites PV-Sva, 227ab:

> sambandhāpauruṣeyatve syat pratītir asamvidaḥ /
> If there were no human activity of connection (= relation), there would be cognitive dawning without recognition.

If one had no relations with people, then upon waking up one would recognize no one, i.e., everyone would be a stranger.

(2) *Individual Presence* (*svabhāva*)

P-Vin-Sva (21*.10-25, 30-35; 22*.1-8, 17-36; 23*.1-4), k. 36-39, k. 41-43, k. 46-51, use PV-Sva, 317-329, in the given order:

svayaṃ rāgādimān nārthaṃ vetti vedasya nānyataḥ /
na vedayati vedo 'pi vedārthasya kuto gatiḥ // 317 /
The person given to lust, etc. neither understands the meaning of the Veda by himself nor from another. The Veda does not cause understanding (of its own meaning). How is there understanding of the Veda's meaning!

tenāgnihotraṃ juhuyāt svargakāma iti srutau /
khādec chvamāṃsam ity eṣa nārtha ity atra kā pramā // 318 /
When it is heard said, "The one desiring heaven should make a burnt offering," or, "One should eat dog flesh," what authority here says, "This is meaningless."?

prasiddho lokavādaś cet tatra ko 'tīndriyārthadṛk /
anekārtheṣu śabdeṣu yenārtho 'yaṃ vivecitaḥ // 319 /
Is the mundane word popularly accepted? In this case, who seeing the extrasensory entity, can analyze this entity in terms of words with multiple meanings?

svargorvaśyādiśabdas ca dṛṣṭo 'rūḍhārthavācakaḥ /
śābdāntareṣu tādṛkṣu tādṛśy evāstu kalpanā // 320 /
When such expressions as 'Urvaśī of the sky' are noticed as expressions of non-popular meaning, let there be constructive thought (*kalpanā*) in such manner in terms of other such expressions!

P-Vin-Sva (21*.26-29), k. 40:

/ don daṅ ldan ma 'grub pa / de rab 'grub pa'i sgrub byed la/
/ raṅ don ma grub nus med de / brgal zhiṅ brtags pa mthuṅs phyir ro //
Having not proven what is possessed of meaning, one proves what has [already] been proven. One is impotent when one's own meaning is unproven because it is the same whether one disputes or examines.

prasiddhiś ca nṛṇāṃ vādaḥ pramāṇaṃ sa ca neṣyate /
tataś ca bhūyo 'rthagatiḥ kim etad dviṣṭakāmitam // 321 /
The word popular among men–is not the one we claim to be (about) an authority. And still again understanding the meaning from that (popular word), what is the use of this aversion and attraction!

atha prasiddhim ullaṅghya kalpane na nibandhanam /
prasiddher apramāṇatvāt tadgrahe kiṃ nibandhanam // 322/
Then transcending the popular acceptance, is there no basis in constructive thought? By reason of the popular acceptance not being an authority, what is the basis in apprehending that (popular acceptance)? [i.e., responding to the opponent with another question].

utpāditā prasiddhyaiva śaṅkā sabdārthaniścaye /
yasmān nānārthavṛttitvaṃ śabdānāṃ tatra dṛśyate // 323 /
Popular acceptance just yields distrust toward certainty of the word meaning, for which reason one notices therein (i.e., popular acceptance) and acceptance of multiple meanings for words.

P-Vin-Sva (22*.9-12), k. 44:

/ gal te 'jig rten pa gaṅ la / rigs pas gnod med de gzuṅ na/
/ rigs pas gnod pa yod min pa'i / rluṅ gi bu de cis mi 'dzin//
If a worldling is full and takes what is not harmed by a principle, by what would the Son of the Wind not be held when he is or is not harmed by a principle?

P-Vin-Sva (22*.13-16), k. 45:

/ dbaṅ po 'das la luṅ don gyi / rten can las gzhan rigs pa med/
/ de yi don yaṅ gnas med phyir / de la rigs pa srid ma yin //
There is no principle different from the basis for the *āgama* meaning that is beyond the sense-organs. Also, because its meaning is placeless, there is no possibility for a principle *there.*

anyathā 'sambhavābhāvān nānāśakteḥ svayaṃ dhvaneḥ /
avasyaṃ śaṅkayā bhāvyaṃ niyāmakam apaśyatām // 324 /
Due to no lack of possibility, there is difference of the word that by itself has variegated force (for multiple meanings) for persons who do not notice a certainty-guide that ought to be, certainly on account of distrust.

eṣa sthāṇur ayaṃ mārga iti vaktīti kaścana /
anyaḥ svayaṃ bravīmīti tayor bhedaḥ parīkṣyatām // 325 /

Someone makes the statement: "This is a post; this is the path." Another says, "I say it myself." Discern the difference between the two! [One person points out something; the other does not point out].

sarvatra yogyasyaikārthadyotane niyamaḥ kutaḥ /
jñātā vātindriyāḥ kena vivakṣāvacanād ṛte // 326 /
What is the certainty in clarifying the single meaning of what is suitable everywhere? Except for expressing what one wants to say, by whom the supra-sensories are known. [It would take a person with extrasensory perceptions to be certain of a single meaning suitable everywhere].

vivakṣā niyame hetuḥ saṃketas tatprakāśanaḥ /
apauruṣeye sā nāsti tasya saikārthatā kutaḥ // 327 /
The wish to speak is a cause for certainty; a sign is a clarification of it. When it does not issue from humans, it (the wish to speak) does not exist. How (then) is there its 'single meaning.'?

svabhāvaniyame 'nyatra na yojyeta tayā punaḥ /
saṃketaś ca nirarthaḥ syād vyaktau ca niyamaḥ kutaḥ // 328/
When there is certainty of an individual presence, it does not work in another place (i.e. meaning) by it (i.e., the wish to speak). The sign would be meaningless; and even when clear, how is there certainty!

yatra svātantryam icchayā niyamo nāma tatra kaḥ /
dyotayet tena saṃketo neṣṭām evāsya yogyatām // 329 /
In which place there is independence by claim; what is there called 'certainty'? Hence, the sign illumines the feasibility not claimed for it.

The P-Vin-Sva k. 36-51 are labelled 'interim verses'.
P-Vin-Sva (23*.22, 28), k. 52:

/ 'jug pa blo sṅon can ñid phyir /
/ de ni mi 'jug 'bras can 'dod /
/ gzhan ni 'jug pa'i 'bras can te /
/de yi rgyu mtshan mthoṅ phyir ro //
Because the cognition which engages [an object] had an earlier state, we claim its nonengagement is fruitional. What has the engagement-result is different, because we can observe its cause.

P-Vin-Sva (24*.10, 20), k. 53:

a. / de yod tsam daṅ rjes 'brel can /
One is bound only with what is present,
b. svabhāvo hetur ātmani /
when itself is the reason: individual presence.
c. / khyad par ltos daṅ dag pa ste /
One especially connecting [cause and effect] and pure,
d. nāśe kāryatvasattvavat //
when passing away has the actuality of the effect-state.

P-Vin-Sva (26*.17-18 and 23-24), k. 54, uses PV-Sva, 193:

ahetutvād vināśasya svabhavād anubandhitā /
sāpekṣāṇāṃ hi bhāvānām nāvaśyaṃbhāvitekṣyate //
Since there is no (remote) cause for the destruction, there is relation through individual presence. One notices no occurrence of certainty for conditional natures.

P-Vin-Sva (27*.3-6), k. 55, uses PV-Sva, 195:

etena vyabhicāritvam uktaṃ kāryāvyavasthiteḥ /
sarveṣām nāśahetūnāṃ hetumannāśavādinām //
Hence, since there is no establishment as a result one declares a mistaken nature for all (remote) causes of destruction stated as 'destruction possessed of (a remote) cause'.

This is an interim verse.

P-Vin-Sva (29.25-28), k. 56 (1st half is PV-Prat, 3ab):

arthakriyāsamartham yat tad atra paramārthasat /
asanto 'kṣaṇikās tasmāt kramākramavirodhataḥ //
The one capable of purposive activity is here said to be absolute existence(*paramārthasat*). Accordingly,thereareno non-momentary ones, since that would contradict series and non-series.

This is called a 'summary verse.' The preceding comments point out if natures were non-momentary, they could not have purposive activity, for it would contradict sequence (or, series) and simultaneity (or, non-series).

P-Vin-Sva (30*.3-4) and P-Vin-Bu, 131b, cite AKBh under AK, I, 7b:

katame te saṃskṛtāḥ . . . skandhapañcakam /
"What are the constructed? The five-set of personal aggregates."

P-Vin-Bu, 131b, cites AK, I, 9ab:

rūpaṃ pañcendriyāṇy arthāḥ pañcāvijñaptir eva ca /
"Form is the five sense-organs, five object-entities, and five non-representations (*avijñapti*)."

P-Vin-Bu, 132a, cites AK, I, 14cd, 15ab, 16a:

vedanā 'nubhavaḥ saṃjñā nimittodgrahaṇātmikā /
caturbhyo 'nye tu saṃskāraskandhaḥ . . .
vijñānaṃ prativijñaptiḥ . . .
Feeling is experience. Idea is the apprehension of sign-sources. Motivation aggregate is those (constructed natures) different from the other four aggregates. Perception is the representation of each (sense object).

The preceding two citations provide the Abhidharma definitions of the five personal aggregates, namely, form, feeling, idea, motivation, and perception.

P-Vin-Bu, 132a, cites AK, I, 14ab:

indriyārthās ta eveṣṭā daśāyatanadhātavaḥ /
Precisely those sense-organs and sense objects are held to be ten sense bases and realms.

P-Vin-bu, 132a, cites AK, I, 16b-d:

manaḥ āyatanaṃ ca tat /
dhātavaḥ sapta ca matāḥ ṣaḍ vijñānāyatho manaḥ //
It is the mind base and it is the seven realms, to wit, the six perceptions and the mind.

P-Vin-Bu, 132a-b, cites AK, I, 17:

ṣaṇṇam anantarātītaṃ vijñānaṃ yad dhi tan manaḥ /
ṣaṣṭhāśrayaprasiddhyarthaṃ dhātavo 'ṣṭādaśa smṛtaḥ //

The *vijñāna* that succeeds any of the six (perceptions)—that is the mind (*manas*). With the purpose of fulfilling the sixth basis (= *manovijñāna*), there are the eighteen realms.

P-Vin-Bu, 132b, cites AK, I, 15b-d:

. . . ete punas trayaḥ /
dharmāyatanadhatvākhyāḥ sahāvijñaptiyasaṃskṛtaiḥ //
These three (aggregates), along with the non-representations and the [three] unconstructed (natures)—are the *dharmāyatana,* the *dharmadhātu.*

The reason for citing these Abhidharma passages is Dharmakīrti's discussion, starting P-Vin-Sva, 29*. 30 about the personal aggregates (*skandha*), realms (*dhātu*), and sense bases (*āyatana*), which taken together are often in this literature called 'all constructed natures' (*sarva-saṃskṛta-dharma*).

(3) ***Result*** **(*kārya*)**
P-Vin-Sva (31*. 27 and 32* 15-17), k. 57, uses PV-Sva, 196:

asāmarthyāc ca taddhetoḥ bhavaty eṣa svabhāvataḥ /
yatra nāma bhavaty asmād anyatrāpi svabhāvataḥ //
Because there is no capability of a cause for that (destruction), it happens through individual presence. Where it in fact happens, even elsewhere than that, (it happens) through individual presence (which is momentary).

P-Vin-Sva (33*. 17), k. 58ab, uses PV-Sva, 2ab:

kāryam svabhāvair yāvadbhir avinābhāvi karaṇe /
Given a cause, the result (*kārya*) has necessary connection with as many individual presences as there are.

P-Vin-Sva (33*. 20, 31), k. 58cd:

/ gtan tshigs de la 'khrul na 'di /
/ rgyu daṅ ldan pa 'das 'gyur //
Should the reason be erroneous, it would transgress the possession of a cause.

P-Vin-Sva (35*. 3-6), k. 59, uses PV-Sva, 35:

nityaṃ sattvam asattvaṃ vā 'hetor anyānapekṣaṇāt /
apekṣāto hi bhāvānāṃ kādācitkatvasaṃbhavaḥ //
Were an actuality or a nonactuality permanent, occasionally there would be something non-caused because not dependent on another; (Impossible!) for things are on-going through dependence.

P-Vin-Sva (36*. 4-11), k. 60-61, use PV–Sva, 36-37:

agnisvabhāvaḥ śakrasya mūrddhā yady agnir eva saḥ /
athānagnisvabhāvo 'sau dhūmas tatra kathaṃ bhavet // 36//
dhūmahetusvabhāvo hi vahnis tacchaktibhedavān /
adhūmahetor dhūmasya bhāve sa syād ahetukaḥ // 37 /
If the individual presence of fire is on Indra's head, it is just fire (*eva,* restriction to the instance, i.e. prior to the emergence of smoke). Then, without the individual presence of fire yonder, how could there be smoke in that place!
For fire has the individual presence, (serving as) the cause of smoke; i.e., possesses a particular capacity for it. Should there be smoke without the cause of smoke, it would be *ahetuka* ('causeless': a heresy for Buddhists).

These two are called 'summary verses' (*saṃgraha-śloka*).
P-Vin-Sva (37*. 19-30), k. 62-64, use PV-Sva, 38, 31-32:

anvayavyatirekād yo yasya dṛṣṭo 'nuvartakaḥ/
svabhāvas tasya taddhetur ato bhinnān na saṃbhavaḥ // 38/
Of what one has been noticed (or, 'seen') the (logical) dependence through *anvaya* and *vyatireka,* the individual presence of that (e.g. fire) is the cause of it (e.g. smoke). Consequently, it (e.g. smoke) does not occur through being particularized.

kāryakāraṇabhāvād vā svabhāvād vā niyāmakāt /
avinābhāvaniyamo 'darśanān na na darśanāt // 31 /
Through on-going cause and result, or through individual presence with certainty, there is certainty of necessary connection, whether or not one sees it.

avaśyaṃbhāvaniyamaḥ kaḥ parasyānyathā paraiḥ /
arthāntaranimitte vā dharme vāsasi rāgavat // 32//
What is the certainty necessarily on-going of another (thesis) by other (means of proof) otherwise (than the two mentioned

in verse 31)? Or when there is the feature (*dharma*) as a sign-source of another entity—like (red) dye on a cloth!

Those three are called 'summary verses'.

P-Vin-Bu, 145a, cites PV-Sva, 60-61 (P-Vin-Sva, 38*. 17-18, uses PV-Sva, 61ab):

dvayor ekābhidhāne 'pi vibhaktir vyatirekiṇī /
bhinnam artham ivānveti vācyaleśaviśeṣataḥ // 60 //
Even when expressing one out of two (exclusion and excluded), by distinction of the remaining reference, it (i.e. the exclusion) follows as though it were a particularized object-entity, i.e. the *vibhakti* (inflection) exhibits *vyatireka* (genitive relation between the two).

bhedāntarapratikṣepāpratikṣepau tayor dvayoḥ /
padaṃ saṃketabhedasya jñātṛvañchānurodhinaḥ // 61 /
The dropping or not dropping of another particular one of those two is the *pada* (T. *gźi*) of a particular sign which works according to the desire of the cognizer.

P-Vin-Sva (37*. 33-34; 39*. 6-7), k. 65, uses PV-Sva, 33:

arthāntaranimitto hi dharmaḥ syād anya eva saḥ /
paścād bhāvān na hetutvaṃ phale 'py ekāntatā kutaḥ //
For the sign-source of another object-entity would be just another feature. Since it would be on-going later, it would not be a cause. Even, when it is a result, how is there certainty!

P-Vin-Bu, 145b, cites PV-Sva, 62-63:

bhedo 'yam eva sarvatra dravyabhāvābhidhāyinoḥ /
śābdayor na tayor vācye viśeṣas tena kaścana // 62 /
Just this is the particularity everywhere of the two terms naming the material and the existent. Still there is scarcely any distinction in the reference (*vācya*) to those two.

jijñāpayiṣur arthaṃ taṃ taddhitena kṛtāpi vā /
anyena vā yadi brūyāt bhedo nāsti tataḥ paraḥ // 63 /
Given the desire to reveal that object-entity, or given the maturation by its benefit, or if one would tell it at another (occasion)—there is no particular thing beyond that!

P-Vin-Bu, 146a-7, "Having become certain about impermanence by observing the last moment, is a cause for delusion in the witness of existence" (skad cig tha ma mthoṅ na mi rtag par ṅes nas yod pa dmigs pa 'khrul rgyu yin te); and cites Dignāga:

> / 'dra ba yis ni bsgribs pa'i phyir /
> / ṅes bzuṅ bas na de mi 'dzin /
> Because one is hindered by similarity, even having taken certainty, one does not (actually) apprehend it.

D. Logical Connection

P-Vin-Sva (39*. 21-24), k. 66, uses PV-Sva 13:

> na cādarśanamātreṇa vipakṣe 'vyabhicāritā /
> saṃbhāvyavyabhicāratvāt sthālītaṇḍulapākavat //
> When there is the discordant locus (*vipakṣa*), one does not avoid a mistake just by not seeing it, because there could be a mistake (anyway), like cooking grain in a pot.

P-Vin-Sva (Steinkellner, 39*. 25-30), Skt. (part of commentary on k. 66) from PVSV 10.15-18 (P-Vin-Bu, 147b-5, ff. including comment on k. 66):

> na hi bahulaṃ pakvadarśane 'pi sthālyantargamanamātreṇa pākaḥ sidhyati / vyabhicāradarśanāt / evaṃ tu syād evaṃsvabhāvā etatsamānapākahetavaḥ pakvā iti / anyathā tu śeṣavad etad anumānaṃ vyabhicāri /
> Even when there are frequent looks at the cooking, the cooking is not accomplished merely by inserting within a pot, because of looking with mistake. Likewise, one would say, "the cooked," when such individual presences are causes of cooking similar to it. Otherwise, the inference would be the mistaken *a posteriori* (*śeṣavat*).

P-Vin-Sva (40*. 1-2, 6-7), k. 67, uses PV-Sva, 14:

> yasyādarśanamātreṇa vyatirekaḥ pradarśyate /
> tasya saṃśayahetutvāc cheṣavat tad udāhṛtam //
> Of which one the *vyatireka* (absence in dissimilar cases) is revealed merely by not looking, of that one, because it is a cause of doubt, there is the term, '*a posteriori*'.

P-Vin-Sva (40*. 13-16), k. 68, uses PV-Sva, 15:

> hetos triṣv api rūpeṣu niścayas tena varṇitaḥ /
> asiddhaviparītārthavyabhicārivipakṣataḥ //
> Certainty was expressed by him (i.e. by the teacher Dignāga), in the event of the three modes of the reason, by way of adversary to the unproven (by applying the *pakṣadharma*), to the reversed meaning (by applying the *anvaya*), and to the mistake (by applying the *vyatireka*).

P-Vin-Sva (41*. 24-27), k. 69, uses PV-Sva, 17:

> na ca nāstīti vacanāt tan nāsty eva yathā yadi /
> nāsti sa khyāpyate nyāyas tadā nāstīti gamyate //
> Not just by saying, "It is not," is it not. If a rule is expressed, to wit, how it is not, then one (easily) understands that it is not.

P-Vin-Bu, 148b-3, "The ācārya Dignāga defined the three modes of the reason" (slob dpon phyogs glaṅ gis gtan tshigs kyi tshul gsum la ṅes pa brjod par mdzad pa yin no).

P-Vin-Bu, 148b-5, cites PS:

> / gñis ka yaṅ rab grub pa / sgrub par byed pa'i ma sun 'byin yin /
> When one fulfills the (condition) of both (the first speaker and the respondent), there is no refuter of the proving-method.

P-Vin-Bu, 149a-6, refers to both PS (kun btus) and NMu (rigs sgo) for the following statement:

> / re zig 'gal ba daṅ na ṅes pa'i gñen por rjes su 'gro ldog gi khyab pa gñis ka brjod par bya ba gaṅ yin pa 'di ni / rigs so źes pa bśad pa gaṅ yin pa de la chos mi mthun pa smos pa ni / ma ṅes pa'i gñen por bśad pas bsal lo /
> As to any explanation asserting, "Now, it is right that both pervasions, *anvaya* and *vyatireka*, are to be mentioned as the adversaries for the contrary and the uncertain,"—this is rejected by the explanation that states the discordant feature as the adversary for uncertainty.

P-Vin-Bu, 150b-6, cites Dignāga's commentary on PS:

> / 'di yaṅ khrul pa'i phyir tshad ma ma yin te gzugs mtshuṅs pas

ro la sogs pa gdon mi za bar mtshuns par 'gyur pa ni ma yin na / de ltar na lhag ma daṅ ldan pa yaṅ dper mi rigs pa yin no /
Besides, because of the error, it is not an authority. Certainly, there is no similitude to flavour, etc. by similitude to form. Accordingly, the *a posteriori* (*śeṣavat*) is not right in the example.

P-Vin-Bu, 152b-6, mentions the *ācārya* (i.e. Dignāga):

/ slob dpon gyis phyogs kyi chos ni rgol ba daṅ phyir rgol ba la ṅes par gzuṅ ṅo /
According to the *ācārya,* the 'first speaker' and the 'respondent' must certainly accept the *pakṣadharma.*

P-Vin-Bu, 153a-4, mentions the *ācārya* (i.e. Dignāga):

/ slob dpon gyis ma ldog pa ma yin te / slob dpon gyis sgra gaṅ źig rgol phyir rgol gñis ka la ṅes pa'i tshul gsum daṅ ma grub pa'i skyon brjod pa de kho na gźan don skabs kyi sgrub pa gaṅ daṅ sun 'byin du gsuṅs pa'i phyir ro /
The *ācārya* denies that there is no exclusion, because the *ācārya* has stated that the three modes should be certain for both the 'first speaker' and the 'respondent'; that any proving on the occasion of a different object is just a reference to the 'nonactual' (*asiddha*) fault; and that there is the 'refuter' (*dūṣaka*).

P-Vin-Bu, 153b-5, cites Dignāga's commentary on PS-Par, 28b:

/ de la daṅ po gñis the tshom / (k. 28b)
Among those, the first two are doubtful.
/ raṅ gi ṅo bo tha dad pas tha dad pa'i don thams cad la spyi daṅ khyad par gyi chos dag ṅes par the tshom byed rgyu yin te / dper na / sgra rtag pa'am mi rtag pa yin te / gźal bya yin pa'i phyir ro / źes bya ba daṅ / de bźin du mñam bya yin pa'i phyir ro / źes bya ba lta bu'o źes pas bsal lo /
That is, they certainly cause doubt about the natures of generality and specialization regarding all the particularized entities because particularized by own nature; for example, the proposition, "Sound is permanent, or impermanent, because it is inferable"; and likewise, "because it is audible". Those should be rejected.

P-Vin-Sva (Steinkellner, pp. 102-107), k. 70:

yady adṛṣṭyā nivṛttiḥ syāc cheṣavad vyabhicāri kim /
vyatireky api hetuḥ syād asiddhiyojanā 'vācyā //
If there could be a reversal (or, cessation) out of sight, how could the *a posteriori* (śeṣavat) be mistaken? The reason would also have reversal; and the combination of nonproof (would be) inexpressible.

P-Vin-Sva 45*. 26-28, 34-35; 46*. 1-2), k. 71, uses PV-Sva, 23; (46*. 8-15), k. 72-73, use PV-Sva, 24-25:

tasmāt tanmātrasaṃbandhaḥ svabhāvo bhāvam eva vā /
nivartayet kāranam vā kāryam avyabhicārataḥ // 23 /
Hence, the individual presence with connection to a *tanmātra* excludes just the presence. Or else, given a material cause, there is a result, for the reason that there is no mistake.

anyathaikanivṛttyānyanivṛttiḥ kathaṃ bhavet /
nāśvavān iti martyena na bhāvyaṃ gomatāpi kim // 24 /
Otherwise, how could there be the inactivity of the other (i.e. *sādhana*) by the inactivity of the one (i.e. the *sādhya*)? What would be the use of a man to say he does not own a cow when he does not own a horse!

saṃnidhānāt tathaikasya katham anyasya saṃnidhiḥ /
gomān ity eva martyena bhāvyam aśvavatāpi kim // 25 /
Likewise, by proximity of the one, how is there proximity of the other? What would be the use of a man to say he owns a cow, when (in fact) he owns a horse!

These three are 'interim verses'.
P-Vin-Sva (46*. 23-24), k. 74ab, uses PV-Sva, 26ab:

tasmād vaidharmyadṛṣṭānte neṣṭo 'vaśyam ihāśrayaḥ /
Therefore, we certainly deny a basis (*āśraya*) here in a discordant example.

P-Vin-Sva (46*. 31; 47*.2), k. 74cd:

/ yaṅ na rgyu yi dṅos por te / me med na yaṅ du ba ste //

Furthermore, as a basis for a reason, smoke in the absence of fire.

P-Vin-Sva (47*. 6-8, 14-15), k. 75, uses PV-Sva, 29:

hetusvabhāvābhāvo 'taḥ pratiṣedhe ca kasyacit /
hetur yuktopalambhasya tasya cānupalambhanam //
When there is exclusion of anything, then the cause is the absence of the individual-presence (kind of) reason; and there is non-apprehension of a feasible apprehension.

P-Vin-Sva (Steinkellner, p. 114-5, final comment by PV-SV 20.9-12):

trividha eva hi pratiṣedhahetuḥ upalabhyasattvasya hetos tathābhāvaniścaye vyāpakasya svātmanaś cānupalabdhir iti... tattadviruddhādyagatigatibhedaprayogato 'nekaprakāra uktaḥ. The exclusion kind of reason is only of three kinds: the non-apprehension of a cause for apprehendability, of a pervader, or of an individual self, given the certainty of absence that way . . . (However), many sorts have been stated by way of variegating through non-comprehending and comprehending the contrary, etc. to this and that.

P-Vin-Bu, f. 148b-3, clarifies the non-apprehension of "an individual self" as that of the 'individual-presence' (*svabhāva*) kind of reason.

III. PARĀRTHĀNUMĀNA (INFERENCE FOR OTHERS)

A. Theory-systems and *śāstras*
B. Examination of *pakṣa* (locus)
   (1) Definition of *pakṣa*
   (2) Examination of *sāmānya*
   (3) Varieties of *pakṣadharma*
C. Communication of the evidence
D. Example and fallacious example

A. Theory-Systems and Śāstras
P-Vin-Bu, f. 148b-3, begins commentary on P-Vin-Par; and on P-Vin-Par; k. lab:

/ gźan don rjes su dpag pa ni /
/ raṅ gis mthoṅ don rab gsal byed /

Parārthānumāna clarifies the *artha* (meaning, entity) that was seen by oneself.

P-Vin-Par, Dharmakīrti on this half-*kārikā* points out that just as oneself has aroused the cognition possessed of the evidence by way of the three-moded evidence (*trirūpa-liṅga*), so, wishing to arouse the cognition possessed of the evidence in others, as one teaches the three-moded evidence—this is inference for others. But, k. 1cd:

/ luṅ las gźan gyis mthoṅ ba ni /
/ raṅ gis mthoṅ ba ma yin yaṅ //
What is seen by others from their Āgama(s) (handed down from the seers) is not what was seen by oneself.

P-Vin-Bu, 161a-7 to 161b-1, to show that inference when operating necessarily excludes direct perception, cites 'Rgyan' (*Alaṃkāra*), PV-Bh-Par, verse citations no. 2:

yathā gṛhītasambandhasmaraṇe vacanāt sati [= smṛti] /
anumānodayas tadvan na pratyakṣodayaḥ kvacit //
Just as when one remembers the perceived relationship, the memory is by way of an utterance; so also when inference occurs, there is no occurrence at all of direct perception.

Since Buddhist logic speaks of two kinds of 'inference'—for oneself and for others, it follows either inference can follow a perception. So Bu-ston mentions (without naming) an opponent here, P-Vin-Bu, 161b-2, f:

/ gzhan don rjes dpag gi mtshan ñid ston pa'i skabs 'dir slob dpon gyis raṅ gis mthoṅ zhes smos pa'am bzuṅ bas ni / gzhan gyis mthoṅ ba gcod de / luṅ las mthoṅ ba ni luṅ mkhaṅ po gzhan kho na rjes mthoṅ ba ni rgol ba raṅ gi tshad mas ma grub pas sgrub byed yaṅ dag min zhiṅ de brjod pa sgrub ṅag yaṅ.dag min no zhes śes par bya ba'i don du'o / don zhes smos pas ni rtags kyi tshul tshad mas gnod med kyi don la med pa rtog pas sgro btags pa las kyaṅ bsgrub bya 'grub pa yin no zhes śes par bya ba'i phyir smos so /
For this section of teaching the character of inference for others (*parārthānumāna*), a (certain) *ācārya* regarding the expression "seen by oneself" decided it was "seen by another." This is 'seeing' according to an *āgama*, and a master of the

> *āgama* who sees only by another. This opponent is incorrect to 'prove' when not proving by one's own Pramāṇa; and is incorrect when stating it, to claim a 'proof, to wit, in the meaning of the knowable. The 'meaning', as stated, is a pretence with constructive thought, denying a meaning for not harming the method of evidence by a Pramāṇa; and which asserts [the fallacy] that the provable is the proof, and so claiming because it is a 'knowable'.

P-Vin-Par, k. 2, uses PV-Par 54:

> riktasya jantor jātasya guṇadoṣam apaśyataḥ /
> vilabdhā bata kenāmī siddhāntaviṣamagrahāḥ //
> Alas, by whom are those wicked demons of theory-systems (*siddhānta*) commissioned for a person born destitute (*rikta*), who does not see (the difference between) virtue and vice!

The word *rikta* in the sense 'devoid of course' is employed in Indian astronomy-astrology. K. 2 is labelled 'interim verse' (*antara-śloka*).

P-Vin-Par, k. 3, uses PV-Par, 14:

> kalpanāgamayoḥ kartur icchāmātrānurodhataḥ /
> vastunaś cānyathābhāvāt tatkṛtā vyabhicāriṇaḥ //
> Due to compliance with just the claim of the agent of the constructive thought and the *āgama*, and due to the presence ottherwise of the given things, the reasons for them are mistaken.

This is a summary verse (*saṃgraha-śloka*).

P-Vin-Par, k. 4, uses PV-Par, 15:

> arthād arthagateḥ śaktiḥ pakṣahetvabhidhānayoḥ /
> nārthe tena tayor nāsti svataḥ sādhanasaṃsthitiḥ //
> Should there be no capacity to define the 'locus' (*pakṣa*) and reason (*hetu*) by understanding the meaning according to the entity when there is an entity, it follows that there would not be for those two (*pakṣa* and *hetu*) a taking shape of proof-method by its own (true nature).

P-Vin-Par, k. 5, uses PV-Par, 17:

sādhyasyaivābhidhānena pāramparyeṇa nāpy alam /
śaktasya sūcakaṃ hetuvaco 'śāktam api svayam //
For demonstrating the capacity, not only does it not suffice for the definition to be in continuous descent from the thesis (*sādhya*) alone, but also that there be no capacity for the reason (*hetu*)-expression by itself.

P-Vin-Par, k. 6, comparable to PV-Par, 29:

asiddhāsādhanārthoktavādyabhyupagatagrahaḥ /
anukto 'pīcchayā vyāptaḥ sādhya ātmārthavan mataḥ //
The apprehending of the disputant's espousal is stated as an object-entity (*artha*) that is nonactual or without proof. Even if not stated, it is pervaded by (such) claim (-belief). It is claimed to be the thesis as in one's own aim (i.e. as in 'inference for oneself').

P-Vin-Bu, 148b-3, cites Dignāga's PS-Par, k. 27:

/ chos daṅ chos can raṅ ṅo bo / yaṅ na de'i khyad par rnams /
/ phyin ci log tu bsgrub pa'i phyir / gnod pa med la 'gal ba yin //
Because demonstrating in 'reversed' (or, wayward) fashion the true feature (*dharma*), factual base (*dharmin*), and their distinctions, (you sir) are contrary to the non-annulment (*abādhaka*).

P-Vin-Bu, 174a-3, cites Vasubandhu (cf. PV-M, p. 374, in comment on PV-Par, 32): "If one inquires, what is the 'other' of the expression 'for others' (*parārtha*); and (someone) suggests that the 'other' is what experiences oneself—in that case, one cannot demonstrate the *anvaya* of 'resting place' as consistent example 'for oneself' (*svārtha*)." Vasubandhu apparently means that a resting place, or bed, serves oneself, is 'for self;' and also serves another, is 'for others;' but a 'resting place' does not 'experience' or 'cognize.' Hence, when one explains the 'other' as the others' senses, eye, etc., this is ridiculous. In short, the theory of 'inference for oneself' and 'inference for others' demands that what we expect others to accept as valid, we should first demonstrate to ourselves as valid. P-Vin-Bu, 174a-5, in comment following the Vasubandhu citation, ties this in with language of the preceding PS-Par, k. 27 citation. That is, the wrong way of explaining the 'other' of 'for others' is the 'reversed' fashion; so "contrary to the non-annulment" amounts to improperly annulling, i.e. destroying the necessary connection.

P-Vin-Par, k. 7-9, use PV-Par, 46-48 (these P-Vin-Par verses begin a series that are termed 'interim verses'):

kaiścit prakaraṇair icchā bhavet sā gamyate ca taiḥ /
balāt taveccheyam iti vyaktam īśvaraceṣṭitam // 46 /
By which occasions (or, books) a claim occurs and is understood by means of them, thinking this claim of yours (to be) willy-nilly, it is clearly inspired by a lord!

vadann akāryaliṅgaṃ taṃ vyabhicāreṇa bādhyate /
anāntarīyake cārthe bādhite 'nyasya kā kṣatiḥ // 47 //
Claiming there is no result-evidence, it (the result-evidence) is annulled by mistake. And (you claim,) what is the harm of another (thesis, *sādhya*) when the entity (*artha*) is annulled by no necessary connection?

uktaṃ ca nāgamāpekṣam anumānaṃ svagocare /
siddhaṃ tena susiddhaṃ tan na tadā śāstram īkṣyate // 48 /
And you say: in its own sphere (i.e. sphere of the thesis), an inference is not dependent upon *āgama*. Hence, when the proven is well proven, not at that time is it dependent upon a *śāstra*.

P-Vin-Par, k. 10-12, use PV-Par 49-51:

vādatyāgas tadā syāc cen na tadānabhyupāyataḥ /
upāyo hy abhyupāye 'yam anaṅgaṃ sa tadāpi san // 49 /
If there would be at that time a rejection of word, it would not be at that time due to no thesis (*abhyupāya* = *sādhya*). For when the means is the thesis, at that time it exists without members.

tadā viśuddhe viṣayadyaye śāstraparigraham /
cikīrṣoḥ sa hi kālaḥ syāt tadā śāstreṇa bādhanam // 50 /
For when the two objects (i.e. of direct perception and of inference) are pure, there may be embrace of the treatise (*śāstra*), for it would be the time for one wishing to perform

(toward the religious goal); at that time there is annulling (of *sādhya* and *sādhana*) by the *śāstra.*

tadvirodhena cintāyās tatsiddhārtheṣv ayogataḥ /
tṛtīyasthānasaṃkrāntau nyāyaḥ śāstraparigrahaḥ // 51 /
For there is no feasibility of examination (*cintā*) in entities proved by it by way of contradicting it! When there is shift to the third place (among *pratyakṣa, parokṣa,* and *atyantaparokṣa*), it is right to embrace the *śāstra.*

P-Vin-Par, k. 13-14, use PV-Par, 52-53:

tatrāpi sādhyadharmasya nāntarīyakabādhanam /
parihāryaṃ na cānyeṣām anavasthāprasaṅgataḥ // 52 /
And in that (i.e. śāstra) one should avoid the annulment of necessary connection of a thesis-feature but not of other (thesis features), or else there would be 'fallacy of infinite regress' (*anavasthā-prasaṅga*).

keneyaṃ sarvacintāsu śāstraṃ grāhyam iti sthitiḥ /
kṛtedānīm asiddhāntair grāhyo dhūmena nānalaḥ // 53 /
The rule (*sthiti*) is: One should embrace the *śāstra* during all the examinations (*sarvacintā*). Done now, there is no apprehension of fire because of the smoke of bad theory-systems.

P-Vin-Par, k. 15-16, use PV-Par, 55-56:

yadi sādhana ekatra sarvaṃ śāstraṃ nidarśane /
darśayet sādhanaṃ syād ity eṣā lokottarā sthitiḥ // 55 //
This is the supramundane rule: (The speaker) should reveal the *sādhana,* if (he claims that) there is a *sādhana* in one case that illustrates every *śāstra.*

asambaddhasya dharmasya kiṃ asiddhau na sidhyati /
hetus tatsādhanāyoktaḥ kiṃ duṣṭas tatra sidhyati // 56 /
When there is no proof of an unrelated feature, will it not be proved? (Or,) if it is proved in this case, is the reason badly stated for proving it?

P-Vin-Par, k. 17, uses in part PV-Par, 57:

dharmān anupanīyaiva dṛṣṭante dharmiṇo 'khilān /
vāgdhūmāder jano 'nveti caitanyadahanādikam // 57 /
Even when an example is not adduced for any features of the factual base, a person infers the fire and so forth in his consciousness from the smoke and so forth of (someone's) word.

P-Vin-Par, k. 18-19, use PV-Par. 58-59:

svabhāvaṃ kāraṇaṃ cārtho 'vyabhicāreṇa sādhayan /
kasyacid vādabādhāyāṃ svabhāvān na nivartate // 58 /
Therebeing no mistake, the entity proving a (given) individual presence and a (given) cause, does not give up the individual presence when there is an annulment of someone's utterance.

prapadyamānas cānyas taṃ nāntarīyakam īpsitaiḥ /
sādhyārthair hetunā tena katham apratipāditaḥ // 59 /
Since the other (='respondent,' *prativādin*) finds out the necessary connection by the accepted thesis entities, why would it not be found out by the reason (*hetu*)!

P-Vin-Par, k. 20-21, use PV-Par, 63-64:

yadi kiñcit kvacic chāstre na yuktaṃ pratiṣidhyate /
bruvāṇo yuktam apy anyad iti rājakulasthitiḥ // 63 /
This is the rule of the royal court: If something is not right anywhere in a *śāstra*, and another declares it right, it is to be invalidated.

sarvān arthān samīkṛtya vaktuṃ śakyaṃ na sādhanam /
sarvatra tenotsanneyaṃ sādhyasādhanasaṃsthitiḥ// 64 /
When one takes all entities to be the same, there is no ability to express a *sādhana*. Therefore, in every case the formation of thesis (*sādhya*) and proof (*sādhana*) is ruined.

P-Vin-Par, k. 7-21, are a continuous sequence entitled 'interim verses' (*antara-śloka*).

The expression *samīkṛtya* of PV-Par, 64, rendered "takes to be the same", can be interpreted two ways: *beneath logic*: the person with poor discrimination who cannot tell the difference between things;

beyond logic: the yogin who realizes the Buddhist *samatā-jñāna* (Sameness Wisdom).

P-Vin-Bu, 183b-4 (end), gives summary of *bādha* (T. *gnod pa*), perhaps in the usual meaning of 'injury' or 'harm', rather than the technical sense of 'annulment'. There is *bādha* to the Āgama, *bādha* to the 'thesis' (*pratijñā*), and *bādha* to the 'evidence' (*liṅga*)—making three. Then another set of three: attending to the Āgama (*luṅ la ltos pa*) by examination (dpyod pa), attending to the Āgama by the pervasion (khyab pa), attending to the Āgama by the locus feature (*pakṣadharma*, phyogs chos). The first one, 'examination', is said to be in three ways (see *Guided Tour*, footnotes 4-5).

B. Examination of Pakṣa (P-Vin-Bu, 187a-3)

(1) *Definition of pakṣa*

P-Vin-Par, k. 22-25, use PV-Par, 84-86, 75 (a series of 'interim verses'):

> hetvādilakṣaṇair bādhyaṃ muktvā pakṣasya lakṣaṇam /
> ucyate parihārārtham avyāptivyatirekayoḥ // 84 /
> The definition of a *pakṣa* (locus) is declared to mean omitting the non-pervasion and the *vyatireka* (absence in dissimilar cases), by leaving out the annulment by such definitions as of the reason (*hetu*).
>
> svayaṃ nipātarūpākhyā vyatirekasya bādhikāḥ /
> sahānirākṛteneṣṭaśrutir avyāptibādhanī // 85 /
> (That is to say), the utterances (i.e. the *śruti*-s) of given nature and by themselves annul the *vyatireka*; and the accepted *śruti* annuls the non-pervasion by means of associated rejection.
>
> sādhyābhyupagamaḥ pakṣalakṣaṇaṃ teṣv apakṣatā /
> nirākṛte bādhanataḥ śeṣe 'lakṣaṇavṛttitaḥ // 86 /
> A locus (*pakṣa*) is defined as the espousal of a thesis (*sādhya*). In those (others), there is no *pakṣa* (locus), due to annulment when there is the rejected, and due to no occurrence of the characteristic when there is the remainder (i.e. the *vyatireka*).
>
> dṛṣṭer vipratipattīnām atrākārṣīt svayaṃ śrutim /
> iṣṭākṣatim asādhyatvam anavasthāṃ ca darśayan // 75 /

> He (the *ācārya*) drew upon his own *śruti* here (i.e. in the sense of *pakṣa* definition) for the view of notions to be rejected—showing the unblemished theory, as well as the false thesis and the infinite regress.

P-Vin-Par, 22-25 are a set of 'interim verses'. P-Vin-Bu, 189a-b, refers to Dignāga to show that 'his own *śruti*' means the five principles. The five, namely, the *svarūpa*, the *eva*, the *svayam* the *iṣṭa*, and the *anirākṛta*, are explained in the *Guided Tour* under Parārthānumāna, "sādhya of genuine evidence for 'aim of others'" and "fallacy of *pakṣa* (locus) for aim of others".

P-Vin-Bu, 190a-6, f. continuing the discussion of the five principles, refers to Dignāga, probably a paraphrase, about the terms 'accepted' (*iṣṭa*) and 'unaccepted' (*aniṣṭa*), which figure in PS-Par, k. 5 (cf. H. Kitagawa, pp. 137-138). The 'first speaker' must have accepted the *pakṣa* (locus).

P-Vin-Par, k. 26-27, comparable to PV-Par, 91-92:

> aniṣiddhaḥ pramāṇābhyāṃ sa copagama iṣyate /
> sandigdhe hetuvacanād vyasto hetor anāśrayaḥ // 91 /
> We claim that the (verbally) uncontradicted espousal is by way of the two authorities. The exclusion is not a basis for the reason (*hetu*) due to expressing the reason when there is doubt.

As to the doubtful reason, cf. PS-Par, k. 25:

> anumānasya bhedena sā bādhoktā caturvidhā /
> tatrābhyupātaḥ kāryāṅgaṃ svabhāvāṅgaṃ jagatsthitiḥ // 92 /
> By variety of inference, the annulment (*bādhā*) is stated to be fourfold. Therein are the espousal (*abhyupāta*), the result-member, the individual-presence member, and the rule of the world.

P-Vin-Par, k. 28-29, use PV-Par, 128-129:

> naimittikyāḥ śruter artham arthaṃ vā pāramārthikam /
> śabdānāṃ pratirundhāno 'bādhanārho hi varṇitaḥ // 128 /
> For we explain that when opposing the entity of *śruti* having a particular cause, or (when opposing) the absolute entity of words, there is no need for annulment.

tasmād viṣayabhedasya darśanāya pṛthakkṛtā /
anumānabahirbhūtā pratītir api pūrvavat // 129 /
Therefore, for showing the variety of sense object, the cognitive dawning is taken separate, outside of inference, as earlier.

P-Vin-Par, k. 28-29, are interim verses.
P-Vin-Bu, 194b-4 (citing Dignāga's *Samuccaya*):

/ dper brjod pa yaṅ 'dra ba ste / gcig tu mdzad de /
gzhal bya'i don can gyi tshad ma dag med do /
"If an example, being similar, were taken as identical, there would be no authorities (*pramāṇa*) having sanctions (*prameya*) as object."

P-Vin-Bu, 195a-6, 7, takes citation from PV-Bh-Par, p. 527, to illustrate 'non-annulment' (*abādha*):

cittam antargataṃ duṣṭaṃ tīrthasnānair na śudhyati /
śataśo pi hi tad dhautaṃ surābhāṇḍam ivaśuci //
gaṅgādvāre kuśāvartte bilvakī nīlaparvate /
snātvā kaṇakhale tīrthe sambhaven na punarbhavaḥ //
The mind that is wicked within, is not purified by bathings at a ford. For even when it is washed a hundred times, it is not clean as a pot (would be).
Nor would there be a (spiritual) rebirth at a quay of the Ganges, on twisted *kuśa*-grass and *bilva*-leaves, or when one has bathed at the Kaṇakhala ford.

P-Vin-Bu, 197b-6 (citing Dignāga's *Samuccaya*):

/ rtsom par byed pa ma yin zhes bya ba ni dam bcaḥ
ba'i skyon yaṅ yin te sṅar khas blaṅs pa daṅ 'gal ba'i phyir ro /
To say, "There is no start," is a fault of thesis (*pratijña*), because it contradicts the prior thesis.

P-Vin-Bu, 198b-3, cites *Rgyan,* i.e. PV-Bh, here on Par, k. 105, the verse no. 166:

parīkṣitaṃ yadi bhavet pramāṇaṃ tatra bādhakaṃ /
parīkṣā na pravṛttā cet svavāco na viśiṣyate //
If it is well examined, the authority in this case is an annulment.

If the examination does not proceed, it (the authority) is no better than one's own word.

(2) ***Examination of the sāmānya (Generality)***
P-Vin-Bu, 199b-4, cites PV-Prat, 2, in part: "(respectively) object of word (sgra'i yul, i.e. generality) and not object of word (yul min, i.e. individual)."

P-Vin-Par, k. 30-32, use PV-Par, 133-135:

tad eva rūpaṃ tatrārthaḥ śeṣaṃ vyāvṛttilakṣaṇam /
avastubhūtaṃ sāmānyam atas tan nākṣagocaraḥ // 133 /
That very form is the entity therein. The remainder has the definition of exclusion (*vyāvṛtti*). The generality is a non-given thing; hence it is nomt in the range of direct perception.

tena sāmānyadharmāṇām apratyakṣatvasiddhitaḥ /
pratikṣepe 'py abādheti śrāvaṇoktyā prakāśitam // 134 /
Thus, since there is no proof of generality features by direct perception, it is taught by audible expression, "Even when rejecting, there is no annulment."

sarvathā 'vācyarūpatvāt siddhyā tasya samāśrayāt /
bādhanāt tadbalenoktaḥ śrāvaṇenākṣagocaraḥ // 135 /
The sensory range in the manner of the audible is stated by way of being a non-reference nature in every sense, by way of its habitation as a proof (*siddhi*), and by way of its strength through annulment.

P-Vin-Par, k. 30-32 are interim verses. PV-Par-M comments on *bādhanāt* as *kāraṇāt* ('through material cause'), implying the purposive activity (*arthakriyā*) attributed in this system to the 'individual character' (*svalakṣaṇa*), which thus has the power to annul; whereas the 'generality character' (alluded to in above verses 133-134) even when rejecting lacks the power to annul.

P-Vin-Bu, 200a-3, cites *Rgyan*, i.e. PV-Bh. -Par, and this verse, p. 529.6, numbered 172:

prasiddhir iṣṭaśabdābhidheyatvaṃ yad akampitaṃ /
prasiddhir vyavahāro hi tajjātatvāt tathocyate //
'Popular acceptance' (*prasiddhi*) is any firm significance of the

accepted word. 'Popular acceptance' is conventional language, namely, it is so stated since it is engendered by that (conventional language).

P-Vin-Bu, 201a-4, cites PV-Par, 110cd:

pratyakṣādimitā mānaśrutyāropena sūcitāḥ //
The (features, *dharma*) judged by perception, etc. are pointed out by the superimposition with *śruti* of authority (*māna* = *pramāṇa*).

PV-M-Par on this verse clarifies that the authority is inference (*anumāna*).

P-Vin-Bu, 201a-4, follows the foregoing citation with the following remarks:

/ ci ste 'dod pa'i sgras brjod bya ñid don rnams la dgag par mi nus śe na / rtog pa' snaṅ yul gyi don thams cad ni chos can / rtog pa snaṅ ba'i ṅo bo ñid kyis snar brda byas pa daṅ sṅar brda ma byas pa'i sgra rnams kyis brjod byar ruṅ ba yin te / rtog pa la snaṅ ba'i·ṅo bo ñid kyis don de la sgra rnams 'dod pa tsam gyis 'jug pa'i phyir /
Is it that there is no capacity to refute the meanings to be expressed by terms as desired? All meanings of the appearing domain of constructive thoughts are the factual base (*dharmin*). By the nature of appearing constructive thought, it is feasible to express by terms of previously constructed words or of the previously unconstructed words—because one uses just as desired the terms for the meanings per the appearing nature of the constructive thought.

P-Vin-Bu, 204a-1, cites PS:

/ 'dir ni śes pa 'aṅ 'phaṅs pa yin /
/ gaṅ phyir śes byed dbaṅ byas phyir ro /
Since one has cast cognition on (evidence, *liṅga*), for this reason one empowers the informing.

P-Vin-Bu, 204a-4, cites the *ācārya*, i.e. PS-Par, k. 23ab (V-version):

/ brjod par 'dod pa'i graṅs gcig ñid /
/ 'gal ba dag la the tshom phyir /

> Because of doubt regarding the (two) contradictories, there is a single amount (= a single factual base) of the 'desire to declare' (*vivakṣā*).

Bu-ston explains that the object is the *āgama*.

P-Vin-Bu, 209a-4 cites PS-SV (or, paraphrase?):

> / raṅ gi chos can la źes smos la khyad par bsal ba sogs 'di bźi/
> Four special rejections are set forth regarding one's (= the first speaker's) factual base (*dharmin*).

Bu-ston precedes the citation with statement of the four:

/ bsgrub byar 'dod pa'i chos daṅ ldan pa'i chos can la gnod na skyon yin gyi / mi 'dod pa'i chos daṅ ldan pa'i chos can la gnod kyaṅ skyon min /

1. While there is a fault when annulling a factual base that has a feature someone has accepted as a thesis (*sādhya*), there is no fault in annulling a factual base that has a feature that one has not accepted (as a thesis).
   / chos can la gnod pas de'i chos la gnod pas tshogs don la gnod na skyon du bstan pa /
2. It is taught as a fault if he annuls the 'global entity' (tshogs don), by annulling the factual base and by annulling its feature.
   / chos can gcig pu la gnod pa skyon du 'dod pa bsal ba /
3. He should reject the claim that there is a fault in annulling a solitary factual base.
   / chos can gyis khyad par du byas pa'i chos la gnod na skyon du bstan pa /
4. It is taught as a fault if one annuls a feature that has been distinguished by the factual base.

(3) *Varieties of pakṣadharma*

P-Vin-Bu, 209a-4, begins treatment of *pakṣadharma* varieties so as to expound fallacies of the reason.

P-Vin-Bu, 209b-1, 2, cites a verse without source mention, with language overlapping PS-Par, k. 8; clearly PV-Bh.-Par, p. 580.1, verse citation no. 352, but exhibiting some text corruption or misediting:

> pakṣadharmo yato hetus tadābhāsāś ca bhūyasā /
> tasmāt tadvistaraḥ [*read* tatprabhedaḥ] pūrvaṃ
> hetvādyārthāt [read hetvābhāsāt] pradarśyate //

On which account the reason (*hetu*) and its fallacies are predominately the *pakṣadharma*, it follows that first its variegation is expounded as fallacies of the reason.

P-Vin-Bu, 209b-7, cites PS:

/ dgos pa med par gtso bo yi /
/ sgra don las 'das' dod ma yin /
If there were no requirement (of applying figuratively), there would be no acceptance beyond the literal word meaning.

P-Vin-Bu, 210a-2, cites PS-Par, k. 10 (K-version):

samudāyārthasādhyatvād dharmamātretha dharmiṇi /
amukhyepy ekadeśatvāt sādhyatvam upacaryate // (cited PV-Bh. p. 580. 29).
Since the thesis has comprisal meaning, when be there just the feature (*dharma*) or else a factual base (*dharmin*), the 'thesis' is used metaphorically by way of a single place, even when it (the feature or the factual base) is not salient, (or, 'primary').

P-Vin-Par, k. 33:

/ phyogs chos mthun phyogs yod med daṅ /
/ rnam gñis re re dag la yaṅ /
/ rnam gsum mi mthun phyogs la yaṅ /
/ yod med rnam pa gñis phyir ro //
Because the *pakṣadharma* is (of the variety) similar locus, present, absent, and both; and each of these of three kinds; while the dissimilar locus is also present, absent, and both; (and each of these of three kinds).

It is well-known that the discussion of the nine kinds of *pakṣadharma* goes back to Dignāga. He treats this briefly in his work *Hetucakra,* and expands upon the matter in PS-Par, starting with his commentary on k. 20. P-Vin-Bu, 213b-1, cites Dignāga's commentary on PS-Par, probably a paraphrase of comments under k. 24.

Dharmakīrti's discussion in his comments under P-Vin-Par, k. 33, gives the same list of nine as in Dignāga's, except for no. 5, where Dignāga has, "Sound is permanent, because it is audible," Dharmakīrti has, "A living body has (an eternal) self because it is possessed of life." Leaving out the occasional factual bases (*dharmin*), "sound," "living body," Dharmakīrti's list of the nine features (*dharma*) and associated reasons (*hetu*) is as follows:

	Dharma ("it is")	*Reason* ("because it is")
1.	permanent	sanctioning (*prameya*)
2.	impermanent	constructed
3.	produced from effort	impermanent
4.	permanent	constructed
5.	having (eternal) self	possessed of life
6.	permanent	produced from effort
7.	not produced from effort	impermanent
8.	impermanent	produced from effort
9.	permanent	incorporeal

The Tibetan arrangement in square fashion is well known (cf. Randle, *Fragments*, p. 31). P-Vin-Bu, 215a-7, uses the term *re'u mig* (S. *koṣṭhaka*), i.e. nine squares with the numbers in this arrangement:

1.	2.	3.
4.	5.	6.
7.	8.	9.

Here, following Dignāga, 2. and 8. are valid; 4. and 6. are contradictory; and the remaining 1, 3, 5, 7, 9 (the odd numbers) are uncertain or doubtful.

P-Vin-Bu, 215a-6, following PS and Dignāga's commentary, for the top row of the square:

> There are three 'present' in the pervasion (*vyāpti*) of the similar locus (*sapakṣa*): 1. "Sound is permanent, because it is sanctioning (= 'object of authority')," is present in the pervasion of the dissimilar locus (*vipakṣa* = *asapakṣa*). 2. "Sound is impermanent, because it is constructed," is surely absent in the dissimilar locus. 3. "Sound, the factual base, is produced from effort, because it is impermanent," is in a single place (*ekadeśa*) of the dissimilar locus, (for example), "If there is lightning, it is not in the sky."

P-Vin-Bu, 215a-7, for the middle row of the square:

> There are three 'absent' in the similar locus: 4. "Sound is

> permanent, because it is constructed," is present in the pervasion of the dissimilar locus. 5. "A living body, the factual base, is endowed with (eternal) self, because it is possessed of life, etc." is absent in both (similar and dissimilar locuses). 6. "Sound is permanent, because it is produced from effort," is present in the dissimilar locus, (for ex.) 'sky,' while 'lightning,' etc. is absent.

P-Vin-Bu, 215b-2, for the bottom row of the square:

> There are three in both parts of the similar locus: 7. "Sound is not produced from effort, because it is impermanent," is in a single place of the similar locus, (for ex.) present in lightning, absent in the sky, while present in the pervasion of the dissimilar locus. 8. "Sound is impermanent, because it is produced from effort," is (present) in both (parts of) the similar locus, and absent in the dissimilar locus. 9. "Sound is permanent, because it is incorporeal," is a claim that atoms are permanent; in the same respect, atoms are absent in the similar locus, while sky is present; and pot, etc. is absent in the dissimilar locus, while action (*karma*) is present.

It will be noticed that only the two valid cases, 2. and 8. satisfy the conditions of pervasion: *anvaya* 'presence in similar locuses,' and *vyatireka* 'absence in dissimilar locuses.'

P-Vin-Par, k. 34, uses PV-Par 195:

> svabhāvakāryasiddhyartham dvau dvau hetuviparyayau /
> vivādād bhedasāmānye śeṣo vyāvṛttisādhanah //
> So as to prove the individual presence and result, there are two reasons and two contradictions. By way of denying (two others) there are the two—particularity (*bheda*) and generality (*sāmānya*). The remainder is the proving method (*sādhana*) of exclusion.

PV-M on this verse follows Dharmakīrti's comments on the P-Vin-Par, k.34. The two reasons are the two valid ones of Dignāga's *Hetucakra*, i.e. nos. 2. and 8.Thus, 'being constructed' (*kṛtakatva*), in the case of self-presence, i.e. literal case, and 'necessary connection with effort' (*prayatnānantarīyakatva*), i.e. use of metaphor, in the case of the results, are for proving the *pakṣadharma* 'impermanence' (*anityatva*). The two contradictions are nos. 4. and 6. (In the square, the two contradictions are at 'cross-purposes'—horizontal—to the two valid ones—the vertical). Particularity and generality are respectively 'too restrictive' (*asādhāraṇa*) and 'unrestricted' (*sādhāraṇa*). No. 1 is 'unrestricted' because of the 'presence' in both the similar and dissimilar locuses. No. 5 is 'too restricted' because of the 'absence' in both the similar and dissimilar locuses. The remainder is therefore nos. 3, 7, 9, to be treated with 'exclusion.' PV-Bh on PV-Par, 195, also mentions that the 'remainder' is three.

C. Communication of the Evidence (*liṅga*)

The title of this section takes its cue from the initial statement in Dharmakīrti's *Nyāyabindu,* III (Inference for Others): "Inference for others is the communication of the evidence with three modes in terms of the material cause (*kāraṇa*) by way of a metaphor for the result (*kārya*)." Previously in P-Vin he had dealt with "the evidence with three modes" in various ways. Now comes the topic of the communication itself, with the expected discussion of cause and result. In P-Vin-Bu, the section apparently begins at 217a-5.

P-Vin-Par, k. 35-36, use PV-Par 197-198:

> prayatnānantaraṃ jñānaṃ prāk sato niyamena na /
> tasyāvṛtyakṣaśabdeṣu sarvathā 'nupayogataḥ // 197 /
> The former cognition right after an effort is certainly not of an existent (= word, śabda), because there is no use (*upayoga*) at all in its words for an ear that is plugged.
>
> kadācin nirapekṣasya kāryā 'kṛtivirodhataḥ /
> kādācitkaphalaṃ siddhaṃ talliṅgaṃ jñānam īdṛśam // 198 /
> At some time of no-dependence, because of opposing the non-doing of a result—such-like cognition proving a sometime result is its evidence.

P-Vin-Par, k. 35-36 are 'summary verses'.

P-Vin-Par, k. 37-39, use PV-Par, 202-204:

> yan nāntarīyakā sattā yo vātmany avībhāgavān /
> sa tenāvyabhicārī syād ity arthaṃ tatprabhedanam // 202 /

One should well analyze the meaning of the assertion, "Whatever is an existent thing with necessary connection or whatever in itself has no parts—it would thereby be without mistake."

saṃyogyādiṣu yeṣv asti pratibandho na tādṛśaḥ /
na te' hetava ity uktaṃ vyabhicārasya sambhavāt // 203 /
We have stated: there is no such connection in those relations; those are not (good) reasons—because of the possibility of mistake.

sati vā pratibandhe 'stu sa eva gatisādhanaḥ /
niyamo hy avinābhāvo 'niyataś ca na sādhanam // 204 /
Or when the connection exists, may it be a proving of understanding! Indeed, a necessary connection is certain, and a proving-means is not uncertain.

P-Vin-Par, k. 37-39 are 'interim verses'.

P-Vin-Par, k. 40-41, use PV-Par, 265-266:

tathānyā nopalabhyeṣu nāstitānupalambhanāt /
tajjñānaśabdāḥ sādhyante tadbhāvāt tannibandhanā // 265 /
Non-existence among the (feasibly) apprehensible is thus not other than non-apprehending. Hence, the words of its discrimination are demonstrated through its presence with that as cause.

siddho hi vyavahāro 'yaṃ dṛśyādṛṣṭāv asann iti /
tasyāḥ siddhāv asandigdhau tatkāryatve 'pi dhīdhvanī // 266 /
For this convention is proved by the remark, "It is not, when the feasibly seen is not seen." When there is its result, i.e. when there is indisputable proof of it (the not-seen of the feasibly seen), it is the word of discrimination.

P-Vin-Par, k. 42-44, use PV-Par, 267-269:

vidyamāne 'pi viṣaye mohād atrānanubruvan /
kevalaṃ siddhasādharmyāt smāryate samayaṃ paraḥ // 267 /
And when the sense object is at hand and through delusion in this case others are not speaking about it, one makes (them) remember the convention only through a proven similar feature.

kāryakāraṇatā yadvat sādhyate dṛṣṭyadṛṣṭitaḥ /
kāryādiśabdā hi tayor vyavahārāya kalpitāḥ // 268 /
In what manner result and material cause are consummated from view and non-view, so are the words of result, and so on, of those two imagined (=constructed, formulated) for conventional language.

kāraṇāt kāryasaṃsiddhiḥ svabhāvāntargamād iyaṃ /
hetuprabhedākhyāne na darśitodāhṛtiḥ pṛthak // 269 /
This accomplishment of a result from a material cause is due to inclusion in individual presence. When expressing a variety of reason (i.e. as individual presence and nonapprehension), the example is not explained as separate (*pṛthag*).

P-Vin-Par, k. 42-44 are interim verses.

P-Vin-Par, k. 45, uses PV-Par, 270:

ekopalambhānubhavād idaṃ nopalabhe iti /
buddher upalabhe veti kalpikāyāḥ samudbhavaḥ //
Due to experiencing a single apprehension, there arises the construction of discrimination, either, "I apprehended," or, "I did not apprehend".

P-Vin-Par, k. 46-47ab, use PV-Par, 273-274ab:

viśiṣṭarūpānubhavād anyathānyanirākriyā /
tadviśiṣṭopalambho 'taḥ tasyāpy anupalambhanam // 273 /
tasmād anupalambho 'yaṃ svayaṃ pratyakṣato gataḥ / 274ab/
By reason of experiencing a distinctive form, there is the rejection of another in every way. Hence, there is the distinctive apprehension; then, belonging to it, the non-apprehension. (274ab:) Therefore, this non-apprehension dawns by itself from a direct perception.

I could not locate in P-Vin-Par, k.47cd. Nor could Steinkellner, *Verse-Index*, p. 223: "vv. 47 and 67 seem to be incomplete." P-Par, 274cd, is as follows: "The understanding is of an event by just itself, i.e. of a separation (*vyavasthiti*) from whatever is absent." (*svamātravṛtter gamakas tadabhāvasvyavasthiteḥ.*)

P-Vin-Par, k. 48, uses PV-Par, 275:

anyathārthasya nāstitvaṃ gamyate 'nupalambhataḥ /
upalambhasya nāstitvam anyenety anavasthitiḥ //

Otherwise, there is no existence to be understood of the entity by way of non-apprehension. In another way (*anyena*), when, there is no existence of the apprehension, there is no separation (either).

P-Vin-Par, k. 49-50, use PV-Par, 276-277:

adṛśye niścayāyogāt sthitir anyatra bādhyate /
yathā 'liṅgo 'nyasattveṣu vikalpādir na sidhyati // 276 /
Just as the rule is annulled elsewhere due to no feasibility of certainty when (something is) not visible, so the constructive thought, etc. that lacks evidence is not proved to other sentient beings.
aniścayaphalā hy eṣā nālaṃ vyāvṛttisādhane /
ādyādhikriyate hetor niścitenaiva sādhane // 277 /
Now, these uncertain results are not enough for proving exclusion. For certainly proving (it), one should at the outset control the reason.

P-Vin-Par, k. 49-50 are interim verses.

P-Vin-Par, k. 51, uses PV-Par, 278:

tasyāḥ svayaṃ prayogeṣu svarūpaṃ vā prayujyate /
arthabādhanarūpaṃ vā bhāve bhāvād abhāvataḥ //
Among the operations of it (=the non-apprehension), either the true nature operates by itself, or the form annulling the (external) entity (operates) when there is a presence due to the presence by reason of absence.

P-Vin-Par, k. 52, uses PV-Par, 279:

anyonyabhedasiddher vā dhruvabhāvavināśavat /
pramāṇāntarabādhād vā sāpekṣadhruvabhāvavat //
Either, because of proof of mutual particularity, like the constant going-on and destruction; Or, because of annulment by other authorities, like the constant going-on of dependence.

It should be noted that the above sequence of PV-Par verses is almost at the end of PV, which has only six more verses (PV-Par, 280-285). From now on Dharmakīrti makes use in P-Vin of verses from various chapters of PV. The place in P-Vin-Bu appears to be 234a-6.

P-Vin-Par, k. 53-54, use PV-Sva, 205-206:

anādivāsanodbhūtavikalpapariniṣṭhitaḥ /
śabdārthas trividho dharmo bhāvābhavobhāyāśrayaḥ// 205 /
A feature (*dharma*) is threefold with word-meaning, to wit, based on presence, absence, and both,—founded on constructive thought arisen from immemorial habit-energy (*vāsanā*).

tasmin bhāvānupādāne sādhye 'syānupalambhanam /
tathā hetur na tasyaivābhāvaḥ śabdaprayogataḥ // 206 /
Among them, when the thesis (*sādhya*) does not assume (take the meaning of) presence, there is the non-apprehension of that (feature). Accordingly, absence is not the reason (*hetu*) for that (word-meaning), (rather) it is due to application of speech.

P-Vin-Par, k. 55-56, use PV-Sva, 207-208:

paramārthaikatānatve śabdānām anibandhanā /
na syāt pravṛttir artheṣu darśanāntarabhediṣu // 207 /
When there is the single side of *paramārtha* there is no cause, nor would there be progress, of words for the entities that differ in the rival philosophical systems.

atītājātayor vāpi na ca syād anṛtārthatā /
vācaḥ kasyāścid ity eṣā bauddhārthaviṣayā matā // 208 /
And there would be no sense to have falsity of any speech, even about the past and the unborn. So we claim that it (the falsity) has as object the entity derived from cognition.

P-Vin-Par, k. 55-56, are labelled 'summary verses' (*saṃgrahaśloka*) both in P-vin-Par. and in PV-SV, 100.15. The 'single side of *paramārtha*' is the individual character (*svalakṣaṇa*), which words cannot reach, so also false words. These words can only be concerned with mentally constructed entities (*kalpitārtha*).

P-Vin-Par, k. 57, uses PV-Sva, 210:

sadasatpakṣabhedena śabdārthānapavādibhiḥ /
vastv eva cintyate hy atra pratibaddhaḥ phalodayaḥ //
Those who refrain from *apavāda* (T. *bsñon pa*, affirmation and then denial) toward word meaning by way of particular 'locuses' of existence and non-existence, should ponder just the given thing (*vastu*) because the arising of a result is tied to this.

P-Vin-Bu, 236a-5, begins a section about word-meaning having no efficiency, and at 236a-7, refers to PS, Dignāga's commentary:

> "The *Samuccaya* explains that the statement, 'There is non-apprehension of the feature thus imagined,' is for the *pradhāna*, etc. imagined by the Sāṃkhya, i.e. a feature non-apprehended."

P-Vin-Bu, 236b-5, cites PV-Par, 260:

> hetusvabhāvanivṛttyaivārthanivṛttivarṇanāt /
> siddhodāharaṇety uktānupalabdhiḥ pṛthag na tu //
> By cessation of the individual-presence (kind of) reason (*hetu*) (and) because of expressing the cessation of the entity (*artha*), the non-apprehension is declared, "the example proved," but not the 'separate' (*pṛthag*) one.

P-Vin-Bu, 237b-4, refers to PS-Par, 2nd half (not in part edited by H. Kitagawa):

> "According to the *Samuccaya*, due to not knowing that the object of inference authority is a generality (*sāmānya*), one takes the existence of a different primary sense (*mukhya*) as an individual character (*svalakṣaṇa*) to be proved."
> / tshad ma'i yul ni mi śes phyir /
> / bsgrub bya'i chos kyaṅ sgrub par byed /
> / rgyas pa'i tshig yin ma brjod do /
> / gtso daṅ rjes 'gro rjes 'gro min //
> Due to not knowing the object of an authority (*pramāṇ-aviṣayājñānād*), when there is a thesis feature (*sādhya-dharma*) (=the *dharma* to be proved), one does not express the extended words that would prove it. Or, given the primary case (*mukhya*) and the metaphoric extension (*anucāra*), there is no similar instance (*anvaya*).

P-Vin-Par, k. 58, uses PV-Sva, 187:

> sattāsvabhāvo hetus cen na sattvā sādhyate katham /
> ananvayo hi bhedānāṃ vyāhato hetusādhyayoḥ //
> If the reason has the individual presence of an existence, how is that existence proved? (It isn't). For the non-*anvaya* of separations is contradictory to the reason and the thesis.

P-Vin-Par, k. 59-60, use PV-Sva, 188-189:

> bhāvopādānamātre tu sādhye sāmānyadharmiṇi /
> na kaścid arthaḥ siddhaḥ syād aniṣiddham ca tādṛśam // 188/
> When a generality factual base has a thesis that is just a distinction of a presence, not any meaning would be proved. And such as this is not subject to contradiction.
>
> upāttabhede sādhye 'smin bhaved dhetur ananvayaḥ /
> sattāyāṃ tena sādhyāyāṃ viśeṣaḥ sādhito bhavet // 189 /
> When in this case a thesis has a particular that is accepted, the reason would be without *anvaya.* Hence, when the thesis is actual, a qualification would be demonstrated.

P-Vin-Par, k. 61 (as numbered by Steinkellner) probably not a P-Vin-Par *kārikā,* since the Tibetan seems to be a variant translation of PS-Sva, 11, per Sanskrit (PVSV, Gnoli ed., p. 95, n.). Here, P-Vin-Par, Dharmakīrti's comments just prior to P-Vin-Par, k. 62 (Steinkellner's number) are identical with PV-SV, 95.1-10:

> tatra ca sādhyanirdeśena na kiṃcit / tatra darśanasambandhākhyānamātrād iṣṭasiddheḥ / tadanirdeśe ca kathaṃ tadviśiṣṭenānvayaḥ / tad ayam agninā 'vinābhāvī siddhaḥ / arthād evāgnes tatpradeśāyogaṃ vyavacchinattīti sa tathā sādhya ucyate / na punas tathā 'syopanyāsapūrvako 'nvayaḥ sādhyokter ihānaṅgatvāt / tatpūrvakatve vā kaḥ pratijñāṃ sādhanād apākaroti / tathā cāha /
> *liṅgasyāvyabhicāras tu dharmeṇānyatra darśyate /*
> *tatra prasiddhaṃ tadyuktaṃ dharmiṇaṃ gamayiṣyati //*
> tasmān nāgnyādisādhanavat sattāsādhanam apy anavadyam iti /
> And in that place there is hardly any [purpose, *prayojana*] to point out the thesis (*sādhya;* but Tib. *bsgrub par byed pa* reads: *sādhana*), because the desired proof is merely through explicating the seeing and the connection. And when not pointing it out, how is there an *anvaya* by way of its qualification? Hence, this is proved to have the necessary connection with fire. This means—the thesis (*sādhya*) is so called, since it rules out the non-connection of that place to fire. Being that way, an *anvaya* does not precede the placement of that (fire), because it has no membership (*aṅgatva*) here for expressing the *sādhya.* Or, if it

did precede it (i.e. the placement), how could the thesis (*pratijñā*) do away with the method of proving (*sādhana*)? For he (i.e. Dignāga) said:

It is not a mistake of evidence that is shown elsewhere by the feature (dharma). One is led to understand that the factual base (dharmin) possessed of that (feature) is well-known at that place.

Therefore, there is no fault that the proving method of existence is not like the proving method of fire, etc.

R. Gnoli in his edition of PVSV, at p. 95, n., identifies the cited stanza as in Dignāga's *Pramāṇasamuccaya*, II, 11. Karṇakagomin's commentary supplies the word *prayojana* in the equivalent passage, placed there between v. 192A and v. 192B in Sankrityayana's numbering. In Gnoli's edition, the passage is between v. 189 and v. 190, translated in this *Analysis*.

P-Vin-Par, k. 62-63; use PV-Sva, 190-191:

aparāmṛṣṭatadbhede vastumātre tu sādhane /
tanṁātravyāpinah sādhyasyānvayo na vihanyate // 190 /
When its particularity is not taken into consideration, i.e., when it is the given thing only, and there is a proving means (*sādhana*), the *anvaya* does not contradict the thesis which pervades only that (given thing).

nāsiddhe bhāvadharmo 'sti vyabhicāryudhayāśrayaḥ /
dharmo viruddho 'bhāvasya sā sattā sādhyate katham // 191 /
When it is unproven, there is no on-going feature; a basis of both (features—on-going and absent) is mistaken. Since a feature opposes absence, how is that existence proved? (It isn't).

P-Vin-Par, k. 64-65, use PV-Sva, 7, 9:

hetunā yaḥ samagreṇa kāryotpado 'numīyate /
arthāntarānapekṣatvāt sa svabhāvo 'nuvarṇitaḥ // 7 /
The arising of a result inferred from a group-reason, is said to be an individual presence, because of non-dependence on another object-entity.

ekasāmagryadhīnasya rūpāde rasato gatiḥ /
hetudharmānumānena dhūmendhanavikāravat // 9 /

A comprehension from taste (as associative condition) of the form, etc. (sense object) that is based on a single group, is by inference from a feature (*dharma*) of the cause, like (inferring) a change of fuel from smoke.

P-Vin-Par, k. 66, 67ab, 68, and 69, do not correspond to PV verses, according to Steinkellner, *Index.*

P-Vin-Par, k. 66:

/ tshogs pa rnam par gźag pa yi /
/ rgyu ni tshogs pa can yin pas /
/ de dag med na de med phyir /
/ ba laṅ ñid las rva can yis //
The reason for establishing a group is to have the (entire) group, because when some (features) are lacking, (the group) is lacking; e.g. the horn from the bull.

P-Vin-Par, k. 67ab, so according to Steinkellner, *Index,* is probably not a half-*kārikā,* because completed by the immediately following phrase:

/ chu yi bdag ñid de 'dra ba /
/ gźi las mṅon par grub pa'i phyir / de'i 'bras yin /
what is like the nature of water, because accomplished from the (water) basis, is its result.

Dharmakīrti goes on to say that in the same manner, inference (*anumāna*) is a result (*kārya*) arising from the evidence (*liṅga*).

P-Vin-Par, k. 68:

/ śes byed yan lag ma grub la /
/ śes byed nus pa yod min phyir /
/ tshul gsum ma grub the tshom za /
/ rtogs pa po yi sgrub byed min //
When the members of communication fail, or there is no capacity of communication—on that account the three modes (of evidence) are nonactual or doubtful, and there is no proving on the part of the one who comprehends (the three modes).

P-Vin-Par, k. 69:

/ gcig rab ma grub the tshom na /
/ ma grub pa daṅ 'khrul pa can /
/ gñis ma grub bam the tshom na /
/ 'gal ba daṅ ni 'khrul pa can //
One person's mistaken object is especially nonactual, or doubtful, or unproven. A second person's mistaken object is nonactual, or doubtful, or contrary.

P-Vin-Bu, f. 243-7, ff., apparently refers to this *kārikā* by stating that the topic has two parts: (a) showing that the feature is mistaken (chos 'khrul par bstan pa); (b) refuting the claim that it is unmistaken (mi 'khrul par' dod pa dgag pa). Hence it is mistaken by being nonactual or doubtful, or unproven; and it is wrongly held to be unmistaken when it is nonactual, or doubtful, or contrary.

Hence, the two *kārikā* present three possibilities: k. 68 refers to the person who understands the three modes but cannot communicate the evidence; k. 69 refers to the person who does not understand the three modes, divided into two possibilities.

P-Vin-Par, k. 70-77, use PV-Sid, 11-16, 18-19 (in given order):

siddhaṃ yādṛg adhiṣṭhātṛbhāvābhāvānuvṛttimat /
sanniveśādi tad yuktaṃ tasmād yad anumīyate // 11 /
Of whatever is the proven shape, etc. patterned after the presence or absence of a Supreme Disposer (*adhiṣṭhātṛ*), one may infer from that just what is valid.

vastubhede prasiddhasya śabdasāmyād abhedinaḥ /
na yuktānumitiḥ pāṇḍudravyād iva hutāśane // 12 /
(Given a valid inference) of something accomplished when the given thing is distinct, there is no valid inference of something (as) not distinct (just) by dint of the same word, any more than from a 'white substance' when there is fire.

anyathā kumbhakāreṇa mṛdvikārasya kasyacit /
ghaṭādeḥ karaṇāt sidhyed valmīkasyāpi tatkṛtiḥ // 13 //
Otherwise, by dint of any pot, etc., made of clay by a potter, one might prove the making by him of an ant-hill (that is made by ants out of clay).

sādhyenānugamāt kārye sāmānyenāpi sādhane /
sambandhibhedād bhedoktidoṣaḥ kāryasamo mataḥ // 14 /

'Equal to the result' (*kāryasama*) we hold to be a fault of stating particulars through pervasion by a 'thesis (*sādhya*) when there is a result, as well as (*api*) (through pervasion) by a generality when there is a means of proof (*sādhana*)—because they are particulars in possession of a connection.

jātyantare prasiddhasya śabdasāmānyadarśanāt /
na yuktaṃ sādhanaṃ gotvād vāgādīnāṃ viṣāṇivat // 15 /
(Given a valid means of proof, *sādhana*) of something accomplished when there is a peculiarity of family (*jāty-uttara*), (for example,) like a horn, there is no valid means of proof by dint of noticing a word generality, i.e. by dint of '*gotva*' ('cowness') among words, etc.

vivakṣāparatantratvān na śabdāḥ santi kutra vā /
tadbhāvād arthasidhau tu sarvaṃ sarvasya sidhyati // 16 /
Since the desire to speak is in others' power, where are there not words! Should there be accomplishment of an object-entity by dint of presence of that (word), all (words) could prove anything (i.e. any thesis, *sādhya*).

vastusvarūpe 'siddhe 'yaṃ nyāyaḥ siddhe viśeṣaṇam /
abādhakam asiddhāv apy ākāśāśrayavad dhvaneḥ // 18 /
There is this means (*nyāya*) when the own form (*svarūpa*) [=literal case] of a given thing (*vastu*) is unproven, like the basis in 'ether' (*ākāśa*) of sound. When it is proven, and even when there is no proof, the qualifier has no annulment.

asiddhāv api śabdasya siddhe vastuni sidhyati /
aulūkyasya yathā bauddhenoktam mūrttyādisādhanam // 19/
Even when there is no proof of a word, like the Vaiśeṣika's means of proof of 'body' (*mūrti*), etc., when the given thing is proved, (the thesis object) is proved—so it is stated by the Buddhist.

P-Vin-Par, k. 70-77, are 'interim verses'.

P-Vin-Bu, 261b-3, cites Dignāga's PS commentary:

/ gcig la yaṅ ldog pa ni mṅon par gsal bar smra ba la byas pa ñid lta bu'o /

"The exclusion of even one (word) is like the pronunciation of distinct speech."

P-Vin-Par, k. 78-79, use PV-Par, 184-185:

yathāsvaṃ bhedaniṣṭhesu pratyayeṣu vivekinaḥ /
dharmī dharmāś ca bhāsante vyavahāras tadāśrayaḥ // 184 /
That habitation is conventional where factual base and separate features manifest in conditions resting upon particulars according to themselves.

vyavahāropanīto 'tra sa evāśliṣṭabhedadhīḥ /
sādhyaḥ sādhanatāṃ nītas tenāsiddhaḥ prakāśitaḥ // 185 /
In this case, it only is posited by convention, while intellect has unclinging differentiation. The thesis (*sādhya*) implicates a proving means (*sādhana*), therefore is revealed as unproved.

P-Vin-Par, k. 78-79 are 'summary verses'.
P-Vin-Par, k. 80-82, use PV-Par, 186-188:

bhedasāmānyayor dharmabhedād aṅgāṅgitā tataḥ /
yathā 'nityaḥ prayatnotthaḥ prayatnotthatayā dhvaniḥ // 186/
By dint of differentiation of dharmas by the two—particularity and generality—there is mutual relation (*aṅga-aṅgitā*, e.g. the *sādhya* and *sādhana*). For instance, by dint of arousal of effort, there is speech, an impermanent arousal of effort.

pakṣāṅgatve 'py abādhatvān nāsiddhir bhinnadharmiṇi /
yathāśvo na viṣāṇitvād esa piṇḍo viṣāṇavān // 187 /
Also, while there is no annulment in *pakṣa* members, there is no proof that it is not in a particular factual base. For example, this 'bodily frame' (*piṇḍa*) (=*dharmin*) has a horn; and because it is horned (= *dharma*), is not a horse.

sādhyakālāṅgatā vā na nivṛtter upalakṣya tat /
viśeṣo 'pi pratijñārtho dharmabhedān na yujyate // 188 /
Or else, due to the inactivity when one closely observes that (factual base), there are no members at the time of the thesis. Also, due to particularity of feature, there is a qualification, while the thesis-meaning is not valid.

P-Vin-Par, k. 80-82, are 'interim verses' (*antara-śloka*).
P-Vin-Par, k. 83, uses PV-Sid, 24:

> svabhāvabhedena vinā vyāpāro 'pi na yujyate /
> nityasyāvyatirekivāt sāmarthyaṃ ca duranvayam //
> Without a particularization of individual presence, the function (*vyāpāra*) is also not valid. And since there is no *vyatireka* (absence in dissimilar cases) of an eternal, the capability would hardly have *anvaya* (presence in similar cases).

P-Vin-Par, k. 83 is a summary verse.
P-Vin-Bu, 272a-6, cites PV-Sid, 196ab:

> duḥkhasantānasaṃsparśamātreṇaivaṃ dayodayaḥ /
> By just contacting (=noticing) a suffering stream of consciousness, there is (his) arising of pity (=compassion).

P-Vin-Bu, 272b-7, cites PV-Sid, 82:

> duḥkhe viparyāsamatis tṛṣṇā cābandhakāraṇaṃ /
> janmino yasya te na sto na sa janmādhigacchati //
> When there is suffering, the wayward mind and craving are the material cause of bondage (*ābandha*). Whoever is born without those two, does not undergo rebirth.

P-Vin-Par, k. 84, uses PV-Par, 244:

> sapakṣāvyatirekī ced dhetur hetur atonvayī /
> nānvayavyatirekī ced anairātmyaṃ na sātmakam //
> If the reason (*hetu*) lacked *vyatireka* (absence in dissimilar locuses) and had a similar locus (*sapakṣa*), then the reason would have *anvaya* (presence in similar locuses). If it had the *vyatireka* and lacked *anvaya*, then lacking non-self would not entail having self.

P-Vin-Par, k. 84 is a summary verse.
P-Vin-Bu, 281a-4, cites PS-Sva, k. 6cd-7 (cf. H. Kitagawa, p. 102):

> / tshul ni re re'aṅ gñis gñis kyis /
> / rtags ni don gyis don byed min / (6cd)
> kṛtakatvād dhvanir nityo mūrtatvād aprameyataḥ /
> amūrta-śrāvaṇatvābhyām anityas cakṣuṣatvataḥ // (7)

> By taking each (of the three) modes in two ways, the evidence (*liṅga*) has no purposive activity by way of the object-entity (i.e. generality character). Sound is 'permanent' due to being constructed, due to being corporeal, and due to being not a sanction. It is 'impermanent' due to being incorporeal and audible, and due to being apprehensible by the eye.

According to Dignāga's commentary on k. 6cd-7, the three reasons for sound being 'permanent' and three for it being 'impermanent' amount to six fallacies of the reason (*hetvābhāsa*). Since the three modes are constructed as *pakṣadharma, anvaya* (presence in similar locuses), and *vyatireka* (absence in dissimilar locuses), for which see Hayes (pgs. 253-4), the set of six can be correlated in part with the nine kinds of *pakṣadharma*. The 'two ways' of k.6cd appear to be the two features (*dharma*) 'permanent' and impermanent.' Since an incompleteness of the three modes is a fallacy of the reason (see in this Vol. One, *Guided Tour*, 'Fallacies of *svārthānumāna*'), there are two possibilities, namely, only one mode, only two modes. Thus, for the feature 'permanent' the fallacies in order exhibit (1) only *pakṣadharma*, (2) only *anvaya*, (3) only *vyatireka;* while for the feature 'impermanent', the fallacies in order exhibit (1) only *pakṣadharma* and *anvaya*, (2) only *pakṣadharma* and *vyatireka*, (3) only *anvaya* and *vyatireka*.

P-Vin-Bu, 281b-1, cites PS-Par, Dignāga's comment under k. 22d (PTT ed., p. 55-1-1, K-version):

> "The five remaining ones are a cause for doubt due to uncertainty in the sense of opposing the reason (*hetu*)."

This remark refers to the nine kinds of *pakṣa-dharma* previously treated, where the five odd-numbered entries (1, 3, 5, 7, 9) were said to be uncertain or doubtful.

P-Vin-Bu, 289a-1, cites PV-Sva, 87:

> saṃsṛjyante na bhidyante svato 'rthāḥ pāramārthikāḥ /
> rūpam ekam anekaṃ ca teṣu buddher upaplavaḥ //
> The entities derived from *paramārtha* are emitted by themselves and not differentiated (by word). Among them, the single form and the multiple form (as the 'generality character') are the 'inundation' of cognition.

This PV-Sva, 87, is among a set of 'summary verses' (*saṃgraha-śloka*).

P-Vin-Bu, 289b-3, mentions *Hetubindu*, probably meaning 'according to':

> "In the *Hetubindu*, it says that the constructive thought (*kalpanā*) apprehending a superimposed nature, is not an authority (*pramāṇa*) because it does not apprehend a purposive activity (*arthakriyā*) as demonstrated."

P-Vin-Bu, 289b-4, cites PV-Prat, 64c:

> aprameyatvād asataś
> Because there is no sanction of a non-existent.

P-Vin-Bu, 290b-5, cites PS-Par, k. 25:

> / thun moṅ min daṅ spyi daṅ ni /
> / 'gal ba 'khrul ba med pa can /
> / chos rnams kun la gaṅ yin pa /
> / de la the tshoṃ gtan tshigs yin //
> Whatever be all the features (*dharma*) of the 'non-inclusion' (*asādhāraṇa*), the generality (*sāmānya*), the opposing, [though] unmistaken (*viruddhāvyabhicārin*), therein is the doubtful reason.

P-Vin-Bu, 291a-7, begins treatment of the Peluka formulation (of the Vaiśeṣika) and the Peṭhara formulation (of the Naiyāyika), applying 'individual presence' (*svabhāva*) to the Peluka, applying 'non-apprehension' (*anupalabdhi*) to the Peṭhara, and demonstrating that both the Peluka and the Peṭhara occasion doubt. (cf. Kamalaśīla on *Nyāyabindu*-Par, 83-121).

P-Vin-Bu, 293b-3, cites PS-Par, Dignaga's comment on k. 23b (PTT ed., p. 55-1-4, 5):

> / kun btus su / gaṅ gi phyir bśad pa'i mtshan ñid can gyi 'gal ba dag gcig la the tshom bskyed pa dag mthoṅ ste / dper na / byas pa daṅ mñan par bya ba dag la sgra la rtag pa dan mi rtag pa dag ñid la the tshom za ba bzhin no / zes ...
> In the *Samuccaya* it says: For the reason that the oppositions have the explained character, one observes the arousals of doubt in (even) one (of them), like the gnawing doubt whether sound is permanent or impermanent, given (the reasons) that it is constructed or that it is audible.

P-Vin-Bu, 293b-5, cites PS-Par, Dignāga's comment on k. 31 (PTT ed., p. 56-2-5), K-edition:

/ kun btus su / de ltar na rtag pa'i spyi khas blaṅs pa la mñan par bya ba ñid daṅ byas pa ñid sgra la spyi rtag gam ma yin nam zhes the tshom gyi rgyu yin no / zhes bśad do /
In the *Samuccaya* it says: Accordingly, in regard to the acceptance of the permanence generality, it occasions doubt to think, "Is sound permanent or impermanent, since it is audible and it is constructed?"

D. Example and Fallacious Example
P-Vin-Bu, 294a-3, f. (From the Tibetan):

/ dpe gtan tshigs las logs su sgrub byed min par bstan / raṅ rgyud du sgrub byed yin pa dgag pa'i daṅ po la / bstan bśad śin tu bśad pa gsum gyi daṅ po ni /
There are two topics, (1) teaching that the example is not a proving method apart from the reason, and (2) refuting that there is a proving method when it is independent (*svatantra*). (1) has three parts—(initial) teaching, explanation, advanced explanation. As to the first part (initial teaching)—
de ltar le'u gñis par rtags kyi mtshan ñid daṅ 'dir sbyor ba daṅ rtags ltar snaṅ gi mtshan ñid bstan nas gtan tshigs kyi sbyor ba ni dpe daṅ bcas pa yin pas dpe'i mtshan ñid brjod dgos so źe na /
Given the manner by which Chapter II (on Svārthānumāna) teaches the character of evidence (*liṅga-lakṣaṇa*), the application (*prayoga*) in this case, and the character of fallacies of evidence (*liṅgābhāsa-lakṣaṇa*); is it necessary that the application of a reason when accompanied by an example, express the character of an example?
/ dpe ni chos can / gtan tshigs las gźan pa'i raṅ rgyud du bsgrub bya bsgrub byed ma yin te / gtan tshigs kyi mtshan ñid tshul gsum ṅes pa'i rtags de tsam gyis bsgrub bya rtogs pa yin pa'i phyir /
When an example is the factual base (*dharmin*), there is no proving method of a thesis with independence differing from the reason; because the thesis is understood by just the certainty evidence of the three modes that define the reason.
/ ṅes naṅ po chos can / de'i mtshan ñid rtags kyi mtshan ñid

> las logs śig tu dṅos su brjod bya yin te / gtan tshigs kyi mtshan ñid bśad ciṅ śes pas de'i mtshan ñid śes pa la / de'i mtshan ñid brjod kyaṅ de'i mtshan ñid śes pa las dgos pa gźan med pa'i phyir ro /
> When the factual base is inherently certain, one may speak directly of its character and apart from the character of evidence; and one knows its character by knowing and expressing the character of the reason (*hetu*), because while mentioning its character there is no other requirement than knowing its character.
> / dpe zhes bya ba chos can / gtan tshigs las logs śig tu bsgrub bya raṅ rgyud du sgrub par byed pa yan lag gzhan ni yod pa ma yin te / gtan tshigs kyi mtshan ñid gsum bśad pa de tsam gyis bsgrub bya'i don rtogs pa'i phyir / bsgrub pa'i yan lag gzhan min mod rtags kyi rjes su 'gro ldog gi khyab bsgrub [f. 294b-1] byed gnod pa can gyi tshad ma dpe la brten pas de'i mtshan ñid brjod dgos so zhe na /
> [Second = explaining], when the factual base is the example, there does not exist another member that proves in Svatantra manner the thesis apart from the reason, because one understands the meaning of the thesis by just explaining the three modes of the reason. Although there be no other member of the proof, when an authority (*pramāṇa*) that annuls the proof (*sādhana*), along with the *anvaya* and *vyatireka* pervasions of the evidence, resorts to the example, is it necessary to speak of the character of that [example]?

The response appears to deny the necessity, thus (f. 294b-1, end): bśad mi dgos te ("It is not necessary to [so] express.").

> / dpe yaṅ dag khyab pa ston byed du bstan / khyab pa ston mi nus na dpe ltar snaṅ du bstan pa gñis ... /
> [Third = further explaining], there are two parts—(1) explanation that shows the pervasion (*vyāpti*) for the genuine example; (2) explanation in the case of an erroneous example, when there is no need to show a pervasion.

I shall not present Bu-don's expansion of the two parts.

P-Vin-Bu, 284b-5, cites PS, chapter *Dṛṣṭānta-dṛṭṭāntābhāsa-parīkṣā* (Examination of the example and the fallacious example), k.1b-d, 2 (K-version):

/ 'dir ni phyogs chos bstan par ni /
/ gnas yin lhag pa'i tshul gñis ni /
/ dpe yis rab tu ston par byed //
/ gtan tshigs bsgrub bya'i rjes 'gro ba /
/ bsgrub bya med la med pa ñid /
/ dpe gaṅ la ni bstan bya ba /
/ de chos mthun dan gcig śos gñis //

"Here for establishing the teaching of the *pakṣadharma*, there are two remaining methods—demonstrating by way of example. Given the reason having *anvaya* of the thesis (*sādhya*), and having absence (= *vyatireka*) in the absence of the thesis—in the case of any example to be shown, there are two, a concordant example (*sādharmyadṛṣṭānta*) and the other one of the two (i.e. a discordant example, *vaidharmyadṛṣṭānta*)."

P-Vin-Bu, 295a-6 to 296a-5, presents the eighteen faults of the example (*dṛṣṭānta*), nine of the concordant example and nine of the discordant example, each of the two sets having three faults of external entity (*artha*), of cognition (*buddhi*), and of speech (*śabda*).

Falsification of the concordant example:

/ dper na / lus can ma yin pa'i phyir / las bzhin / zhes pa bsgrub par bya ba'i chos rtag(s) pas stoṅ pa yin no / rdul phra rab bzhin / zhes pa bye brag pa rdul phran rtag par 'dod pa daṅ sgo bstun nas chos kyis mi stoṅ yaṅ la sogs pa rtags lus can ma yin pas stoṅ ste / lus can yin pa'i phyir ro / bum pa bzhin no / zhes bya ba ni rtags chos gñis kas stoṅ ste gsum po don skyon no / mi 'di 'dod chags la sogs pa daṅ ldan pa yin te / smra ba'i phyir / lam po che'i mi bzhin no / zhes bya ba ni bsgrub bya'i chos la the tshom za ba yin no / la sogs pa / mi 'di 'chi ba'i chos can yin te / 'dod chags la sogs pa daṅ ldan pa'i phyir / lam po che'i mi bzhin / zhes pa rtags yod par the tshom za ba yin no / mi 'di thams cad mkhyen pa ma yin te / 'dod chags la sogs pa daṅ ldan pa'i phyir. / lam po che'i mi bzhin / zhes pa chos rtags gñis ka la the tshom za ba ste gsum po blo skyon no / rtags chos lhan cig tu srid par mthoṅ yaṅ khyab pa med pa rjes 'gro med pa'i dpe ni / dper na gaṅ smra ba de ni 'dod chags la sogs pa daṅ ldan pa yin te / 'dod pa'i mi bdag gam phyir rgol bzhin no zhes bya ba daṅ / rjes su 'gro ba yod kyaṅ skyes bus rab tu ma bstan pa ni / sgra mi rtag pa ste / byas pa'i phyir / bum pa bzhin no / zes bya ba lta bu'o / de bzhin du rjes su 'gro ba phyin ci log tu bstan pa'i dpe ni / gaṅ mi rtag pa de ni byas pa ste / bum pa bzhin no / zhes bya ba lta bu mi rtag pa la byas pas khyab pa bstan pas byas pa mi rtag pa las gzhan 'jug par dogs pa mchod pas go byed du mi 'gyur te / gñis po de smra ba po'i skyon te /

(a) faults of the external entity:

1. void of the thesis feature (*sādhyadharma*), e.g., "Sound is permanent, because it is incorporeal, like *karma.*
2. void of evidence (*liṅga*) e.g. "(ditto), like atoms".
3. void of both, e.g. "(ditto), like a pot".

(b) faults of cognition:

4. doubt as to the *sādhyadharma,* e.g. "This man has lust, etc., because he speaks, like a travellor."
5. doubt as to existence of evidence, e.g. "This man has the nature of death, because he has lust, etc., like a travellor."
6. doubt as to both, e.g. "These men are not omniscient, because they possess lust, like a travellor."

(c) faults of speech:

7. while it is possible to notice together the evidence and the *sādhyadharma,* the example lacks pervasion (*vyāpti*), or *anvaya,* e.g., "Whoever speaks, he has lust, etc., like a lustful man, be it myself or the respondent."
8. while there is the *anvaya,* a person does not demonstrate it, e.g., "Sound is impermanent, because it is created, like a pot."
9. likewise the example which exhibits the *anvaya* waywardly, e.g. "Whatever is impermanent, it is created, like a pot."

Falsification of the discordant example:

[begins B-Vin-Bu, f. 295b-5 (end)] / sgra rtag ste / lus can ma yin pa'i phyir / rdul phra rab bzhin / zhes pa bsgrub bya'i chos rtags pa ldog pa med pa yin no / las bzhin no / zhes pa rtags ldog pa med pa'o / nam mkha' bzhin no / zhes bya ba ni la sogs pa chos rtags gñis ka ldog pa med pa'o / don skyon can gsum po de bzhin du ldog pa la the tshom za la blo skyon can gsum po ni / ser skya la sogs pa chos can / thaṁs cad mkhyen pa 'am yid ches pa chags bral ma yin te / de'i rtags phul du phyin pa skar ma śes pa'i bstan bcos ma bstan pa'i phyir / mkha' gos can gyi ston pa khyu mchog daṅ sdoṅ ris bzhin zhes pa bsgrub bya'i chos ldog par the tshom za'o / ser skya la sogs pa chos can / de'i tshig ṅes brjod sñan dṅags mchod sbyin gsum rig pa'i bram zes tshad mar mi gzuṅ ste / 'dod chags la sogs pa daṅ ldan pa'i phyir / go-u-ta-ma daṅ rgyas pa daṅ yid las byuṅ ba la sogs pa chos kyi bstan bcos dran pa de bzhin / zhes pa rtags ldog par the tshom za'o / ser skya la sogs pa chos can / chags bral min te / byin pa 'am thob pa bdag gir byin pa yoṅs su 'dzin pa daṅ de rjes zhen pa'i kun tu 'dzin pa daṅ ldan pa'i phyir / khyu mchog la sogs pa bzin / zhes chos rtags gñis ka ldog par the tshom za ba'o / ldog pa yod kyaṅ rab tu ma bstan pa'i dpe ni / sgra gcig ste / byas pa'i phyir / nam mkha' bzhin / zhes pa'o / la sogs pa'i sgras ldog par brjod pa ni / gaṅ chags bral de ni smra ba ma yin te / rdo'i dum bu bzhin / zhes pa gñis ka log par mthoṅ yaṅ khyab pa ston mi nus pa'o / ldog pa phyin ci log ni / gaṅ ma byas pa de ni rtag pa ste / nam mkha' bzhin / zhes pa phyin ci log tu smras pa'i skyon du yaṅ brjod par bya'o /

(a) faults of the external entity:

1. there is no *vyatireka* (dissimilar absence) of a thesis feature (*sādhyadharma*), like 'permanence'; e.g. "Sound is permanent, because it is incorporeal, like atoms."
2. there is no *vyatireka* of the evidence, e.g. "like karma".
3. there is no *vyatireka* of both, e.g. "like space".

(b) faults of cognition:

4. doubt as to *vyatireka* of the thesis feature (*sādhyadharma*); e.g. "Given the factual base (*dharmin*) Kapila, etc. an omniscient person, or an *āpta* (trusted sage), is not free from passion, because he, having attained excellence of evidence, does not teach the treatises (conveying) knowledge of the stars, like Ṛṣabha and Vardhamāna, who teach the Digambara."
5. doubt as to *vyatireka* of the evidence, e.g. "Given the *dharmin* Kapila, etc., a brahmin of the three Vedas—Ṛg, Sāma, and Yajur, does not accept his (Kapila's) words as authority, because he has lust, etc., as (in) the Smṛti of Dharmaśāstra-s, of Gautama, (?)Vyāsa, and Mānava.

6. doubt as to *vyatireka* of both, e.g. "Given the *dharmin* Kapila, etc., he is not free from lust, etc. because he is given over to personal acquisition of the donated or obtained and to clinging to it, like Ṛṣabha, etc."

(c) faults of speech:

7. even though there be the *vyatireka*, the example does not well demonstrate it, e.g., "It is a single word, because it is created, like the sky."
8. expression of the *vyatireka* with an 'etc.-word' ('whoever'), e.g. "Whoever is free from lust, he does not speak, like a piece of stone." This observes the two (*dharma* and evidence) obliquely, and is incapable of showing pervasion.
9. the wayward *vyatireka*, e.g. "Whatever is not created, it is permanent, like the sky."

P-Vin-Bu, 298a-3, begins to treat final section of P-Vin, on sophistries (*jāti*), to which Dignāga devotes the final chapter of PS (*Jātiparīkṣa*), which especially involves fallacious examples (*dṛṣṭāntābhāsa*) and fault-finder (*dūṣaka*). P-Vin-Bu, 289a-7, says that fourteen *jāti* are found in PS, and 289a-7 to 289b-1, provides a summary verse (*phrad ma phrad* ...). At 299a-7, Bu-ston provides another verse with a list of ten, *'phel* (S. *atiśaya*), *'grib* (S. *nirhrāsa*), and so on. At 299b-4, Bu-ston mentions the twenty-four *jāti* (T. *ltag chod*), so this number is presumably the sum of fourteen and ten, and represents an increase of the list after the time of Dignāga.

As to P-Vin-Par *kārikā* after no. 84, Steinkellner counts up to 87, where no. 87 is a final verse in 9-syllable lines. However, using my version of the Tibetan text for P-Vin, I failed to find *kārikā* to be counted as nos. 85 and 86. The final verse ('*kārikā* 87') is worth presenting and translating (P-Vin-Bu, 300a-6):

/ don yod lugs gzigs mdo don 'di rigs śes /
/ luṅ yaṅ dor nas ṅas bśad ṅas par ni /
/ rnam dag thugs de'i dgoṅs pa'aṅ 'di ñid de /
/ mi gsal blo can skye bos rtogs ma yin //

P-Vin-Bu-300b-2, discusses the reading "*luṅ yaṅ dor nas*" ("having rejected the *āgama*") which was a disputed matter, since Tibetans after the time of the translator Blo-ldan-śes-rab suspected a corruption. So Bu-ston mentions an alternate rendering of "*luṅ ni ma spaṅs par*" ("having not rejected the *āgama*"), which has an extra syllable. Bu-ston himself takes the phrase as indicating an attempt to decide between alternatives:

> "Be the *āgama* [an authority], or be it not—that is also good" (luṅ yod dam med kyaṅ bla ste). (We shall see in *Guided Tour* that Tsong-kha-pa opts for the *āgama* as authority.) So the translation:
>
> I (=Dharmakīrti), having viewed the school (*lugs*) (of logicians) that is fruitful (*don yod*), knowing the principles (*rigs śes*) (of validity) whereby Īśvarasena's position is rejected), have explained (i.e. commented upon) this Sūtra's (i.e., upon Dignāga's *Pramāṇasamuccaya*) meaning; and whether the *āgama* be (an authority) or rejected (for that role) I, remembering that pure heart (the Sugata's profound Dharma) which persons (i.e., Sāṃkhya, etc.) of dull intellect (*buddhi*) cannot understand.

TSONG-KHA-PA'S GUIDED TOUR THROUGH THE SEVEN BOOKS OF DHARMAKĪRTI

The work on Buddhist logic here presented in Tibetan and translated is by Tsoṅ-kha-pa (1357-1419), founder of the Gelugpa order of Tibetan Buddhism. His own sect does not accept him as the authority for Buddhist logic. That sect's curriculum uses Rgyal-tshab-rje's commentary on Dharmakīrti's *Pramāṇavārttika* for the logic course. The selection of Tsoṅ-kha-pa's little text on logic present volume needs justification. First, the Tibetan title is *Sde bdun la 'jug pa'i sgo don gñer yid kyi mun sel*, which I render: "Dispelling the darkness of mind by aiming to understand the seven books (of Dharmakīrti).[1] I refer to it as the *Guided Tour* through the seven books of Dharmakirti.

Tsoṅ-kha-pa's biography shows that before leaving for Central Tibet, when given final instructions by his boyhood teacher, Don-grub-rin-chen, he was told to study the seven works on logic by Dharmakīrti. After taking courses in the traditional topics of monastery curriculums, which included the study of Buddhist logic, Tson-kha-pa became an enthusiastic student of the *Pramāṇavārttika.* The biography shows that the autumn of 1378 was mainly given over to the study of this text.[2] This was about two years after he met and began to travel together for years with Red-mda'-pa (1349-1412), his guru and a master of the Sa-skya-pa sect in the fields of Mādhyamika and Buddhist logic. The text here translated (*Guided Tour*) mentions

---

1. This text lacks in the Peking edition of Tsoṅ-kha-pa's works, PTT, extra volumes. I first used the Sarnath edition of the text (1969), which in my copy had a mix-up around the 50s and a defective colophon. I also have the Sarnath re-edition (1972) with correct pages and the full colophon, as well as the 1984 reissue of the same. The text is in the author's collected works, Tashilunpo edition, Vol. Tsha.
2. See the biographical sketch in Alex Wayman, tr. *Calming the Mind and Discerning the Real; Buddhist Meditation and the Middle View,* from the *Lam rim chen mo* of Tsoṅ-kha-pa (New York: Columbia University Press, 1978), pp.16-18.

at the end that it was exhorted by some notable of his day, named Grags-pa'i-rgyal-mtshan; but inside the text there is a passage naming Red-mda'-pa as the source, so the text is presumably composed during the time Tsoṅ-kha-pa was still travelling with his master.

My colleague in lexical studies, who helped me with my translation, Dr. Lozang Jamspal, told me that he heard from his own Tibetan teacher that this work on the seven books is a product of Tsoṅ-kha-pa's youth—a remark which has an implication of downgrading the text. Years later, after completing the *Lam rim chen mo* in 1402, and when Rgyal-tshab-rje met him and became a leading disciple, he may have polished up the *Guided Tour* into its present form, or it might be that he never changed a word from its original form. Rgyal-tshab-rje recorded Tsoṅ-kha-pa's lectures on logic, now in the latter's collected works, Vols. Pha and Ba, such as the *Tshad ma'i brjed byaṅ chen mo* (chief things to remember about logic) (in Pha, 44 fols.), and the *Mṅon sum le'u'i brjed byaṅ* (things to remember about the PV-Prat chapter) (in Ba, 25 fols.). Presumably when Tsoṅ-kha-pa again lectured on the PV-Prat at or soon after 1407 when Mkhas-grub-rje (1385-1438) became a disciple, the latter recorded it (Tsoṅ-khāpa, collected works, Ma, 93 fols.). Also, Tsoṅ-kha-pa used Buddhist logic for problems of Mādhyamika philosophy in this period berween 1402 and 1407, such as the *Dka' gnad kyi zin bris* (in Vol. Ba) and the *Dbu ma rgyan gyi brjed byaṅ* (in Vol. Ma), both on Śāntarakṣita's *Madhyamakālaṃkāra,* the latter one recorded by Rgyal-tshab-rje; and the work called *Legs bśad sñiṅ po* (in Vol. Pha, 114 fols.) on the two meanings of Buddhist scriptures.

Now, for including this early work of Tsoṅ-kha-pa herein, we should note a peculiarity that differentiates it from his all other works, written to teach this and that. His *Mun sel* is not meant to teach fundamentals of Buddhist logic derived from the seven books. It is rather how Tsoṅ-kha-pa studied the topic. Thus it has a disadvantage for the translator, since when pandits write to teach and are successful in the aim, they so write as to help the translator. When the text is just as the topic was studied, which happens in the present case, it has an advantage that the topic was studied by an extraordinary student, thus including important elements of the system, some of which might be missed by the pandit who wishes to teach Buddhist logic. In short, the title's words, "Dispelling the darkness of mind" appears to refer to the author's own mind, not the mind or minds of intended readers. To support this conclusion, we may note that Mkhas-grub-rje, Tsoṅ-kha-pa's disciple, has a work of similar, not identical title, in his Vol. Tha, collected works. The agreement is in the *yid kyi mun sel* "dispelling the darkness of mind." We may conclude that Mkhas-grub-rje's work also shows how he studied Buddhist logic, not how he taught it. The fact that it is much bigger than Tsoṅ-khāpa's work, suggests that Mkhas-grub-rje intended it as a preparation for writing his commentary on the *Pramāṇavārttika* called *Rigs pa'i rgya mtsho.*

That in both cases the expression "Dispelling the darkness of mind" refers to the mind of the respective authors is supported by a work by Go-rams-pa (1429-89), his commentary on Sa-pan's *Rigs gter,* namely the *Sde bdun mdo daṅ bcas pa'i dgoṅs pa phyin ci ma log par 'grel pa tshad ma rigs pa'i gter gyi don gsal bar byed pa* (Clarifying the *Pramāṇayuktinidhi* by errorless commentary on the purport of the seven works [of Dharmakīrti] along with [Dignāga's] Sūtra).[3] We see at once that Go-rams-pa claims to clarify a certain text, and so does not use such an expression as "Dispelling the darkness of mind." Go-rams-pa does start out somewhat like Tsoṅ-kha-pa in the *Mun sel,* but does it differently and from the beginning is on the attack. He soon mentions a position to refute: "Some Tibetans assert that the appearing sense object (*snaṅ yul*) and the prima facie object (*gzuṅ yul*) are the same thing (*don gcig pas*), on which account there is an appearing sense object for the realization of the object generality (*don spyi de rtog pa'i gzuṅ yul*) and it is (also) the prima facie object for the deviant cognition failing to realize that the appearance is not (so) (*med pa gsal ba de rtog med log śes kyi gzuṅ yul yin*). There are two principles for refuting this (*'di dgag pa la rigs pa gñis*).... We notice that Tsoṅ-kha-pa's *Guided Tour* does treat the prima facie object as the appearing sense object, but this does not mean that Go-rams-pa had Tsoṅ-kha-pa's text in mind for his attack. Later in the *Guided Tour* Tsoṅ-kha-pa defines 'deviant cognition' (*log śes*) as the cognition apprehending something as being in a place when it is not so.

The evidence from Go-rams's work and from Tsoṅ-kha-pa's *Mun sel* allows a conclusion that such 7-books treatises were a sort of *genre* in the Sa-skya-pa sect. Tsoṅ-kha-pa probably had several of such treatises and prepared his own with the help of Red-mda'-pa. By usually avoiding arguments with others, Tsoṅ-kha-pa manages to

3. Abbreviated title: *Rigs gter gsal byed,* by Go-rams-pa Bsod-rnams Seng-ge (Mussoorie, India: Sakya College, 1975).

incorporate an extensive coverage of the material.

Of course, such 7-books treatises are not a substitute for studying the basic texts, e.g. the *Pramāṇavārttika.* They amount to an introduction to the terminology and topics of the system. There were in India various introductions for the 'beginners'. The present *Guided Tour* adds touches from advanced studies to serve the interests of the 'beginner' on the Tibetan scene.

The reader will notice in this translation the ubiquitous use of definitions. This important topic was worked up by the Tibetan Chapa (= Chos seng, 1109-1169) (see him in the P-Vin lineage list, my Vol. Two, the two Tibetan lineage lists). Tsoṅ-kha-pa also has a section on the topic of definitions, the definable, and so on, which was treated by Sa-skya Paṇḍita (Sa-Paṇ, 1182-1252) in his *Tshad ma rigs pa'i gter,* 8th chapter. Go-rams-pa's commentary on Sa-Paṇ's *Rigs gter* has a large section on definitions, especially disagreeing with others.

Tsoṅ-kha-pa's eight pairs in III. Means of Understanding the Object, are certainly helpful, and probably due to the earlier lineage.

There is a striking difference as to the inclusion of certain matters under Svārthānumana and Parārthānumāna, found herein, from the respective inclusion in the P-Vin account (for which see, supra, introductory remarks to the Analysis of P-Vin).

While as was mentioned, Dr. Jamspal gave valuable advice for the translation, the form below presented, with whatever imperfections, is my own. For one thing, I have tried to help the reader in terms of organization. For example, when the author mentions, say, three items to be defined, and then the three definitions, I reordered the material so that the respective definitions went together with the terms defined.

THE TEXT AND TRANSLATION

/ phyogs bcu'i rgyal ba sras daṅ bcas pa thams cad la phyag 'tshal lo /

/ mkhyen rab dbaṅ phyug 'jam pa'i dbyaṅs /
/ bdud bźi pham mdzad mi g'yo mgon /
/ ṅag dbaṅ lha mo dbyaṅs can ma /
/ rtsom 'chad rtsod pa'i blo gros spel //

Homage to all the Jinas of the ten directions and their spiritual sons (= the Bodhisattvas).

May Mañjughoṣa, the lord of divine knowledge; Acala-nātha, who defeats the four Māras; and Devī Sarasvatī, queen of speech—enhance the intelligence of composition, explanation, and debate.

/ yul daṅ yul can yul de rtogs pa'i thabs / rnam pa 'di gsum gtan la dbab par bya /

I shall establish these three aspects—sense object (*viṣaya,* yul), subject (*viṣayin,* yul can), and means of understanding (rtog pa'i thabs) that sense object.

/ de la yul daṅ śes bya gźal bya rnams gtso bor don gcig yin pas / yul gyi mtshan ñid go bar bya'i rig par bya / śes bya'i mtshan ñid blo'i yul du byar ruṅ ba / gźal bya'i mtshan ñid tshad mas rtogs par bya ba /

I. OBJECT

Among them, a sense object, a knowable (*jñeya,* śes bya), and a sanction (*prameya,* gźal bya) are mainly the same thing. Thus, the definition of a sense object is to be perceived, i.e. to be apprehended. The definition of a knowable is to be feasibly the sense object of cognition (*buddhi,* blo). The definition of a sanction is to be comprehended by an authority (*pramāna,* tshad ma).

/ yul la ṅo bo'i sgo nas dbye na / dṅos po daṅ dṅos med / 'dus byas daṅ 'dus ma byas / rtag pa daṅ mi rtag pa'o / mtshan ñid rim pa bźin / don byed nus pa / don byed nus stoṅ / dper na nam mkha' lta bu / raṅ gi rgyu rkyen las skyes pa / raṅ gi rgyu rkyen las ma skyes pa / mi 'jig pa'i chos / raṅ grub dus las dus gñis par mi sdod pa'i dṅos po rnams so /

Variegating sense objects by way of their individual nature, they are:

1. discrete thing (*bhāva,* dṅos po), defined as a purposive activity (don byed nus pa); and non-discrete thing (*abhāva,* dṅos med), defined as a nonpurposive activity, for example, like space (*ākāśa*).
2. constructed thing (*saṃskṛta,* 'dus byas), defined as arising by its cause (*hetu*) and condition (*pratyaya*); and unconstructed thing (*asaṃskṛta,* 'dus ma byas), defined as not arising by a cause and a condition.
3. permanent thing (*nitya,* rtag pa), defined as having indestructable features; and impermanent thing (*anitya,* mi

rtag pa), defined as an entity with individual actuality (raṅ grub) that does not last from one time to the next.

/ dṅos po la ṅo bo'i sgo nas dbye na / bem rig gñis / daṅ po'i mtshan ñid rdul du grub pa / gñis pa'i mtshan ñid yul rig pa /

Variegating a 'discrete thing' by way of its individual nature, there is the unconscious thing (bem), defined as atomic reality (rdul du grub pa); and the apprehending thing (rig), defined as the apprehension of sense object (yul rig pa).

/ bem po la dbye na / phyi don bem po daṅ naṅ don bem po gñis / mtshan ñid rim bźin / phyi'i rdul du grub pa / naṅ gi rdul du grub pa /

Variegating an unconscious thing (bem po), there is the external entity, with character of external atomic reality; and the inner entity, with character of inner atomic reality.

/ phyi don bem po la dbye na / gzugs sgra dri ro reg bya lṅa / mtshan ñid rim bźin / bem po gaṅ źig / mig gi dbaṅ śes kyi dṅos yul du gyur pa / gan źig rna ba'i / gaṅ źig sna'i / gaṅ źig lce'i / gaṅ źig lus kyi dṅos yul du gyur pa / gzugs la dkar nag sogs kha dog gi gzugs dan / gru bźi sogs dbyibs kyi gzugs gñis / sgra la ṅag tshig sogs / luṅ du ston pa'i sgra / chu sgra sogs luṅ du mi ston pa'i sgra gñis / dri la źim mi źim gñis / ro la / źim mi źim gñis / reg bya la / 'jam rtsub gñis /

Unconscious things, as external entities, are five in number:

1. formation, a particular unconscious thing that is the actual object of eye-sense-cognition; to wit, the formation of white, black, etc. color (*varṇa*), and the formation of square, etc. shape (*saṃsthāna*).
2. sound, a particular one, of the ear; to wit, two kinds of sounds—sound that is a means of communication, such as speech words; and sound that is not a means of communication, such as the sound of water.
3. odor, a particular one, of the nose; to wit, two kinds of odor, agreeable and disagreeable.
4. taste, a particular one, of the tongue; to wit, two kinds of taste, agreeable and disagreeable.
5. tangible, a particular one that is the actual body surface as object, to wit, smooth or rough.

/ naṅ don bem po la dbye na / mig gi dbaṅ po gzugs can / rna'i / sna'i / lce'i / lus kyi dbaṅ po gzugs can daṅ lṅa / mtshan ñid rim pa bźin / naṅ don bem po gaṅ źig / mig gi dbaṅ źes kyi bdag rkyen

/ gaṅ źig rna ba'i / gan źig sna'i / gaṅ źig lce'i / gaṅ źig lus kyi dbaṅ śes kyi bdag rkyen du ruṅ ba / dbye na / re re la / mig gis yul la 'jug dus kyi mig dbaṅ lta bu rten bcas kyi dbaṅ po gzugs can daṅ / mig gis yul la mi 'jug dus kyi mig dbaṅ lta bu / de mtshuṅs kyi dbaṅ po gzugs can gñis gñis su yod /

Unconscious things, as 'inner' entities, are five in number:

1. the formed eye-sense organ, a certain inner unconscious thing serving as the governing condition (*adhipati-pratyaya*) of eye-sense cognition.
2. the formed ear, ditto of ear-sense cognition.
3. the formed nose, ditto of nose-sense cognition.
4. the formed tongue, ditto of tongue-sense cognition.
5. the formed corporeal sense-organ, ditto of corporeal-sense cognition. Variegating each one, there are two cases: At the time when the eye, for example, engages the object, there is the formed sense-organ along with its basis [the object]. At the time when the eye (for example) does not engage the object, the formed sense-organ matches the eye-organ.

/ dṅos po la byed pa'i sgo nas dbye na / rgyu daṅ 'bras bu gñis / mtshan ñid rim bźin / chos de yod med kyi rjes su 'gro ldog byed pa'i don gźan phyi ma /

Variegating a discrete thing by way of causation, there is a cause, defined as a feature's activation (*pravṛtti*, rjes su 'gro) as existent or deactivation (*nivṛtti*, ldog) as nonexistent; and there is an effect as a later different object-entity of the causation (byed pa).

/ rgyu la ṅo bo'i sgo nas dbye na / dṅos rgyu daṅ brgyud rgyu gñis / mtshan ñid rim bźin / chos de'i rgyu gaṅ źig / chos de'i rgyu daṅ khyod kyi 'bras bu gñis ka yin pa med pa / gaṅ źig chos de'i rgyu daṅ khyod kyi 'bras bu gñis ka yin pa yod pa /

Variegating the cause by individual nature, there are:

1. implicit cause (*bhāvahetu*), to wit: the feature has a particular cause, while there is not both the feature's cause and your effect.
2. explicit cause (*parampara-hetu*), to wit: there is both a particular feature's cause and your effect.

/ rgyu la gtso phal gyi sgo nas dbye na / ñer len daṅ lhan cig byed rkyen gñis / mtshan ñid rim bźin / chos de'i lhan cig byed rken la bltos nas chos de skyed pa / chos de'i ñer len gyis chos de skyed pa'i grogs su gyur pa /

Variegating the cause by 1. chief and 2. secondary, there are:

1. Material cause (*upādāna*[-hetu]), defined as what generates the feature in relation to associative conditions for that feature.
2. Associative conditions (*sahakārin-pratyaya*), defined as associating with the material cause that generates the feature.

/spyir rkyen la dbye na / dmigs rkyen / bdag rkyen / de ma thag rkyen gsum / mtshan ñid rim bźin / chos de yul gyi rnañ ldan du dṅos su skyed byed kyi phyi don / chos de raṅ dbaṅ du skyed byed / chos de gsal rig gi ṅo bor gtso bor dṅos su skyed byed /

Variegating the condition in a general way, there are three:

1. Mental-support condition (*ālambana-pratyaya*), defined as that (mental) nature (*dharma*) having the image of a sense object, while there is an on-going external entity as generator.
2. Governing condition (*adhipati-pratyaya*), defined as what generates the feature independently.
3. Immediately preceding condition (*samanantara-pratyaya*), defined as the on-going generator in the individual principal sense of the clear apprehension of the feature.

/ źar byuṅ dus gsum daṅ / rags rgyun sogs 'chad pa la / 'das pa'i mtshan ñid thal zin pa / ma 'oṅs pa'i mtshan ñid ma sleb ciṅ thal ma zin pa / da ltar gyi mtshan ñid skyes la ma 'gags pa / rags pa'i mtshan ñid raṅ gi bdag ñid du gyur pa'i phyogs cha yod pa'i rdul / dpe bum pa ltar bu / cha med kyi rdul gyi mtshan ñid / raṅ gi bdag ñid du gyur pa'i phyogs cha med pa'i rdul / dpe mdun gi rdul chuṅ tha gcig lta bu'o / rgyun gyi mtshan ñid / raṅ gi bdag ñid du gyur pa'i skad cig sṅa phyi du ma yod pa'i dṅos po / dpe lo lta bu'o / skad cig cha med kyi mtshan ñid / raṅ gi bdag ñid du gyur pa'i skad cig sṅa phyi med pa'i dṅos po / dpe yi ge'i cha śas su gyur pa'i skad cig drug cu'i daṅ po lta bu'o /

Along those lines (źar byuṅ), one explains the three times, the coarse, continuity, etc.

The definition of the past is to have elasped. The definition of the future is to have not arrived. The definition of the present is to be born but not stopped.

The definition of coarse is an item individually with parts; for example, a pot. The definition of a partless item is an item individually without parts; for example, a tiny item of one piece in front of you.

The definition of continuity is a state which individually has many earlier and later moments; for example, a year. The definition of a partless moment is a state which individually lacks earlier and later moments; for example, the first of sixty seconds of the syllable-timing (*akṣara-kalā*).

/ yul la yul du byas tshul mi 'dra ba'i sgo nas dbye na / snaṅ yul lam / gzuṅ yul / źen yul / 'jug yul daṅ gsum /

Variegating the sense objects by way of diverse manners of taking them as objects, there are three: 1. appearing sense object (*pratibhāsa-viṣaya*) = prima facie object (*grāhya-viṣaya*), 2. claimed object (*adhyavasita-viṣaya*), 3. involvement object (*praveśa-viṣaya*).

/ gzuṅ yul gyi mtshan ñid / snaṅ nas rig par bya ba / dbye na / mṅon sum gyi gzuṅ yul / rtog pa'i gzuṅ yul / rtog med 'khrul śes kyi gzuṅ yul daṅ gsum / daṅ po la dbye na / gźan rig mṅon sum gyi gzuṅ yul / raṅ rig mṅon sum gyi gzuṅ yul daṅ gñis / rim pa bźin / chos de la raṅ 'dra'i rnam pa dṅos su gtod byed kyi phyi don / dper na dbaṅ yid la ltos te gzugs sogs lṅa lta bu'o / gzuṅ yul phyi ma gñis don spyi lta bu daṅ / zla gñis lta bu'o /

1. The prima facie object is defined as to be apprehended by its appearance. There are three kinds:
   (1) the prima facie object of perception (*pratyakṣa*), which is either (a) the externally directed (*parasaṃvedana*) perception, or (b) the introspective (*svasaṃvedana*) perception; (for a) the on-going fixation on an external entity, for example, the five, formation, etc., (for b) imagery (*ākāra*) resembling a feature (*dharma*), for example, when those five depend on the mental sense-organ.
   (2) the prima facie object of constructive thought (*kalpanā*), e.g. a generality feature (*sāmānya-dharma*).
   (3) the prima facie object of delusive cognition (*bhrānti-jñāna*) without constructive thought, e.g. the double moon.

/ źen yul gyi mtshan ñid / źen nas rig par bya ba / dbye na / yod ṅes med ṅes / bskal don daṅ gsum / yod ṅes kyi mtshan ñid / tshad mas dmigs pa / med ṅes kyi mtshan ñid / tshad mas snaṅ ruṅ ma dmigs pa / gaṅ zag de'i bskal don gyi mtshan ñid / yod kyaṅ gaṅ zag de'i tshad ma la bltar mi ruṅ ba / dbye na / gaṅ zag de la yul gyi bskal ba'i bskal don / dus kyi bskal ba'i bskal don / raṅ bźin gyi bskal ba'i bskal don daṅ gsum / dpe rim bźin khaṅ ba gźan na gnas pa'i mi'i sdod lugs lta bu daṅ / saṅ mdun gyi gźi 'dir mi'i sdod lugs lta bu daṅ / mdun gyi gźir śa za lta bu'o /

2. The claimed object is defined as to be [possibly] apprehended after being claimed. In variegation, there are three:

(1) certainty of existence, namely, the visualization by an authority (*pramāṇa*).

(2) certainty of nonexistence, namely, nonvisualization feasibility by an authority.

(3) inaccessibility of object-entity, to wit, an object-entity exists for a given person but cannot come within the scope of a person's authority.

The object-entity is inaccessible in three ways:

a. inaccessibility of place, e.g. the lay-out of a man dwelling in another house.

b. inaccessibility of time, e.g. the lay-out tomorrow of a man in this spot.

c. inaccessibility of individual presence (*svabhāva*), e.g. a demon (*piśāca*) in a spot in front.

/ 'jug yul gyi mtshan ñid / blaṅ dor bya ba'i phyir źugs pa na mi slu ba / dper na / sgra mi rtag rtogs kyi rjes dpag la mi rtag pa lta bu / sṅon po'i dbaṅ po'i mṅon sum la sṅon po lta bu daṅ / bum pa'i sgra rtog khyad par can la bum pa lta bu daṅ / so nam byed pa'i skyes bu la sa bon daṅ chu lud drod gśer tshogs pa'i źiṅ lta bu'o /

3. The involvement object is defined as non-deception when one is involved for accepting (the correct) and rejecting (the incorrect). Examples: When there is an inference understanding sound to be impermanent, this is indeed impermanent. When there is (outer) sense organ perception of blue, there is indeed (the color) blue. When one has a discursive thought, to wit, "There is a pot," there is indeed a pot. When a person is engaged in farming, there is a field with the set of seeds, damp manure, warmth, and moisture.

/ gźal bya la rtogs tshul gyi sgo nas dbye na / raṅ mtshan daṅ spyi mtshan gñis sam / yaṅ na / gźal bya mṅon gyur la sogs pa gsum / raṅ mtshan gyi mtshan ñid / don dam par don byed nus pa / dper na sṅon po lta bu'o / yaṅ na yul dus ma 'dres par gnas pa'i dṅos po / dpyi mtshan gyi mtshan ñid don dam par don byed mi nus pa'i chos / yaṅ na rtogs pa la yul dus 'dres par snaṅ ba'i snaṅ yul / dper na rtog pa la lto ldir źabs źum snaṅ ba lta bu'o / gźal bya mṅon gyur gyi mtshan ñid mṅon sum tshad mas rtogs par bya ba / dper na sṅon po lta bu'o / gźal bya ldog gyur gyi mtshan ñid rjes dpag tshad mas rtogs par bya ba / dper na sṅon po mi rtag pa lta bu'o / yaṅ na de gñis kyi mtshan ñid / myoṅ stobs kyi sgro 'dogs dpyad par bya daṅ / rtags stobs kyis sgro 'dogs dpyad par bya ba / gźal bya śin tu lkog gyur gyi mtshan ñid dpyad pa gsum gyis dag pa'i luṅ la brten nas rtogs par bya ba / dper na / sbyin pas loṅs spyod khrims kyis bde / źes pa'i luṅ raṅ gi bstan bya'i don la mi slu ba lta bu'o /

One may variegate the sanction (*prameya*) by way of the mode of comprehension, in two ways:

1. individual character (*svalakṣaṇa*), which is purposive activity in the absolute sense, for example, (the color) blue. Besides, the object-entity is disposed without admixture of space and time.
2. generality character (*sāmānyalakṣaṇa*), which is a feature without purposive activity in the absolute sense. Besides, the object appearing to constructive thought appears with admixture of space and time, for example, to constructive thought a pot with a large bulb becoming slender at the bottom.

One may variegate the sanction in three further ways:

1. sanction directly realized (*sākṣāt*), which is comprehended by the direct-perception authority (*pratyakṣa-pramāṇa*), for example, blue. This examines the superimposition (on object-entities) by the power of experience (*anubhava-bala*).
2. sanction 'beyond sight' (*parokṣa*)' which is comprehended by inference authority (*anumāna-pramāṇa*), for example, "The blue is impermanent." This examines the superimposition by the power of understanding (*adhigama-bala*).
3. sanction further beyond sight (*atyantaparokṣa*), which is comprehended by recourse to a pure scripture by three examinations in all.[4] For example, "By giving, there is possession; by morality, there is happiness," a scripture which is without deception in regard to its individual indicated aim.[5]

/ źar byuṅ brjod bya'i mtshan ñid / brda las go bar bya ba / dbye na gñis las / źen pa'i brjod bya'i mtshan ñid / ṅag kun sloṅ gi śes pas źen pa'i dbaṅ gis ṅag las go bar bya ba / źen pa'i brjod byas zlas draṅs pa'i dṅos kyi brjod bya'i mtshan ñid / ṅag kun sloṅ gi rtog pa la snaṅ ba'i dbaṅ gis ṅag las go bar bya ba / dper na bum pa'i don spyi lta bu'o / źen pa'i brjod bya la dbye na / dṅos kyi źen pa'i brjod bya daṅ / śugs kyi źen pa'i brjod bya gñis / dper na bum pa mi rtag ces pa'i

4. Cf. Kamalaśīla's *Nyāyabindupūrvapakṣasaṃkṣipti* (supra), with the three examinations in analogy with how experts test gold.
5. A fuller list is given by the translator Dpal-brtsegs, PTT edn. of Tanjur, Vol. 145, p. 116, for the instrumental attribution to the six perfections (*pāramitā*): "By giving, possessions; by morality, heaven; by forbearance, (good) appearance (*ākṛti*); by striving, uninterrupted increase of virtues; by meditation and by insight, skill in the five sciences (*vidyāsthāna*)."

sgra la bltos nas bum pa mi rtag pa lta bu daṅ / bum pa rtag pa ma yin pa lta bu'o / yaṅ brjod bya la 'chad dus kyi brjod bya daṅ / 'jug dus kyi brjod bya gñis / daṅ po la dbye na / źen pa'i brjod bya daṅ / dṅos kyi brjod bya gñis / phyi ma la dbye ba med do /

Along those lines, the reference (*vācya*) is defined as the making understood through a signal (*saṃketa*). In variegation, there are two:

1. claimed reference (źen pa'i brjod bya) is defined as using a knowledge of speech medium to render understood through speech, by the power of being claimed. This is of two kinds:
   (1) reference claiming directly; for example, that the pot is impermanent, using the remark, "The pot is impermanent."
   (2) reference claiming indirectly; for example, that there is no pot that is permanent.
2. conceded reference (dṅos kyi brjod bya), drawing on the spoken claimed reference, is defined as a mental construct (*kalpanā*) given over to speech, and to be understood by a remark empowered by an appearance, For example, the generality feature (*sāmānya-dharma*) of a pot.

Moreover, there is the reference at the time of a (doctrinal) explanation, of two kinds: claimed reference and conceded reference; and there is the reference at the time of engagement (i.e. putting into practice), which has no division.

/ yul gyi skabs bśad zin to /

This concludes the section of object (*viṣaya*).

II. SUBJECT

/ yul can gyi mtshan ñid go byed dam rig byed / dbye na rjod byed daṅ śes pa gñis /

'Subject' (*viṣayin*, yul can) is defined as what makes understood or makes apprehended. There are two kinds: referral, and cognition.

/ rjod byed kyi mtshan ñid / brda'i dbaṅ gis brjod bya go byed / ṅo bo'i sgo nas dbye na / miṅ tshig ṅag gsum / miṅ gi mtshan ñid yul gyi no bo tsam rjod byed / dper na bum pa źes pa lta bu'o / dbye na gñis las / don de'i dṅos miṅ gi mtshan ñid / don de la daṅ por brda sbyar ba'i miṅ gaṅ źig / don de 'khrul med du go bar byed nus pa / dper na ri dvags rgyal po la seṅ ge źes pa'i sgra lta bu'o / don de'i btags miṅ gi mtshan ñid / khyod dṅos miṅ du 'jug pa'i yul de daṅ don de chos 'ga' źig mtshuṅs pa rgyu mtshan du byas nas / don de la phyis brda sbyar ba'i miṅ / dper na bram ze'i khye'u kha che sna ñag la seṅ ge źes pa'i sgra lta bu / tshig gi mtshan ñid / yul gyi ṅo bo yaṅ khyad chos daṅ sbyar nas rjod byed / dper na / bum pa chuṅ ṅu źes pa'i sgra lta bu / ṅag gi mtshan ñid / yul gyi khyad chos kyaṅ 'jug ldog gi gźi daṅ sbyar nas rjod byed / dper na bum pa chuṅ ṅus chu 'on cig ces pa'i sgra lta bu'o /

Referral (*vācaka*, rjod byed) is defined as making understood the reference (*vācya*, brjod bya) by dint of a (verbal) signal (*saṃketa*, brda). In variegation by individual nature, there are three—name (*nāma*, miṅ), phrase (*pāda*, tshig), and sentence (*vyañjana*, ṅag).

1. 'Name' is defined as a referring to just the individual nature (ṅo bo) of the sense-object (*viṣaya*), for example, (the name) 'pot'. There are two kinds:
   (1) actual name of an object-entity, to wit, to that entity one initially applies a name as a signal, capable of making that entity understood without error, for example, calling a lion 'king of the deer'.
   (2) nickname for the entity, to wit, given the object involved in your actual name, then by virtue of taking some feature of that entity as equivalent (to the whole entity), one later applies to that entity a name as a signal, for example, to call a brahmin who is big-mouthed and flat-nosed a 'lion'.
2. 'Phrase' is defined as a referral that adds a differentiating feature (khyad chos) to the individual nature of the sense object; for example, 'a small pot'.
3. 'Sentence' is defined as a referral that adds an active (*pravṛtti*) or inactive (*nivṛtti*) support ('jug ldog gi gźi) to the differentiating feature of the sense object; for example, "Bring water by means of the small pot."

/ rjod byed la brjod bya'i sgo nas dbye na / rigs rjod kyi sgra daṅ tshogs rjod kyi sgra daṅ gñis / daṅ po'i mtshan ñid raṅ gis zin par brjod pa'i brjod bya'i don de yin na rigs spyi yin pa / dper na gzugs źes pa'i sgra lta bu'o / tshogs rjod kyi sgra'i mtshan ñid / raṅ gis zin par brjod pa'i brjod bya yin na / rdul rdzas brgyad 'dus kyi goṅ bu yin pa / dper na ri bo gaṅs can źes pa'i sgra lta bu'o /

In variegation of the referral by way of the reference, there are two kinds of speech—referring to the genus and referring to the group.

1. speech referring to the genus (*jāti*, rigs) is defined as, given an object-entity of reference referred to, taking it as the subject

(raṅ gis zin par), to wit, the genus-generality (*jāti-sāmānya*, rigs spyi). For example, the remark, "There is form."

2. speech referring to the group (*sāmagrī*, tshogs) is defined as a reference (i.e. a name) referred to, taking it as the subject, e.g. the mass comprising the eight material atoms. For example, the expression "the Himalaya mountain."

/ brjod bya la brjod tshul gyi sgo nas dbye na / chos brjod kyi sgra daṅ / chos can brjod pa'i sgra gñis / daṅ po'i mtshan ñid raṅ gis zin par brjod pa'i brjod bya'i khyad chos gźan rnams raṅ gi brjod byar spaṅs pa'i sgo nas brjod bya go byed / dper na ba glaṅ rta min pa ñid yin no / źes pa'i sgra lta bu'o / chos can brjod pa'i sgra'i mtshan ñid / raṅ gis zin par brjod pa'i brjod bya'i khyad chos gźan rnams raṅ gi brjod byar ma spaṅs pa'i sgo nas brjod bya go byed / dper na ba glaṅ rta ma yin pa yin no /

In variegation by the manner of referring to the reference, there are two kinds:

1. Speech referring to a feature (*dharma*) is defined as making understood the reference—while other differentiated features of the reference are referred to, taking it as the subject—by way of its own rejection of a (different) reference. For example, the remark, "A cow (feature) is not a horse (feature)."
2. Speech referring to a factual base (*dharmin*) is defined as making understood the reference—while other differentiated features of the reference are referred to, taking it as the subject—by way of its own non-rejection of a (different) reference. For example, the remark, "It is a cow, not a horse" (ba glan rta ma yin pa).

/ rjod byed la rnam gcod kyi sgo nas dbye na / mi ldan rnam gcod kyi sgra daṅ / gźan ldan rnam gcod kyi sgra daṅ / mi srid rnam gcod kyi sgra daṅ gsum / mtshan ñid rim pa bźin / tshig phrad khyad chos kyi 'og de ma thag par sbyar nas rjod byed / khyad gźi'i 'og de ma thag par sbyar nas rjod byed / bya ba srid pa'i 'og de ma thag par sbyar nas rjod byed / dpe rim bźin / nag pa 'phoṅs skyen pa kho na źes brjod pa'i sgra daṅ / srid sgrub kho na 'phaṅs skyen źes brjod pa'i sgra daṅ / mtsho skyes la sṅon po srid pa kho na źes brjod pa'i sgra lta bu'o /

In variegation of the referral by way of ruling out (*vyavaccheda*, rnam gcod), there are three propositions (sgra).

1. Proposition ruling out non-connection (*ayogavyavaccheda*, mi ldan rnam gcod) is defined as a referral by adding a post-

particle immediately after the differentiating feature. For example, the proposition, "Caitra is an archer indeed (*eva*)."

2. Proposition ruling out connection with something else (*anyayogavyavaccheda*, gźan ldan rnam gcod) is defined as a referral by adding a post-particle immediately after the differentiable support (=factual base). For example, the proposition, "Pārtha (i.e. Arjuna) alone (*eva*) is the archer."
3. Proposition ruling out impossibility (*atyantayogavyavaccheda*, mi srid rnam gcod) is defined as a referral by adding a post-particle immediately after the possible activity. For example, the proposition, "A lotus might be (*eva*) blue."

/ rjod byed la 'chad dus kyi sgo nas dbye na / źen pa'i rjod byed daṅ / des zlas draṅs pa'i dṅos kyi rjod byed gñis / phyi ma ni bum pa'i sgra spyi lta bu / źen pa'i rjod byed la dbye na / dṅos kyi źen pa'i rjod byed daṅ / śugs kyi źen pa'i rjod byed gñis / dpe rim bźin / bum pa mi rtag pa daṅ bum pa rtag pa ma yin pa la bltos te bum pa mi rtag ces pa'i sgra lta bu'o /

In variegation by the time of stating the referral, there are two kinds:

1. a claimed referral, of two kinds:
   (1) a referral with a direct claim; for example, noticing that the pot is impermanent, the remark, "the impermanent pot."
   (2) a referral with an indirect claim; for example, noticing that there is no pot that is permanent, the (same) remark, "the impermanent pot."
2. a material referral, citing the foregoing (claimed referral); for example, the generality remark, "It is a pot."

/ źar byuṅ yi ge daṅ gaṅ zag gñis las / yi ge'i mtshan ñid re re bas don ston mi nus kyaṅ phyed daṅ gñis yan chad tshogs na don ston ruṅ gi skad cig du ma can gyi sgra / dbye na A I sogs dbyaṅs yig daṅ / KA, KHA sogs gsal byed gñis so / gaṅ zag gi mtshan ñid / phuṅ po lṅa 'am gźi'i tshogs rgyun la btags pa'i btags yod / dper na lha sbyin lta bu'o / saṅs ma rgyas pa'i dbaṅ du byas so /

Along those lines, there are syllables (yi ge) and persons (gaṅ zag):

1. Syllables are individually incapable of showing meaning, but a set of one and a half or more may show meaning, as may also the speech in multiple moments. They are divided into the vowels, A, I, etc., and the consonents, KA, KHA, etc.
2. Persons are defined as the designation designating a continutiy

of the five aggregates (*skandha*), or of the suppport-group (*ādhāra-sāmagrī*, gźi'i tshogs); for example, Devadatta. It (i.e. as so defined) refers to a person who did not become a Buddha.

/ blo daṅ rig pa / śes pa mams don gcig yin la / mtshan ñid sṅar bśad zin ciṅ / dbye na / tshad ma / tshad min / rtog pa / rtog med / 'khrul ma 'khrul / raṅ rig / gźan rig / sems sems byuṅ rnams su yod pa las /

Cognition (*buddhi*, blo), meaning the same as apperception (rig pȧ) and knowing (śes pa), has been already defined.[6] In variegation, there are A. authority amd nonauthority, B. constructive thought and non-constructive thought, C. delusion and nondelusion, D. introspection and outward-directed cognition, E. thought and thought derivative.

/ tshad ma'i mtshan ñid raṅ yul gsar du rtogs pa'i blo / des na / tshad ma slu med can śes pa / źes pa'i don mi slu ba tsam min gyi / gsar du rtogs pa 'di lta yin źes pa'i phyir du / ma śes don gyis gsal byed kyaṅ / źes pas gźuṅ sṅa ma'i don gsal du btaṅ ba yin no / 'o na kyaṅ gi don gaṅ źe na / gźuṅ sṅa ma'i don la / sgra byuṅ tshad ma la ma khyab pa'i sk̇yon med par ma zad / kun rdzob śes pa la khyab ches pa'i skyon yaṅ med / ces pa'i don no /

A. Authority and non-Authority

Authority (*pramāṇa*, tshad ma) is defined as the cognition which comprehends newly its own sense-object (yul). Hence (the text), "Authority is a cognition without deception." This (passage of the *Pramāṇavārttika*) does not mean only nondeception, because it refers to this understanding as "newly". The former version laid down meaning clearly by (the words) "Or, it clarifies the (previously) unknown entity." What is the meaning (here) of "or" (*vā*, 'on kyaṅ)? As to the meaning of the former text, not only should there be no fault of nonpervasion (as found) in the 'derived belief' (*śabda*) authority, but *also* (="or") there should be no fault of pervasive feature (as found) in conventional (kun rdzob) cognition. That is the meaning (of "or").

/ tshad min blo'i mtshan ñid / raṅ yul gsar du rtogs pa ma yin pa'i blo /

6. The author means that when beginning the topic "II. SUBJECT," the author said that the 'subject' is what makes understood or makes apprehended; and that there are two kinds, referral and cognition. He then sets forth the first kind, referral, and now treats the second kind, cognition.

Nonauthority (*apramāṇa*) cognition is defined as the cognition (*buddhi*) that does not comprehend newly its sense object (*viṣaya*).

/ dbye na / bcad śes log śes the tshom yid dpyod snaṅ la ma ṅes kyi blo daṅ lṅa /

In variegation, there are five kinds of cognition: 1. deciding cognition. 2. deviant cognition, 3. doubt, 4. mental analysis, and 5. the cognition uncertain as to the appearance.

/ bcad śes kyi mtshan ñid / raṅ 'dren byed kyi tshad ma sṅa mas rtogs zin byed pa ma ñaṃs pa'i yul la sgro 'dogs gcod nus su 'jug pa'i blo / dbye na / mṅon sum tshad mas draṅs pa'i bcad śes gñis / dpe rim bźin / sṅon 'dzin dbaṅ po'i mṅon sum gyis draṅs pa'i sṅon po ṅes pa'i blo lta bu daṅ/ sgra mi rtag par rtogs pa'i rjes dpag tshad mas draṅs pa'i sgra mi rtag par ṅes pa'i blo lta bu'o / mṅon sum tshad mas draṅs pa'i mṅon sum phyi ma rnams kyaṅ bcad śes yin no /

1. Deciding cognition (bcad śes) is defined as the cognition proceeding capable of deciding the superimposition (sgro 'dogs) on the sense object, given that it (the object) was not lost when already comprehended by a prior authority that individually conveys it. In variegation there are two deciding cognitions.
   (1) (object) conveyed by perception (*pratyakṣa*) authority; for example, a cognition certain of blue, conveyed by a sense-organ perception that has apprehended blue.
   (2) (object conveyed by inference authority); for example, the cognition certain that sound is impermanent, conveyed by an inference authority that has comprehended sound to be impermanent.

The later perceptions (*pratyakṣa*) conveyed by a perception authority are also deciding cognitions.

/ log śes kyi mtshan ñid / de ma yin pa la der 'dzin pa'i śes pa / dbye na / sgra rtag 'dzin gyi rtog pa lta bu / rtog pa log śes daṅ zla ba gñis snaṅ gi dbaṅ śes lta bu rtog med log śes gñis /

2. Deviant cognition (log śes) is defined as the cognition apprehending something as being in a place when it is not so. In variegation, there is the deviant reflection like the constructive thought which apprehends sound as permanent, and the nonconstructive thought like the sense-organ cognition with appearance of the double moon.

/ the tshom kyi mtshan ñid / yul ma ṅes par źen pa'i blo / dbye na / the tshom sṅon du-rgyu daṅ bag la ñal gñis / daṅ po la dbye na

/ cha mñam du 'dzin pa daṅ / śas cher 'dzin pa gñis / daṅ po ni dper na sgra rtag gam mi rtag sñam pa / gñis pa la / don 'gyur gyi the tshom daṅ / don mi 'gyur gyi the tshom gñis / dpe rim bzin / sgra phal cher mi rtag sñam pa'i blo lta bu / the tshom bag la ñal la dbye na / rtags la ma brten pa daṅ brten pa gñis / dpe rim bźin / khron pa na chu yod sñam pa'i blo lta bu daṅ / ma ṅes pa'i rtags la brten pa'i blo mtha' dag go /

3. Doubt is defined as the cognition which professes uncertainty about the object. In variegation there are two kinds:
   (1) doubt about a prior happening, of two kinds:
      a. grasping in equal parts; for example, wondering whether a (heard) sound is permanent or impermanent.
      b. grasping with a preponderance, of two kinds:
         b-1. doubt as to whether something is the case; for example, wondering whether a (heard) sound is prevalently permanent.
         b-2. doubt as to whether a something is the case; for example, wondering whether a (heard) sound is prevalently impermanent.
   (2) 'traces' (*anuśaya*) of doubt, of two kinds:
      a. not based on evidence (*liṅga*); for example, the mind wondering if there is water in the well.
      b. based on evidence; for example, any notion based on uncertain evidence (*anaikāntika-liṅga*).

/ yid dpyod kyi dgag sgrub gźan du bźad do /

4. Mental analysis (yid dpyod) using exclusion (*pratiṣedha*) and affirmation (*pratipatti*) will be explained later on.[7]

/ snaṅ la ma rtogs pa'i blo'i mtshan ñid / raṅ mtshan snaṅ źiṅ de la sgro 'dogs gcod mi nus pa / dbye na / 'khrul pa'i rgyu mtshan gyis snaṅ la ma rtogs pa daṅ / yid ma gtad pa'i rgyu mtshan gyis snaṅ la ma rtogs pa'i blo gñis / dpe rim bźin sṅon po mi rtag pa la sṅon po'i dbaṅ po'i mṅon sum lta bu daṅ / ser po la yid gtad dus kyi dbaṅ po'i mṅon sum lta bu'o /

5. Cognition that does not comprehend the appearance (snaṅ la ma rtogs pa'i blo) is defined as the incapacity of deciding,

7. The remark about 'mental analysis' came no. 4 in the introductory list, but in fact appears in the text right after the next paragraph, labelled no. 5. I moved the remark to the present location to agree with the order in the introductory list.

when an individual character (*svalakṣaṇa*) appears, that there is a superimposition upon it. In variegation there are two kinds:

(1) cognition not comprehending the appearance by reason of delusion; for example, for blue being impermanent, has sense perception of (continuous) blue.

(2) cognition not comprehending the appearance by reason of not fixing attention upon it; for example, sense perception (of e.g. blue) at the time the mind is preoccupied with yellow (imagery).

/ tshad ma la graṅs ṅes kyi sgo nas dbye na / mṅon sum tshad ma daṅ / rjes dpag tshad ma gñis /

If one variegates the authority by way of numerical certitude (graṅs ṅes), there are two kinds— 'direct perception' authority and 'inference' authority.

/ mṅon sum tshad ma'i mtshan ñid / rtog bral ma 'khrul ba gaṅ źig / raṅ yul gsar du rtogs pa / 'di mṅon sum bźi ka la 'gre'o / mṅon sum gyi mtshan ñid rtog bral ma 'khrul ba'i śes pa / dbye na / dbaṅ po i / yid kyi mṅon sum / raṅ rig / rnal 'byor mṅon sum daṅ bźi'o /

***Pratyakṣa* (*Direct Perception*)**

Pratyakṣa authority is defined as one free from constructive thought (*kalpanā*) and free from delusion (*bhrānti*). It comprehends newly its object. This direct perception is of four kinds. When one variegates direct perception, as defined, i.e. free from constructive thought and free from delusion, the four are direct perception belonging to the sense-organs, to the mind, to introspection, and to the yogin.

/ rim pa bźin du / In the given order:

/ raṅ gi bdag rkyen dbaṅ po gzugs can las dṅos su skyes pa'i gźan rig gi śes pa rtog bral ma 'khrul pa / dbye na / gzugs 'dzin dbaṅ po'i mṅon sum / sgra 'dzin / dri 'dzin / ro 'dzin / reg 'dzin dbaṅ po'i mṅon sum daṅ lṅa'o / mtshan ñid rim bźin / raṅ gi bdag rkyen mig dbaṅ / rna ba'i / sna'i / lce'i / lus kyi dbaṅ po las dṅos su skyes pa'i gźan rig gi śes pa rtog bral ma 'khrul pa /

1. (Outer) sense perception (*indriya-pratyakṣa*) grasps formation, grasps sound, grasps odor, grasps taste, grasps tangibles— five sense perceptions in all. They are the outward-directed cognitions (*parasaṃvitti*), free from constructive thought and free from delusion, arisen from and on-going (dṅos su) with

the eye-organ, ear-, nose-, tongue-, corpus-sense organ, (each) an individual controlling condition (*adhipatti-pratyaya*, bdag rkyen).

/ raṅ gi bdag rkyen yid kyi dbaṅ po las dṅos su skyes pa'i gźan rig gi śes pa rtog bral ma 'khrul pa / dbye na / gzugs 'dzin yid kyi dbaṅ po'i mṅon sum nas / reg 'dzin yid kyi dbaṅ po'i mṅon sum gyi bar lṅa'o / mtshan ñid rim pa bźin / raṅ gi bdag rkyen gzugs 'dzin / sgra 'dzin / dri 'dzin / ro 'dzin / reg 'dzin yid kyi dbaṅ po las dṅos su skyes ba'i gźan rig gi śes pa rtog bral ma 'khrul pa / dbaṅ mṅon skad cig phyi ma rnams yid mṅon yin te / raṅ gi gzuṅ don grogs su yod pa'i dbaṅ mṅon gcig gis de ma thag rkyen byas pa la byuṅ ba'i gźan rig gi śes pa rtog bral ma 'khrul pa yin pa'i phyir / yid śes yin te / raṅ gi bdag rkyen yid dbaṅ las dṅos su skyes pa'i śes pa yin pa'i phyir te / raṅ daṅ rigs mthun pa'i rnam śes sṅa ma bkag kha ma las skyes pa'i śes pa yin pa'i phyir / źes 'chad pa 'thad pa 'dra'o /

2. Mental perception (*mānasa-pratyakṣa*) is an outward directed cognition (*parasaṃvitti*), free from constructive thought, free from delusion, arisen from and on-going with the mind sense-organ (*manas-indriya*), an individual controlling condition. In variegation, there is the perception through mind organ grasping formation, and so on, up to the perception through mind organ grasping tangibles, five in all. They are outward directed cognitions free from constructive thought, free from delusion, arisen from and on-going with the mind organ, the controlling condition that grasps form, sound, odor, taste, tangible. At the second moment, the mind (*manas*) perceives the perceptions of the (five) senses. It is the outward directed cognition, free from constructive thought, free from delusion, arisen from the immediately preceding condition by way of a single sense perception of its related (grogs su yod pa) individual grasped object. Hence, it is mind cognition. It is the cognition arisen directly from the mind-organ (*manas-indriya*), its controlling condition. It is the cognition arisen from its individual and affiliated perception (*vijñāna*), which had just finished stopping. The explanations seem to be right.

/ raṅ rig mṅon sum gyi mtshan ñid / kha naṅ kho nar phyogs pa'i 'dzin rnam / śes pa kun gyi steṅ na yod /

3. Introspective perception (*svasaṃvedana-pratyakṣa*) is the one that grasps only on the inner side (of the mind) while based on all cognition as imagery (*ākāra*).

/ rnal 'byor mṅon sum gyi mtshan ñid / yaṅ dag pa'i don bsgoms pa'i stobs las byuṅ ba'i 'phags pa'i śes pa rtog bral ma 'khrul ba / dbye na / ñan thos raṅ rgyal theg chen gyi rnal 'byor mṅon sum daṅ gsum / dpe rim bźin / ñan thos kyi mthoṅ lam daṅ / raṅ rgyal gyi mthoṅ lam lta bu'o /

4. Yogin's perception (*yogi-pratyakṣa*) is the cognition of the nobles (*ārya*), free from constructive thought, free from delusion, arisen from the power of contemplating a right topic (*artha*). In variegation, there are three—that of the disciples (*śrāvaka*); for example, the 'path of vision' (*darśana-mārga*) of the Śrāvaka. That of the self-enlightened (*pratyekabuddha*); for example, the path of vision of the Pratyekabuddha. That of the Mahāyāna [and for example, the path of vision of the Bodhisattva].[8]

/ rjes dpag tshad ma'i mtshan ñid / tshul gsum tshaṅ ba'i rtags la brten nas raṅ yul lkog gyur gsar du rtogs pa'i blo / dbye na gsum las / dṅos po stobs źugs kyi rjes dpag ni / byas pa'i rtags la brten nas sgra mi rtag par rtogs pa'i blo lta bu / grags pa'i rjes dpag ni / rtogs yul na yod pa'i rtags la brten nas ri boṅ can zla ba'i sgras brjod ruṅ du rtogs pa'i rjes dpag lta bu / yid ches rjes dpag ni / dpyad pa gsum gyis dag pa'i luṅ la brten nas sbyin pas loṅs spyod ces sogs kyi luṅ raṅ gi bstan bya'i don la mi slu bar rtogs pa'i blo lta bu'o /

***Anumāna* (*Inference*)**

Inference authority is defined as the cognition that comprehends newly its object beyond sight (*parokṣa*) by recourse to evidence (*liṅga*) having the complete three modes (tshul gsum). In variegation, there are three kinds:

1. inference aroused on the strength of a given thing (dṅos po stobs śugs), e.g. the cognition comprehending a sound as impermanent by recourse to the evidence that it is created (*kṛta*).
2. popular (*prasiddha, pratīta,* grags pa) inference, e.g. the inference comprehending the feasibility of calling the moon 'rabbit possessor' by recourse to the evidence that is present in the domain of understanding.

8. For the 'path of vision' (*darśana-mārga,* mthoṅ lam), cf. E. Obermiller, *The Doctrine of Prajñā-pāramitā as exposed in the Abhisamayālaṃkāra of Maitreya,* reprint from Acta Orientalia, Vol. XI (1932), Index, p. 112, entry for *darśana-mārga.*

3. inference of the master (lineage) (*āpta*, yid ches), e.g. taking recourse to a pure scripture by three examinations, the cognition which is without deception regarding its individual indicated aim in regard to such a scripture as 'By giving, there is possession ...'"[9]

/ tshad ma la yul can la ṅes pa 'dren nus kyi sgo nas dbye na / raṅ las ṅes kyi tshad ma daṅ / gźan las ṅes kyi tshad ma gñis / daṅ po'i mtshan ñid / tshad ma gaṅ zig raṅ ñid tshad ma yin par raṅ stobs kyis ṅes pa 'dren pa / dper na / raṅ ñid tshad ma yin par raṅ stobs kyis ṅes pa 'dren pa'i rjes dpag daṅ / mṅon sum bźi lta bu'o / gñis pa'i mtshan ñid / thad ma gaṅ źig raṅ ñid tshad ma yin par gźan stobs kyis ṅes pa 'dren pa / dper na / raṅ ñid tshad ma yin par gźan stobs kyis ṅes pa 'dren pa'i rjes dpag daṅ / mṅon sum tshad ma gsum lta bu'o / yaṅ na de gñis kyi dpe rim bźin tshad ma'i brda la byaṅ ba'i skyes bu'i rgyud kyi tshad ma lta bu daṅ / tshad ma'i brda la ma byaṅ ba'i skyes bu'i rgyud kyi tshad ma lta bu'o /

Variegating the authority by the ability to convey certainty (ṅes pa 'dren nus) regarding the subject (*viṣayin*), there are two—authority with certainty from oneself, and authority with certainty from another.

1. Authority with certainty from oneself is defined as the authority which conveys certainty by one's own power (raṅ stobs) that it is an authority; for example, the inference that conveys certainty by one's own power that it is an authority, and the four kinds of perception (*pratyakṣa*). Besides, for example, it is the authority of a person's stream of consciousness (rgyud) who is familiar with the sign of authority.
2. Authority with certainty from another is defined as the authority which conveys certainty by another power (gźan stobs) that it is an authority; for example, the inference which conveys certainty by another power that it is an authority, and three perception authorities.[10] Besides, for example, it is the authority of a person's stream of consciousness who is not familiar with the sign of authority.

---

9. See the previous notes 4 and 5.
10. It is not clear which 'perception authority' is omitted to leave three. We may suppose that since the authority came from another, this may cause an omission of the perception authority for the five outer-directed senses, leaving the mental one, the introspection, and the yogin's *pratyakṣa*.

/ mkhas pa kha cig / raṅ las ṅes daṅ gźan las ṅes kyi tshad ma'i mtshan ñid rim bźin tshad ma gaṅ źig raṅ ñid mi slu ba can du raṅ stobs kyis ṅes pa 'dren nus pa daṅ / gźan stobs kyis ṅes pa 'dren pa gñis / daṅ po la dbye na / rjes dpag tshad ma daṅ / raṅ rig mṅon sum tshad daṅ / don byed snaṅ gi mṅon sum tshad ma daṅ / goms pa can gyi mṅon sum tshad ma daṅ / gźan las ṅes ni 'khrul rgyu caṅ gyi mṅon sum tshad ma ste / da lta rgyaṅ riṅ po'i 'bar ba me'i kha dog yin min du the tshom skyed ciṅ phyis tshad gźan la brten nas raṅ ñid rgyaṅ riṅ po'i dmar 'bar ba me'i kha dog yin pa la mi slu ba lta bu can du ṅes rgyu'i rgyaṅ riṅ po'i dmar 'bar ba 'dzin pa'i dbaṅ mṅon lta bu'o /

Some savants say that the kind with certainty from oneself is defined as the kind with ability to convey certainty by one's own power while not deceiving oneself; and that the kind with certainty from another conveys certainty through another power while not deceiving oneself. Variegating the first kind (certainty from oneself), there is the inference authority, the introspective perception authority, the perception authority that illumines purposive activity (don byed snaṅ gi mṅon sum tshad ma), and the perception authority that is continually practiced (*abhyāsin*, goms pa can). The kind with certainty from another is the perception authority for a cause of error; for example should in the present time doubt arise as to whether or not the far-off blazing red is the color of a fire, later by reliance on another authority, there is a cause of certainty (believing) that oneself is not deceived in taking the far-off blazing red to be the color of a fire; i.e. (someone else's) sense perception (? stronger than one's own) grasps what has the far-off blazing red color [and reports it as a fire].

B. Constructive Thought and Nonconstructive Thought

/ rtog pa'i mtshan ñid / raṅ gi snaṅ yul yin na spyi mtshan yin dgos pa / rtog med śes pa'i mtshan ñid / śes pa gaṅ źig / raṅ gi snaṅ yul yin na raṅ mtshan gaṅ gźi ma grub gaṅ ruṅ yin dgos pa /

Constructive thought (*kalpanā*) is defined as requiring, in the case when (a cognition has) its appearing sense object (*viṣaya*), that this be a "generality character" (*sāmānya-lakṣaṇa*). Nonconstructive thought (*akalpanā*) is defined as requiring, in the case when a cognition has its appearing object, that this be either an "individual character" (*svalakṣaṇa*) or a nonactual support (gźi ma grub).

/ rtog pa la sbyor tshul gyi sgo nas dbye na / sgra sbyor rtog pa daṅ don sbyor rtog pa gñis / daṅ po'i mtshan ñid brda dus kyi miṅ daṅ tha sñad kyi don gñis sbyar nas 'dzin pa'i śes pa / dper na yal 'dab can gyi śiṅ ṅo sñam pa'i blo lta bu'o / gñis pa'i mtshan ñid / khyad gźi khyad chos sbyar nas 'dzin pa'i śes pa / dper na skyes bu dbyug pa can no sñam du 'dzin pa'i blo lta bu'o /

Variegating constructive thought by the method of application (sbyor tshul), there are two kinds:

1. Constructive thought with application to speech is defined as the cognition—at the time of a signal—that apprehends by combining the two object-entities of name and conventional description; for example, a cognition that imagines, "The tree has leaves and branches."
2. Constructive thought with application to a feature is defined as the cognition apprehending by combining the specialized support (= factual base) and the specialized feature (*dharma*); for example, the cognition that imagines, "That person has a stick."

/ rtog pa la snaṅ yul gyi sgo nas dbye na / sgra spyi rkyaṅ ba la snaṅ ba daṅ / don spyi rkyaṅ ba la snaṅ ba daṅ / gñis ka snaṅ ba'i rtog pa gsum / dpe rim bźin brda la ma yaṅ ba'i rgyud kyi bum pa'i sgra spyi snaṅ ba'i blo lta bu daṅ / brda la ma byaṅ ba'i skyes bu'i rgyud kyi bum pa'i don spyi snaṅ ba'i blo lta bu daṅ / brda la byaṅ ba'i skyes bu'i rgyud kyi bum 'dzin rtog pa lta bu /

Variegating constructive thought by the appearing sense object (snaṅ yul), there are three kinds:

1. constructive thought of the appearance, restricted to the generality speech; for example, given a signal, the cognition of appearance with generality speech, "It's a pot," in the stream of consciousness of a person not familiar with the signal (or, sign).
2. constructive thought of the appearance, restricted to the generality feature (*dharma*); for example, given a signal, the cognition of appearance with generality of a pot's feature in the stream of consciousness of a person not familiar with the signal (or, sign).
3. constructive thought of the appearance of both; for example, given a signal, the constructive thought which apprehends the pot, to wit, in the stream of consciousness of a person familiar with the signal.

/ rtog pa la dgos pa'i sgo nas dbye na / brda rten can gyi rtog pa daṅ / don gźan la sgro 'dogs pa'i rtog pa daṅ / lkog tu gyur pa'i don gyi rtog pa gsum / daṅ po ni bum pa'i spyi 'dzin śes pa lta bu / gñis pa ni / mig rgyu la chur 'dzin gyi śes pa lta bu / gsum pa la bźi las / rtags 'dzin pa'i sems ni de sgrub kyi rjes dpag gi ñer len du gyur pa'i sgrub kyi tshul gsum gaṅ ruṅ ṅes pa'i blo / rjes dpag ni bśad zin no / dran pa ni / 'das pa la dmigs pa'i rtog pa / mṅon 'dod las byuṅ ba'i rtog pa ni / sgra tsam gyi rjes su 'braṅs pa'i rtog pa'o /

Variegating constructive thought by the occasion (*prayojana*, dgos), there are three kinds:

1. constructive thought with a signal as a basis, e.g. the cognition which apprehends the generality of a pot.
2. constructive thought which superimposes another entity, e.g. the cognition which apprehends water in a mirage.
3. constructive thought of an entity that is out of sight (*parokṣa*), which is of four kinds:
   (1) The thought that holds the evidence is the cognition certain of any one of the three modes of proof that are the [necessary] condition (*upādāna*) for the inference of that proof.
   (2) **ānumānika*[11] (the derivative of inference) has been explained.
   (3) *smārta* (the derivative of memory) is the constructive thought which perceives the past.
   (4) *ābhilaṣika* (derived belief) is the constructive thought which only follows speech.

/ rtog med śes pa la dbye na / rtog med 'khrul śes daṅ / rtog med ma 'khrul ba'i śes pa gñis / daṅ po'i mtshan ñid / raṅ gi bdag rkyen dbaṅ po bslad pa las byuṅ ba'i śes pa / dbye na / dbaṅ śes 'khrul pa daṅ / rtog med yid śes 'khrul ba gñis / dpe rim bźin / zla ba gñis snaṅ gi dbaṅ śes lta bu daṅ / rmi lam gsal snaṅ gi śes pa lta bu'o /

Variegating nonconstructive thought, there are two kinds:

1. delusive cognition without constructive thought, to wit, the cognition of a defective sense organ, its controlling condition. There are two kinds:
   (1) delusion of sense cognition, e.g. sense cognition with appearance of a double moon.
   (2) delusion of mental cognition free from constructive thought, e.g. cognition with a vivid appearance in dream.
2. nondelusive cognition without constructive thought, to wit, all the previously mentioned direct perceptions (*pratyakṣa*).

---

11. The derivative form is a correction of the Tibetan *rjes dpag*.

C. Delusion and Nondelusion

/ 'khrul rgyu ni rnam pa bźi ste / gnas la yod pa grur źug pa'i dbaṅ gis ljon śiṅ 'gror snaṅ gi śes pa lta bu / rten la yod pa mig dbaṅ rab rib kyis dkrugs pa'i dbaṅ gis duṅ ser por snaṅ ba'i śes pa lta bu daṅ / yul la yod pa mgal me myur du bskor ba'i dbaṅ gis 'khor lor snaṅ ba'i śes pa lta bu daṅ / de ma thag rkyen la yod pa źe sdaṅ drag pos yid śes 'khrugs pa'i blo lta bu'o /

There are four instruments of error (*vibhramakāraṇa*):

1. found in a place; for example, the cognition of an appearance that while embarking in a boat, the trees on the shore are moving.
2. found in a basis (the sense organ); for example, the cognition of an appearance that, by dint of the eye-organ's caul, by reason of the impaired sense organ, the conchshell is yellow.
3. found in the sense object; for example, the cognition of an appearance, by dint of a speedily whirling torch, that there is a wheel.
4. found in the immediately preceding condition; for example, by reason of a fierce hatred the mind cognition is agitated.

/ źar la mṅon sum ltar snaṅ gi mtshan ñid / raṅ gi snaṅ yul la 'khrul pa'i śes pa / dbye na rtog med mṅon sum ltar snaṅ daṅ rtog pa mṅon sum ltar snaṅ / mtshan ñid daṅ dbye ba sṅar bśad zin to / 'khrul śes kyi mtshan ñid / de ma yin pa la der 'dzin gyi śes pa / dbye na gñis las / rtog pa 'khrul śes ni / sgra rtag 'dzin gyi rtog pa lta bu daṅ / rtog med 'khrul śes ni bśad zin to / ma 'khrul pa'i śes pa'i mtshan ñid / yul gyi gnas lugs rig pa'i śes pa / dbye na / mṅon sum daṅ / źen yul la ma 'khrul pa'i rtog pa gñis / gñis pa ni / rjes dpag lta bu'o /

Along those lines, semblance of perception (mṅon sum ltar snaṅ) is defined as the delusive cognition toward its own appearing object. In variegation there is the semblance of perception without constructive thought, and the semblance of perception with constructive thought. The definitions and variety have been already expounded.

Delusive cognition ('khrul śes) is defined as the cognition that apprehends something some way and it is not that way. In variegation there are two kinds. Of these, the delusive cognition with constructive thought is, e.g. the constructive thought that apprehends sound as eternal. The delusive cognition without constructive thought has already been explained.

Non-delusive cognition is defined as the cognition aware of the situation (or lay-out) of the object. In variegation there are two:

direct perception (*pratyakṣa*); and a non-delusive constructive thought toward the claimed sense object, e.g. inference.

/ raṅ rig gi mtshan ñid / 'dzin rnam / gźan rig gi mtshan ñid gzuṅ rnam /

D. Introspection and Outward Directed Cognition

Introspection (*svasaṃvedana*) is defined as the subject-imagery ('dzin rnam). Outward directed (cognition) is defined as the object-imagery (gzuṅ rnam).

/ sems kyi mtshan ñid / yul daṅ yul gyi khyad par gñis kyi naṅ nas yul tsam rig pa / dbye na / rnam śes tshogs drug gam brgyad / sems byuṅ gi mtshan ñid / yul gyi khyad par rig pa / dbye na / lṅa bcu rtsa gcig /

E. Thought and Thought Derivative

Thought (*citta*) is defined as awareness of only the sense object (*viṣaya-mātra*) among the two, sense object and differentiated sense object. In variegation, there is the set of perceptions (*vijñāna*), six [as in the Mādhyamika school] or eight [as in the Yogācāra school]. Thought derivative (*caitta* or *caitasika*) is defined as the awareness of the differentiated sense object (*viṣaya-viśeṣa*). In variegation, there are fifty-one.[12]

/ źar la tshad 'bras kyi rnam gźag 'chad pa ni /

Authority as a Result

Along those lines, there is the exposition establishing authority as result (*kārya*).

/ 'bras rtogs daṅ po'i skabs su / sṅon po gźal bya / sṅon po'i rnam pa śar nas sṅon po la gsar du mi slu ba'i śes pa tshad ma / sṅon po dṅos su rtogs pa'i tshad ma 'bras bur 'jog pa /

1. In the first phase of realizing the result, there is blue as the sanction. Given that the imagery of blue has arisen (in the mind), the authority is the new non-deceiving cognition of blue. The authority with implicit realization of the blue, is established as the result.

12. Stcherbatsky, *The Central Conception of Buddhism and the Meaning of the Word "Dharma"* (Calcutta: Susil Gupta, 1961) did not help: but in my essay "Supports and other objects" (Millennium, Vol. Two) I show that the 51 number is the list in Asaṅga's *Abhidharmasamuccaya*.

/ 'bras rtogs gñis pa'i skabs su / gzuṅ rnam gźal bya / gzuṅ rnam yoṅs su dpyod byed 'dzin rnam tshad ma / gzuṅ rnam ñams su myoṅ ba'i raṅ rig 'bras bur 'jog ciṅ /

2. In the second phase of realizing the result, there is the object-imagery as the sanction. Given that the object-imagery is pondered, the authority is the subject-imagery. The introspection that experiences the object-imagery is established as the result.

/ 'bras rtogs gñis pa'i skabs su / sṅon po gźal bya / sṅon po'i rnam pa śar nas sṅon po la gsar du mi slu ba'i śes pa tshad ma / sṅon po la ltos nas ran gi bdag nid du gyur ba'i yul dṅos su rtogs pa'i tshad ma 'bras bur 'jog go /

3. In the third phase of realizing the result, there is the sanction of blue. The authority is the new non-deceptive cognition of blue while blue is arising (in the mind). In respect to blue, the authority with implicit realization of the sense object which is itself the controlling condition, is established as the result.

/ rjes dpag gi tshad 'bras ni / sgra mi rtag pa gźal bya / sgra mi rtag par sgrub pa'i tshul gsum tshaṅ ba'i rtags las sgra mi rtag pa'i rnam pa śar nas sgra mi rtag pa la gsar du mi slu ba'i śes pa tshad ma / sgra mi rtag par dṅos su rtogs pa'i rjes dpag 'bras bu /

4. Regarding the inference authority as the result, a sanction is (the proposition) "Sound is impermanent." Given that the (auditory) imagery "Sound is impermanent" has arisen through the evidence which has the complete three modes proving "Sound is impermanent," it follows that the authority is the new nondeceiving cognition that sound is impermanent. The inference with implicit realization that sound is impermanent, is the result.

/ sems tsam pa'i skabs su / dbaṅ śes kyi rkyen gsum gyi / go don ji lta bu źe na /

The 'Mind-only' (*cittamātra*) School

In the school of Cittamātra, what is the aim of understanding their three conditions (*pratyaya*) of sense-cognitions?

/ dbaṅ śes kyi dmigs rkyen gyi mtshan ñid / ran gis bsgos pa'i bag chags kyi dbaṅ gis raṅ 'bras dbaṅ śes yul gyi rnam ldan du gtso bor skyed byed / dper na sṅor snaṅ dbaṅ śes sṅa ma ni śes pa gźan gyis par bar chod dam ma chod kyaṅ ruṅ / raṅ gi rigs 'dra sṅor snaṅ dbaṅ śes phyi ma'i dmigs rkyen yin pa bźin no / gzuṅ rnam dmigs rkyen du bśad pa ni / tha sñad du yin gyi spyir ma yin no /

1. The support-condition (*ālambana-pratyaya*) of sense-cognition is defined as what chiefly generates, by dint of habit-energy (*vāsanā*) (previously) cultivated by oneself, the sense-cognition by its own result into possession of sense object-imagery (*viṣaya-ākāra*). For example, the previous sense-cognition of green appearance is either interrupted or not interrupted, as the case may be, by another cognition. Its affiliated green appearance is the later support-condition of sense-cognition. The explanation that the object-imagery (gzuṅ rnam) is the support-condition (dmigs rkyen) is conventionally said, but is not general.

/ dbaṅ śes kyi bdag rkyen gyi mtshan ñid / dbaṅ śes yul 'dzin du gtso bor skyed byed kyi sa bon / dper na sṅor snaṅ dbaṅ śes sṅa ma'i nus pa'i dbaṅ gis sṅor snaṅ dbaṅ śes sṅon po 'dzin nus su gtso bor skyed pa'i kun gźi'i steṅ gi nus pa lta bu'o /

2. The controlling-condition (*adhipati-pratyaya*) of sense-cognition is defined as the seed which chiefly generates the sense-cognition into apprehension of the object. For example, the capacity within the *ālaya-vijñāna* which chiefly generates the sense-cognition of a green appearance into a capacity for apprehending green, by dint of the former capacity of sense-cognition of a green appearance.

/ de ma thag rkyen gyi mtshan ñid sṅar bźin la dper na śes pa sṅa ma'i nus pa'i dbaṅ gis sṅor snaṅ dbaṅ śes myoṅ ba'i ṅo bor gtso bor dṅos su skyed pa śes rgyud kyi steṅ gi nus pa lta bu'o /

3. The immediately-preceding condition (samanantarapratyaya) is defined as previously; for example, by dint of a prior capacity of-cognition, there is a capacity within the cognition-series for chiefly an implicit generation as the form of experience, to wit, the sense-cognition of green appearance.

/ yul rtogs pa'i thabs la / 'gal ba / 'brel pa / dgag pa / sgrub pa / spyi / bye brag / gcig daṅ tha dad / sel 'jug daṅ / sgrub 'jug / mtshan ñid daṅ mtshon bya / rdzas chos daṅ ldog chos / rjes dpag rnam gñis gtan la dbab pa'o /

III. MEANS OF UNDERSTANDING THE OBJECT

As to the means of understanding the sense object (*viṣaya,* yul), one establishes (pairs) as follows:

A' Opposition (*virodha,* 'gal ba)	A" Connection (*sambandha,* 'brel pa)

B'	Exclusion (*pratiṣedha,* dgag pa)	B"	Affirmation (*pratipatti,* sgrub pa)
C'	Generality (*sāmānya,* spyi)	C"	Particularity (*bheda,* bye brag)
D'	Oneness (*ekākībhāva,* gcig)	D"	Multiplicity (*nānātva,* tha dad)
E'	Selective Exclusion (*vyāvṛtti-anuvṛtti,* sel 'jug)	E"	Total Acceptance (*prayoga-pravṛtti,* sgrub 'jug)
F'	Definition (*lakṣaṇa,* mtshan ñid)	F"	Detail (*lakṣman,* mtshon bya)
G'	Feature of a material thing (*dravyadharma,* rdzas chos)	G"	Excluded Feature (*vyāvṛtta-dharma,* ldog chos)
H'	Inference for oneself (*svārthānumāna,* raṅ don rjes dpag)	H"	Inference for others (*parārthānumāna,* gźan don rjes dpag)

/ 'gal ba'i mtshan ñid mi mthun par gnas pa'o / dbye na / lhan cig mi gnas 'gal daṅ / phan tshun spaṅ 'gal / tshad mas gnod 'gal daṅ gsum / rim pa bźin /

A' Opposition

Opposition is defined as contrariety (mi mthun par gnas pa). In variegation there are three kinds: incompatibility-opposition, mutually exclusive opposition, and annulling opposition by authority. In their sequence:

/ phan tshun byed pa 'gal stobs mñam du 'grogs su mi ruṅ ba / dbye na / bem por gyur pa'i lhan cig mi gnas 'gal / śes par gyur pa'i / srog chags su gyur pa'i lhan cig mi gnas 'gal gsum / dpe daṅ po tsha reg daṅ graṅ reg lta bu / snaṅ mun lta bu / gñis pa'i dpe sgra mi rtag rtogs kyi rjes dpag daṅ sgra rtag 'dzin gyi sgro 'dogs kun brtags mṅon gyur lta bu / gsum pa sbrul daṅ ne'u le lta bu /

1. [Incompatibility-opposition (*sahābhava-virodha,* lhan cig mi gnas 'gal)] is the unfeasibility of congregating in equal strength. In variegation, there are three kinds:
    (1) unconscious (bem por gyur pa) incompatibility; for example, heat and cold; light and darkness.
    (2) conscious (śes par gyur pa) incompatibility; for example, the inference that comprehends sound as impermanent (against) the conspicuous imagination with superimposition that grasps sound as permanent.
    (3) incompatibility of living beings (srog chags su gyur pa);

for example, the snake and the mongoose.

/ phan tshun spaṅ 'gal gyi mtshan ñid / chos de las tha dad / khyod kyaṅ yin chos de yin pa'i gźi mthun mi srid pa / dbye na / dṅos 'gal daṅ brgyud 'gal gñis / dañ po'i mtshan ñid / chos de daṅ mi mthun par gnas pa'i gtso bo gaṅ źig / khyod daṅ chos de gaṅ yaṅ ma yin pa'i phuṅ gsum med pa / dper na rtag pa dan mi rtag pa lta bu / brgyud 'gal gyi mtshan ñid / chos de daṅ mi mthun par gnas pa gaṅ źig / chos de rnam par bcad ldog tu nas pa ma yin pa / dper na byas pa daṅ rtag pa lta bu'o /

2. Mutually exclusive opposition (*anyonyaparihāra-virodha,* phan tshun span 'gal) is defined as the difference from that *dharma,* (such that) you exist and that *dharma* exists, but there is no possibility of a common placement (gźi mthun). In variegation, there are two kinds:
    1. Implicit opposition (dṅos 'gal) is defined as any salient contrariety with that *dharma,* (such that) the *dharma* does not exist with you at all, while there is no third possibility (*vinā-rāśi-traya,* phun gsum med pa); for example, permanence and impermanence.
    2. Explicit opposition (brgyud 'gal) is defined as any contrariety with that *dharma* (such that) there does not exist a situation that averts a ruling out of that *dharma*; for example, (the statements) "It is created" and "It is permanent."

/ źar la raṅ bźin gyi 'gal ba'i mtshan ñid / khyad chos de daṅ mi mthun par gnas pa'i gtso bo yin pa / tsha graṅ lta bu/

Along those lines, opposition by individual presence (*svabhāva-virodha*) is defined (such that) your main thing is the contrariety with that *dharma,* like hot and cold.

/ tshad mas gnod 'gal gyi mtshan ñid / gaṅ ruṅ gcig gis cig śos dṅos su 'gog byed sgrub pa'i gcig nas cig śos daṅ mi mthun pa / dper na byas pa daṅ rtag pa lta bu /

3. Annulling opposition by authority (*pramāṇena bādhavirodha,* tshad mas gnod 'gal) is defined as the implicit opposition to any one of two by the other one, (such that) one being proved it is inconsistent with the other one of two; for example, (the statements) "It is created" and "It is permanent."

/ 'brel ba'i mtshan ñid / khyod chos de las tha dad / chos de bkag na khyod khegs pa / dbye na bdag gcig 'brel daṅ de byuṅ 'brel gñis / mtshan ñid rim bźin / chos de'i khyab bya gaṅ źig / chos de las don gźan ma yin pa daṅ yin pa/

A" Connection

Connection is defined as follows: You differ from that *dharma,* (but) if that *dharma* is negated, you have to be (no longer) differentiated. In variegation, there are two kinds:

1. Connection between oneself and the identical (bdag gcig 'brel) is defined as follows: Anything pervaded that belongs to that *dharma* is not a different entity from that *dharma.*
2. Connection arising therefrom (de byuṅ 'brel) is defined as follows: anything pervaded that belongs to that *dharma* is a different entity from that *dharma.*

/ khyab bya'i mtshan ñid / 'brel ba dan gcig / khyab byed kyi mtshan ñid / chos de khyod las tha dad / khyod bkag na chos de khegs pa / khyab mñam gyi mtshan ñid / khyod chos de las tha dad / khyod bkag na yaṅ chos de khegs / chos de bkag na yaṅ khyod khegs pa /

Thing pervaded (*vyāpya,* khyab bya) is defined as identity with the connection.

Pervader (*vyapaka,* khyab byed) is defined as follows: That *dharma* differs from you, (such that) if you are negated, that *dharma* has to be (no longer) differentiated.

Same pervasion (*samavyāpti,* khyab mnam) is defined as follows: You differ from that *dharma* (such that) if you are negated that *dharma* has to be (no longer) differentiated; and if that *dharma* is negated you too have to be (no longer) differentiated.

/ dus mñam gyi mtshan ñid / khyod chos de las tha dad / khyod kyi dus na yaṅ chos de grub / chos de'i dus na yaṅ khyod grub pa /

Same time (*samakāla,* dus mñam) is defined as follows: You differ from that *dharma,* (such that) at the time you exist that *dharma* exists, and at the time that *dharma* exists you exist.

/ dgag pa'i mtshan ñid / chos gan zig / khyod kyi don spyi 'char ba / khyod kyi dgag bya'i don spyi 'char ba la bltos pa / sgrub pa'i mtshan ñid / chos gaṅ źig / khyod kyi don spyi 'char ba khyod kyi dgag bya'i don spyi 'char ba la mi bltos pa / dper na / bum pa lta bu /

B' Exclusion and B" Affirmation

Exclusion is defined as follows: Any *dharma* (such that) when your objectivity-generality (don spyi) arises, it should depend on the arising of your excludable objectivity-generality.

Affirmation is defined as follows: Any *dharma* (such that) when your objectivity-generality arises, it should not depend on the arising of your excludable objetivity-generality; for example, like a pot.

/ dgag pa la dbye na / med dgag daṅ ma yin dgag gñis /

In variegation of exclusion, there are two kinds: entailed exclusion (*prasajya-pariṣedha,* med par dgag pa) and implicative exclusion (*paryudāsa,* ma yin par dgag pa).

/ med dgag gi mtshan ñid / dgag pa gaṅ źig / raṅ brjod pa'i sgras raṅ gi dgag bya bkag śul du chos gźan mi 'phen pa/dper na bum med lta bu'o/

1. Entailed exclusion is defined as any exclusion that denies what is excluded by it, through its own proposition, without implicating another *dharma*; for example "It is not a jar."

ma yin dgag gi mtshan ñid/dgag pa gaṅ źig/raṅ brjod pa'i sgras raṅ gi dgag bya bkag śul du chos gźan 'phen pa / dbye na / chos gźan śugs la 'phen pa'i ma yin dgag / chos gźan dṅos su 'phen pa'i ma yin dgag / dṅos śugs gñis ka la 'phen pa'i ma yin dgag / chos gźan skabs stobs kyis 'phen pa'i ma yin dgag daṅ bźi / dpe rim bźin/ lha sbyin tshon po ñin par zan mi za ba lta bu/bum med yod pa lta bu/lha sbyin tshon po ñin par zab mi za ba riṅ pa ma yin pa yod pa daṅ / 'di bram gdol gaṅ yin dris pa na bram ze ma yin źes brjod pa'i tshe 'di bram ze ma yin pa lta bu'o /

2. Implicative exclusion is defined as any exclusion that denies what is excluded by it, through its own proposition, but does implicate another *dharma*. In variegation, there are four kinds:
   (1) implicative exclusion that implicates another activity of a *dharma*; for example, "Fat Devadatta does not eat food during the daytime" [implicating an eating activity at night].
   (2) implicative exclusion that implicates another substance; for example, "The absent pot exists" [implicating a pot substance somewhere else].
   (3) implicative exclusion that implicates both substance and activity; for example, "The food which fat Devadatta does not eat during the daytime is not spoiled" [implicating both the nighttime eating and other food that is spoiled].
   (4) implicative exclusion implicating another *dharma* by force of circumstances; for example, when the question is asked, "Is he a brahmin or an outcaste?" and the answer at this time is "He is not a brahmin," then his not being

a brahmin [implicates his being an outcaste].

/ spyi'i mtshan ñid / du ma la rjes 'gro byed pa / bye brag gi mtshan ñid / khyod chos de yin / chos de la bdag gcig tu 'brel / khyod ma yin źiṅ chos de yin pa du ma grub pa /

A generality is defined as what creates a necessary association (*anvaya*) for many. Particularity is defined as follows: You are that feature (*dharma*). You are connected to it as an identical nature. If you were not, that *dharma* would (still) be; and many (particulars) exist.

/ spyi la dbye na / rig spyi / tshogs spyi / don spyi / sgra spyi daṅ bźi'o /

In variegation of generality, there are four kinds: genus (*jāti*) generality (rigs spyi), group (*sāmagrī*) generality (tshogs spyi), objectivity (*artha*) generality (don spyi) and speech (*śabda*) generality (sgra spyi).

/ chos de'i rigs spyi'i mtshan ñid / chos de khyod yin / de khyod daṅ bdag gcig tu 'brel / de ma yin źiṅ khyod yin pa du ma grub pa / dper na gser bum la bltos te bum pa lta bu /

1. Genus generality for a feature (*dharma*) is defined as follows: That feature is you. That feature is connected to you as an identical nature. There are many kinds of you besides that feature; for example, a pot vis-à-vis a golden pot.

/ tshogs spyi'i mtshan ñid / ya gyal du ma tshogs pa / dper na nags sam / bum pa lta bu /

2. Group generality is defined as a collection of many members; for example, a forest or a pot.

/ chos de'i don spyi'i mtshan ñid / rtog pa la chos de'i don du snaṅ ba gaṅ źig / dṅos po ma yin pa / dbye na / dṅos po dṅos med gñis ka la brten pa'i sgra don gsum / dpe rim bźin rtog pa la lta ldiṅ źabs źum du snaṅ ba lta bu daṅ / rtog pa la nam mkhar snaṅ ba lta bu daṅ / rtog pa la śes byar snaṅ ba lta bu'o /

3. Objectivity generality of a feature is defined as any appearance to reflection (or, constructive thought) as the objectivity of the feature (such that) it is not an individual character (= *svalakṣaṇa*). In variegation there are three kinds:
   (1) objectivity of words based on an individual object; for example, appearance in reflection of the words "pot with a large bulb becoming slender at the bottom".
   (2) objectivity of words based on a non-individual object; for example, appearance in reflection of the word "sky".
   (3) objectivity of words based on both; for example, appear-

ance in reflection of the words "It is knowable".

/ sgra spyi'i mtshan ñid rtog pa la miṅ du snaṅ ba gaṅ źig / dṅos po ma yin pa / dper na / rtog pa la bum pa źes pa'i sgrar snaṅ ba lta bu'o /

4. Speech generality is defined as any appearance in constructive thought of a name (such that) it is not an individual character (= *svalaksana*); for example, the appearance of the word "pot" in constructive thought.

/ spyi bye brag la bltos pa'i tshig rkyaṅ daṅ / gñis tshogs bźag pa'i dgag sgrub gźan du 'chad do /

In regard to generality and particularity, the denying or the proving (of them) when taken as separate terms or when lumping the two together, are explained elsewhere.

/ gcig gi mtshan ñid / chos gan źig / rtog pa la tha dad du mi 'char ba / du ma'i mtshan ñid / chos gaṅ źig / rtog pa la tha dad du 'char ba /

D' Oneness and D" Multiplicity

Oneness is defined as any *dharma* that does not arise in constructive thought (*kalpanā*) as multiple.

Multiplicity is defined as any *dharma* that arises in constructive thought as multiple.

/ gcig la dbye na / rdzas gcig daṅ ldog pa gcig / rdzas gcig gi mtshan ñid / mṅon sum la snaṅ ba gaṅ źig / tha dad du mi snaṅ ba / dper na byas mi rtag lta bu / rdzas gcig la gcig gis ma khyab bo / ldog pa gcig ni bum pa daṅ bum pa lta bu /

If one variegates the oneness, there are two kinds:

1. Substantially one (rdzas gcig) is defined as something appearing to direct perception (such that) it does not appear different; for example, created and impermanent. 'One' has a larger scope than 'substantially one'.
2. Exclusively one (ldog pa gcig) is like a pot, a pot.

/ tha dad kyi mtshan ñid / gźi grub chos de daṅ dṅos miṅ tha dad du go bya / dbye na / rdzas tha dad / ldog pa tha dad gñis / rdzas tha dad kyi mtshan ñid / mnon sum la tha dad du snaṅ ba / dper na / ka bum lta bu / ldog pa tha dad ni byas mi rtag lta bu /

Difference is defined as the difference to be understood between the name of an entity and the feature which 'proves' the basis. In variegation there are two kinds:

1. Substantially different (rdzas tha dad) is defined as the appearance of difference to direct perception; for example, a pillar

and a pot.

2. exclusively different (ldog pa tha dad); for example, created and impermanent.

E' Selective Exclusion and E" Total Acceptance

/ sel 'jug gi mtshan ñid / chos de'i yul can gaṅ źig / chos de daṅ yin khyab mñam pa'i chos kun yod kyaṅ khyod kyis yul du mi byed pa / dbye na / sel 'jug phyin ci log ma log gñis / dpe rim bźin / sgra rtag 'dzin gyi rtog pa lta bu daṅ / sgra mi rtag par rtogs pa'i blo lta bu'o / yaṅ na / sel 'jug la rjod byed kyi sgra daṅ / rtog pa daṅ / rtags rnams su yod do /

Selective Exclusion is defined as any subject (*viṣayin*) of that *dharma* (such that) there exist all the *dharmas* that are equivalent to that *dharma*, but you (as the subject) do not necessarily make them your objects (*viṣaya*). In variegation, there are two kinds:

1. wrong Selective Exclusion; for example, constructive thought which posits sound as impermanent.
2. right Selective Exclusion; for example, cognition which understands sound to be impermanent.

Moreover, Selective Exclusion exists in the words of a referral (rjod byed), in constructive thought (rtog pa), and in the evidences (rtags) (i.e. of the three modes).

/ sgrub 'jug gi mtshan ñid / chos de'i yul can gaṅ źig / chos de daṅ yin khyab mñam pa'i chos kun yod na / khyod kyis yul du byed pa / dbye na / sgrub 'jug 'khrul śes daṅ / ma 'khrul pa'i śes pa gñis / dper na zla ba gñis snaṅ gi dbaṅ śes lta bu daṅ / sṅar bśad pa'i mṅon sum thams cad do /

Total Acceptance is defined as any subject of a *dharma* (such that) there exist all the *dharmas* that are equivalent to that *dharma*, and you (as subject) make them your objects (*viṣaya*). In variegation of Total Acceptance, there are two kinds:

1. delusive cognition; for example, sense cognition of a double-moon appearance.
2. non-delusive cognition; for example, all the previously mentioned direct perceptions.

/ yaṅ na de gñis kyi mtshan ñid / cha śas su phye nas yul du byed pa daṅ cha śas su phye nas yul du mi byed pa źes ruṅ ṅo /

Or, feasible definitions for those two are (for selective exclusion) to not take the whole thing as the sense object, after analysis into parts; and (for total acceptance) to accept the whole of the sense object, after analysis into parts.

/ gźan sel gyi mtshan ñid / raṅ gi bsal bya tshig gis zin par bcad nas rtogs par bya ba'i chos / dbye na / gñis las / med dgag gi sel ba ni / bum min gyi steṅ du bum pas dben pa lta bu / ma yin dgag gi gźan sel la dbye na / don gyi gźan sel daṅ / blo'i gźan sel gñis / daṅ po ni / bum pa yin pa las log pa lta bu / gñis pa ni / rtog pa la bum ma yin las log par snaṅ ba lta bu /

Exclusion of the Other (*anyāpoha,* gźan sel) is defined as a *dharma* to be comprehended by exhaustively cutting away by word what by itself is rejected. In variegation there are two kinds:

1. exclusion in terms of entailed exclusion (*prasajya-pariṣedha*); for example, in the state of non-pot, there is seclusion from pots.
2. exclusion in terms of implicative exclusion (*paryudāsa*), variegated into two kinds:
   (1) exclusion in terms of 'object-entity'; for example, when a pot exists, what diverges from it.
   (2) exclusion in terms of 'cognition'; for example, when a pot does not exist in constructive thought, what appears to diverge from it.

F' Definition and F" Distinct Detail

/ mtshan ñid kyi mtshan ñid / don chos gsum tshaṅ ba / mtshan ñid ma yin pa'i mtshan ñid / don chos gsum ma tshaṅ ba /

A definition (*lakṣaṇa,* mtshan ñid) is defined as being complete with three objective features (don chos). A non-definition is defined as being not complete with three objective features.

/ mtshon bya'i mtshan ñid / tha sñad chos gsum tshaṅ ba /

mtshon bya ma yin pa'i mtshan ñid / tha sñad chos gsum ma tshaṅ ba /

The distinct detail (*lakṣman,* mtshon bya) is defined as being complete with three features of conventional expression (tha sñad chos). The indistinct (or unfocussed) is defined as being not complete with three features of conventional expression.

/ yaṅ na / mtshan ñid daṅ / mtshon bya'i mtshan ñid / rdzas yod chos gsum tshaṅ ba daṅ / 'jog byed chos gsum tshaṅ ba źes daṅ / rtags yod chos gsum tshaṅ ba daṅ / gźag bya chos gsum tshaṅ ba / źes kyaṅ ruṅ ṅo /

Moreover, (both) the definition and the distinct detail are defined as complete with the three material features (rdzas yod chos) and with the three fixing features ('jog byed chos); and as feasible, complete with the three evidential features (rtags yod chos) and with the three features to be established (gźag bya).[13]

/ mtshan gźi'i mtshan ñid / mtshan ñid kyis mtshon bya mtshon pa'i gźir gyur ba /

A definable *(lakṣya,* mtshan gźi) is defined as a span (**tala,* gźi) with distinct detail (*lakṣman,* mtshon bya) and with relevance (*lakṣaṇā,* mtshon pa) for the definition (*lakṣaṇa,* mtshan ñid).[14]

/ mtshan ñid kyi skyon la dbye na / ma khyab pa'i mtshan ñid kyi skyon / khyab ches pa'i mtshan ñid kyi skyon / mtshan gźi la mi gnas pa'i mtshan ñid kyi skyon daṅ gsum / dpe rim bźin / ba laṅ gi mtshan ñid du nog sogs 'dus pa khra bo bkod pa'i tshe / nog sogs 'dus pa khra bos ba laṅ la ma khyab pa lta bu daṅ / ba laṅ gi mtshan ñid du mgo ldan bkod pa'i tshe mgo ldan gyis ba laṅ la khyab ches pa lta bu daṅ / rta ba laṅ du mtshon pa la nog sogs 'dus pa bkod pa'i tshe / nog sogs 'dus pa rta la mi gnas pa lta bu'o /

In variegation of the faults (*doṣa*) of definition, there are three kinds:

1. The fault of non-pervasion definition is defined by example: At the time of formulating a dappled assemblage of humped back, etc. among the cow's characteristics, the cow is not pervaded by the dappled assemblage of humped back, etc.
2. The fault of over-pervasion definition is defined by example: At the time of formulating that possession of a head is in the cow's characteristics, the cow is over-pervaded by head-possession.
3. The fault of no locus (i.e. impossibility) in the definable is defined by example: At the time of formulating the assemblage of humped back, etc. in clear view of a horse and a cow, the assemblage of humped back is impossible in the horse.

/ yaṅ na / mtshan ñid ltar snaṅ la dbye na / raṅ ldog rdzas ma grub / don ldog gźan 'gyur / mtshan ñid mtshan gźi la mi gnas pa'i mtshan ñid ltar snaṅ daṅ gsum / dpe rim bźin / ba laṅ gi mtshan ñid du ba laṅ bkod pa lta bu daṅ / rta'i mtshan ñid du nog sogs 'dus pa bkod pa lta bu'o /

13. The present writer expects to explain these triads in an essay in Vol. Two.

14. The Sanskrit equivalents for the main Sanskrit terms are due especially to the Mahāyāna treatise *Sūtrālaṃkāra* (ed. by Sylvain Lévi), XI, 36, where the term *lakṣya* is rendered by Tib. *mtshan gźi; lakṣaṇa* by *mtshan ñid;* and *lakṣaṇā* by *mtshon pa.* Then the Lokesh Chandra Tibetan-Sanskrit Dictionary for Tib. *mtshon bya* gives Sanskrit *lakṣman.* Hence, the above solution.

Moreover, in variegation of fallacies (*ābhāsa*) of definition there are three kinds:

1. A substance fails to exclude itself; for example, use of the word 'cow' in the definition of 'cow'.
2. A divergence excludes the entity; for example, ...[15]
3. The definition and the definable do not share a locus; for example, the words "assemblage of humped back, etc." in the characteristics of a horse.

/ mtshon bya ltar snaṅ la dbye na / raṅ ldog tha sñad du ma grub pa / tha sñad gźan 'gyur / tha sñad mtshan gźi la mi gnas pa daṅ gsum /

In variegation of the fallacies of the distinct detail, there are three fallacies:

1. The exclusion of itself has failed in the conventional language.
2. There is a divergence of the conventional language.
3. The conventional term is not found in the definable.

/ mtshan ñid ltar snaṅ la / mtshan ñid mi rten pa daṅ / mtshon bya mi rten pa gñis te / mdor na ltar snaṅ brgyad po re re la gñis te sum cu rtsa gñis su bśad kyaṅ 'gal ba cher med do /

Among the fallacies of the definition, there are the two: nonbasis of definition and nonbasis of distinct detail. In short, each of the eight fallacies (3 + 3 + 2) is multiplied two by two to make thirty-two, and there is not much dispute about this.

/ rdzas kyi mtshan ñid skyes bu'i dgos don sgrub nus gzugs lta bu / rdzas chos kyi mtshan ñid rdzas kyi bdag ñid du gyur pa'i gzugs kyi yon tan / gzugs kyi mi rtag pa lta bu /

G' Feature of a Material Thing

A material thing is defined as being capable of accomplishing human aims; for example, material form (*rūpa*).

A feature of a material thing is defined as a virtuality (*guṇa*) of the formation that identifies the material thing; for example, impermanence of the formation.

/ ldog pa'i mtshan ñid / rtog pa la rigs mi mthun las log par snaṅ ba'i chos gaṅ źig / dṅos po ma yin pa / rtog pa la gzugs su snaṅ ba lta bu /

---

15. The example is missing in the Sarnath edn. It also is missing in Tsoṅ-kha-pa's collected works, Tashilunpo edn., Vol. Tsha, signal Mun sel, fol. 12b-3, 4.

G" Excluded Feature

The definition of 'exclusion' is any feature (*dharma*) which in constructive thought (*kalpanā*) appears to exclude the incompatible genus. It is not an individual thing (= *svalakṣaṇa*); for example, an appearance in constructive thought as a formation.

/ ldog chos kyi mtshan ñid / rtog pa la rdzas kyi yon tan du snaṅ ba'i chos gaṅ źig dṅos po ma yin pa / rtog pa la gzugs mi rtag par snaṅ ba lta bu /

An excluded feature is defined as any feature that appears in constructive thought as a material quality (**vāstava-guṇa*). It is not a discrete entity (**bhāva*). For example, an appearance in constructive thought that a formation is impermanent.

/ rdzas ldog gi bśad pa ni rje btsun red mda'-pa'i bźed par snaṅ ṅo /

The foregoing explanation of the material thing and exclusion is approximately the venerable Red-mda'-pa's idea.

/ deṅ saṅ grags tshod la rdzas ldog gi mtshan nid rim bzin / khyod gzi grub / khyod khyod raṅ yin / khyod ma yin de khyod ma yin pa / khyod gźi grub / khyod khyod raṅ ma yin pa 'am / khyod ma yin de khyod yin pa gaṅ ruṅ yin pa / daṅ po gzugs lta bu / ldog chos la dbye na / gñis las / raṅ ma yin gyi ldog chos kyi mtshan ñid / khyod gźi grub / khyod khyod ran ma yin pa / mtshan ñid lta bu / raṅ yin gyi ldog chos kyi mtshan ñid / khyod gźi grub/ khyod khyod raṅ yin khyod ma yin de khyod yin pa/ mtshon bya lta bu'o / raṅ yin daṅ raṅ ma yin daṅ raṅ yin sogs śin tu khas len dgos śin / 'di dag la rdzas ldog gi tha sñad du bźag pa la yid brtan mi snaṅ ṅo /

Nowadays what appears commonly for (defining) a material thing and exclusion is this: You exist; you are you; non-you is not you; for example, like a formation. (for exclusion:) You exist; either you are not you, or non-you is you. Excluded feature is of two kinds:

1. The excluded feature of not being you is defined as: You exist; you are not you, like the definition.
2. The excluded feature of being self is defined as: You exist; you are you; not you is you, like the distinct detail. (According to that) one must certainly accept that itself exists; itself does not exist; (and) itself exists. About these matters, there is much verbiage relating to a material thing and exclusion, but not trustworthy.

/ raṅ don rjes dpag gtan la dbab pa la / rtags yaṅ dag gi mtshan ñid / tshul gsum tshaṅ ba /

H' Inference for Oneself (*svārthānumāna*)

For establishing the 'inference for oneself,' genuine evidence (*liṅga*) is defined as the complete three modes (*trirūpa*).

/ tshul gsum po gan źe na / phyogs chos kyi mtshan ñid / rtags de sgrub kyi śes 'dod chos can gyi steṅ du 'god tshul daṅ mthun par tshad mas ṅes pa'i tshul / rjes khyab kyi mtshan ñid / rtags de sgrub kyi sgrub tshul ltar mthun phyogs kho na la yod par ṅes pa'i tshul / ldog khyab kyi mtshan ñid / rtags de sgrub kyi sgrub tshul ltar mi mthun phyogs la med pa kho nar ṅes pa'i tshul /

What are the three modes? (As follows:)

1. The *pakṣadharma* (the locus-feature) is defined as the evidence (*liṅga*) that is the method of certainty by an authority consistent with the method of disposing upon the factual base when one desires to know (*jijñāsita*) the proof.
2. The *anvaya-vyāpti* (the inclusive pervasion) is defined as the evidence that is the means of certainty affirming just the similar locus (*sapakṣa*) according to the method of processing the proof.
3. The *vyatireka-vyāpti* (the exclusive pervasion) is defined as the evidence that is the means of certainty denying just the nonsimilar locus (*asapakṣa*) according to the method of processing the proof.

/ yaṅ na rtags yaṅ dag gi mtshan ñid / bsgrub bya raṅ ñid kyis tshad mas ma grub pa'i gaṅ zag gis tshul gsum tshad mas grub pa'i rtags / de'i phyogs chos kyi mtshan ñid / bsgrub bya la raṅ ñid kyi tshad mas grub bsal gaṅ yaṅ ma źugs pa'i gaṅ zag gis rtags de sgrub kyi śes 'dod chos can gyi steṅ du tha dad pa'i tshul gis 'dod tshul daṅ mthun par tshad mas grub pa'i tshul /

Moreover, genuine evidence is defined as the evidence by which a person proves with authority of the three modes (or, means), having himself/herself not already proven with authority (the thesis (*sādhya*, bsgrub bya). Its locus-feature (*pakṣadharma*) is defined as the evidence, by a person who refrains from any rejection (*pratyākhyeya*) of the thesis (*sādhya*); and who desires to know the proof, where the means of proof is by an authority consistent with the desired means, to wit, by a different means upon the factual base (*dharmin*).

/ phyogs chos can du soṅ ba'i gaṅ zag gis grub pa'i rjes khyab kyi mtshan ñid / phyogs chos can du soṅ ba'i gaṅ zag gis rtags de sgrub kyi sgrub tshul ltar mthun phyogs kho na la yod par ṅes pa'i tshul /

The inclusive pervasion (*anvaya-vyāpti*) of proof by a person who resorts to the locus factual base (*pakṣadharmin*) is defined as the evidence, by this person who resorts to the locus factual base, when there is the means of certainty present only in the similar locus (*sapakṣa*) according to the means of processing the proof.

/ des grub pa'i ldog khyab kyi mtshan ñid / phyogs chos can du soṅ ba'i gaṅ zag gis rtags de sgrub kyi mi mthun phyogs la med pa kho nar ṅes pa'i tshul /

The exclusive pervasion (*vyatireka-vyāpti*) for proof by that one, is defined as the evidence by the person resorting to the locus factual base, when there is the means of certainty which avoids precisely the dissimilar locus (*asapakṣa*) for the proof.

/ des na / rjes ldog gi mtshan ñid goṅ ma gñis rtags kyi rjes ldog tsam gyi mtshan ñid yin no /

Hence, the two foregoing definitions of *anvaya* and *vyatireka* are definitions of just the *anvaya* or *vyatireka* belonging to the evidence.

/ śes 'dod chos can nam / bsgrub bya'i chos can gyi mtshan ñid / de sgrub kyi phyogs btags pa ba gaṅ źig / de sgrub kyi bsgrub bya'i chos kyi dpag gźir gzuṅ ba / sgra lta bu /

The factual base (*dharmin*) which one desires to cognize, also (called) the factual base of the thesis (*sādhya-dharmin*), is defined as any metaphorical transfer of the 'locus of proof' (*sādhana-pakṣa*) which takes as basis the inferring of the thesis feature (*sādhya-dharma*) of that proof; for example, 'sound'.

/ bsgrub bya'i chos kyi mtshan ñid / de sgrub kyi phyogs btags pa ba gaṅ źig / de sgrub kyi bsgrub bya'i chos can gyi steṅ du rtags kyis dpag par bya ba / mi rtag pa lta bu /

The thesis feature (*sadhya-dharma*) is defined as any metaphorical transfer of the 'locus of proof' that is to be inferred by evidence (centered) upon the thesis factual base (*sadhya-dharmin*) for that proof; for example, 'impermanence'.

/ mthun phyogs kyi mtshan ñid / sgrub tshul ltar bsgrub bya'i chos kyis mi ston ba / bum pa lta bu'o /

The similar locus (*sapakṣa*) is defined as one not void of the thesis feature (*sadhyadharma*) according to the means of proof; for example, 'a pot'.

/ mi mthun phyogs kyi mtshan ñid / de go ldog / dbye na / gźan pa / 'gal ba / med pa mi mthun phyogs daṅ gsum mo / dpe rim bźin / sgra mi rtag par sgrub pa la ses bya lta bu daṅ rtag pa lta bu daṅ / ri boṅ gi ra lta bu'o /

The dissimilar locus (*asapakṣa*) is defined as the exclusion of a referent (*tadgamakavyavrtti*). In variegation there are three dissimilar locuses.

1. 'other than that' (*tato 'nyaḥ*); for example, the proof that sound is impermanent as the knowable.
2. 'contrary to that' (*tad-viruddhaḥ*); for example, permanence.
3. 'absence of that' (*tad-abhāvaḥ*); for example, horn of a rabbit.

/ rtags yaṅ dag la graṅs ṅes kyi sgo nas dbye na / 'bras raṅ ma dmigs pa'i rtags gsum / 'bras bu'i rtags yaṅ dag gi mtshan ñid / tshul gsum tshaṅ ba'i gtan tshigs gaṅ źig / raṅ las rdzas tha dad du gyur ba'i bsgrub bya'i chos daṅ de byuṅ du 'brel ba / raṅ bźin gyi rtags yaṅ dag gi mtshan ñid / sgrub rtags yaṅ dag gaṅ źig / de sgrub kyi bsgrub bya'i chos yin na khyod kyi bdag gcig pa'i khyab byed yin pa / ma dmigs pa'i rtags yaṅ dag gi mtshan ñid / tshul gsum tshaṅ ba'i rtags yaṅ dag gaṅ źig / de sgrub kyi dṅos kyi bsgrub bya'i chos yin na / dgag pa yin pa /

Variegating the number certainty for the genuine evidence, there are three kinds of evidence, namely result (*kārya*), individual-presence (*svabhāva*), and non-apprehension (*anupalabdhi*).

1. Genuine evidence of result is defined as any reason (*hetu*) with complete three modes (such that) there should be a thesis feature (*sādhyadharma*) which is a different substance from itself, and a connection arising therefrom.
2. Genuine evidence of individual-presence is defined as any genuine evidence for the proof (such that) if there is a thesis feature of that proof, it must be a pervader identical with you (= the individual).
3. Genuine evidence of nonapprehension is defined as any genuine evidence with complete three modes (such that) if there is an obvious thesis feature of that proof, it should be an exclusion (*pratiṣedha*).

/ 'bras rtags la dbye na / rgyu chos sgrub / rgyu dṅos sgrub / rgyu sṅon soṅ sgrub / rgyu'i khyad par sgrub / rgyu'i spyi sgrub pa'i 'bras rtags daṅ lṅa / daṅ po'i mtshan ñid / de sgrub kyi 'bras rtags gaṅ źig / khyod kyi dus na de sgrub kyi bsgrub bya'i chos de grub pas khyab pa / dper na kha naṅ bu ram goṅ bu'i steṅ du bu ram gyi gzugs da ltar ba yod par sgrub pa la bu ram gyi ro da ltar ba rtags su bkod pa lta bu'o / gñis pa'i mtshan ñid / tshul gsum tshaṅ ba'i gtan tshigs yaṅ dag gaṅ źig / raṅ la rdzas tha dad du gyur ba'i de sgrub kyi bsgrub bya'i chos kyi 'bras bu yin pa/dper na du ldan la me yod du sgrub pa la / du ba rtags su bkod pa lta bu'o / phyi ma gsum po dpe rim bźin rig byed kyi sgra 'dzin ñan śes raṅ rgyu sgra mi rtag pa sṅon du soṅ sgrub pa la rtsol byuṅ ñan śes rtags su bkod pa lta bu'o / gzugs 'dzin dbaṅ śes la dbaṅ yid las gźan pa'i rgyu yod par sgrub pa la dbaṅ yid las gźan pa'i rgyu med na mi skye ba'i d'ṅos po rtags su bkod pa lta bu'o/sdug bden raṅ rgyu yod par sgrub pa la res 'ga' 'byuṅ ba bkod pa lta bu'o/

In variegation of 'result' evidence, there are five result-evidences, namely, 1. proving a feature of a cause (*hetu*), 2. proving the actual cause, 3. proving that the cause precedes, 4. proving a different kind of cause, 5. proving the generality (*sāmānya*) of the cause.

1. The first one (i.e. proving a feature of a cause) is defined as any result evidence of that proof (such that) at your time (of evidence) the thesis feature of that proof must exist. For example, one proves that now there is the form of molasses on a pile of molasses in a vessel, and uses as reason that now there is the flavor of molasses.
2. The second one (i.e. proving the actual cause) is defined as any genuine reason complete with the three modes (such that) it is the result of the thesis feature of the proof which is a different substance than itself. For example, one proves that on a place having smoke, there is fire; and uses as a reason that there is smoke (at that place).
3. (Proving that the cause precedes); for example, one proves that when there is auditory cognition grasping sound that informs, it was preceded by its own cause, the impermanent sound; and uses as a reason that auditory cognition arises from the effort (of paying attention).
4. (Proving a different kind of cause); for example, one proves that when sense cognition grasps form there is a cause different from the mind organ; and uses as a reason that if there were no cause different from the mind organ, the given thing would not arise (in cognition).
5. (Proving the generality); for example, one proves that there is an own-cause for the Truth of Suffering; and uses as a reason the occasionality (*kādācitkatva*).

/ raṅ bźin gyi rtags yaṅ dag la gñis las / khyad par dag pa ba'i raṅ bźin gyi rtags yaṅ dag gi mtshan ñid / raṅ bźin kyi rtags yaṅ dag gaṅ źig / khyod ces brjod pa'i sgras khyod kyi ldog pa byed chos ma 'phaṅs pa /dper na sgra mi rtag sgrub la dṅos po bkod pa lta bu / khyad par ltos pa ba'i ran bźin gyi rtags yaṅ dag gi mtshan ñid / gaṅ źig / khyod ces brjod pa'i sgras khyod kyi ltos pa byed chos 'phaṅs pa / dbye na / tha mi dad bltos pa ba daṅ / tha dad bltos pa'i raṅ bźin gyi rtags gñis / daṅ po ni / sgra mi rtag sgrub la skye ldan rtags su bkod pa lta bu'o / gñis pa la / bltos pa dṅos su 'phaṅs pa daṅ/ śugs la 'phaṅs pa'i raṅ bźin gyi rtags gñis / dpe rim bźin / sgra mi rtag sgrub la rgyu rkyen las skyes pa rtags su bkod pa lta bu daṅ / byas pa rtags su bkod pa lta bu'o /

Genuine evidence of individual-presence (*svabhāva*) is twofold:

1. The genuine evidence of individual-presence independent of distinctions is defined as any genuine evidence of individual-presence (such that) the speech referral "You" does not implicate a *dharma* that excludes you; for example, while proving sound to be impermanent, one uses as a reason that it (i.e. sound) is a particular thing.
2. The genuine evidence of individual-presence involved with distinctions is defined as any one (such that) the speech referral "You" implicates a dharma (feature) that constitutes a relation of yours. In variegation there are two kinds:
   (1) individual-presence evidence related without differentiation; for example, while proving that sound is impermanent, one uses as a reason that it (i. e. sound) possesses arising.
   (2) individual-presence evidence related with differentiation. There are two kinds:
      a. one that implicates relation directly; for example, while proving that sound is impermanent, one uses as a reason that it arises through cause and conditions.
      b. one that implicates indirectly; for example, (while proving that sound is impermanent) one uses as a reason that it has been created.

/ ma dmigs pa'i rtags yaṅ dag la gñis / mi snaṅ ba ma dmigs pa'i rtags yaṅ dag gi mtshan ñid / de sgrub kyi dgag bya'i chos kyi yul de yod kyaṅ / de phyogs chos gyi gaṅ zag la bltar mi ruṅ ba / dper na mdun gyi gźi 'dir śa za bskal don du soṅ ba'i skyes bus śa za yod ṅes kyi tha sñad don mthun mi 'jug par sgrub pa la śa za bskal don du soṅ ba'i gaṅ zag gis śa za ma dmigs pa bkod pa lta bu / snaṅ ruṅ ma dmigs pa'i rtags yaṅ dag gi mtshan ñid / gaṅ źig / de sgrub kyi dgag bya'i chos kyi yul de yod na de sgrub kyi phyogs chos can gyi gaṅ zag la bltar ruṅ ba / dbye na gñis las /

Genuine evidence of nonapprehension (*anupalabdhi*) has two kinds:

1. Genuine evidence of nonapprehension of what does not appear is defined as follows: While there is the object (*viṣaya*) consisting of the excludable feature (*dharma*) being proved, and there is a locus factual base (*pakṣadharmin*), it (the excludable feature) is not visible to a person. For example, a person refers to an entity inaccessible for seeking, namely, a demon at this spot in front. To prove that one does not encounter an existing demon, consistent with conventional language of certitude, the person who refers to the entity inaccessible for seeking uses as a reason that there is no apprehension of an inaccessible demon.
2. Genuine evidence of nonapprehension of what may feasibly appear is defined as any (evidence such that) if there exists a sense object amounting to the excludable feature of the proof, it should be visible to that person; and the locus feature (*pakṣadharma*) should be visible to that person. In variegation, there are two kinds.

/ 'brel yul ma dmigs pa'i rtags yaṅ dag gi mtshan ñid / ma dmigs pa'i rtags yaṅ dag gaṅ źig / med dgag yin pa / 'gal zla dmigs pa'i rtags yaṅ dag gi mtshan ñid / gaṅ źig / ma yin dgag gam sgrub pa gaṅ ruṅ yin pa / 'brel yul ma dmigs pa'i rtags yaṅ dag la dbye na / rgyu ma dmigs / khyab byed ma dmigs / raṅ bźin / dṅos 'bras ma dmigs pa'i rtags daṅ bźi /

(1) Genuine evidence of nonapprehension that there is a sense object as connection ('brel yul) is defined as any genuine evidence of nonapprehension (such that) it is an entailed exclusion (*prasajya-pratiṣedha*).

(2) Genuine evidence of adversary apprehension ('gal zla dmigs) is defined as any one (such that) it is either an implicative exclusion (*paryudāsa*), or an affirmation, as the case may be. [For variegation of (2), see below].

In variegation of (1), genuine evidence of nonapprehension of a sense object as a connection, there are four kinds, nonapprehension of a cause (*hetu*), of a pervader (*vyāpaka*), of individual-presence (*svabhāva*), and of on-going result (*kārya*).

/ rgyu ma dmigs pa'i rtags yaṅ dag gi mtshan ñid / 'brel yul ma dmigs pa'i rtags yaṅ dag gaṅ źig / de sgrub kyi dgag bya'i chos su gyur pa'i dṅos po yin na / de las rdzas tha dad du gyur pa'i khyod kyi dṅos kyi log phyogs la de byuṅ du 'brel źiṅ de'i rgyu yin pa / dper na / sṅo 'phyur ba daṅ ldan pa'i me med kyi mtshan mo'i rgya mtsho du med du sgrub pa la me med bkod pa lta bu /

a. Genuine evidence of nonapprehension of a [material] cause is defined as any genuine evidence of nonapprehension of a sense object as the connection (such that) if there is an entity being the excludable feature of that proof, it should be connected as arising from it as the [material] cause to your [= the evidence's] direct opposite, which is a different substance. For example, proving that since there is no fire possessing a rising greenish mist, it (a fire) is not on the ocean at night; and one uses as the reason that there is no smoke because there is no fire.

/ khyab byed ma dmigs pa'i rtags yaṅ dag gi mtshan ñid / gaṅ źig de sgrub kyi dgag bya'i chos de yin na / de khyod kyi dṅos kyi ldog chos gaṅ yin la bdag gcig tu 'brel ba / dper na / śiṅ med kyi brag rdzoṅ na śa pa med par sgrub pa la śiṅ med bkod pa lta bu'o /

b. Genuine evidence of nonapprehension of a pervader is defined as any excludable feature of the proof (such that) it should be connected in an identical way to the direct opposite of that proof. For example, when proving that on a rocky crag devoid of trees there is no Śiṃśapa tree, one uses as a reason that there are no trees (there).

/ raṅ bźin ma dmigs pa'i rtags yaṅ dag gi mtshan ñid / tha sñad 'ba' źig sgrub kyi ma dmigs pa'i rtags yaṅ dag gaṅ źig / khyod kyi dṅos kyi ldog phyogs yin na / de sgrub kyi dgag bya'i chos kyi raṅ bźin yin pa / dper na / lto ldir źabs źum gyis dag pa'i sa phyogs na bum pa med par sgrub pa la lto ldir źabs źum snaṅ ruṅ ma dmigs pa lta bu /

c. Genuine evidence of nonapprehension of individual-presence is defined as any genuine evidence of nonapprehensi[illegible] being proved with just conventional language (such tha[illegible] there is the direct divergent locus (*pakṣa*) of you (the proo[illegible]), it should be of identical nature with the excludable feature of that proof. For example, when proving that there is no pot on a spot bare of a pot with a large bulb becoming slender at the bottom, there is nonapprehension of the pot with large bulb becoming slender at the bottom, which, if it were there, would be visible.

/ dṅos 'bras ma dmigs pa'i rtags yaṅ dag gi mtshan ñid / 'brel yul ma dmigs pa'i ma dmigs pa'i rtags yaṅ dag gaṅ źig / khyod kyi dṅos kyi ldog chos su gyur pa'i dṅos po yin na de sgrub kyi dgag bya'i chos su gyur pa'i dṅos po'i dnos 'bras yin pa / dper na / du bas dben pa'i rtsig sgor du rgyu nus pa thogs med med par sgrub pa la du ba med pa bkod pa lta bu'o /

d. Genuine evidence of nonapprehension of an on-going result is defined as any genuine evidence of nonapprehension of a sense object of the connection (such that) if there is a given thing that is the on-going divergent feature of you (this proof), it should be the on-going result of the given thing that is the excludable feature of this proof. For example, when proving that in a wall-cavity that is devoid of smoke there is no impediment to the cause of smoke, to prove there is no (impediment), one uses as reason a lack of smoke.

/ 'gal zla dmigs pa'i rtags yaṅ dag la dbye na / phan tshun spaṅ 'gal la brten pa'i 'gal zla dmigs pa'i rtags yaṅ dag daṅ / lhan cig mi gnas 'gal la brten pa'i de daṅ gñis / daṅ po'i mtshan ñid / 'gal zla dmigs pa'i rtags yaṅ dag gaṅ źig / phan tshun spaṅs 'gal gyi sgo nas de sgrub kyi dgag bya 'gog pa / gñis pa'i mtshan ñid / gaṅ źig / lhan cig mi gnas 'gal gyi sgo nas de sgrub kyi dgag bya 'gog pa /

(2) [See above, for (1) and (2) of 2. "Genuine evidence of nonapprehension of what may feasibly appear"]. In variegation of adversary apprehension, there are two kinds: a. Genuine evidence of adversary apprehension based on opposition through mutual exclusion, is defined as any genuine evidence of apprehension (such that) it is the excludable opposition of that proof by opposition through mutual exclusion. b. Genuine evidence of adversary apprehension based on opposition through incompatibility is defined as any one (such that) it is the excludable opposition of that proof by opposition through incompatibility.

/ daṅ po la dbye na phan tshun spaṅs 'gal la brten pa'i khyab byed 'gal dmigs kyi rtags yaṅ dag daṅ / de la brten pa'i 'gal khyab dmigs pa'i rtags yaṅ dag gñis / dpe rim bźin / sgra rtag dṅos kyis stoṅ par sgrub pa la byas pa bkod pa lta bu / bum pa 'jig pa phyis rgyu don gźan la mi bltos par sgrub pa la raṅ grub tsam nas 'jig pa bkod pa lta bu'o /

In variegation of a. there are two kinds:

(a) genuine evidence of apprehension of pervader opposition, based on opposition through mutual exclusion; for example, when proving that sound is void of a permanent going-on, one uses as reason that it is created.

(b) genuine evidence of apprehension of opposing pervasion based thereon; for example, when proving that there is a later break-up of the pot without depending on another cause-entity, one uses as a reason its break-up through just its own agency ['self-destruct'].

/ lhan cig mi gnas 'gal la brten pa'i 'gal zla dmigs pa'i rtags yaṅ dag la dbye na / lhan cig mi gnas 'gal la brten pa'i raṅ bźin 'gal dmigs / khyab byed 'gal dmigs / rgyu 'gal dmigs / 'bras bu 'gal dmigs / 'gal 'bras dmigs pa / rgyu daṅ 'gal ba'i 'bras bu dmigs pa'i rtags daṅ drug / dpe rim bźin / me stobs chen rgyun chags pas khyab par non pa'i sa phyogs// na grań reg stobs chen rgyun chags med par sgrub pa la me stobs chen pas khyab par non pa rtags su bkod pa lta bu daṅ / des khyab par non pa'i sa phyogs na graṅ reg rgyun chags med par sgrub pa la rtags 'dra / des khyab par non pa'i sa phyogs na graṅ 'bras spu loṅ byed rgyun chags med par sgrub pa la rtags 'dra / des khyab par non pa'i sa phyogs na graṅ rgyu nus pa thogs med stobs chen rgyun chags med par sgrub pa la rtags 'dra / du ba drag 'phyur bas khyab par non pa'i sa phyogs na graṅ reg stobs chen rgyun chags med par sgrub pa la du ba drag 'phyur bas khyab par non pa rtags su bkod pa lta bu / des khyab par non pa'i sa phyogs na gra' 'bras spu loṅ byed rgyun chags med par sgrub pa la du drag 'phyur bas khyab par non pa rtags su bkod pa lta bu'o/

In variegation of b. there are six kinds:

(a) adversary apprehension of individual-presence (*svabhāva*) based on opposition through incompatibility. For example, when proving that if a place is set upon pervasively by a stream of great strength of fire it is not a stream of great strength to touch cold, one uses as a reason that it is set upon pervasively by a great strength of fire.

(b) adversary apprehension of pervader (*vyāpaka*) based on opposition through incompatibility. For example, when proving that in a place set upon pervasively by it, there is no stream to touch cold, one uses a like reason.

(c) adversary apprehension of cause (*hetu*) based on opposition through incompatibility. For example, when proving that in a place set upon pervasively by it, there is no stream causing bristling of (one's) hair as the result of cold, one uses a like reason.

(d) adversary apprehension of result (*kārya*) based on opposition through incompatibility. For example, when proving that in a place set upon pervasively by it, there is no stream of great strength without impediment to the ability to cause cold, one uses a like reason.

(e) adversary apprehension of opposition-result (*virodha-kārya*) based on opposition through incompatibility. For example, when proving that in a place set upon pervasively by a furious rising of smoke there is no stream of great power to touch cold, one uses as a reason that it is set upon pervasively by a furious rising of smoke.

(f) adversary apprehension of result in terms of cause and opposition (*hetu-virodha-kārya).* For example, when proving that in a place set upon pervasively by it, there is no stream to make hair bristle as a result of cold, one uses as a reason that it is set upon pervasively by a furious rising of smoke.

/ yaṅ lhan cig mi gnas 'gal la brten pa'i 'gal zla dmigs pa'i rtags yaṅ dag la dbye na / 'gal ba'i raṅ bźin dmigs pa bźi / 'gal ba'i 'bras bu dmigs pa bźi / 'gal ba'i khyab bya dmigs pa bźi ste bcu gñis su bśad kyaṅ 'gal ba cher med do /

Moreover, if one variegates the genuine evidence of adversary apprehension based on opposition through incompatibility, it is explained that there are four apprehensions of the individual-presence of opposition ('gal ba'i raṅ bźin dmigs pa), four apprehensions of the result of opposition ('gal ba'i 'bras bu dmigs pa), and four apprehensions of the pervadable of opposition ('gal ba'i khyab bya dmigs pa) twelve in all; and there is no disputing this.

/ rtags yaṅ dag la bsgrub bya'i chos kyi sgo nas dbye na / sgrub rtags yaṅ dag daṅ / dgag rtags yaṅ dag gñis / mtshan ñid rim bźin / de sgrub kyi rtags yaṅ dag gaṅ źig / de sgrub kyi dṅos kyi bsgrub bya'i chos yin na sgrub pa yin pa / de gaṅ źig / de yin na dgag pa yin pa /

In variegation of genuine evidence by way of the thesis feature (*sādhyadharma*), there are two kinds:

1. Genuine evidence of affirmation (*pratipatti*) is defined as any genuine evidence of that proof (such that) if there is a material *sādhyadharma* of that proof, it is an affirmation.
2. Genuine evidence of exclusion (*pratiṣedha*) is defined as any genuine evidence of that proof (such that) when there is a material *sādhyadharma* of that proof, it is an exclusion. Whatever it is, if it exists, it is an exclusion.

/ daṅ po ni / 'bras raṅ gi rtags thams cad yin la / phyi ma ni / ma dmigs pa'i rtags thams cad yin no /

The former (i.e. affirmation) is all the evidence going with result (*kārya*) and individual-presence (*svabhāva*). The latter (i.e. exclusion) is all the evidence going with nonapprehension (*anupalabdhi*).

/ rtags yaṅ dag la dgos pa'i sgo nas dbye na / raṅ don gyi rtags yaṅ dag daṅ / gźan don gyi rtags yaṅ dag gñis las / mtshan ñid rim pa bźin / rtags yaṅ dag gaṅ źig / sṅa rgol gyis phyir rgol gyi don du ma bkod pa daṅ bkod pa / dpe rim bźin / sṅa rgol med pa'i gaṅ zag raṅ ñid la du bas du ldan la me yod du sgrub pa'i tshe du ba lta bu daṅ / rgol bas phyir rtol la byas pas sgra mi rtag par sgrub pa'i tshe byas pa lta bu'o /

In variegation of genuine evidence by way of the purpose (*abhiprāya*, dgos), there are two kinds:

1. Genuine evidence of 'own aim' (*svārtha*) is defined as any genuine evidence (such that) the 'first speaker' (*pūrvavādin*) does not use a reason for the sake of the respondent (*prativādin*). For example, the 'first speaker', without (another) person, because to himself there is smoke, proves that on a mountain possessing smoke, there is fire; e.g. at that time saying, "There is smoke."
2. Genuine evidence of 'aim for others' (*parārtha*) is defined as any genuine evidence (such that) the first speaker does use a reason for the sake of the respondent. For example, the first speaker proves to the respondent that sound is impermanent because it is created; e.g. at that time saying, "It is created".

/ rtags yaṅ dag la sgrub tshul gyi sgo nas dbye na / don sgrub kyi rtags yaṅ dag daṅ / tha sñad 'ba' źig sgrub kyi rtags yaṅ dag gñis / daṅ po'i mtshan ñid / gaṅ źig / de sgrub kyi dgag bya'i chos kyi don de śes 'dod chos can gyi steṅ na yod kyaṅ de der phyogs chos can gyi tshad ma la bltar mi ruṅ ba / dper na sṅo 'phyur ba daṅ ldan pa'i me med kyi mtshan mo'i rgya mtsho na du ba med par sgrub pa la me med bkod pa lta bu / gñis pa'i mtshan ñid / gaṅ źig / dgag bya'i chos kyi don de śes 'dod chos can gyi steṅ na yod na de der phyogs chos can gyi tshad ma la bltar ruṅ ba / dper na / lto ldir źabs źum gyis dag pa'i sa phyogs na bum pa med par sgrub pa la lto ldir źabs źum snaṅ ruṅ ma dmigs pa bkod pa lta bu'o / tha sñad sgrub kyi rtags yaṅ dag gi mtshan ñid / gaṅ źig / de sgrub kyi dgag bya'i chos kyi tha sñad de śes 'dod chos can gyi steṅ na yod kyaṅ / de der phyogs chos can gyi tshad ma la bltar mi ruṅ ba /

In variegation of genuine evidence by way of the method of proof (*sādhana*), there are two kinds, namely, 1. genuine evidence for proof of an object-entity (*artha*), and 2. genuine evidence for proof of just conventional language (*vyavahāra*).

1. Genuine evidence for proof of an object-entity is defined two ways:
   (1) It is first defined as any one (such that) even though the object-entity constituting the excludable feature of that proof exists on the factual base (*dharmin*) desired to be known, it is not visible there for the authority of the person who has (for the time being) the locus feature (*pakṣadharma*). For example, since a fire does not possess a rising blue-green mist, for proving there is no smoke on the lake at night, one uses as a reason that there is no fire (there).
   (2) It is next defined as any one (such that) if the object-entity constituting the excludable feature exists on the factual base desired to be known, at that place it is visible for the authority of the person who has (for the time being) the locus-feature. For example, if a spot is bare of a pot becoming slender at the bottom, one proves the non-apprehension of the pot, using the reason if a pot becoming slender at the bottom were there, it is would be visible, but it is not apprehended.
2. Genuine evidence for a proof of conventional language is defined as any one (such that) even though the conventional language constituting the excludable feature of that proof exists on the factual base desired to be known, it is not witnessed there for the authority of the person who has (for the time being) the locus feature (*pakṣadharma*).

/ yaṅ na rtags yaṅ dag la sgrub tshul gyi sgo nas dbye na / don sgrub kyi rtags yaṅ dag daṅ / tha sñad sgrub kyi rtags yaṅ dag gñis / mtshan ñid rim bźin / tshul gsum tshaṅ ba'i rtags yaṅ dag gaṅ źig / de sgrub kyi dṅos kyi bsgrub bya'i chos yin na mtshan ñid yin pa daṅ / gaṅ źig de sgrub kyi dṅos kyi bsgrub bya'i chos yin na mtshon bya yin pa / dpe rim bźin / skad cig ma sgrub pa la rgyu rkyen las skyes pa bkod pa lta bu daṅ / sgra mi rtag par sgrub pa la byas pa bkod pa lta bu'o /

In an alternate variegation of genuine evidence by way of the method of proof, there are also two:

1. Genuine evidence for proving an object-entity is defined as any genuine evidence complete with the three modes (such that) if there is a material thesis feature (*sādhyadharma*) of the proof, it should be a definition (*lakṣaṇa*). For example, when proving

(a thing is) momentary [= the definition] one uses the reason that it has arisen from cause and conditions.

2. Genuine evidence for proving conventional language is defined as any (genuine evidence complete with the three modes such that) if there is a material thesis feature of the proof, it should be the distinct detail (*lakṣman*). For example, when proving that sound is impermanent [= the distinct detail] one uses the reason that it is created.

/ rtags yaṅ dag la 'jug tshul gyi sgo nas dbye na / mthun phyogs la khyab byed du 'jug pa'i rtags yaṅ dag daṅ / rnam pa gñis su 'jug pa'i rtags yaṅ dag gñis / gaṅ źig / sgrub tshul ltar mthun phyogs mtha' dag la yod pa / gaṅ źig / sgrub tshul ltar mthun phyogs 'ba' źig la med pa / duṅ sgra mi rtag par sgrub pa la byas pa bkod pa lta bu daṅ / tshol byuṅ bkod pa lta bu'o /

In variegation of genuine evidence by way of the method of engaging, there are two kinds:

1. Genuine evidence that engages the similar locus in a pervader way; to wit, any one present in all similar locuses according to the method of proof; for example, when proving the sound of the conch to be impermanent, one uses the reason "It is created".
2. Genuine evidence that engages (the similar locus) in two ways; to wit, anyone that exists in all similar locuses according to the method of proof, and anyone that is absent in some similar locuses according to the method of proof; for example, when proving the sound of the conch to be impermanent, one uses the reason "It arises from effort".

/ rtags yaṅ dag la bsgrub bya'i sgo nas dbye na gsum las / dṅos po stobs źugs kyi rtags yaṅ dag gi mtshan ñid / tshul gsum tshaṅ baṅ gtan tshigs gaṅ źig / de sgrub kyi bsgrub bya yin na sgra byuṅ grags pa daṅ de 'grub pa luṅ la ltos pa gaṅ yaṅ ma yin pa / dper na / sgra mi rtag par sgrub pa la byas pa bkod pa lta bu / grags pa'i rtags yaṅ dag gi mtshan ñid / gaṅ źig / de sgrub kyi bsgrub bya yin na sgra byuṅ grags pa yin pa / dper na ri boṅ can zla ba'i sgras brjod ruṅ du sgrub pa la rtog yul na yod pa rtags su bkod pa lta bu / yid ces kyi rtags yaṅ dag gi mtshan ñid / gaṅ źig / de sgrub kyi bsgrub bya yin na / de tshur mthoṅ gi tshad mas 'grub pa ṅes par luṅ la bltos pa / dper na / sbyin pas loṅs spyod khrims kyis bde źes pa'i luṅ raṅ gi bstan bya'i don la mi slu bar sgrub pa la / dpyad pa gsum gyis dag pa'i luṅ bkod pa lta bu'o /

In variegation of genuine evidence by way of the thesis (*sādhya*), there are three kinds:

1. Genuine evidence aroused on the strength of a given thing (= first kind of inference) is defined as any reason with complete three modes (such that) when there is a thesis of the proof, there is no reliance at all for proving it on the popular kind arising from a saying or on scripture (= the second and third kinds of inference). For example, when proving that sound is impermanent, one uses the reason that it is created.
2. Genuine evidence that is popular (*prasiddha*) is defined as any one (such that) when there is a thesis of the proof, there is the popular kind arising from a saying. For example, when proving the feasibility that the moon can be expressed by (the name) "one having a rabbit," one uses the reason that it exists in the realm of constructive thought.
3. Genuine evidence of the master (lineage) is defined as any one (such that), if it is the thesis of that proof, it depends on a trustworthy scripture that is proved by an authority that 'looks hither' (*arvāg-darśana*). For example, when proving that the scripture 'By giving, (there results) possessions; by morality, happiness" is without deception regarding its indicated aim, one uses the reason that it is a pure scripture by means of the three examinations.[16]

Fallacies

/ rtags ltar snaṅ gi mtshan ñid / rtags su bkod pa gaṅ źig / tshul gsum ma tshaṅ ba / yaṅ na de'i mtshan ñid / bsgrub bya raṅ gis tshad mas ma grub pa'i gaṅ zag gis tshul gsum tshad mas 'grub mi srid pa'i rtags / dbye na gñis las / 'gal ba'i rtags kyi mtshan ñid / phyogs chos grub ciṅ khyab pa phyin ci log tu ṅes pa'i rtags / ma ṅes pa'i rtags kyi mtshan ñid / phyogs chos grub ciṅ khyab pa rnal ma daṅ phyin ci log gaṅ du yaṅ ma ṅes pa / yaṅ ṅa phyogs chos grub ciṅ phyogs chos can du soṅ ba'i gaṅ zag gis khyab pa rnal ma daṅ phyin ci log gaṅ du 'aṅ ma ṅes pa / ma grub pa'i rtags kyi mtshan ñid / rtags su bkod pa gaṅ źig / phyogs chos ma grub pa /

A fallacy (*ābhāsa*, ltar snaṅ) of evidence (*liṅga*, rtags) is defined as any use of a reason with incompleteness of the three modes (tshul

16. See notes 4 and 5, above.

gsum ma tshaṅ ba). Moreover, its character is an impossible evidence for proof by authority of the three modes by a person who has not realized with his own authority the thesis (*sādhya*). In variegation there are two kinds:

1. Contrary evidence (*viruddha-liṅga*, 'gal ba'i rtags) is defined as an evidence with the locus feature (*pakṣadharma*) proven, while the pervasion (*vyāpti*) is certainly wayward.
2. Uncertain evidence (*anaikāntika-liṅga*, ma ṅes pa'i rtags) is defined as an evidence with the locus feature proven, while it is not certain as to whether the pervasion is right or wrong. Or, it is (an evidence) with the locus feature proven, while there is no certainty of right or wrong of the pervasion on the part of the person who has accepted the locus feature.

Nonactual evidence (*asiddha-liṅga*, ma grub pa'i rtags) is defined as any use of a reason (such that) the locus feature is unproven.

/ 'gal rtags la sbyor ba'i sgo nas dbye na / 'bras raṅ ma dmigs pa'i 'gal rtags gsum / mtshan ñid rim bźin / 'gal rtags gaṅ źig / khyod raṅ las rdzas tha dad pa'i de sgrub kyi dgag bya'i chos la de byuṅ du 'brel ba / sgrub pa'i 'gal rtags gaṅ źig / de sgrub kyi dgag bya'i chos yin na / khyod kyi bdag gcig pa'i khyab byed yin pa / gan źig / de sgrub kyi dṅos kyi dgag bya'i chos yin na / dgag pa yin pa / dpe rim bźin / du ldan la me med du sgrub pa la du ba rtags su bkod pa lta bu daṅ / sgra rtag par sgrub pa la byas pa rtags su bkod pa lta bu daṅ / śiṅ med kyi brag rdzoṅ du śa pa yod par sgrub pa la śiṅ med bkod pa lta bu'o /

In variegation of the contrary evidence, there are three kinds, namely, of the result (*kārya*), of the individual-presence (*svabhāva*), and of the nonapprehension (*anupalabdhi*).

1. (That of the result) is defined as any contrary evidence (such that) when the proof should be a different substance from you yourself, the proof is related to the excludable *dharma* by way of arising from it. For example, when proving there is no fire on a mountain possessing smoke, one uses the reason that there is smoke.
2. (That of the individual-presence) is defined as any contrary evidence (such that) if there is a refutable feature of the proof, it should be a pervader in an identical way with you. For example, when proving that sound is eternal, one uses the reason that it is created.
3. (That of the nonapprehension) is defined as any contrary evidence (such that) if there a material (= on-going) refutable

feature of the proof, it should be an exclusion (*pratiṣedha*). For example, when proving that there is a Śiṃśapa tree on a treeless rocky ledge, one uses the reason that there are no trees (there).

/ 'gal rtags la brjod tshul gyi sgo nas dbye na / bźi las / chos kyi ṅo bo sgrub pa'i 'gal rtags kyi mtshan ñid / phyog chos grub ciṅ de sgrub kyi bsgrub bya'i chos kyi ṅo bo daṅ khyab pa phyin ci log tu ṅes pa / dper na / sgra rtag par sgrub pa la byas pa rtags su bkod pa lta bu'o / chos kyi khyad par sgrub pa'i 'gal rtags kyi mtshan ñid / phyogs chos grub ciṅ że 'dod la bsgrub bya'i chos kyi ṅo bor bzuṅs śiṅ brjod tshul la bsgrub bya'i chos kyi khyad par du bzuṅ ba'i chos daṅ khyab pa phyin ci log tu ṅes pa / dper na mig sogs de 'dus pa ma yin pa'i yul can gźan [gyi] don byed par sgrub pa la 'dus śiṅ bsags pa bkod pa lta bu'o / chos can gyi ṅo bo bsgrub pa'i 'gal rtags kyi mtshan ñid / phyogs chos grub cin że 'dod la bsgrub bya'i chos kyi ṅo bor bzuṅ la / brjod tshul la chos can gyi ṅo bor bzuṅ ba'i chos daṅ / khyab pa phyin ci log tu ṅes pa / dper na / dṅos gyur gyi nam mkha' rtag par sgrub pa la 'dus ma byas bkod pa lta bu'o / chos kyi khyad par sgrub pa'i 'gal rtags kyi mtshan ñid / że 'dod kyi chos can gyi steṅ du phyogs chos grub ciṅ / że 'dod la bsgrub bya'i chos kyi ṅo bor bzuṅ la / brjod tshul la chos can gyi khyad par bzuṅ ba'i chos daṅ khyab pa phyin ci log tu ṅes pa / dper na mig sogs 'dus pa ma yin pa'i yul can de gźan don byed par sgrub pa la 'dus śiṅ bsags pa bkod pa lta bu /

In variegation of the contrary evidence by way of the manner of referring (brjod tshul), there are four kinds:

1. The contrary evidence for proving the true nature of a feature (*dharmasvarūpa*, chos kyi ṅo bo) is defined as (the evidence) with proven case feature, while it is certain the thesis feature of that proof and the pervasion are wayward. For example, when proving that sound is eternal, one uses the reason that it is created.
2. The contrary evidence for proving a feature-distinction is defined as (the evidence) with proven locus feature, while it is certain that the personal preference that accepts the nature of the thesis feature, the manner of referring that accepts the nature of the thesis feature—(such) a feature, and the pervasion, are wayward. For example, when proving the eye, etc. perform a purpose for the other one, the nonaccumulated subject, one uses the reason that the eye, etc. are accumulated.

3. The contrary evidence for proving the nature of a factual base (*dharmi-svarūpa,* chos can gyi ṅo bo) is defined as (the evidence) with proven locus feature, while it is certain that the personal preference that accepts the nature of the thesis feature, the manner of referring that accepts the nature of the factual base—(such) a feature, and the pervasion, are wayward. For example, when proving that the on-going space is eternal, one uses the reason that it is 'unconstructed' (*sic.* 'dus ma byas) [But it should be: 'produced from effort', rtsol ba las byuṅ ba].
4. The contrary evidence for proving a *dharmin*-distinction [correction of chos kyi khyad par = *dharma*-distinction] is defined as (the evidence) with proven locus feature on the factual base (*dharmin*) of personal preference, while it is certain that the personal preference that accepts the nature of the thesis feature, the manner of referring that accepts the factual-base distinction—such a feature, and the pervasion, are wayward. For example, when proving that the eye, etc., perform a purpose for the other, the nonaccumulated subject, one uses the reason that it is accumulated.

/ ma ṅes pa'i rtags la dbye na gñis las / thun moṅ ma yin pa'i ma ṅes pa'i rtags kyi mtshan ñid / phyogs chos grub ciṅ de sgrub kyi mthun phyogs mi mthun phyogs gaṅ la yaṅ ma mthoṅ ba / yaṅ na / phyogs chos grub ciṅ de sgrub kyi phyogs chos can du soṅ ba'i gaṅ zag gis mthun phyogs mi mthun phyogs gaṅ la yaṅ ma mthoṅ ba / dper na / sgra rtag par sgrub pa la mñan bya bkod pa daṅ / gson lus bdag bcas su sgrub pa la srog bkod pa lta bu'o / thun moṅ gi ma ṅes pa'i rtags kyi mtshan ñid / ma ṅes pa'i rtags gaṅ źig / phyogs chos can du soṅ ba'i gaṅ zag gis de sgrub kyi mthun phyogs la mthoṅ ba 'am mi mthun phyogs la mthoṅ ba gaṅ ruṅ yin pa / dbye na /

In variegation of the uncertain evidence (*anaikāntika-liṅga,* ma ṅes pa'i rtags), there are two kinds:

1. Uncertain evidence that is too restricted (*asādhāraṇa,* thun moṅ ma yin pa) is defined as (the evidence) with proven locus feature, but which one does not see in the similar locus or the dissimilar locus of that proof. Or, it is (the evidence) with proven locus feature, but which the person who accepts the locus feature of that proof does not see in any similar locus or dissimilar locus of that proof. For example, when proving that sound is eternal, one uses the reason that it is audible. Again,

when proving that a living being has a self, one uses the reason that it is alive.

2. Uncertain evidence that is unrestricted (*sādhāraṇa*, thun moṅ) is defined as (the evidence) which a person who has accepted the locus feature either sees in the similar locus or in the dissimilar locus, of that proof. In variegation:

/ dṅos kyi ma ṅes pa daṅ lhag ldan gyi ma ṅes pa gñis / mtshan ñid rim bźin / thun moṅ gi ma ṅes pa'i rtags gaṅ źig / phyogs chos can du soṅ ba'i gaṅ zag gis mthun phyogs mi mthun phyogs gñis ka la mthoṅ ba / gñis pa'i mtshan ñid / de gaṅ źig / phyogs chos can du soṅ ba'i gaṅ zag gis mthun phyogs mi mthun phyogs gñis ka la mthoṅ bas ma khyab pa /

(In variegation of 2.—)

(1) material uncertainty (*vāstava-anaikāntika*, dnos kyi ma ṅes pa) is defined as (the evidence) which the person who has accepted the locus feature sees in both the similar locus and the dissimilar locus.

(2) *a posteriori* uncertainty (*śeṣavat-anaikāntika*, lhag ldan gi ma ṅes) is defined as (the evidence) which the person who has accepted the locus feature does not necessarily see in both the similar locus and the dissimilar locus.

/ daṅ po la dbye na / mthun phyogs mi mthun phyogs gñis ka la khyab byed du 'jug / gñis ka la rnam gñis su 'jug / gñis ka la rnam gñis su 'jug / mthun phyogs la rnam gñis su 'jug mi mthun phyogs la khyab byed du 'jug pa / mi mthun phyogs la rnam gñis su 'jug mthun phyogs la khyab byed du 'jug pa'i dṅos kyi ma ṅes pa'i rtags dan bźi / dpe rim bźin / sgra rtag par sgrub pa la gźal bya bkod pa lta bu / bye brag pa'i ṅor sgra rtag par sgrub pa la reg bya can ma yin pa rtags su bkod ba lta bu / sgra rtsol ma byuṅ du sgrub pa la mi rtag pa rtags su bkod pa lta bu'o / sgra rtsol byuṅ du sgrub pa la mi rtag pa bkod pa lta bu'o /

In variegation of (1) material uncertainty, there are four kinds:

a. engaging (the evidence) by way of pervader in both the similar and the dissimilar case. For example, when proving that sound is eternal, one uses the reason that it is a sanction (*prameya*).

b. engaging (the evidence) in two ways in both (the similar and the dissimilar cases). For example, when proving sound to be eternal for the Vaiśeṣika school, one uses the reason that it (i.e. sound) is intangible.

c. engaging (the evidence) in two ways in the similar locus, and engaging (the evidence) by way of pervader in the dissimilar locus. For example, when proving that sound does not arise from effort, one uses the reason that it (i.e. sound) is impermanent.

d. engaging (the evidence) in two ways in the dissimilar locus, and engaging (the evidence) by way of pervader in the similar locus. For example, when proving that sound arises from effort, one uses the reason that it (i.e. sound) is impermanent.

/ lhag ldan ma ṅes pa'i rtags la dbye na gñis / 'gal ba lhag ldan gyi ma ṅes pa'i rtags kyi mtshan ñid / gaṅ źig / phyogs chos can du soṅ ba'i gaṅ zag gis de sgrub kyi mi mthun phyogs la mthoṅ ba / dper na / ṅag smra ba'i skyes bu pha rol po kun mkhyen yin par sgrub pa la ṅag smra ba bkod pa lta bu'o / yaṅ dag lhag ldan gyi ma ṅes pa'i rtags kyi mtshan ñid / gaṅ źig / phyogs chos can du soṅ ba'i gaṅ zag gis mthun phyogs la mthoṅ ba / dper na ṅag smra ba'i skyes bu pha rol po kun mkhyen ma yin par sgrub pa la ṅag smra ba bkod pa lta bu'o /

In variegation of (2) *a posteriori* uncertainty, there are two kinds:

a. Uncertain evidence, contrary *a posteriori* ('gal ba lhag ldan), is defined as (the evidence) which the person who has accepted the locus feature sees in the dissimilar locus of that proof. For example, when proving that the other person who speaks is omniscient, one uses the reason that this one is speaking.

b. Uncertain evidence, genuine *a posteriori* (yaṅ dag lhag ldan) is defined as (the evidence) which the person who has accepted the locus feature sees in the similar locus. For example, when proving that the other person who speaks is not omniscient, one uses the reason that this one is speaking.

/ ma grub pa'i rtags la dbye na / don la bltos nas ma grub / blo la bltos nas ma grub / gaṅ zag la bltos nas ma grub pa'i rtags daṅ gsum /

In variegation of nonactual evidence (*asiddhitva-liṅga*, ma grub pa'i rtags), there are three such:

1. nonactual in respect to the object-entity (*artha*).
2. nonactual in respect to the discriminating mind (*buddhi*).
3. nonactual in respect to a person (*pudgala*).

/ daṅ po la dbye na / gźi ma grub nas ma grub / tha dad med nas ma grub / phyogs gcig la bltos nas ma grub pa'i rtags daṅ gsum / daṅ po la dbye na / rtags kyi ṅo bo mi srid nas ma grub / chos kyi ṅo bo mi srid nas ma grub pa gñis / dpe rim bźin / skyes bu bdag bcas su sgrub pa la bdag gi yon tan daṅ ldan pa bkod pa lta bu daṅ / bdag khyab pa yin par sgrub pa la bde sdug yon tan kun la dmigs pa bkod pa lta bu'o / tha dad med nas ma grub pa'i rtags la dbye na / gzi rtags tha dad med nas ma grub / gźi chos tha dad med nas ma grub / chos rtags tha dad med nas ma grub pa gsum mo / dpe rim bzin / sgra mi rtag par sgrub pa la sgra dan / sgra sgrar sgrub pa la mi rtag pa bkod pa daṅ / sgra mi rtag par sgrub pa la mi rtag pa bkod pa lta bu'o / phyogs gcig la bltos nas ma grub pa'i rtags ni / dper na / zla ba gñis snaṅ gi dbaṅ śes mṅon sum du sgrub pa la rtog bral ma 'khrul ba rtags su bkod pa lta bu'o /

In variegation of the first one (nonactual in respect to the object-entity), there are three cases of nonactual evidence:

(1) nonactual by nonactual support (*āśrayāsiddha*) is of two kinds:
   a. nonactual by no possibility of a true form of evidence. For example, when proving that a person has a self, one uses the reason that this one possesses the virtualities of a self.
   b. nonactual by no possibility of a true form of a feature (*dharma*). For example, when proving that the self pervades, one uses the reason that it apprehends all virtualities of pleasure and pain.

(2) nonactual by no difference has three kinds:
   a. nonactual by the support and evidence not shown as different. For example, when proving that sound is impermanent, one uses the reason that it is sound.
   b. nonactual by the support and feature not shown as different. For example, when proving that sound is sound, one uses the reason that it is impermanent.
   c. nonactual by the feature and evidence not shown as different. For example, when proving that sound is impermanent, one uses the reason that it is impermanent.

(3) nonactual evidence in respect to one part (phyogs gcig la bltos nas ma grub pa). For example, when proving that sense cognition of the appearance of a double moon is 'direct perception' (*pratyakṣa*), one uses the reason that the evidence is free from constructive thought (*kalpanā*) and undeluded (*abhrānta*).

/ blo ṅo la ltos nas ma grub pa'i rtags la dbye na / the tshom za nas ma grub / śes 'dod med nas ma grub pa'i rtags gñis / daṅ po la dbye na / chos can la the tshom za nas ma grub / rtags la the tshom za nas ma grub / de gñis kyi 'brel pa la the tshom za nas ma grub pa daṅ gsum / dpe rim bźin / źa za'i bum pa mi rtag par sgrub pa'la byas pa bkod pa lta bu dan / du ba'am rlaṅs pa yin min the tshom za ba'i sṅo loṅ po yod pa'i sa phyogs su me yod par sgrub pa la du ba yod pa rtags su bkod pa lta bu / ri sul gsum kyi dbus ma na rma bya yod par sgrub pa la rma bya'i sgra grag pa bkod pa lta bu'o / gñis pa ni / dper na sgra mi rtag par grub zin ma brjed pa'i ṅor sgra chos can / mi rtag ste / byas pa'i phyir / źes pa lta bu'o /

In variegation of the second one (nonactual in respect to the discriminating mind), there are two kinds of nonactual evidence:

(1) nonactual by doubt (the tshom za nas ma grub) is of three kinds:
   a. nonactual by doubt toward the factual base. For example, when proving that a *piśāca*-pot[17] is impermanent, one uses the reason that it is created.
   b. nonactual by doubt toward the evidence. For example, when proving that there is fire in a place for which previously it was doubtful whether there was smoke or rather vapor (such as the rising greenish mist), one uses the reason in evidence that there is existence of smoke.
   c. nonactual by doubt as to the relation of those two (i.e. the factual base and the evidence). for example, when proving that there is a peacock in the middle one of those ravines of a moutain,[18] one uses the reason that the the cry (heard) was of a peacock.

(2) nonactual by not wishing to cognize (śes 'dod med nas ma grub pa). For example, (someone) has previously proved that sound is impermanent; then takes an unforgotten sound as the factual base, asserting that it is impermanent because it is created.

/ gaṅ zag la bltos nas ma grub pa'i rtags la dbye na / rgol ba la bltos nas ma grub / phyir rgol la bltos nas ma grub / gñis ka la bltos nas ma grub pa'i rtags gsum . dpe rim bźin / graṅs can pas saṅs rgyas pa la blo bde sems med du sgrub pa la skye 'jig can bkod pa lta bu / gcer bu pas śiṅ sems ldan du sgrub pa la / śun pa bśus na·'chi ba bkod pa

17. Said to be one carried by a nonvisible demon.
18. The example supports my translation of the term *dharmin* as 'factual base' because the doubt is toward whether the peacock is in the right, left, or middle ravine.

lta bu / sgra mi rtag par ṡgrub pa la mig ṡes kyi bzuṅ bya bkod pa lta bu'o /

In varieation of the third one (nonactual in respect to a person), there are three kinds of nonactual evidence:

(1) nonactual in respect to the 'first speaker' (*vādin*) (rgol ba la bltos nas ma grub). For example, the Sāṃkhya, when proving that an enlightened being has a blissful mind (*buddhi*) without thoughts, uses as a reason that this (mind) possesses arising and passing away.

(2) nonactual in respect to the 'respondent' (*prativādin*) (phyir rgol la bltos nas ma grub). For example, the Nirgranthas, when proving that a tree is conscious, use as a reason that it would die if the bark is peeled.

(3) nonactual in respect to both. For example, when proving that sound is impermanent, one uses as a reason that it is perceptible by eye-cognition.

Example

/ dpe yaṅ dag gi mtshan ñid / bsgrub bya ṅes pa'i snon du khyab pa ṅes pa'i gźir gyur pa / dbye na gñis las / mthun dpe yaṅ dag gi gźir gyur pa / dbye na / dṅos kyi mthun dpe yaṅ dag daṅ / rigs 'dra'i mthun dpe yaṅ dag gñis / dpe rim bźin / byas pas sgra mi rtag par sgrub pa'i mthun dper bum pa bkod pa lta bu daṅ / lto ldir ba snaṅ ruṅ ma dmigs pas lto ldir bas dag pa'i sa phyogs su bum pa med par sgrub pa la / ri boṅ gi mgo la rva bkod pa lta bu'o / mi mthum dpe yaṅ dag gi mtshan ñid / bsgrub bya ṅes pa'i sṅon du ldog khyab dṅos su ṅes pa'i gźir gyur pa / dper na byas pas sgra mi rtag par sgrub pa'i mi mthun dper nam mkha' bkod pa lta bu'o /

A genuine example (*dṛṣṭānta,* dpe) is defined as the basis of certainty of pervasion prior to the certainty of the thesis (*sādhya*). In variegation there are two kinds:

1. Genuine concordant example (*sādharmyadṛṣṭānta,* mthun dpe) is defined as the basis of certainty prior to the *anvaya*-pervasion (presence in all similar case), which is prior to certainty of the thesis. In variegation there are two:

   (1) genuine discrete (or individualized) (dṅos kyi) concordant example. For example, when proving that sound is impermanent because created, one formulates a concordant example, to wit, "like a pot."

(2) genuine homogeneous (rigs 'dra'i)[19] concordant example. For example, when proving that there is no pot in a place bare of the large-bulbed (kind of pot), because there is no apprehension of the large-bulbed (kind of pot) which could feasibly appear, one formulates (a concordant example), "like a horn on the head of a rabbit."

2. Genuine discordant example (*vaidharmyadṛṣṭānta,* mi mthun dpe) is defined as the on-going (dṅos su) basis of certainty of the *vyatireka*-pervasion (absence in all dissimilar cases) that precedes the certainty of the thesis. For example, when proving that sound is impermanent because created, one formulates a discordant example, to wit, "like space".

Fallacy of Example

/ dpe ltar snaṅ gi mtshan ñid / bsgrub bya ṅes pa'i sṅon du rjes khyab pa ṅes pa'i gźir gzuṅ źiṅ/ ṅes par mi nus pa / dbye na / mthun dpe ltar snaṅ daṅ mi mthun dpe ltar snaṅ gñis /

Fallacy of the example is defined as follows: while accepting a support of certainty of the pervasion that precedes certainty of the thesis, (in fact) there is no ability to be certain. In variegation there are two kinds: 1. fallacy of concordant example, 2. fallacy of discordant example.

/ daṅ po'i mtshan ñid / bsgrub bya ṅes pa'i sṅon du rjes khyab dṅos su ṅes pa'i gźir bzuṅ źiṅ ṅes par mi nus pa / dbye na / don skyon can / blo skyon can / skra skyon can gyi mthun dpe daṅ gsum / daṅ po la dbye na / chos kyis / rtags kyis stoṅ / de gñis kas stoṅ pa'i mthun dpe ltar snaṅ gsum / dpe rim bźin / lus can ma yin pas sgra rtag par sgrub pa'i mthun dper las daṅ / rdul pra rab daṅ bum pa bkod pa lta bu'o / gźan gñis re źig gźog /

1. Fallacy of concordant example is defined as follows: While accepting an on-going certainty support of the *anvaya*-pervasion that precedes the certainty of the thesis, (in fact) there is no ability to be certain. In variegation, there are three kinds of

19. The Tib. *rigs 'dra'i* = *rigs mthun* = S. *sājātiya,* does not here mean 'affiliated'. Rather, it is as the Monier-Williams Sanskrti-English dictonary states under the word it spells *sājātya,* with the meaning 'homogeneousness'. This shows that the contrasting term *dṅos kyi* must be rendered as 'discrete'. Hence, the two examples, first the 'pot' as an individual thing; then, since homogeneity does not allow for an individual to emerge, a pot with a large bulb is not seen.

fallacious concordant example: faulty object-entity (*artha*), faulty discriminative mind (*buddhi*), and faulty word (*śabda*). Faulty object-entity is in variegation three kinds of fallacy of concordant example, namely, void of a feature (*dharma*), void of evidence (*liṅga*), void of both. For example, when proving that sound is permanent because it is is incorporeal, one formulates a concordant example (for void of a feature) "like *karma*"; (for void of evidence) "like an atom"; (for void of both) "like a pot". The other two (i.e. faulty discrimination and faulty word) are left (aside) for the time being.

/mi mthun dpe ltar snan gi mtshan ñid / bsgrub bya ṅes pa'i sṅon du ldog khyab dṅos ṅes pa'i gźir bzuṅ źiṅ ṅes par mi nus pa / dbye na / don skyon can sogs gsum gyi mi mthun dpe ltar snaṅ gsum / daṅ po la / chos kyis mi stoṅ / rtags gyis mi stoṅ / de gṅis kas mi stoṅ ba'i mi mthun dpe ltar snaṅ gsum / dper na / lus can ma yin pas sgra rtag par sgrub pa'i mi mthun dper / rdul phra rab daṅ las daṅ nam mkha' bkod pa lta bu'o /

2. Fallacy of discordant example is defined as follows. While accepting an on-going certainty-support of the vyatireka-pervasion that precedes the certainty of the thesis, (in fact) there is no ability to be certain. In variegation there are three kinds of fallacious discordant example: faulty object-entity, etc. as above. Faulty object-enity is in variegation three kinds of the fallacy of discordant example, namely, not void of feature, not void of evidence, not void of both. For example, when (the opponent is) proving that sound is permanent because it is incorporeal, that (person) formulates a discordant example (for not void of a feature) "like an atom," (for not void of evidence) "like *karma*," (for not void of both) "like space".

/ źar byun rtags dpe'i skyon 'chad pa la / rtags skyon gyi mtshan ñid / de sgrub kyi rtags su bkod le'o de kho na la ldan źiṅ rtags su bkod le'o de de sgrub kyi rtags yaṅ dag ma yin par sgrub pa'i tshul gsum tshaṅ ba'i rtags gaṅ śig / bsgrub bya sgrub nus daṅ tshul gsum gaṅ ruṅ gi dṅos kyi ldog phyogs gaṅ ruṅ yin pa / dbye na / ma grub pa'i rtags kyi skyon / 'gal rtags kyi skyon / ma ṅes pa'i rtags kyi skyon daṅ gsum / dpe rim bźin / sgra mi rtag par sgrub pa la mig śes kyi gzuṅ bya bkod pa'i tshe sgra mi rtag sgrub kyi rtags su bkod na phyogs chos ma grub pa lta bu daṅ / sgra mi rtag par sgrub pa la byas pa bkod pa'i tshe sgra rtag sgrub kyi rtags su bkod na khyab pa phyin ci log tu ṅes pa lta bu daṅ / sgra rtag par sgrub pa la gźal bya bkod pa'i tshe sgra rtag par sgrub kyi rtags su bkod na khyab pa rnal ma daṅ phyin ci log gaṅ du yaṅ ma ṅes pa lta bu'o /

Along those lines, for explaining example-faults of evidence, fault of evidence is defined as any evidence (*liṅga*) complete with the three modes of proof, while possessed of only the so-called use of a reason as evidence for the proof; and while the so-called use of a reason as evidence is not genuine evidence for the proof, (such that) there is ability to prove the thesis, or there are the three modes, or an on-going exclusion-locus, as the case may be. In variegation there are three kinds:

1. fault of nonactual evidence. For example, when proving that sound is impermanent, one uses as a reason "It is perceptible by eye-cognition"; and at that time when using the reason as evidence for proving sound is impermanent, there is no proof of the locus-feature (*pakṣadharma*).
2. fault of contrary evidence. For example, when proving that sound is impermanent, one uses as a reason "It is created"; and at that time, when using a reason as evidence for proving sound is permanent, waywardness of the pervasion is certain.
3. fault of uncertain evidence. For example, when proving that sound is permanent, one formulates a sanction (*prameya*); and at that time, when using it (the sanction) as a reason in evidence for proving sound is permanent, there is uncertainty as to (whether one is right or wrong) regarding the pervasion and support, and even regarding where is the waywardness.

/ des na rtags skyon la gźi grub pas khyab la / rtags skyon can la gźi grub ma grub ci rigs su yod do / rtags yaṅ dag gi mtshan ñid kyi bsal bya yin na gźi ma grub dgos te / byas pa sgra mi rtag par sgrub pa'i rtags yaṅ dag ma yin pa daṅ mig śes kyi gzuṅ bya sgra mi rtag par sgrub pa'i rtags yaṅ dag yin pa lta bu ni rtags yaṅ dag gi bsal bya yin pa'i phyir ro / 'di ni dpe dan phyogs kyi skabs su yaṅ go bar bya'o/

Hence, when the fault of evidence is pervaded by proof of the support, what principle can decide whether the support which holds the fault of evidence is proven or disproven? If the definition of genuine evidence is rejected, the support is necessarily disproven. This is because when there is no genuine evidence for proving that a created sound is impermanent; and when there is genuine evidence for proving a sound to be impermanent, but then perceptible by eye-cognition—(in both cases) it is a rejection of genuine evidence. This should also be understood for the phases of example and locus (*pakṣa*).

/ dpe skyon gyi mtshan ñid / de sgrub kyi dper bkod le'o de kho na la ldan źiṅ / de sgrub kyi dper bkod le'o de de sgrub kyi dpe yaṅ dag ma yin par sgrub pa'i tshul gsum tshaṅ ba'i rtags gaṅ źig / bsgrub bya ṅes pa'i sṅon du khyab pa ṅes pa'i gźir gyur pa'i dṅos kyi ldog phyogs yin pa / dbye na / mthun dpe'i skyon daṅ / mi mthun dpe'i skyon gñis / dpe rim bźin / lus can ma yin pas sgra rtag par sgrub pa'i mthun dper bum pa bkod pa'i tshe / rtag pas stoṅ pa lta bu daṅ / lus can ma yin pas sgra rtag par sgrub pa'i mi mthun dper nam mkha' bkod pa'i tshe rtags pas mi stoṅ pa lta bu'o /

A fault of example (dpe skyon) is defined as any evidence with complete three modes for the proof, (such that) while there is a sort of use of a reason, then the example for the proof; that sort of use of a reason, then the example for the proof, involves an example that is not genuine for the proof; (namely, that evidence) is the material exclusion-locus that is the certainty-support of the pervasion that precedes the certainty of the thesis. In variegation there are two faults:

1. fault of concordant example. For example, when proving that sound is permanent because it is incorporeal, one uses a concordant example "like a pot"; at that time it (the pot) is void of permanence.
2. fault of discordant example. For example, when proving that sound is permanent because it is incorporeal, one uses a discordant example "like space"; at that time, it (space) is not void of permanence.

/ gźan don rjes dpag gtan la dbab pa la / dṅos daṅ bsgrub bya sun 'byin sogs bśad pa la gsum las /

H" Inference for Others (*parārthānumāna*)

For establishing 'inference for others' one explains the fault-finder (*dūṣaka*, sun 'byin) for both the present thing (*bhāva*, dṅos) and the thesis (*sādhya*, bsgrub bya). There are three parts to this.

/gźan don rjes dpag gam / sgrub ṅag yaṅ dag gi mtshan ñid / rgol ba raṅ gis tshad mas grub pa'i rtags kyis tshul gsum phyir rgol la lhag chad med par ston pa'i ṅag yan lag gñis ldan / dbye na / gñis las / chos mthun sbyor gyi sgrub ṅag yaṅ dag gi mtshan ñid / rgol ba raṅ gis tshad mas grub pa'i phyogs chos daṅ rjes khyab phyir rgol la dṅos su lhag chad med par ston pa'i ṅag yan lag gñis ldan / dper na / gaṅ byas mi rtag dper na bum pa bźin sgra ni byas źes pa'i ṅag lta bu'o

/ chos mi mthun sbyor gyis sgrub ṅag yaṅ dag gi mtshan ñid / rgol ba raṅ gis tshad mas grub pa'i phyogs chos daṅ ldog khyab phyir rgol la lhag chad med par ston pa'i ṅag yan lag gñis ldan / dper na / gaṅ rtag pa ma byas nam mkha' bźin sgra ni byas so źes pa'i ṅag lta bu'o /

1. Inference for another, or the genuine syllogism (sgrub ṅag) is defined as having two ancillaries, to wit, the three modes by way of the evidence which the 'first speaker' (*vādin*) has proved by his own authority; and the utterance (*vāda*) explaining it to the 'respondent' (*prativādin*) without violating (the first speaker's proof). In variegation there are two kinds:
   (1) genuine syllogism of concordant application (*sādharmya-prayoga*, chos mthun sbyor) is defined as the two ancillaries: a. the locus feature and the *anvaya*-pervasion which the 'first speaker' has proven by his own authority; and b. the actual utterance teaching it without violating (the first speaker's proof) to the 'respondent'. For example, the 'first speaker' saying, "Whatever is created is impermanent, like a pot; and sound is created."
   (2) genuine syllogism of discordant application (*vaidharmya-prayoga*, chos mi mthun sbyor) is defined as the two ancillaries: a. the locus feature and the *vyatireka*-pervasion which the 'first' has proven by his own authority; and b. the utterance teaching it without violating (the first speaker's proof) to the 'respondent'. For example, the 'first speaker' says, "Whatever is permanent is uncreate, like space; but sound is created."

/ sgrub ṅag ltar snaṅ gi mtshan ñid / sgrub ṅag tu bkod pa gaṅ źig / skyon gaṅ ruṅ daṅ ldan pa / dbye ba gsum las / blo skyon can gyi sgrub ṅag ltar snaṅ ni / blo bde chos can / sems med yin te / skye 'jig can yin pa'i phyir / gzugs sogs bźin źes pa'i ṅag lta bu'o / don skyon can gyi sgrub ṅag ltar snaṅ ni / sgra ni rtag pa yin te / phyogs daṅ mthun phyogs gaṅ ruṅ yin pa'i phyir / źes pa'i ṅag lta bu / sgra skyon can gyi sgrub ṅag ltar snaṅ ni / dper na sgra ni mi rtag ste byas pa yin pa'i phyir / dper na bum pa bźin / sgra yaṅ byas / de'i phyir sgra mi rtag ces pa'i ṅag lta bu'o /

2. Fallacy (*ābhāsa*) of the syllogism is defined as any formulation as a syllogism that has some particular fault (*doṣa*). In variegation there are three kinds:
   (1) Fallacy of syllogism that has the fault of *buddhi* (cognition, or discriminating mind) is, e.g. the 'first speaker. saying, "The cognition that is the factual base of pleasure

is unconscious (sems med), because it has arising and passing away, like a formation, etc."

(2) Fallacy of syllogism that has the fault of object-entity (*artha*) is, e.g. the 'first speaker' saying, "Sound is permanent, because it is the locus (*pakṣa*) or similar locus (*sapakṣa*) as appropriate..

(3) Fallacy of syllogism that has the fault of word (rational utterance) is, e.g. the 'first speaker' saying, "Sound is impermanent, because it is created; for example, like a pot. Sound is also created; therefore, sound is impermanent."

/rtags yaṅ dag gi bsgrub bya'i mtshan ñid / rtags yaṅ dag la brten nas gzod go bar bya ba / dbye na / raṅ don gyi rtags yaṅ dag gi bsgrub bya daṅ / gźan don gyi rtags yaṅ dag gi bsgrub bya gñis /

3. The thesis (*sādhya*) of genuine evidence is defined as what is to be understood newly after taking recourse to genuine evidence. In variegation there are two kinds, of 'own aim' and 'aim of others' / daṅ po'i mtshan ñid / glo bur du rtags tshad mas grub pa la brten nas gzod go bar·bya ba /

(1) The thesis of genuine evidence for 'own aim' is defined as what is to be understood newly in a 'flash' (*āgantuka*) after taking recourse to proving with an authority of evidence.

/ gźan don gyi rtags yaṅ dag gi bsgrub bya'i mtshan ñid / ṅo bo'i don sogs chos lṅa tshaṅ ba / yaṅ na bsgrub byar 'os śiṅ rgol bas bsgrub byar khas blaṅs pa / chos lṅa ni / kun las btus las / ṅo bo kho du / de sgrub kyi phyir rgol gyis tshad mas grub zin ma lried pa ma na raṅ ñid daṅ / 'dod' gyur ma bsal bstan bya ba / źes 'byuṅ ba ltar du / de sgrub kyi phyir rgol gyis tshad mas grub zin ma brjed pa ma yin pa daṅ / de sgrub kyi sgrub byed du bkod bźin pa ma yin pa daṅ/ de sgrub kyi rgol bas dpag 'dod kyi yul du byas pa daṅ / de sgrub kyi rgol ba źe bas 'dod pa daṅ / de sgrub kyi phyir rgol gyis tshad mas ma bsal rnams so /

(2) The Thesis of genuine evidence for 'aim of others' is defined as the complete five *dharmas* of *svarūpa*, etc. Besides, it is worthy of being a thesis and is accepted as a thesis by the 'first speaker'. The five dharmas are as found in (Dignāga's) *Samuccaya*: "the *svarūpa*, the *eva*, the *svayam*, the *iṣṭa*, and the *anirākṛta* will be explained." To wit:

a. For proving it, one should not forget that it has not been realized by the 'respondent' to that proof.

b. For proving it, it should not be the same as what is used as the means of proof (*sādhana*) of that proof.

c. For proving it, it should be an object which the respondent desires to consider.

d. For proving it, the respondent should admit the claim.

e. For proving it, the respondent must not have rejected it with an authority.[20]

/ gźan don gyi phyog ltar snaṅ gi mtshan ñid / sna rgol gyis dam bcas pa'i tshogs don gaṅ źig / no bo'i don sogs chos lṅa ma tshaṅ ba / dbye na lṅa las /

The fallacy of locus (*pakṣa*) for the aim of others is defined as any feature of the set associated with the thesis (*pratijñā*) by the first speaker, among the five features (*dharma*) of *svarūpa-artha* and so on (i.e., the fivefold group announced by Dignāga, clarified by the five above sentences) (such that) it is incomplete. In variegation, there are five kinds:

/grub zin pa'i phyogs ltar snaṅ ni / sgra mi rtag par tshad mas grub zin pa'i gaṅ zag gi ṅor / sgra mi rtag par dam bcas pa'i tshe sgra mi rtag pa lta bu'o /

1. Fallacy of the locus (*pakṣa*) that was already proved is illustrated as follows: A person had already proven by authority that sound is impermanent At the time he makes a claim that sound is impermanent, the saying of "Sound is impermanent" [is redundent].

/sgrub byed du bkod bźin pa'i phyogs ltar snan ni / sgra mi rtag par sgrub pa la sgra mi rtag pa bkod pa'i tshe sgra mi rtag pa lta bu'o/

2. Fallacy of the locus (pakṣa) according to the reason used in proving is illustrated as follows: When proving sound to be impermanent, at the time one uses the reason in evidence that sound is impermanent, the saying of "Sound is impermanent" [is evidence equal to the thesis].

/rgol ba dpag 'dod med pa'i phyogs ltar snaṅ ni / rgol bas sṅar gzegs zan gyi luṅ khas blaṅs nas / phyis sgra mi rtag sgrub la byas pa rtags su bkod pa'i tshe / sgra rtag pa nam yon lta bu'o /

3. Fallacy of the locus which the 'first speaker'[21] does not desire

20. Since the full form in Tibetan for 'first speaker' is *sṅa rgol*, for the 'respondent' *phyir rgol*, to keep them separate, the text should have been using the full forms in the above discussion, since *rgol* by itself is ambiguous. However, since the text is the author's own study of the topic, he uses a full form *phyir rgol*, followed by several instances of *rgol*, intending also *phyir rgol*.

21. Again the *rgol ba* here and a following one are ambiguous. Here, the 'first speaker' is intended in the sense that this person has the fallacious presentation which the Buddhist (as the respondent) attempts to refute.

to infer is illustrated as follows: The 'first speaker' formerly accepted the scripture of Kaṇāda [founder of the Vaiśeṣika school]. Later, when proving that sound is impermanent, at that time this person uses the reason in evidence that it (i.e. sound) is created, (but) mentions the option that sound is eternal.

/rgol bas źe bas mi 'dod pa'i phyogs ltar snaṅ ni / graṅs can pas mig sogs bdag don byed par sgrub par 'dod nas / ṅag tu mig sogs gźan don byed par dam bcas pa'i tshe sogs gźan don byed pa lta bu'o /

4. Fallacy of the locus when the 'first speaker' does not personally accept it, is illustrated as follows: The Sāṃkhya claim to have proved that the eye, etc. serve the purpose of the self (*aham*). But in their words, claiming that the eye, etc. serve the purpose of another, their saying "The eye, etc., serve the purpose of another" [would mean in their system the Purusa, not the Ahaṃ(*kāra*) which is equivalent to Prakṛti].

/ bsal ba źugs pa'i phyogs ltar snaṅ ni / sgra mñan bya ma yin pa lta bu /

5. Fallacy of the locus which is subject to rejection is illustrated as follows: (the proponent says:) "The sound is inaudible" [but how can it be called a 'sound' if no one hears it?].

/ bsal ba'i mtshan ñid / dam bca' ltar snaṅ gaṅ źig khyod kyi ldog phyogs kyi don tshad mas grub pa / dbye na gñis las /

Refusal *(pratyākhyā*, bsal ba) is defined as any fallacy of (announced) thesis (*pratijñā*) (such that) your object-entity (*artha*) belongs to the excluded locus (*vyāvṛttapakṣa*), is proved by authority. In variegation there are two kinds:

/ mṅon sum bsal ba'i mtshan ñid / gaṅ źig / khyod kyi dṅos kyi ldog phyogs kyi don mṅon sum tshad mas grub pa / dper na sgra mñan bya ma yin pa lta bu'o /

1. Rejection of a direct perception (*pratyakṣa*) is defined as any one (such that) your discrete object-entity belongs to the excluded side, is proved by authority of direct perception; for example, "The sound is inaudible."

/ dṅos po stobs źugs kyi rjes dpag gi bsal ba'i mtshan ñid / gaṅ źig / khyod kyi dṅos kyi ldog phyogs kyi don dṅos po stobs źugs kyi rjes dpag gis grub pa / dper na / sgra rtag pa lta bu /

2. [Rejection of an inference (*anumāna*), variegation of three kinds]:

(1) Rejection of an inference aroused on the strength of a discrete thing is defined as any one (such that) your discrete object-entity belongs to the excluded locus, is proved by an inference aroused on the strength of a discrete thing; for example, "Sound is eternal."

/ grags pa'i rjes dpag gi bsal ba'i mtshan ñid / gaṅ źig / khyod kyi dṅos kyi ldog phyogs kyi don grags pa'i rjes dpag gis grub pa / dper na / ri boṅ can zla ba'i sgras brjod mi ruṅ lta bu /

(2) Rejection of a popular inference is defined as any one (such that) your discrete object-entity belongs to the excluded locus, is proved by a popular inference; for example, "It is not proper to make the saying 'The moon has a rabbit.' "

/ yid ches bsal ba'i mtshan ñid / sṅar khas blaṅs pa'i dam bca' ṅag phyi mas ñams par byas pa'i dam bca' ltar snaṅ gi don / dper na / raṅ tshig sṅa phyi 'gal ba'i sgo nas khas blaṅs kyis bsal ba daṅ / yid ches pa'i bsal ba gñis /

(3) Rejection of a master (*āpta*) lineage is defined as follows: Having previously announced the espousal of a thesis, later one disavows the thesis. As to the meaning of this fallacy, there are two kinds: a. rejection of espousal by way of opposition (or contradiction) between the earlier and the later (versions of) one's words; b. rejection of a master (lineage).

/ daṅ po'i mtshan ñid / raṅ tshig sṅa mas bźag pa raṅ tshig phyi mas ñams par byas pa'i dam bca' ltar snaṅ gi don / dper bud med gcig sṅar mar daṅ bcas nas phyis mo gśam du dam bcas pa'i tshe bud med bu skyed pa'i nus ldan yod med gñis ka yin pa lta bu /

a. The rejection of espousal by way of opposition is defined as opposition between one's prior and later word. This is the meaning of the fallacy where a thesis is previously established by one's word and later disavowed. For example, having previously made the thesis that a certain woman is a mother, and later on the thesis that she is a barren woman; at that time, the woman both is and is not capable of generating a child.

/ gñis pa'i mtshan ñid / dam bca' ltar snaṅ gi don gaṅ źig / raṅ gi dṅos kyi log phyogs kyi don yid ches rjes dpag gis grub pa / dper na / sṅar saṅs rgyas kyi luṅ tshad mar khas blaṅs nas / phyis sbyin sogs dkar chos la spyad pa las ma 'oṅs pa na bde ba mi 'byuṅ bar dam bcas pa'i don lta bu'o /

b. Rejection of a master lineage is defined as any meaning of the fallacy of thesis (such that) one's own discrete object-entity belongs to the excluded locus, is proved by inference of the master (*āpta*) (variety). For example, having previously announced the thesis that the Buddha's scripture is an authority, later on, being not prone to practising the 'white' (i.e. virtuous) *dharma* of giving (*dāna*), and so on, one takes the thesis as not pleasurable (or, is dissatisfying).

/ des na / yid ches bsal ba yin pa la yid ches rjes dpag gis bsal ba yin pas ma khyab ciṅ / spyir yid ches bsal ba daṅ dṅos po stobs źugs kyi bsal ba yaṅ mi 'gal lo / yaṅ kun las btus su / yid ches / źes gcig tu bsdus nas bśad pa'i raṅ tshig daṅ luṅ tshig gi mtshan ñid / rim pa bźin rgol ba raṅ gis bden źen gyis smras pa'i bsgrub bya brjod pa'i tshig daṅ / dpyad pa gsum gyis dag pa'i luṅ yin pa / bla ma sṅa ma dag gyis po'i mtshan ñid rim bźin / bsgrub bya brjod pa'i tshig gaṅ źig / chos can yod na tshur mthoṅ gis dṅos po stobs źugs kyis 'grub pa luṅ la mi bltos pa daṅ bltos pa źes gsuns te dpyad do /

Hence, rejection of a master lineage is not pervaded by rejection through inference. In general rejection of a master lineage and rejection of (inference) aroused on the strength of a given thing, are not in opposition. Moreover, (Dignāga's) *Samuccaya* says, "*āptavāda*..." Thus (Dharmakīrti's) own words as well as the *āgama* words (i.e. of the *Samuccaya*), explained by condensing into one, are defined, in the given order (i.e. Dignāga's and then Dharmakīrti's words), as the words telling the thesis (*sādhya*) which is expressed by the 'first speaker' himself through his ascertainment of truth; and the pure scripture with three examinations.[22] One should ponder what was said to be the definition (*lakṣaṇa*) going with the two former gurus (Dignāga and Dharmakīrti) in the given order, namely, that it is any words telling the thesis (such that) when there is a factual base (*dharmin*), a person 'looking hither' (*arvāg-darśana*) proves with (inference) aroused on the strength of a discrete thing; and (in the given order) does not pay attention to, or does pay attention to a scripture.

/ źar la phyogs skyon gyi mtshan ñid / phyogs su bzuṅ le'o de kho na la ldan źiṅ / de de sgrub kyi phyogs mtshan ñid pa ma yin par sgrub pa'i tshul gsum tshaṅ ba'i rtags gaṅ źig / ṅo bo'i don sogs chos lṅa gaṅ run gi dṅos kyi log phyogs yin pa / dbye na lṅa las / grub zin pa'i phyogs ltar snaṅ gi skyon ni / sgra mñam bya yin pa la sgra mñan bya yin par sgrub pa'i phyir rgol gyi tshad mas grub pa źugs pa lta bu'o / lhag ma bźi'aṅ des 'gre'o /

Along those lines, the fault (*doṣa*) of a locus (*pakṣa*) is defined as any one possessing only a so-called embracing of a 'locus', where the

22. See footnotes above, no. 4 and 5.

evidence is complete with the three modes of proof while lacking the characteristics of a 'locus' for proving this and that, (such that) it is the material contrary locus of any one of the five features (*dharma*), the *svarūpa-artha*, and so on. In variegation there are five: 1. fault of fallacy of the locus (*pakṣa*) already proven, e.g. "A sound is audible," when the 'first speaker' proved by authority (the thesis) to be proved that sound is audible. The remaining four (2-5) may be treated accordingly.

/sun 'byin bśad pa la / sun 'byin yaṅ dag gi mtshan ñid / skyon las skyon du brjod pas skyọn can go nus pa'i ṅag / dbye na /raṅ rgyud kyi sun 'byin yaṅ dag daṅ / thal 'gyur gyi sun 'byin yaṅ dag gñis / raṅ rgyud ni sgrub ṅag yaṅ dag yin pas bśad zin no / sun 'byin ltar snaṅ gi mtshan ñid / sun 'byin du bkod pa gaṅ źig / skyon la skyon du brjod pas skyon du go mi nus pa /

For explaining the fault-finding (*dūṣana*), the genuine fault-finding is defined as the announcing able to express a fault, pointing out the fault with the words, "It is faulty." In variegation there are two kinds, the genuine independent (*svatantra*) fault-finding, and the genuine 'reductio absurdum' (*prasaṅga*) fault-finding. The 'independent' (*svatantra*) (kind) has already been explained by way of the genuine means of proof. A fallacy of fault-finding is defined as any formulation as fault-finding (such that) it cannot admit that there was a fault in calling a fault a fault.

/ thal 'gyur yaṅ dag gi mtshan ñid / lan gyis ldog ni nus pa'i tha dag / dbye na / sgrub byed 'phen pa daṅ / mi 'phen pa'i thal 'gyur yaṅ dag gñis /

A genuine 'reductio absurdum' (*prasaṅga*) is defined as a refutation that cannot be warded off by a reply. In variegation there are two kinds: the genuine *prasaṅga* which implicates, or does not implicate a means of proof (*sādhana*).

/ daṅ po'i mtshan ñid / thal 'gyur yaṅ dag gaṅ źig / chos log gis ran gi chos can gyi steṅ du / rtags log sgrub ba tshul gsum tshaṅ ba / dbye na / raṅ rigs daṅ gźan rigs 'phen pa'i thal 'gyur yaṅ dag gñis /

1. A genuine *prasaṅga* which implicates a means of proof is defined as any genuine *prasaṅga* complete with the three modes (of evidence) when proving that an evidence is wayward in terms of a wayward feature (*dharma*) on its own factual base. In variegation there is the genuine *prasaṅga* which implicates one's own principle or another's principle.

/ daṅ po'i mtshan ñid / gaṅ źig / chos log gis raṅ gi chos can gyi steṅ du / rtags log sgrub na raṅ daṅ rigs gcig pa'i tshul gsum tshaṅ ba yin pa / dper na pha rol pos me stobs chen pos khyab par non pa'i sa phyogs na graṅ reg rgyun chags yod par khas len pa la / me stobs chen pas khyad par non pa'i sa phyogs chos can / me stobs chen gyis khyab par non pa ma yin par thal / graṅ reg stobs chen rgyun chags yod pa'i phyir / źes pa'i thal 'gyur lta bu /

(1) A genuine 'reductio absurdum' (prasanga) which implicates one's own principle is defined as any one complete with the three modes of principle identical with one's own, when proving that an evidence is wayward in terms of a wayward feature on its own factual base. For example, the other person accepts that in a place set upon pervasively by a fire of great power, there is a continuity of touching cold. This reduces to the absurdity that the place, i.e. the factual base, that is set upon pervasively by a great power of fire, is not (after all) set upon pervasively by a great power of fire, since there is a continuity of great power to touch cold. Such is the reductio absurdum (*prasaṅga*).

/ gźan rigs 'phen pa'i thal 'gyur yaṅ dag gi mtshan ñid / gaṅ źig chos log gis raṅ gi chos can gyi steṅ du / rtags log sgrub na raṅ daṅ rigs mi gcig pa'i tshul gsum tshaṅ ba / dper na pha rol pos sṅo 'phyur ba daṅ ldan pa'i mtshan mo'i rgya mtshor du ba yod par khas len pa na / sṅo 'phyur ba daṅ ldan pa'i mtshan mo'i rgya mtsho na chos can / me yod par thal / du ba yod pa'i phyir / źes pa'i thal 'gyur lta bu /

(2) A genuine *prasaṅga* which implicates another's principle is defined as any one complete with the three modes of principle not identical with one's own, when proving that an evidence is wayward in terms of a wayward feature on its own factual base. For example, the other person accepts that there is smoke on a lake at night having a rising greenish mist. This reduces to the absurdity that there is fire on the lake, the factual base, at night and having a rising greenish mist, because there is 'smoke'. Such is the reductio absurdum.

/ sgrub byed mi 'phen pa'i thal 'gyur yaṅ dag gi mtshan ñid / gaṅ źig / chos log gis raṅ gi chos can gyi steṅ du / rtags log sgrub na tshul gsum ma tshaṅ ba / dper na / pha rol pos lto ldir źabs źum gyis dag pa'i sa phyogs na bum pa yod par khas blaṅs pa la / lto ldir bas dag pa'i sa phyogs chos can / bum pa med par thal / lto ldir ba snaṅ ruṅ ma dmigs pa'i phyir / źes pa'i thal 'gyur lta bu /

2. A genuine *prasaṅga* that does not implicate a means of proof is defined as any one not complete with the three modes (of evidence) when proving that an evidence is wayward in terms of a wayward feature on its own factual base. For example, the

other person accepts that there is a pot on a spot bare of a large-bulbed and slender legged (pot). This reduces to the absurdity that there is no pot on the spot, which is the factual base bare of a large bulbed (type of pot), because one does not apprehend a visible large bulbed (type of pot). Such is the reductio absurdum.[23]

/ thal 'gyur ltar snaṅ ba'i mtshan ñid / lan gyis ldog par nus pa'i thal 'gyur / dper na pha rol pos sgra rtag par khas blaṅs pa la / sgra chos can / mi rtag par thal / mñan bya yin pa'i phyir / źes pa lta bu'o /

Fallacy of a 'reductio absurdum' (*prasaṅga*) is defined as a *prasaṅga* that can be warded off by a reply. For example, the other person accepts that sound is eternal, (or says that) when sound is the factual base, it is wrong that it is impermanent because it is audible.

/ rgol ba'i mtshan ñid phyogs sṅa ma 'jog nus par khas len pa'i gaṅ zag / phyir rgol gyi mtshan ñid / phyogs sṅa ma sun 'byin par khas len pa'i gaṅ zag / dbaṅ po'i mtshan ñid / rgol ba gñis kyi rtsod pa rgyal pham śan 'byed par khas len pa'i gaṅ zag /

A 'first speaker' (rgol ba) is defined as a person who espouses (a thesis) and is able to posit the former side (*pūrvapakṣa*). A 'respondent' (*phyir rgol ba*) is defined as a person who espouses (a thesis) and is able to find fault with the former side.

A referee (dbaṅ po) is defined as a person who accepts (the role) to assess victory or defeat in the argument of the two debaters.

/ gźan yaṅ thal 'gyur ltar snaṅ la lan 'debs tshul bśad par bya ste /sgra rtag par thal byas pa yin pa'i phyir la / khyab pa 'gal źes pa lta bu daṅ / sgra mi rtag par thal mñan bya yin pa'i phyir la khyab pa ma ṅes źes pa lta bu daṅ / sgra mi rtag par thal mig gi gzuṅ bya yin pa'i phyir la / rtags ma grub ces pa lta bu daṅ / mdun gyi gźi 'dir śa za'i bum pa chos can / mi rtag par thal / byas pa'i phyir la / rtags la the tshom za źes pa lta bu daṅ / draṅ don gyi luṅ bstan bya'i don la mi bslu bar thal / dpyad pa gsum gyis dag pa'i luṅ yin pa'i phyir la 'dod ces pa lta bu'i lan 'debs par bya'o //

Moreover, for the case of a fallacy of *prasaṅga*, I shall explain the method of replying. For the *prasaṅga* that sound is permanent because it is constructed, one replies, "There is opposition of pervasion." For the *prasaṅga* that sound is impermanent because it

23. Here, the opponent is assailed for claiming that there is a pot in a place devoid of a certain kind of pot. This claim seems to go astray in not realizing that there is no pot in a place unless it is a kind of pot.

is audible, one replies that the pervasion is uncertain. For the *prasaṅga* that sound is impermanent because it is visible, one replies that the evidence has not proven (the thesis). For the *prasaṅga* that when the *piśāca*-pot on this spot in front is the factual base, it is impermanent because it is created, one replies that the evidence is doubtful. For the *prasaṅga* that there is no deception in the meaning to be taught by a scripture of provisional meaning (*neyārtha*) because it is a scripture by the three examinations, one replies, "(So) you believe!"

'dir 'bad dge bas daṅ po'i las can rnams /
gnas skabs rigs pa'i sgo la 'jug pa daṅ /
mthar thug blaṅ dor gnas la tshul bźin du /
sbyaṅs nas byaṅ chub dam pa thob par śog /

bstan pa daṅ sems can la phan pa rgya chen po 'byuṅ bar gyur cig /

Aspiration

By reason of the virtuous endeavor in this world,
may the beginners enter the gateway of the principles
of the occasion; and may they, having exercised methodically
in the ultimate points of accepting (the right) and
rejecting (the wrong), attain the sublime enlightenment.

May there be widespread benefit to the Teaching and to sentient beings.

mtha' bral lta bas chos kun stoṅ par gzigs /
yaṅ dag rigs pas rtsod ṅan dregs pa 'joms /
dmigs med thugs rjes kun la bu ltar brtse /
'phags mchog klu sgrub yab sras la phyag 'tshal //

Maṅgala Verses

I bow to the best Noble Nāgārjuna and son (=Āryadeva), who by the view free from the extremes, have seen the void of all *dharmas*; who by genuine principles have subdued the pride of bad disputants; and who by aimless compassion love all like a son.

kun bkra'i gzugs la mig gis blta ba bźin /
rnam maṅ rgyal ba'i gsuṅ rab ji sñed la /

rnam dag mkhyen pa thogs pa med 'jug pa /
thogs med sku mched źabs la phyag 'tshal lo //

I bow to Asaṅga and brother (= Vasubandhu), who to the extent they see with eye (=eye of *dharma*) the manifold forms, engage with unimpeded (*asaṅga*) pure knowledge to the same extent as is the numerous teachings of the Buddha.

gnas gsum gzal bya'i de ñid ma lus pa /
tshad ma gsum gyis gtan la phab pa'i don /
sgrub daṅ suṇ 'byin ṅag gis 'doms mdzad pa /
rigs pa'i dbaṅ phyug gñis la phyag 'tshal lo //

I bow to the two Lords of Principles (=Dignāga and Dharmakīrti) who, for every single real of sanction for the three modes have established the object-entity by three authorities;[24] and have counselled by words of affirmation and fault-finding.

tshul khrims rgya mtsho'i dbus na gnas bcas śiṅ /
'bum phrag 'dul ba'i gźuṅ gi gdeṅs kas brjid /
rnam grol thar pa'i nor bu gtsug na mdzes /
mchog gñis klu yi dbaṅ po la phyag 'tshal //

I bow to the two best lords of serpents (=Guṇaprabha and Śākyaprabha) who taking their dwelling place within the ocean of morality, glistening with heads (made) of the thousandfold Vinaya-texts, are beautified on their crowns with the gem of liberation.

/ ces pa rigs rus phun sum tshogs pa'i bdag ñid bdag po grags pa rgyal mtshan pas bskul ba'i don du / śar tson kha pa blo bzaṅ grags pa'i dpal gyis sbyar ba'o //

Colophon

So I, Śar-Tsoṅ-kha-pa[25] Blo-bzaṅ-grags-pa'i-dpal, equipped with the lineage of principles, and because exhorted by his honor Grags-pa'i-rgyal mtshan, have composed the foregoing.[26]

// Maṅgalaṃ //

---

24. These seem to be *pratyakṣa,* and *anumāna,* (2 kinds).
25. The name means "the man from East Onion Vallery".
26. This colophon does not include the title which was presented at the outset on my introduction, with the abbreviation *Mun sel.* Such a title is given at the outset; if. the text is in the form of folios, then presented on the initial folio.

BIBLIOGRAPHY

A

Asaṅga. *Abhidharmasamuccaya.* See Pradhan, Pralhad; see Tatia, Nathmal.

Asaṅga. Hetu-vidyā ("Rules of Debate"), Tibetan in PTT, Vol. 109, starting p. 298-1-6; see Pāṇḍeya, J., Wayman, A., and Yaita, H.

Asaṅga. *Yogācārabhūmi,* Part I ed. by Vidhushekhara Bhattacharya (Univ. of Calcutta, 1957).

B

Biardeau, Madeleine. "Le role du l'example dans l'inference indienne," Journal Asiatique, 1957.

Bod rgyal tshig mdzod chen mo, 3 vols. (Peking: Mi rigs dpe skrun khang, 1985).

Brough, John, "Some Indian Theories of Meaning," *Transactions of the Philological Society,* 1953, p. 176c.

Bu-ston. *History of Buddhism,* tr. from the Tibetan by E. Obermiller (Heidelberg, 1931).

Bu-ston. Collected Works, Part 24 (Ya) (Delhi: International Academy of Indian Culture, 1971): comment on the Tibetan version of Dharmakīrti's *Pramāṇa-viniścaya.*

C

Chandra, Lokesh. *Tibetan-Sanskrit Dictionary;* Compact Edition (Kyoto: Rinsen Book Co., 1982).

D

Dhaky, M.A. "the Date and Authorship of Nyāyāvatāra," in *Nirgrantha,* Vol. 1 (Ahmedabad, 1995).

Dharmakīrti. *Hetubindu* II, tr. by Ernst Steinkellner (Wien, 1967).

Dharmakīrti. *Nyāyabindu,* with Dharmottara's commentary (Banaras: Chowkhamba Skt. Series, 1954). See Stcherbatsky, Th.

Dharmakīrti. *Pramāṇavārttikam*, with the Vṛtti commentary of Manorathanandin, ed. by Dwarikadas Shastri (Varanasi: Bauddha Bharati, 1968); Tib. version (Sarnath, Varanasi: Central Institute of Tibetan Higher Studies, 1974); Sanskrit-Tibetan and Tibetan-Sanskrit Indexes, compiled by Miyasaka, Y. (Narita: Naritasan Shinshoji), *Acta Indologica*, III, 1975 and IV, 1976.

Dharmakīrti. *Pramāṇaviniścaya*; its separate printing of the Tibetan version, *Tshad ma rnam par ṅes* pa (Delhi: Karmapae Chodhey, 1976); a Tibetan commentary, see Bu-ston. See also Steinkellner, E. and Vetter, T.

Dharmakīrti. *Svavṛtti* on PV-Sva. See Gnoli, R. and Malvaniya, D.; also Karnakagomin.

Dharmottara. Commentary on P-Vin (as cited by Bu-ston, Vol. Ya).

Dignāga. *Pramāṇa-samuccaya* (=PS) and his own *Vṛtti* (= PS-vṛtti). Tibetan versions: Derge Tanjur, Tshad ma, PS tr. by Vasudhararakṣita and Sha-ma Seṅ-rgyal, Vol. Ce, starting 1b; PS-Vṛtti tr. by same translators, Ce, starting 14b. PIT version, Tanjur, Tshad ma, PS tr. by Gser gyi go-cha (= Kanakavarman) and Dad pa'i ses-rab, starting Vol. Ce; PS-vṛtti tr. by same translators, starting Ce 93b; and in between, PS-vṛtti also tr. by Vasudhararakṣita and Seṅ-rgyal, starting Ce 13a. See also Hattori, M. and Kitagawa, H.

Dpal-brtsegs (translator). PTT edn. of Tanjur, Vol. 145, p. 116.

E

Edgerton, Franklin. *Buddhist Hybrid Sanskrit Dictionary* (New Haven: Yale Univ. Press, 1953).

G

Gnoli, Raniero. *The Pramāṇavārttika of Dharmakīrti; The First chapter with the autocommentary* (Roma, 1960).

Go-rams-pa. Rigs gter gsal byed (Mussooorie, India: Sakya College, 1975).

H

Hahn, Michael. "On the Pratyaya Rules of Ratnākaraśānti," *Journal of the Oriental Institute*, XXX, 1-2, Sept.-Dec. 1980, pp. 61-77.

Hattori, Masaaki. *Dignāga, On Perception* (Cambridge, Mass.: Harvard Univ. Press, 1968), starting p. 173 the Tibetan texts (in transcription) of PS-vṛtti, the Pratyakṣa chapter, both the Kanakavarman and the Vasudhararakṣita renditions.

Hayes, Richard P. "Dignāga's Views on Reasoning *(Svārthānumāna)*, *Journal of Indian Philosophy*, 8 (1980).

J

Jaini, P. *Sāratama*, Ratnākaraśānti's *Pañjikā* on the *Aṣṭasāhasrikā Prajñāpāramitā* (Patna, 1979).

Jha, Ganganatha. *The Pūrvamīmāṃsā-sūtras of Jaimini* (Varanasi, Delhi, 1979); *Pūrva-Mīmāṃsā in its Sources* (Varanasi, 1964).

Jñānaśrī. Commentary on P-Vin (as cited by Bu-ston, Vol. Ya).

Joshi, S.D. and J.A.P. Roodbergen. *Patañjali's Vyākaraṇa Mahābhāṣya*, Tatpuruṣāhnika (Poona: University of Poona, 1973).

K

Kajiyama, Yuichi. "Three kinds of Affirmation and Two kinds of Negation in Buddhist Philosophy," *WZKS*, XVII, 1973, pp. 161-75.

Kalyāṇarakṣita. *Sarvajñāsiddhi* (as cited by Bu-ston, Vol. Ya).

Kamalaśīla. *Nyāyabindukārikā-pūrvapakṣa-saṃkṣipti*, Tibetan tr. in PTT Vol. 137, p. 191-3-1 to 195-2-6.

Karṇakagomin. *Commentary on the Pramāṇavārttikavṛtti of Dharmakīrti* (Kyoto: Rinsen Book Co., 1982).

Kesamutti-sutta. From the Aṅguttara-Nikāya, Book of Threes, and addressed to the Kālāmas.

Kitagawa, Hidenori. *A Study of Indian Classical Logic—Dignāga's System* [in Japanese], tr. of Dharmakīrti's *Saṃtānāntarasiddhi*, in English, pp. 407ff. (Tokyo, 1965), starting p. 447, the Tibetan (in transcription) for PS and PS-vṛtti, both the Kanakavarman and Vasudhararakṣita renditions, 1st halves of the chapters Svārthānumāna, Parārthānumāna, Dṛṣṭānta-dṛṣṭāntabhāsa-parīkṣā, Jāti-parīkṣā; starting p. 555, both the K and the V renditions for paragraphs of PS critisizing certain Naiyāyika theories; starting p. 577, K and V for criticism of a Vādavidhi theory.

Kitagawa, Hidenori. "A Note on the Methodology in the Study of Indian Logic," *Journal of Indian and Buddhist Studies* (Tokyo), Vol. VIII: 1 (January 1960).

M

Malvaniya, Dhalsukhbhai. Ed. *Svārthānumāna* Chapter of PV and Dharmakīrti's *Svavṛtti* thereon (Banaras, 1959).

McDermott, A.C. Senape, *An Eleventh-Ccentury Buddhist Logic of*

'Exists' (Dordrecht, 1970).

Mimaki, K. *Le réfutation bouddhique de la permanence des choses* (Paris, 1976).

Mimaki, K. "Sur le rôle de l'*antaraśloka ou du saṃgrahaśloka,*" in *Indianisme et Bouddhisme*, Mélanges offerts a Mgr Étienne Lamotte (Louvain, 1980), pp. 233-244.

Mkhas grub rje. Collected works, Vol. Tha, *Tshad ma sde bdun gyi rgyan yid kyi mun sel zhes bya ba* [cited as his 'Mun sel'].

Muktakalaśa. *Kṣaṇabhaṅgasiddhivivaraṇa,* in PTT, Vo. 138, p. 85-3-3, ff.

N

Nagatomi, Masatoshi. "*Mānasa-Pratyakṣa*: a Conundrum in the Buddhist *Pramāṇa* system," in *Sanskrit and Indian Studies; Essays in Honour of Daniel H.H. Ingalls,* ed. by M. Nagatomi, et al. (Dordrecht, 1980), pp. 243-60.

O

Obermiller, E. *The Doctrine of Prajñā-pāramitā as exposed in the Abhisamayālaṃkāra of Maitreya,* Acta Orientalia, Vol. XI (1932).

P

Pāṇḍeya, Jagadīśvara. Editor of Asaṅga, *Hetu-vidyā, in Homage to Bhikkhu Jagdish Kashyap,* ed. by P.N. Ojha (Nalanda, Bihar: Siri Nava Nalanda Mahavihara, 1986), Part II, pp. 315-49.

Pradhan, Pralhad, Ed. *Abhidharmasamuccaya* (Santiniketan: Visva-Bharati, 1950).

Prajñākaragupta. *Pramāṇavārttikabhāṣyam,* ed. by Rāhula Sāṅkṛtyāyana (Patna: Kashi Prasad Jayaswal Research Institute, 1953).

R

Ratnākaraśānti. *Antarvyāptisamarthana;* Sanskrit text in Shastri, H. *Six Buddhist Nyāya Tracts*; Tibetan version, PTT, Vol. 138, p. 104-3-6 to p. 106-4-4.

Ratnakīrti. *Kṣaṇabhaṅgasiddhi-vyatirekātmikā,* in Anantalal Thakur, ed., *Ratnakīrti-Nibandhāvaliḥ* (Patna 1957, and revised edition 1975).

Ruegg, D.S. *The Life of Bu ston Rin po che with the Tibetan text of the Bu ston rNam thar* (Rome: Istituto italiano per il Medio ed Estremo Oriente, 1966).

S

Sa-skya-Pandita. *Tshad ma rigs pa'i gter* (xylograph reproduced from blocks at Simtokha, 1976).

Shastri, Dharmendra Nath. *Critique of Indian Realism* (Agra, 1964).

Shastri, Dwarikadas. See Dharmakīrti. *Pramāṇavārttikam.*

Shastri, Haraprasād. *Six Buddhist Nyāya Tracts* (Calcutta: Asiatic Society, 1910).

Staal, J. F. "The Concept of *Pakṣa* in Indian Logic, *Journal of Indian Philosophy* 2 (1973) 156-66.

Stcherbatsky, Th. *Buddhist Logic,* Vol. II (New York: Dover Publications, 1962), containing annotated translation of Dharmakriti's *Nyāyabindu with Dharmottara's* commentary.

Stcherbatsky, Th. *The Central Conception of Buddhism* (Calcutta: Susil Gupta, 1961).

Steinkellner, Ernst. *Dharmakīrti's Pramāṇaviniścayaḥ;* Zweites Kapitel: Svārthānumāna (Wien, 1973).

Steinkellner, Ernst, See Dharmakīrti, *Hetubindu.*

Steinkellner, Ernst, *Verse-Index of Dharmakīrti's Works (Tibetan Versions)* (Wien, 1977).

Sūtrālaṃkāra (*=Mahāyāna-S.*). Ed. by Sylvain Lévi (Paris, 1907).

T

Tatia, Nathmal, Ed. *Abhidharmasamuccaya-bhāṣyam* (Patna: Jayaswal Research Institute, 1976).

Thakur, A. See Ratnakīrti.

Tsong-kha-pa. Lectures on logic (*Tshad ma'i brjed byaṅ chen mo,* Vol. Pha; *Mṅon sum le'u'i brjed byaṅ,* vol. Ba) [for his use of logic in Mādhyamika works, see introduction to the translation of his *Mun sel*].

Tsong-kha-pa. *Sde bdun la 'jug pa'i sgo don gñer yid kyi mun sel,* Tashilunpo edition Vol. Tsha; Sarnath edition, 1972, 1984 (referred to as his *Mun sel*).

Tucci, Giuseppe, "Buddhist logic before Dignāga (Asaṅga, Vasubandhu, Tarkaśāstras)," *JRAS,* 1929.

V

Vetter, Tilmann, *Dharmakīrti's Pramāṇaviniścayah;* 1. Kapitel: Pratyakṣam (Wien, 1966).

Vidyabhusana, Satis Chandra, *A History of Indian Logic* (1920; Delhi edn., Motilal Banarsidass, 1971).

Vidyabhusana, Satis Chandra. *Nyāyāvatara*, edited and translated (Arrah, India: The Central Jain Publishing House, 1915).

Vinitadeva. *Nyāyabindu-ṭīka* (Sanskrit said to be reconstructed from Tibetan, with English translation, by Mrinalkanti Gangopadhyaya (Calcutta, 1971).

W

Wayman, A. Tr. *ABHIDHĀNAVIŚVALOCANAM OF ŚRĪDHARASENA* (Narita: Naritasan Shinshoji, 1994).

Wayman, A. *Analysis of the Śrāvakabhūmi Manuscript,* University of California Publications in Classical Philology, vol. 17 (Berkeley, Calif., 1961).

Wayman, A. Tr. *Calming the Mind and Discerning the Real,* from Tsong-kha-pa's Lam rim chen mo (New York: Columbia University Press, 1978; Delhi reprint: Motilal Banarsidass, 1979 and 1997).

Wayman, A. Editor of Asaṅga, *Hetu-vidyā,* in present Vol. One.

Wayman, A. "An Historical Review of Buddhist Tantras," *Journal of Rare Buddhist Texts Research Project* (Sarnath, Varanasi: Central Institute of Higher Tibetan Studies, 1995).

Wayman, A. "The Nyāyāvatāra and Buddhist Logical Works by Dignāga and Ratnākaraśānti." in *Nirgrantha* II (1997).

Wayman, A. Review of Hattori, M. Dignāga, On Perception, in *JAOS,* 89:2 (April-June 1969), pp. 434-7.

Wayman, A. "The rules of debate according to Asaṅga," *JAOS* 78:1 (1958).

Wayman A. "Ratnākaraśānti's *Antarvyāptisamarthana,*" *Journal of the Asiatic Society* (Calcutta), XXVII: 2 (1985).

Wayman, A. Tr. *The Sarvarahasyatantra* [with notes from Ratnākaraśānti's commentary], in *Studies of Mysticism in Honor of the 1150th Anniversary of Kōbō's Nirvanam* (Narita: Naritasan Shinshoji, 1984).

Wayman, A. *Untying the Knots in Buddhism* (Delhi: Motilal Banarsidass, 1997).

Y

Yaita, H. Editor of Asaṅga, *Hetu-vidyā,* in *Naritasan Bukkyō Kenkyūsho,* Kiyo 15 (Narita: Naritasan Shinshoji, 1992), pp. 505-76.

INDEX

a posteriori (uncertainty: contrary and genuine) 82, 213-6, 313
ābhāsa (fallacy) 308 (and elsewhere)
Abhidharma 80, 161, 209
Ācala-nātha 258
Acta indologica 122
actuality (*sattva*) (and non-) 54, 65, 105, 107-8, 113-5, 117-22, 208, 211, 215, 220, 239, 241-2
āgama 142-4, 206, 218-9, 221, 224, 253-4, 275
Ālambanaparīkṣa 162
ālayavijñāna 283
annulment (*bādhaka*) 114-8, 120-1, 133, 220-4, 226-7, 229, 236, 243-4
antarvyāpti (inner pervasion) 103
anumāna (inference, qv) X, XVI, XIX, 126, 275-7
anumeya (inferable) XIX, 82
anuvāda (doctrinally consistent discussions) 8
anvaya (similar presence) XX, 102, 119-20, 232, 238-40, 245-6, 249-51, 288, 295 (*-vyāpti*), 296, 316-7, 321
anyāpoha 291
apavāda 8, 237
Apoha 152
application, concordant and discordant 321
apprehension, adversary 303-4
āptāgama (lineage of the masters) X, XIX, 22-5, 33, 218-9, 275
Aristotle XIV
Arjuna 269
artha (meaning, object entity) 36, 218
arthakriyā (see 'purposeful activity')
arthāpatti (presumption from a circumstance) 192
Asaṅga IX, X, XXIII, 3 ff., 154
arvāg-darśana ('looking hither') 326
asapakṣa XVI, 295
Aśoka (a tree) 47
assembly (*parṣat*) 39
attributes (*dharma*) 40
atyantaparokṣa ('further beyond sight') XIX, 79-80, 157
authority (see *pramāṇa*) XVII, XVIII, (as a result): 45, 176-83, 281-2; 16, 18, 76, 78-80, 83, 90, 95, 100, 107, 115, 118, 126-7, 129, 131-6, 140, 144, 147, 149, 154-9, 169, 174, 205-6, 215, 225-6, 238, 246, 249, 252-4, 259, 263-4, 270-7 (and non-), 306, 308, 320-2, 324, 326, 331
avavāda (precepts) 8
Aviddhakarṇa 77, 168
avijñapti 209

bādha (annulment, or injury) 224
bādhaka (see 'nullification') XVI, XVIII
Bārhaspatya-s (= Cārvākas) 76
Bhartṛhari XIV
bhrānti (delusion) 16-7, 182, 184
Biardeau, Madeleine 102, 107
Blo-ldan-śes-rab 253
Bodhisattva 89
Brough, John XIII, XIV
buddhi (cognition, discriminative mind) 254, 313, 317, 321
Bu-ston X, XV, 127-9, 147, 152-7, 174, 177, 184, 193, 201, 218, 229, 253

Calming the Mind and Discerning the Real 255
Candrakīrti 128
Caraka (author of a medical text) 76
cause (*hetu*) 12, 22, 25, 87, 89, 121, 140-1, 170, 177, 180, 185, 202, 207-8, 210, 259, 261, 298, 300, 303-4, 185, 202, 207-8, 210-4, 217, 225,

233, 237, 241, 259, 261, 298, 300, 303-4
cause (material, *kāraṇa*) 49-51, 54, 63, 107, 114, 140-1, 200, 202, 261-2, 300-2, 216, 227, 233, 235
Chandoratnākara 122
Chandra, Lokesh 28, 34, 292
Cha-pa (= Chos-seng) 258
Cittamātra (a school of Buddhism) 282-3
cognition (*buddhi*) 137, 185, 259, 270; 44 (*jñāna*); faults of: 251-2;—of a sense 44, 314; cognitive dawning (*pratīti*) 45
Commentary on the Pramāṇavārttika of Dharmakīrti 204
compatibility (*avirodha*) (with certainty) 24-5
condition (*pratyaya*) 259, 262, 273, 282-3
confidence (*vaiśāradya*) 29, 40
connection (or, relation) 204, 239, 243, 285-6, 299-300
connection, necessary 89, 95, 103, 106, 138-140, 155, 221-3, 233-4
constructive thought(s) (*vikalpa* or *kalpanā*) 44, 75-80, 195, 205-6, 219, 228, 235-6, 246, 263, 289-90, 308; (—and nonconstructive thought) 277-9
continuity (defined) 262
continuum (*dharmatā*) 11-2
contradictions 232-3, 239; 58-9 (contradicted); 192 (contradicting); 242 (contrary)
Critique of Indian Realism 103

Dbu ma rgyan gyi brjed byari 256
Debate IX, X, XXIII; 3 ff. (Asaṅga's Rules of Debate); 259, 329
deception (*visaṃvādana*) 132-3, 185
defilement (*saṃkleśa*) 23
definition (*lakṣaṇa*) 220, 224, 306, 326; definable 292; Definition and Distinct Detail 291-3; distinct detail (*lakṣman*) 307
definition of *pakṣa* 224-7
delusion(s) (*bhrānti*) 16, 76, 80, 95, 185, 187, 198, 213, 279; delusive 95; undeluded 314; delusion and nondelusion 279-80; (*moha*) 134, 154
demons 199, 219, 264, 315
Devadatta 269
Devendrabuddhi 156, 194
Devī Sarasvatī 259
Dhaky, M.A. 102-3
dharma (as 'feature' qv, or 'attribute' qv) 47-8, 90, 104-5, 139, 188-9, 231, 253, 288; (as 'natures') 12, 21-2, 24-5; (as 'doctrine') 9, 23, 25, 27, 30, 36, 90, 254, 325
Dharmakīrti IX, X, XX, XXIII-XXIV, 44 ff., 83-8, 90-8, 100, 103, 110, 125, 127, 132-3, 135-6, 140, 142-3, 147-8, 150-3, 161-2, 172, 174, 180, 184, 190, 197, 201, 218, 230-3, 241, 254-5, 257, 326, 331
Dharmakīrti's Pramāṇaviniścaya 148
dharmadhātu 210
Dharmaśāstra(s) 73, 252
dharmatā (as a group of category *dharmas;* as a continuum, qv) 11
dharmin ('factual base' and 'feature base') 89, 104, 119, 139, 189-90, 252, 311, 315
Dharmottara 43, 68, 102, 147-8, 156, 194, 202
Digambara (Jains) 93, 97-9, 252
Dignāga X, IX, XV, XVI, XIX, 67-8, 102, 125-7, 129, 134-6, 139, 147-50, 152-3, 156, 161-4, 169, 174, 179, 186-7, 191-2, 197, 213-5, 220, 225-6, 230-2, 238, 240, 243, 246-7, 254, 257, 323, 326, 331
Dignāga-Dharmakīrti System 125 ff., 127, 132, 142, 149, 156, 161, 169, 188
Dignāga, on Perception 127-8, 152
Direct Perception (see *pratyakṣa,* and 'perception') 12, 14, 26, 33, 51, 59, 76-80, 85, 94, 106-7, 112, 126, 129, 135-6, 142, 155-6, 160, 163-4, 218, 221, 227, 235, 280, 289-90, 324
discursive thought 264
disputant 220
dissimilar absence (*vyatireka*) 55, 62, 65-7, 72-4
dissimilarity (*vairūpya*) 12, 33
distinct detail (see 'definition')

Dka' gnad kyi zin bris 256
Don-grub-rin-chen 255
Dpal-brtsegs 265
dream 173-4, 279
dṛṣṭānta (example) 103
Dṛṣṭānta-dṛṣṭāntābhāsa 152
Dṛṣṭāntadṛṣṭāntābhāsa-parikṣapariccheda 192

Edgerton 28, 34
effect (or 'result', *phala*) 12, 15, 22, 25, 87, 114, 261
elements (earth, etc.) 15-6
evidence (see *liṅga*) XX, 19-20, 45-7, 51, 55, 59, 62-5, 67, 82, 84-6, 89, 91, 95-6, 103, 106, 109, 111, 120-1, 138-41, 143, 145, 149, 155, 184-5, 187-96: (on definition) 188-90; (on varieties) 190-1; (on the connection with feature) 191-6, 196-213, 218-9, 221, 224, 228, 233, 236, 240-2, 245-6, 248-9, 253, 272, 275, 282, 290, 295-6, 299-300, 304-9: (its fallacy) 308; (contrary—) 309; (uncertain—) 309; (nonactual—) 309; 310-4, 317-20, 322-3, 326-9; Communication of the—233-48; (fallacies of—) 248; (doubt of—) 251; (void of—) 251; (—whose *vyatireka* is doubtful) 252; (—lacking *vyatireka*) 252
example (*dṛṣṭānta* or *udāharaṇa*) 11, 26, 84, 90-1, 102, 106, 108, 117-8, 220, 223, 226, 235, 238, 248-9, 316-7, 319; (—generally speaking) 103, 112-3, 116, 121, 135, 143, 149, 153; (external—) 104, 106, 111; (faults of external—) 251-2; (fallacies of—) 25, 98, 125, 143, 149, 153; (concordant—) 316-7; (discordant—) 215-6, 250-3, 317-8, 320; (falsification of concordant—) 250-1; (falsification of discordant—) 251-3; Example and Fallacious Example 248-50; (fallacious—) 253; (—lacking pervasion or *anvaya*) 251; (—not lacking *anvaya* but not expressing it) 251; (—exhibiting *anvaya* waywardly) 251
exclusion (*pratiṣedha* or *vyāvṛtti*) 47-8, 50-1, 120, 158, 192, 198, 200, 294, 297; (in general) 212, 215-7, 225, 227, 233, 236, 243, 309, 318; Exclusion and Affirmation 286-9; (mutual—) 302; (entailed—) 300; (implicative—) 300; exclusion (of the other) (*anyāpoha*) 196, 291; (—by the grammatical particle *eva*) 189, 191, 211, 268-9

factual base (*dharmin, qv*) 46, 60-1, 84, 94 ('feature base'), 105-11, 113-8, 120-2, 166, 188-90, 194-7, 199, 220, 223, 228-30, 239-40, 244, 248-9, 252, 268, 295-6, 300, 306, 310-1, 326-9
fallacy (*ābhāsa* qv) 75, 95-6, 98, 102 (*doṣa*), 125, 138-40, 292-3, 308-16
fault-finder (*dūṣaka*) 253, 320; fault-finding (*dūṣana*) 327
feature(s) (*dharma* qv) 71, 73, 80, 82, 84-5, 105-6, 108-9, 111-2, 114, 119, 139, 141, 149, 160, 182, 188-91, 194-8, 212, 220, 222-4, 228-30, 234, 237-8, 240-2, 244, 246-7, 261-3, 268, 278, 288, 293-4, 299-302, 304-6, 309-10; —concordance (*sādharmya*) and discordance (*vaidharmya*) 52, 54-6, 73-4, 82, 91, 100; excluded—293-4, 305-6, 309;—of a material thing 293; (discordant—) 214; (refutable—) 309; (its contrary evidence) 310-12, 314, 317-8, 327-8; five clarified by five sentences 322-3
function (*vyāpāra* qv) 157, 159, 245

Ganges 226
Gautama (author of a Ḍharmaśāstra text) 73, 252
generality (*sāmānya* qv) 93, 97, 106, 109-11, 119, 134-5, 144, 156, 167, 187-8, 196, 215, 227, 232-3, 238-9, 243-4, 247-8, 266-7, 269, 278, 288, 298;—character (*sāmānya-lakṣaṇa*) XIX, 45, 74, 78, 126, 132, 136-7, 157, 164, 176, 184, 186-8, 227, 245-6, 277;—and particularity 288
gerundive XVIII
global (*sāmānya* qv) XV, 68-9, 136-8, 161
Gnoli, R. 240

Go-rams-pa 257-8
Grags-pa'i-rgyal-mtshan 256
group reason 240-1
Guṇaprabha 331

Hahn, Michael 122
Hansen, Chad X
Hattori, Masaaki 127-9, 152-3, 161, 176
Hayes, Richard P. 246
hetu (as 'a reason' qv) X, XIV, XV, XVI, 10, 26; (as 'cause' qv) 12
Hetubindu 110, 163
Hetucakra 230, 232
hetuvidyā 5
History of Buddhism 153
Hu-Shih X

image (*ākāra*) 126, 134, 159, 263, 274, 281-3
impermanence 127, 132, 134-5
Indianisme et Bouddhisme 153
inaccessibility (*viprakarṣa*) 14
Index [of Steinkellner's] 241
individual character (*svalakṣaṇa* qv) XIX, 45, 78, 80, 126, 132, 134, 137, 157, 160, 167, 184-6, 227, 237-8, 277, 289
individual presence (*svabhāva* qv) XX, 11, 20, 46-8, 51-5, 53-5, 64, 67-70, 88-9, 91, 105, 138, 141, 145, 149, 159, 171-2, 180, 184, 195-8, 202, 204-11, 213, 216-7, 223, 225, 232, 235, 238, 240, 245, 247, 264, 285, 297, 299-300, 303-4; (—defined) 140; (its contrary evidence) 309
Indra 211
inferable (*anumeya* qv) 46, 84-5, 93, 111-2, 119, 177, 188, 190
inference (*anumāna* qv) 18-22, 26, 33, 51, 58-9, 67-8, 76, 78-80, 82-3, 85, 89, 94-5, 97, 102-3, 106-9, 111, 114, 126, 129, 132, 135-6, 141-4, 149, 155-6, 175-6, 183-6, 195, 213, 216, 218, 221, 225-6, 228, 238, 241-2, 264-5, 271, 273, 279-80, 324-6; (as result) 282; (—for oneself [*svārthānumāna*, 45-51, 294-308] and others [*parārthānumāna*, 51-75, 320-9]) X, 90, 218, 220, 233
inherence (*samavāya*) 87
intention (or, purpose) (*abhiprāya*) 133
introspection-[perception] *svasaṃvedana-pratyaṣa* qv) 44, 94, 126, 131, 170, 178-81, 183, 281; introspection and outward directed cognition 281-2
Īśvarakṛṣṇa 171
Īśvarasena 147, 190, 254

Jaiminīya 76-8, 83, 88, 94, 97-8
Jaini, Padmanabh S. 122
Jamspal, Lozang 256, 258
jāti (as a 'class' or 'genus') 198, 267
Jāti-parīkṣā 152, 253
Jha, Ganganatha XIV
Jñānaśrībhadra 147-8, 172
Joshi, S.D. XVIII
Journal Asiatique 102
Journal of Rare Buddhist Texts 104
Journal of the Asiatic Society 101
Journal of the Oriental Institute 122
Jyotiṣ (astronomy-astrology) 72

Kajiyama, J. 101-2, 110
kalpanā (discursive or constructive thought) XX, 129, 132, 154, 160-1, 163, 166, 170, 174, 184, 266, 277, 314
Kalyāṇarakṣita 174
Kamalaśīla IX, XXIII, 43, 75 ff., 102, 148, 154, 247, 265
Kaṇāda 323
Kanakavarman (Dignāga translator) 129, 152
Kapila 72-3, 85, 98, 252
karma (as 'activity') 11, 21, 24, 71, 81, 98, 136, 171, 251-2
Karṇakagomin 204, 240
kārya (as 'result') 197
Kitagawa, Hidenori XIV, 139, 152, 186, 225
kriyā 189
Kṣaṇabhaṅgasiddhi 102
Kṣaṇabhaṅgasiddhivivaraṇa 102
Kṣaṇabhaṅgasiddhivyatirekātmika 105

La Vallée Poussin 128
lakṣaṇa (character) XV, XX, 129
Lam rim chen mo 255
Legs bśad sñiṅ po 256

Lévi, Sylvain
Life of Bu-ston Rin po che 153
Lineage (of Masters) (see *āptāgama*) 26, 308, 325-6
lineage of principles 331
liṅga (see 'evidence') XVI, 188, 196
locus (*pakṣa* qv) 26, 53, 56-7, 82, 92-3, 95-6, 99, 106, 108-9, 111-2, 114, 117, 139, 149, 219, 237, 293, 295-6, 300-1, 306, 319, 321, 323-4, 326; (no locus) 292; (—exclusion) 318, 320, 324-5; locus, discordant (*vipakṣa*) 213; locus similar (*sapakṣa*) 46, 55, 61-2, 64, 69, 74, 84-5, 119, 245-6, 295-6, 307, 311-3, 321, 330-3; locus, dissimilar (*asapakṣa*) 46, 55, 61-2, 64, 69, 74, 83-5, 119, 139, 191, 230-3, 246, 295-6, 311-3
locus feature (*pakṣadharma* qv) 224, 309-13, 319, 321
logic 223-4
Logical Connection 213-7
Lokāyata 95

Madhyamakakārikā 128
Madhyamakālaṃkāra 256
Mādhyamika (a school of Buddhism) XIX, 255-6, 281
Mahāvyutpatti 90
Mānasa-pratyakṣa XV, 126, 130, 136, 149, 161, 169, 179
manaskāra (attention, mindfulness) 12
Mānava 252
Mañjughoṣa 258
Mano-indriya 161
Mano-vijñāna 161-2
Māras, four 259
McDermott, A.C. Senape 105
measures (*māna*) 135-6
meditation 171
memory 48, 111, 126-7, 129, 131, 167, 174-5, 185, 188, 218, 279
mental object 159
mental perception 44
merits and demerits (*guṇa-doṣa*) 38
metaphoric transfer (*upacāra*) 51, 202
Mimaki, Katsumi 101, 152
Mīmāṃsaka(s) XVI, 88, 97, 99, 133
mind organ 298
Mkhas-grub-rje 257
Mṅon-sum le'u'i brjed byaṅ 256
momentariness (*kṣaṇikatva*) 105-7, 120, 306; momentary (*kṣaṇika*) 118
Monier-Williams Sanskrit-English Dictionary 316
Muktākalaśa 102
Mun sel 256-7

Nāgārjuna 128
Nagatomi, Masatoshi 148
Naiyāyika(s) XVI, 76, 78, 82, 85, 87, 90, 95, 97-9, 247
nimitta (sign-causes) 137, 141, 203, 209
Nirgrantha 102, 104, 316
nirvikalpika XX
non-apprehension (*anupalabdhi*) 46-51, 54, 56, 67, 76, 88-90, 121, 138, 140, 145, 149, 156, 158, 184, 196-204, 217, 234-8, 247, 297, 299-302, 304, 306, 309, 317
not contradicted (*nirākṛta*) 57-8
numbers (from two kinds to twenty-seven kinds)

A. Two Kinds

a. Of presence and absence, causes, etc.: times for involvement object 264; identity with that, or arising from that 55, 87; either a product or due to effort 64; presence and absence 63; connection 286; oneness 289; difference 289; bases (for presence and absence) 193; non-actual by non-actual support 314; opposition to sign-causes 141; causes 261; causes (again) 261
b. Speech in general: formulations 192; speech conventions 193-4; verses 151-2
c. Speech as references and referrals: reference 266; claimed reference 266; names (actual and nicknames) 267; referrals by reference 267; referring to the reference 268; times of the referral 269
d. Exclusions: exclusion (entailed and implicative) 200, 287; selective exclusion(wrong and right) 290; exclusions of the other 291;

exclusion by implicative exclusion 291; opposition through mutual exclusion 302; excluded features 294; mutually exclusive opposition 285

e. Rejections, faults, fallacies: refusal (or rejection) (*pratyākhyā*) 324; (genuine) fault-finding 326; example-faults 320; example fallacy 317-8; of master-lineage 325-6; of evidence 309; of the definition 293

f. The Syllogism: thesis 10; thesis topics 9; genuine syllogism 321; genuine 'reductio absurdum' 327-8

g. Evidence: uncertain evidence 311; unrestricted uncertain evidence 312; *a posteriori* uncertainty 313; non-actual evidence 315; 'individual presence' evidence 299; 'individual presence' involved with distinctions 299; 'non-apprehension' 158; 'individual presence' evidence related with differentiation 299; non-apprehesion evidence 299-300; 'non-apprehension' evidence of what may feasibly appear 300; adversary apprehension 302; genuine evidence by thesis feature 304; genuine evidence by purpose 305; genuine evidence by method of proof 305-6; alternate of the foregoing 306-7; genuine evidence as to engaging 307; to be demonstrated—for 'result' an origin, for 'individual presence' a connection therewith 69-70

h. cognitions (in general): cognitions 131, 183, 185; deciding cognitions 271; doubt 272; delusion (of thought, of view) 16-7; deception and delusion 185; mental analysis usage 272; constructive thought 278 and non-constructive thought 279; (both) 176; cognition not comprehending 272-3; delusive cognition 279-80; nondelusive cognition 280; semblances of perception 280

i. Authorities and their objects: authority 276-7; authorities XIX, 157, 159, 184, 187, 225; (their) sanctions 157, 159, 187; *prameya* XIX, 265; inference 183-8; inference objects XIX; inference for others 51-2; inference (for oneself, for others) XXIII, 149; inference according to Kapila 85; characters (of direct perception and inference) 79; direct perception 155; conditions for introspection 178

j. Miscellaneous: total acceptance 290; aims (one's own and of others) 322; subject (apparently = 'topic') 266

B. Three Kinds

a. Existence, nonexistence, the objects: object (*viṣaya*) 263; apprehensions of prima facie object 263; claimed object 263-4; inaccessible ways of object entity 264; dissimilar locuses (non-actual, contrary, and uncertain) 139, 297; meanings of objects (*pratyakṣa's* one object, *anumāna's* two) 79-80; *pakṣadharma* (present, absent, and both) 230-2; (also) bases of feature (*dharma*) 237; non-actual re the object entity 314; non-actual by no difference 314; non-actual by doubt 315; non-actual re a person 315-6; *lakṣaṇa* (objects of direct perception and inference) XIX

b. Definitions: complete definitions 291; distinct details 291; faults of a definition 292; fallacies (*ābhāsa*) of a definition 292-3; fallacies of distinct detail 293

c. Cognition (general): constructive thought by appearances 278; constructive thought by occasion 279; conditions of sense cognition (in Cittamātra) 282-3; *kalpanā* (constructive thought) 176

d. Evidence: (modes of) evidence XX, etc.; contrary evidence 313; non-actual evidence 313; genuine evidence 297; genuine evidences as to the thesis 307-8; examination of the result 178-9; the undemonstrated per Vaiśeṣika 96

e. Examples: concordant example fallacy 317; discordant example fallacy 318; further kinds of discordant example fallacy 318; example faults of evidence 319

f. Conditions: rulings out (*avacchedaka*) [by the particle *eva*] 188-9; counterparts (*pratiyogin*) [to the three *eva*] 189; conditions (*pratyaya*) 262; times (past, present, future) 262; opposition 284; incompatibility-opposition 284; ways to avoid doubt 154; referrals (name, phrase, sentence) 267; referral by ruling out 268-9

g. Syllogism (generalities): fallacies of the thesis 97; modes of the reason 69, etc.; fallacies of the reason 67; only exclusion kinds of reason 217

h. Authorities and Sanctions: authorities 10, 203-4; inference 275, 307; (three) Parts to Inference for Others 320-2; further rejections of an inference 324-5; sanctions (prameya) 265; phases of sanction for result 281-2; particulars (re introspection) 181; Yogin's perception 275; inference per Naiyāyika 85

i. Debate consideration: considerations to undertake a debate 37; attributes of debate utility 40; lineages of the master 23; Vedas 72, 252; faults (of external entity, cognition, speech) 250-3; examinations of a pure scripture 224, 265, 308, 326, 329

C. Four Kinds

Cognition (general): *aviparokṣa* (not out-of-sight) (the 4 aspects) 12-4; *anāvaraṇa* (lack of obscuration) (the 4 aspects) 13-4; direct perception 17-8, 126, 160, 163, 273; semblance of perception 130, 175; certainty from oneself 277; non-apprehension of a sense object as connection 300-2; non-apprehension of absent objects 140, 200-1; constructive thoughts of unseen entities 279; instruments of error 280; wayward constructive thought (of count, of individual nature, of sense object, of result) 75-9

Logic (general): implicative exclusion 287; generalities (*sāmānya*) 288-9; evidence (*liṅga*) 190-1; fallacies of locus 59; annulment (*bādhā*) 225; special rejections re one's factual base 229; contrary evidence by the manner of referring 310-1

D. Five Kinds
E. Six Kinds
F. Seven Kinds,
G. Eight Kinds
H. Nine Kinds
I. Eleven Kinds,
J. Thirteen Kinds
K. Twenty-seven Kinds

D. Five Kinds: similarities 11; delusions 16-7; formal sense organs 18; inference sources 18-9; merits of speech 27-8; cognition (deciding, deviant, doubt, mental analysis, and uncertain) 271-3; *kalpanā* (constructive thought) 176; relations according to Naiyāyika 87; member-terms in Inference for Others per the Naiyāyika 90; syllogism members 92: fallacies of reason (per the Naiyāyika) 95-6; entities, external and unconscious 260; entities, inner and unconscious 261; 'aim of others' 322; fallacy of locus for 'aim of others' 323-4; principles of *śruti* (*svarūpa*, etc.) [cf. the preceding two entries] 225, faults of a locus 326; result-evidence 298

E. Six Kinds: settings of the debate 9; worldly direct perceptions 18: claim of six characters 82; perfections (*pāramitā*) (with instrumental attribution) 265; apprehensions of

opposing pervasion 303-4
F. Seven Kinds: Dharmakīrti's books XXIV; Sāṃkhya relations 86-7; delusions (2+5) 16
G. Eight Kinds: proving 10
H. Nine Kinds: perfect aspects of speaker's words, 28; faults of the discussion 35-7; groups of evidence 139; faults of concordant example 251; faults of discordant example 252-3
I. Eleven Kinds: initial verses XXIV and 125 ff., 149
J. Thirteen Kinds: vocal candor (*vāgvijñapti*) 32; collapse of discussion (*kathāsāda*) 33-5
K. Twenty-seven Kinds: benefits from speech ornaments 30-1
Nyāyabindu XX, 139, 152, 161, 201, 233, 247
Nyayabindupūrvapakṣasaṃkṣipti 265
Nyāya-Vaiśeṣika 103, 133, 136, 171
Nyāyavatāra 102-4

Obermiller, E. 147, 153
object, inaccessible 88, 199, 203-4
object, sense 14-6, 45, 77-8, 86, 91, 127, 130-8, 141, 143-5, 155-7, 159-62, 164-5, 167-8, 175, 177-80, 182, 194-7, 199-200, 209, 212, 220-1, 226, 234, 240-2, 245, 259-64, 267, 270, 277, 280-2, 283 ff., 299-300, 305-6, 313-4, 317-8, 321, 324, 331; in both the mental and supramental range 18;—of introspection 169-70; an entity 223, 238
object(s) (generally) 221
obscuration (*āvaraṇa*) 13-4
occurrence (*utpatti*) 12-3
omniscience 88, 203, 313
Oneness and Multiplicity 289
opposition (*virodha* or *viruddha*) 49, 247, 284-5, 302-4
opposition-result (*virodha-kārya*) 303
ornament (its meaning) (*alaṃkāra*) 31

pakṣa [see 'locus'] XVI, 57-9, 104, 139, 143, 149, 224-5, 244; Pakṣa, Examination of 224-33
pakṣadharma 138-40, 143, 149, 184, 203, 214-5, 229-33 (Varieties), 246, 250, 295
Pandeya, Jagadīśvara 4
paramārtha (the absolute) 25, 139, 152; —sat 137, 237, 246
parārthānumāna (inference for others) 218
parokṣa ('beyond sight') XIX, 79, 95, 157, 176, 265, 275
particularity (*bheda*) 172, 212, 215, 232-3, 236, 239-40, 243-5
Pātrasvāmin 82
Peluka (= Pailuka) 97, 247
perception, direct (*pratyakṣa* qv) XIX, 16-8, 126, 136, 154-5, 182, 184; (defined) 130, 164;—(general) 195, 209-10, 218, 263-4, 271, 281, 316, perception-only 15; outer—149, 154, 160, 163-4, 167, 273; mental—149, 161-4, 167-9, 274; introspective—149, 154, 163, 167 (*svasaṃvitti*), 169-70, 274-5; yogin's—149, 154, 163, 173-4, 275;—semblance 126, 130, 135, 149, 154, 174-6
person 313-4
pervadable 304; pervader 49, 217, 240 300, 302-3, 307, 309, 312; pervasively 303-4
pervasion (*vyāpti* qv) 49, 89, 94, (over-), 106-8, 113-6, 121, 139, 191-2; (inner [*antar*]) and (external [*bahir*]) 103, 109-12, 117-8; (in terms of *anvaya* or *vyatireka*) 49, 286; *anvaya* 214, 317, 321; *vyatireka* 214, 317-8; (non-) and (over-) 224, 292; exclusive—296-6; opposing—302;—right or wrong 224, 231-2, 243, 253, 309, 317, 320, 329; wayward—309, 311, 319
Peṭhara (=Paiṭhara) 97, 247
Pradhan, Pralhad 4
Prajñākaragupta 169
Prakṛti 171
pramāṇa (authority) XVI, XVII, XVIII, XIX, XX, 26, 78, 83, 125, 127, 219, 228; non-*pramāṇa* 132; *pramānya* ('authorizing') 157 (defined), 179
Pramānasamuccaya X, XVII, 147, 152, 191, 226, 238, 240, 243, 247-8, 254, 326

Pramāṇavārttika 103, 110 (Chap. IV), 149, 153, 255, 257-8
Pramāṇaviniścaya X, 127, 132, 147, 153; *-ṭik* 29
prameya XVI, XVII, XVIII, XIX, XX, 126-7, 265
prasajya-pariṣedha 193
pratijñā (as 'thesis') IX, X, 10, 26
pratīti (cognitive dawning) 104, 204, 226
pratiyogin (counterpart to) 189
pratyakṣa (direct perception, qv; or perception, direct, qv) X, XI, XV, 44-5, 149; —, *parokṣa, atyantaparokṣa* 222; *-ābhāsa* (fallacies of *pratyakṣa*) 129, 174
presence (*bhāva*) 187
proof (*sādhana*) or proving (and non-proof) 57-64, 73-5, 78, 84-6, 89, 92-4, 99-100, 104, 106, 111-2, 114-8, 120-1, 135, 143-5, 177, 186, 190-2, 196-8, 205, 279, 295-6, 301-4, 319-20
purposeful activity (*arthakriyā*) 45, 105, 132-3, 135-7, 155-6, 185-7, 208, 227, 245, 247, 259
Pūrvamīmāṃsā 107

quarrels 7, 120-1

Randle (*Fragments*) 231
Ratnākaraśānti IX, X, XXIII, 101 ff.
Ratnakīrti 101-2, 105
Ratnakīrtinibandhāvaliḥ 105
reason, a (see *hetu*) 10, 26, 33, 47, 52-5, 61-4, 67-9, 82, 84-6, 89-93, 95-6, 97 (uncertain), 98-100, 103, 106, 109-101, 112-20, 125, 138-41, 145, 156, 190, 192, 196-7, 204, 210, 214-7, 219-20, 222-5, 230, 231 (9 kinds), 232, 234-9, 245-6, 247 (doubtful), 248-50, 301-8, 311-6, 318-20, 323; fallacies of—143, 145, 229-30, 246, 248-9
Red-mda'-pa 255-7, 294
referral (*vācaka*) 267, 290
refusal (= rejection) 324-6
refutation (*dūṣanā*) 75, 97
result, a (*phala* or *kārya*) 47-51, 53-4, 63-4, 67, 69-70 74, 78, 86, 89, 107, 131, 138, 140-1, 145, 149, 154, 157, 176-80, 183-4, 196, 202-4, 208, 210-3, 216, 221, 225, 232-3, 235-7, 240-2, 281-2, 297-8, 300-4; (its contrary evidence) 309
Rgyal-tshab-rje 255-6
Rigs gter 258;——*gsal byed* 257
Rigs pa'i rgya mtsho 257
rikta 219
Rin-chen bzang po 104
Roodbergen, A.F. XVIII
Ṛṣabha 72-3, 252
Ruegg,. D.S. 153

Sa-skya-pa sect 255, 257
Sa-skya Paṇḍita (= Sa Pan) 257-8
sādhana (proof, qv) 9-10, 53, 102, 107-8, 111-2, 118, 121, 134, 144, 216, 222-3, 243-4
sādharmya XX
sādhya (thesis) IX, XVI, 9, 26, 36, 139 (defined), 144, 216, 222-3, 239, 293-4
Śakraprabha 331
sākṣāt XX, XIX
Śākyabuddhi 156, 191, 201-2
sāmānya XV, 149, 158, 171;—*lakṣaṇa* (generality character) XV, XVI, XIX;—*gocara* (global scope) XV, 68, 161; examination of—227-9
same time 286
saṃketa (signal or sign) 165, 176, 207
Sāṃkhya 60, 76, 82-3, 85-7, 93-4, 97, 143, 171, 238, 254, 315, 324
Sāṃkhya-kārikā 84, 171
saṃvṛti-sat 137
samyak-dṛṣṭi (right views) 132
sanction (*prameya* qv) XVII, XVIII, XIX, XX, 129, 131, 155, 157, 176-7, 180-1, 183, 186-7, 190, 226, 231, 246, 259, 281-2, 312, 319, 331
Sankrityayana 240
Sanskrit and Indian Studies; Essays in Honour of Daniel H.H. Ingalls 148
Śāntarakṣita 102, 148, 162, 193, 256
Śānti-pā (= Ratnākaraśānti) 101-4, 107, 121-2
sapakṣa XVI, 295
Sāratamā 122
Sarvajña-siddhi-(*kārikā*) 174

Sarvarahasyatantra 122
sarvasaṃskṛtadharma 210
śāstra 30, 133-4, 143, 154, 156, 203-4; (in sense of *āgama*) 221-3
sattva (actuality, qv) 103, 208
satyavādin XVII
Sautrāntika 180
scripture, pure, trustworthy 308
Selective Exclusion and Total Acceptance 290-1
self 66, 68, 77-8, 140, 183, 217, 220, 314;—destruct 302
semblance of perception (see under 'perception'—semblance) 280
sense organs 44, 126, 130, 156, 161, 164-7, 169, 175, 177, 181, 195, 206, 209, 227, 246-7, 261, 279-80
sequence (*krama*) 105, 121, 208
Shastri, D.N. 103
Shastri, Dvarikadas 149
Shastri, Haraprasad 101
Siddhānta (theory-system) 96, 219
Siddhasena Divakara 102
Siddhasena Siddharṣi 102
sign-source (see 'signal') 212
signal (*saṃketa* qv) 266-7, 278-9
similar presence (*anvaya*) 55-6, 65-7, 71, 191
similarity (*sārūpya, sādṛśya*) 11-2, 33
simultaneity (*yaugapadya*) 105, 121, 208
Six Buddhist Nyāya Tracts 101
skandha (personal aggregates) 209
skill (*kauśalya*) 39-40
Smṛti 252
Smṛtijñānakīrti 188
sophistries (*jāti*) 75, 253
speaker (and speech) 5, 9, 27-9; speaker (defined) 157; first—(*pūrvavādin* or *vādin*) 39-40, 315; respondent (*prativādin*) 316; 214-5, 222, 305, 320, 322-4, 329; (desire to speak) 229, 242-3; speech 63-4, 241, 244; utterance 233-4, accepted word 225, 227-8, conventional language 235; speech ornaments 39-1; of two kinds, referring to a feature or to a factual base 268; faults of—251-3; end of discussion 32-37; other kinds: quarrels (*vivāda*) 6-7, noxious talk (*apavāda*), and precepts of guidance (*avavāda*). Finally: Vāgīśvara (Lord of Speech) 75; *śruti* (proper or scriptual utterance) 224-5, 228
Staal J.F. XIV
Stcherbatsky 43
Steinkellner, Ernst 110, 148, 160, 163, 174, 235, 239, 241, 253
Sthīrasiddhidūṣaṇa 101
A Study of Indian Classical Logic—Dignāga's System 152
subject (*viṣayin*) 259, 266
Sugata 254
superimposition (T. sgro btags pa) 186
svabhāva (see 'individual presence') XIX, XX, 9, 11, 197; *-hetu* XX
svalakṣaṇa XV, XVI, XIX, 161, 294
svārthānumāna 138-9, 152
svasaṃvedana-pratyakṣa XV, XVI, XX, 77, 130 (spelled *svasaṃvitti-*), 149, 161
Svatantra manner 249
syllogism 92, 102, 118, 144

tārkika (logician) 91
Tathāgata(s) 132
Tatia, Nathmal 4
Tattvasaṃgraha 102, 148, 162, 193
Thakur, Anantalal 105
theory-systems (see 'syllogism') 222; Theory Systems and Śāstras 217-224
thesis (*sādhya* qv) 9-10, 26, 33, 47, 53-4, 55, 57-8, 59-62, 64-5, 67, 71-3, 78, 90, 92, 94-6, 99-100, 102-4, 106-11, 114-7, 119-21, 191, 196, 197-8, 212, 220-4, 226, 229-30, 237-40, 248-50, 295-6, 304, 306-8, 316, 320, 322-6, 329; cetainty of—317;—feature (*sādhyadharma*) 310-1, void of 251, doubt of 251, lacking *vyatireka* 252, whose *vyatireka* is doubful 252
thought and thought derivative 281
Tibet-Sanskrit Dictionary 28, 34, 292
translation (of terms) XIII ff.
Trikulabrahmana 98
trirūpa (three forms) [cf. above, 'B, Three Kinds' under d, Evidence, i.e. 3 modes] XVI

Tshad ma'i brjed byaṅ chen mo 256
Tshad ma rigs gter 258
Tshad ma rnam par ṅes pa 151
Tshad ma rnam par ṅes pa'i ṭik tshig don rab gsal 147
Tsong-kha-pa IX, X, XXIII, 4, 154, 254, 255 ff. (255-351)
Tucci, Guiseppe 3

udāharaṇa ('example') 10
understanding, means of 259
upāya (means) 203

Vacanamukha 188
vāda (debate) 5, 26
Vaiśeṣika 76-7, 83, 85, 91, 93-4, 96, 98, 243, 247, 312, 323
Vaiyākaraṇa (grammarians) 81
Vardhamāna 72, 252
Vārṣagaṇya 7
Vasubandhu 3, 83, 92, 220
Vātsiputrīya 86
Vātsyāyana 102
Vedānta 133
Verse Index of Dharmakīrti's Works 148, 235
Vetter, Tilmann 148, 150, 179
Vidyābhūṣana, M.M. Satis Chandra XIV, 103
views (*dṛṣṭi*) 7; delusion of 17
vijñāna 76, 180, 188, 210
vikalpa (=*kalpanā* qv) (constructive thought) 164; *vikalpika* XX
Vinaya (disciplinary code) 8
Vinītadeva 43
vipakṣa (opposing side) (cf. 'locus,' discordant) 114
viśeṣa (qualification) 9-10
Viṣṇu 86
Vyatireka (dissimilar absence) XX, 119, 137-8, 158, 184, 211-2, 214, 224, 232, 245-6, 249-50, 252-3, 295-6, 317-8, 321
vyāpāra (function) 127, 131, 136, 157, 176
vyāpti (pervasion qv) XIV
Vyāsa 252
vyavaccheda(ka) 104, 110 (3 kinds), 191, 268

Wayman, Alex XVII, 3, 11, 101, 104

Yaita, H. 4
yid kyi mun sel (dispelling the darkness of mind) 257
Yogācāra School 281
Yogācārabhūmi 154
Yogācārin 180
yogakṣema 163-4
yogin's perception 44-5, 126, 130, 154, 173-4, 199